CATHOLIC THEOLOGICAL ETHICS
PAST, PRESENT, AND FUTURE

CATHOLIC THEOLOGICAL ETHICS IN THE WORLD CHURCH
James F. Keenan, Series Editor

Since theological ethics is so diffuse today, since practitioners and scholars are caught up in their own specific cultures, and since their interlocutors tend to be in other disciplines, there is the need for an international exchange of ideas in Catholic theological ethics.

Catholic Theological Ethics in the World Church (CTEWC) recognizes the need: to appreciate the challenge of pluralism; to dialogue from and beyond local culture; and, to interconnect within a world church not dominated solely by a northern paradigm. In this light, CTEWC is undertaking four areas of activity: fostering new scholars in theological ethics, sponsoring regional conferencing, supporting the exchange of ideas via our web site (catholicethics.com), and publishing a book series.

The book series will pursue critical and emerging issues in theological ethics. It will proceed in a manner that reflects local cultures and engages in cross-cultural, interdisciplinary conversations motivated by mercy and care and shaped by shared visions of hope.

CATHOLIC
THEOLOGICAL ETHICS
PAST, PRESENT, AND FUTURE

The Trento Conference

Edited by

JAMES F. KEENAN

ORBIS BOOKS

Maryknoll, New York 10545

Founded in 1970, Orbis Books endeavors to publish works that enlighten the mind, nourish the spirit, and challenge the conscience. The publishing arm of the Maryknoll Fathers and Brothers, Orbis seeks to explore the global dimensions of the Christian faith and mission, to invite dialogue with diverse cultures and religious traditions, and to serve the cause of reconciliation and peace. The books published reflect the views of their authors and do not represent the official position of the Maryknoll Society. To learn more about Maryknoll and Orbis Books, please visit our website at www.maryknollsociety.org.

Library of Congress Cataloging-in-Publication Data

Catholic theological ethics, past, present, and future : the Trento conference / James F. Keenan, editor.
    p. cm.
    Conference held in July 2010.
    Includes index.
    ISBN 978-1-57075-941-3
    1. Christian ethics—Catholic authors—Congresses. 2. Catholic Church—Doctrines—Congresses. I. Keenan, James F.
    BJ1249.C195 2012
    241'.042—dc23

                                                              2011021168

*To the people of the Province and City of Trento
and, most especially, Antonio Autiero*

CONTENTS

Part IV
THE FUTURE

ACKNOWLEDGMENTS

I want to thank Brian McNeil for his translations of the essays by Reinhard Marx, Antônio Moser, Simone Morandini, Éric Gaziaux, Bénézet Bujo, Paolo Prodi, and Alberto Bondolfi; and Margaret Wilde for her translations of the essays by Diego Alonso-Lasheras and Miguel Ángel Sánchez Carlos.

I want to thank all the contributors who delivered admirable reflections for advancing our discussions.

I want to thank my most able, thorough, and conscientious assistant, Kevin Vander Schel, a Ph.D. student here at Boston College.

Finally, to Susan Perry at Orbis Books, a warm and sustained sense of gratitude for shepherding this entire project through and for her no-nonsense editorial eyes and pen!

Welcome to Trento

Monsignor Luigi Bressan
Archbishop of Trento

Dear friends, I am most honored to welcome you to our town and the archdiocese of Trento for this important meeting on ethics. In the sixteenth century our beloved town was chosen for a well-known ecumenical council because it appeared to be the best place for an encounter between the Protestants, who had requested a council in German territory, and the Catholics, who refused to go to Germany. The discussions on the venue for the gathering went on for several years; and finally, after a suggestion made to the emperor by the bishop of Trento, Cardinal Bernardo Clesio, the decision was made in favor of our town. We know that, unfortunately, a real encounter did not take place, and Western Christianity remained divided. But we in Trento realize that we have a mission to build bridges for a better understanding.

At the same time, we are aware of the great positive impact the Council of Trent had on the life of the Christian community, and we share with the rest of the universal church the mission God entrusted to his children in Jesus Christ. Trento is not, as in the case of other historical councils such as Nicaea or Chalcedon, just a name in the theological development of the discipline and doctrine of the church, but a living community, spread over 452 parishes with about 400 diocesan priests, 200 religious men, 500 religious women, other consecrated people in secular institutes and church movements, about 400 missionaries in many countries of the world, and numerous lay people generously committed to pastoral work and social service. Our relations with the public authorities are good and respectful. Not everything is perfect in Trentino; however, we try to respond to the challenges of today aware that, as Christians, we are the heirs of a great tradition and the beneficiaries of the grace of God.

When the theologians and bishops came to Trento for the Council, they discovered the town was small and had problems accommodating up to two thousand guests. There are not so many of us for this gathering, and I hope you will not meet any inconveniences during your stay. While I thank you for choosing Trento for such an important gathering, I express my appreciation for the support we have received not only from the seminary but also from the Institute for Superior Religious Studies and the Bruno Kessler Foundation as well as from the public authorities, the university, and other institutions.

The Conference

At Trento, we had 31 plenary presenters, 30 posters, and 240 concurrent presenters. Among the latter, there were four sessions where one could choose from twenty different panels of three presenters. Let us just consider some panels within one session. On one entitled "Refugees, Immigration, and National Sovereignty," U.S. ethicist David Hollenbach spoke on the responsibility to protect; Filipina Gemma Cruz spoke on a Catholic ethics of risk for immigration reform; and the English scholar Anna Rowlands addressed the issue of subsidiarity and asylum. On another, three U.S. professors, Patricia Beattie Jung, Susan Ross, and John McCarthy spoke on what evolutionary biology is bringing to sexual diversity. Since the panels were differentiated by language (English, French, Spanish, and Italian), one of the Italian panels had Italy's Giovanni Del Missier, Brazil's Rogerio Gomes, and Argentina's Maria Martha Cuneo discussing vulnerability and bioethics.

During another session three speakers spoke on HIV/AIDS: Mary Jo Iozzio (United States); Lillian Dube (Zimbabwe); and Uzochukwu Jude Njoku (Nigeria). During that same session, there were panels on economics, the right to food, the common good, dying, human rights, bioethics, global sustainability and the personal life, children as moral agents, and teaching casuistry and truth-telling. Sixteen presentations were on virtue ethics; and though all were in English, the presenters came from the United States, the United Kingdom, Germany, Poland, Nigeria, and Belgium. In returning home to their countries, many participants submitted their presentations for publications. On our Web site (www.catholicethics. com), we post either a PDF or a link to the published essay, as well as the entire program itself, and the dozens of commentaries on the conference that appeared around the world. You can also read there our plans for the future.

Apart from the opening plenary on interreligious dialogue, the remaining plenaries were divided into three groups, with the second day on the past; the third on the present; and the last on the future. In order to have a large number and variety of presenters, we adopted a rule that allowed each plenary presenter fifteen minutes. We asked each presenter, in light of the discussions that followed their presentations, to expand their insights into a fully developed argument, which we happily publish here.

I think we learned many lessons at Trento, above all something about our vocation. We theological ethicists are by our very nature critical: our vocation is based on the premise that we are needed because things are not as they could be. As the critics and reformers of society and church, we seek to practically bridge the gulf between who we are and who we can be. Thus, we always begin with the premise that there is a deficit in our location, and, therefore, we need to work together to find a way to remedy it.

Often when church leaders or church laity hear presentations by ethicists, they wonder why we are not more positive. We cannot be. By nature we are teleologists: we aim at a better future. Not surprisingly then, at our final session, complaints were raised, above all, "Why did not Archbishop Marx stay for questions?" Others responded, "It was about time ethicists sat and listened to archbishops!" It took Linda Hogan, Antonio Autiero, and I nearly thirty minutes to insist that the decision to not hold questions was ours not his, a decision due to time constraints. Then, later, at the closing dinner, in the farewell address, Charles Curran emboldened us to be more critical![6]

We ethicists believe that we must find the truth, and in part that means naming what is lacking, not yet seen, not understood, or not articulated. It also means being aware of those not heard, rejected, oppressed, or abandoned. We are called to read the signs of the times as they actually are. Yet, still, we are not an unhappy lot of nay-sayers. On the contrary. To do what we do, we need to listen, dream, imagine, cajole, and laugh at ourselves, anticipating discord and hoping for better outcomes; we are fairly resilient, sanguine, and affable, as we were throughout the conference.

What I found at Trento and on my way to Trento, is precisely what the young women scholars from Africa said to me as the conference closed. "Jim, we are so surprised that we actually belong to something so big, so dedicated, and so dynamic." I smiled. At Trento, we discovered our catholic vocation. I hope you find it here in these pages.

Notes

1. James F. Keenan, ed., *Catholic Theological Ethics in the World Church: The Plenary Papers from the First Cross-cultural Conference on Catholic Theological Ethics* (New York: Continuum, 2007).

2. Linda Hogan, *Applied Ethics in a World Church: The Padua Conference* (Maryknoll, NY: Orbis Books, 2008).

3. James F. Keenan, ed., *Catholic Theological Ethics in the World Church: The Plenary Papers from the First Cross-cultural Conference on Catholic Theological Ethics* (Quezon City: Ateneo de Manila, 2008); *Los Desafíos Éticos del Mundo Actual: Una Mirada Intercultural Primera Conference Intercontinental e Intercultural sobre Ética Teológica Católica en la Iglesia Mundial* (Buenos Aires: Editorial San Benito, 2008); *Etica Teologica Cattolica nella Chiesa Universale: Atti del primo Congresso interculturale di teologia morale* (Bologna: Edizioni Dehoniane, 2009); *Catholic Theological Ethics in the World Church: The Plenary Papers from the First Cross-cultural Conference on Catholic Theological Ethics* (Bangalore: Asian Trading Company, 2009); *Ética Teológica Católica no Contexto Mundial* (Sao Paolo: Editora Santuario, 2010).

4. Linda Hogan, *Applied Ethics in a World Church: The Padua Conference* (Quezon City: Ateneo de Manila, 2009).

5. William C. Mattison III, ed., *New Wine, New Wineskins: A Next Generation Reflects on Key Issues in Catholic Moral Theology* (Lanham, MD: Rowman & Littlefield, 2005).

6. Charles Curran, "We Cannot Put Our Heads in the Sand," *National Catholic Reporter*, September 7, 2010, 1, http://ncronline.org/print/20049.

Part I
ETHICS AND INTERRELIGIOUS DIALOGUE
IN A GLOBALIZED WORLD

Catholic, Protestant, and Muslim Perspectives

A Catholic Perspective
Archbishop Bruno Forte (Italy)

A Protestant Perspective
Mercy Amba Oduyoye (Ghana)

A Muslim Perspective
Ahmad Syafii Ma'arif (Indonesia)

INTRODUCTION

Since the heritage of sixteenth-century Trento provided an immediate backdrop to the conference, the planning committee wanted to signal that our discourses belonged very much to twenty-first-century Trento. For the opening we decided to highlight exactly what the sixteenth century did not do (and could not do): interreligious dialogue.

Our speakers were major figures on the world stage. Knowing that our discussion would later pursue exclusively Catholic theological ethics, they forcefully reminded us that other believers shared similar concerns and expectations. Archbishop Bruno Forte of Chieti-Vasto, Italy, known for his work on aesthetics and an ethics of the transcendence,[1] and a member of the newly formed Pontifical Council for Promoting the New Evangelization, gave the first presentation. He proposed four theses: (1) that there is no ethics without transcendence; (2) nor any ethics without gratuitousness and responsibility; (3) nor without justice and solidarity; and (4) that ethics points us toward that free, sovereign, ultimate, and absolute transcendence that has first turned toward us.

From Ghana, Mercy Amba Oduyoye, from the Circle of Concerned African Women Theologians, found in interreligious dialogue the hope of greater justice, stability, and equity.[2] She saw this discourse as among Christians and Muslims, but in her paper she also underlined two specific constituencies from and on her continent: believers in African Traditional Religion and women of faith of each of these three traditions.

9

Finally, the third speaker was Indonesian Ahmad Syafii Ma'arif, who previously chaired (1998-2005) the Muhammadiyah, the world's second largest Muslim organization with thirty million members. Dr. Ma'arif won the prestigious Ramon Magasasy award (2008) for his work in advancing peace, dialogue, and tolerance.[3] Invoking the Qu'ran, Ma'arif reminded us that, as opposed to secularists, people of faith share a cosmology, an anthropology, and a vision of the source and end of morality that is necessary for attending to the challenges of today.

Notes

1. Bruno Forte, *The Portal of Beauty: Towards a Theology of Aesthetics* (Grand Rapids, MI: Eerdmans, 2008); *L'Uno per L'altro: Per un'etica della transcendenza* (Brescia: Morcelliana, 2003).

2. Mercy Amba Oduyoye, *Daughters of Anowa: African Women and Patriarchy* (Maryknoll, NY: Orbis Books, 1995); *Introducing African Women's Theology* (Boston: Pilgrim Press, 2001); *Beads and Strands: Reflections of an African Woman on Christianity in Africa* (Maryknoll, NY: Orbis Books, 2004); and *Hearing and Knowing: Theological Reflections on Christianity in Africa* (Eugene, OR: Wipf & Stock, 2009).

3. See Ma'arif Institute, http://www.maarifinstitute.org/.

A CATHOLIC PERSPECTIVE

Archbishop Bruno Forte

What are the challenges emerging for ethics and interreligious dialogue from today's "global village"? I will first attempt to answer this question by way of metaphor, for the various layers of meaning in metaphors allow us to draw out the sense of what is afoot without making banal the complexity of the real situation. Using three "fluid" metaphors—shipwreck, liquidity, and seafaring—and one "solid"— the tower of Babel—I would like to outline what might possibly be the task of ethics and interreligious dialogue in our globalized world.

The Metaphor of Shipwreck

Hans Blumenberg[1] has used the metaphor of *shipwreck* as a tool to interpret the modern age and its crisis. The image refers back to a text from Lucretius, in which the *condition humaine* in the "classic" era was to find its voice: "What a beautiful thing it is, when the winds clash over the sea, and the dark vastness of the waters churn beneath, to watch the distant shipwreck from dry land: it is not the other's disaster that brings you joy, but the distance that separates you from a similar destiny."[2] The power of this metaphor derives from the contrasts it makes between the dry land with all its steadiness and safety and the fluid, inconstant sea. Lucretius's spectators observe the scene of the shipwreck from the *terra firma* of their certitudes.

Modern observers, however, no longer enjoy such certainties; on the contrary, they experience the evident truth of Pascal's words: *Vous êtes embarqués,*[3] we are all on board the ship! As Blumenberg comments, the steady vantage point from which the historian can be a detached spectator no longer exists. What is new— beginning from the "age of lights" onward—is that the observer is ever less to be distinguished from the shipwreck itself. Having lost the certainties offered us by positivism and the ideologies of the modern age, we have all been shipwrecked heirs of modernity and dwellers in postmodernity.

Here we can grasp the far-from-secondary difference between the crisis of 1929 and that of the present day. Then, the universe of ideological certainties presented itself as a feasible alternative to the crisis, like a rising sun. Today, following the end of ideologies and the collapse of the system of competing blocs, things are no longer thus. We are like sailors who have to rebuild their ship on the open sea. Our only hope of salvation lies in creating a ship with what remains of the wreck. On the great sea of history planks continue to appear that we can take hold of, but where do they come from? Maybe from earlier wrecks? Or from some totally other "elsewhere"? On the horizon of this scene of shipwreck, in which the spectators themselves have been thrown into the sea, a sense of expectation begins to emerge. Perhaps, in the questions thus arising from the shipwreck, we may find, in its most essential form, the currently sensed collective need for ethics and religious meaning.

The Metaphor of Liquidity

The image of the ever-restless sea recalls the metaphor of *liquidity*, employed with singular versatility by the British sociologist of Polish-Jewish roots, Zygmunt Baumann.[4] In our times, models and configurations are no longer "given," and even less "axiomatic." There are just too many of them. They clash with one another, and they contradict the commandments to which they refer, so that each of them has been deprived of a good measure of its power to coerce. It would be imprudent to deny, or even to minimize, the deep change that the advent of fluid modernity has introduced into the human condition. In the absence of dependable points of reference, everything seems fluid and, as such, justified or justifiable in relation to the passing wave of the moment. The very ethical parameters that the "great Code" of the Bible had entrusted to the West now seem to have been diluted and are no longer obvious nor readily at hand. The talk is of "relativism," "nihilism," "weak thought," and the "ontology of decline."

With remarkable foresight, Dietrich Bonhoeffer, who died a martyr of Nazi barbarity in the Flossenbürg concentration camp on April 9, 1945, had grasped how such a situation was to challenge the ethics of the world that would be born from the ashes of totalitarianism: "Since there is nothing lasting, the foundation of life in history, which is trust, fails in all its forms."[5] The human being drowns in the crowd of solitudes represented by the masses, and the dream of emancipation breaks against the wall of totalitarianism. "The master of the machine becomes its slave, and the machine becomes the enemy of man. Creatures rise up against their creator: a remarkable repetition of Adam's sin! The emancipation of the masses issues in the terror of the guillotine. . . . The path we have walked since the French revolution leads to nihilism."[6]

This *liquidity* finds particular expression today in the volatility of the certainties promised by the "virtual economy" of international finance, in fact ever more separated from the real economy. Now that the mask of maximum profit for minimum risk has fallen away, we are left with the ruins of a fluid situation at all levels. To find points of reference so as to indicate ways forward that can be trusted is the titanic challenge facing those charged with government and administration. Economics, too, in its search for salvation, knocks at ethics' door!

The Metaphor of Seafaring

And yet, on the sea of history there appear other planks to hold on to, fragments allowing us to assemble a skiff still able to sail. What are they? I do not consider it unfounded to find here a metaphor for the meaning offered to human beings by the various *religious creeds*. The religions are summoned to the sickbed of *homo oeconomicus*. In their turn, they are challenged by the whole process of globalization and so become aware of a new need to meet and work together.

Samuel P. Huntington identifies the challenge of the immediate future in the conflictual nature of this encounter.[7] After the wars between nation-states that typified the nineteenth century, and those between ideologies characteristic of the twentieth, in his view the twenty-first century will be marked by the clash of civilizations, themselves to be identified with the religious traditions in which they find inspiration. What needs to be established, therefore, is if and in what measure the religions can play a role in overcoming conflict and in building a new world order. Christianity and Islam, especially, are to be found at the heart of this debate, not only because of their links respectively with Western and Arab culture, but also because of the threat constituted by the alliance between some anti-Western movements and certain religious outlooks that claim to be founded on the Islamic faith. Yet, no less important for the cause of peace is the role that could be played by Judaism and the great religions of Asia.

The challenge, then, is to choose between two models: "clash" or "covenant" between civilizations and religions. Certainly, the encounter between them cannot simply be a matter of juxtaposition. The alternative to the barbarity of total clash appears to be the possibility of *métissage*.[8] This confluence of multiple identities, certainly linked to the great migratory movements now underway, is no less related to the overcoming of distance achieved through the various means of communication, especially the Internet. We refer here to the experience, hitherto unknown to the majority of people, of the encounter between very different identities, leading to the formation of plural, nomadic, "mixed" identities, which at one and the same time are both self-assertive and flexible.[9]

The succession of events, from fateful 1989 to September 11, 2001, and what then followed reveal the urgency of this challenge. We have moved from a world where frictions were fundamentally ideological to one where they are essentially a matter of identity. For many years to come this problem of identity will poison history, weaken intellectual debate, and spread hatred, violence, and destruction on all sides. A basic choice has to be made. *Métissage* has always been part of the history of peoples and cultures. The illusion of purity of identity and race is pure folly. If a culture is fully alive, it is also able to enter into a process of mutual exchange and reciprocal understanding with the identity of those who come to dwell within it. Certainly, this "assembling" is neither easy nor risk free. What is decisive, though, is that persons and cultures come to recognize a code of common values, capable of serving as a basis for relations of mutual respect, mutual recognition, and dialogue. What might be the sources of such a code? And what might be the route for this boat put together on the seas of the great village?

The Tower of Babel

An ethics founded on *biblical revelation* offers a decisive possibility for defining such a code, and it helps to indicate the route to be followed. Such an ethics finds its fundamental point of reference in the centrality of the human person standing before the mystery of the living God. Beyond the shipwreck, on the waves of liquid modernity, the boat is now built together, with everyone agreeing to shared, stable, and reliable rules, rooted in the dignity of the human being and in the binding nature of the moral imperative, making possible the voyage together across the wide sea toward the harbor—only ever glimpsed in hope and never fully reached in reality—of universal peace and justice for all. The notion of the absolute uniqueness of every human being provides the theoretical bulwark against every possible manipulation of persons, and it grounds the recognition of their inalienable dignity.

Yet the recognition of this dignity also leads us back to its ultimate foundation. In this connection, we may be helped by a "solid" metaphor, the "tower of Babel." Genesis 11 paints a picture of divisive confusion, originating from the split between the virtual—imagined or claimed—and the real, truly lived and at personal cost. The tower of Babel, though, offers another level of meaning that escapes the majority of commentators but was already noticed by Voltaire, when he underlined that the name "Babel" means that *El*—God—is father. Jacques Derrida draws out an important implication of this, when he observes that God punishes the builders of the tower "for having thus sought to make a name for themselves, to choose their own name, to build their own name, to unite themselves around this name as in a place that is at one and the same time a language and a tower, both the one and the other. He punishes them for having thus sought to generate for themselves a unique and universal genealogy."[10]

The Babel metaphor implies that the future of humanity does not lie in the cancellation of all differences but in their ability to live together, in their mutual knowledge and acceptance, based on the common foundation of the absolute dignity of each human being before God, the only master of history. The great code constituted by the Decalogue translates this project into the commandment, call, and impulse written deep in each person for the good of all. The God of the covenant is not in competition with human beings but is that friend and neighbor who reveals and guarantees the dignity of the total humanity of every person. This is the God of Jesus Christ, the God who is love (see 1 John 4:8-16).

In the divine *Logos* made flesh is revealed not only the *logos* that underpins the world and all life but also the plan of God's love that precedes the world and goes into it gratuitously. In the global village, where the different religious traditions are called to dialogue, the incarnation and the paschal mystery of Jesus Christ offer a totally new horizon: one of a possible, impossible love, impossible for our human strength alone, made possible by God's drawing near, God with us, the eternal Emmanuel. To witness to this foundation, not against anyone but out of love for all, to live it through the presence of the Risen One in his body the church, is the task of Christian ethics in this age of the global village and of the urgent need for a meeting of religions and civilizations, respectful of the differences. The Christian witness, given courageously "in season and out of season" (2 Tim 4:2), offers light and help to the navigation of human beings.

An Ethics Based on the Bible

I would like to conclude these reflections by moving from the metaphors to the theses that underlie them. I will offer four such theses, aimed at developing an ethics founded on biblical revelation and capable—it seems to me—of speaking to the whole global village.

First thesis: *There is no ethics without transcendence.* There can be no moral action where the presence of the other is not acknowledged in all the depth of his or her irreducible difference. There can be no foundation for ethics without this acknowledgment: whenever we assert ourselves to such a degree as to deny the existence of others over against whom we are called to measure ourselves, we deny the very possibility of a choice between good and evil, and drown all difference in the deep ocean of our own solipsism. No one is an island! Beyond the ideologies and totalitarianisms of the modern era, there is the need for an ethics of closeness and interpersonal relations. When we are shipwrecked on the great sea of history we need one another to bind together the single planks to which we hold!

Second thesis: *There is no ethics without gratuitousness and responsibility.* This movement of transcendence has a gratuitous and potentially infinite character. To relate to the other in terms of some selfish calculation is to empty moral decision of all value, rendering it a mere act of commerce or a simple exchange between equals. Here Kant's teaching retains all its truth: either the moral imperative is categorical, and hence unconditional, or it does not exist. In this gratuitous and potentially infinite nature of ethical transcendence we grasp how it is always "an exodus from self without return" (Emmanuel Levinas) and how at its very heart lies love, giving without counting the cost and without measure, by the unadulterated, radiant power of gift. When we are shipwrecked, we will only find salvation together in an act of mutual generosity, one to the other, and all of us to each one.

Third thesis: *There is no ethics without solidarity and justice.* In this same movement of transcendence, we experience the cluster of others surrounding our individual selves as the source of a complex network of ethical demands. To temper and reconcile these demands so that the gift made to the one does not become a wound to the other, or a barrier raised against him or her, means that we have to find a way of conjugating ethics with justice. As together we seek to regulate this network of the requirements of justice, we discover that we have to make sense of the notion of rights. It is not abstract, objective norms, nor a despotic authority that provides law with its claim to be obeyed, but rather the urgent need to temper ethical relations so that no such relation be to the exclusive advantage of some or to the detriment of the dignity of others. Here an ethics of solidarity completes an ethics of responsibility, guarding the latter against the ever-present risk of an intemperate and fruitless absolutism of intention. The common good is the measure and norm of individual action, especially in the area of civil duties. Only thus can the boat be put together and sail toward an agreed destination!

Fourth thesis: *Ethics points us toward that free, sovereign, ultimate, and absolute transcendence that has first turned toward us.* When we recognize that this movement of transcendence toward the other and the network of others in which we are placed carry with them an inner, infinite call, another transcendence, ultimate and hidden, begins to take shape on the horizon. In the intimate yet penultimate transcendence we discover that we have already recognized the footfall and memory of this greater transcendence. In others whose faces are familiar to us we meet the categorical imperative of that absolute love that comes to meet us, and in the absolute demand of solidarity toward the weakest we find an infinitely needful love that calls to us.

This absolute transcendence turned toward us, this absolute need for love that calls to us in the very act of offering itself, opens us up to theological ethics. Here the demand of being one-for-the-other sends us back to a deeper and foundational relation with the living God, One in the mutual self-giving of the Three. Here the ethics of responsibility and solidarity call us to the ethics of grace, and to the communion of the church, to whom this divine gift is entrusted to be shared and offered, particularly to the communion with those who have in the church the responsibility of the magisterium, as it was authoritatively remembered by the encyclical *Veritatis splendor* of Pope John Paul II (1993), and by the instruction by the Congregation for the Doctrine of the Faith entitled *Donum veritatis* (1990) on the ecclesial vocation of the theologian. Here our penultimate love leads us back to a love that is ultimate and sovereign, in the eternal interpersonal event of the one God in three Persons. Here, autonomy meets its founding and liberating heteronomy, and in the varied forms of our being one-for-the-other this possible-impossible love comes to tell its story in time. Love "never ends" (1 Cor 13:8).

Against this love will be measured the deep truth of our choices. At the evening of our lives we will be judged on love! The harbor toward which we sail the ship rebuilt on the sea of history is the future of the promise that at the end God will be all in all, and the whole world will be God's home. This future—of which the divine life shared in the church is anticipation and promise—works on ethics like magnetism on the compass. The ethics of transcendence is inseparable from the ethics of love and of hope, founded on the promise of the faith that the God of the covenant has lit in the history of human persons. Thanks to this compass the boat will be able to find its way forward, and the sea of time—which touches every shore of the "global village"—will be able to flow into the ocean of eternity. In this sense, too, I like to understand the beautiful image attributed to Antoine de Saint-Exupéry: "If you want to build a ship, don't drum up the men to gather wood, divide the work and give orders. Instead, teach them to yearn for the vast and endless sea."

Notes

1. Hans Blumenberg, *Schiffbruch mit Zuschauer: Paradigma einer Daseinsmetapher* (Frankfurt am Main: Suhrkamp, 1979).

2. Lucretius, *De rerum natura*, 2.1-4.

3. Blaise Pascal, *Pensées*, in *Oeuvres complètes* (Paris: J. Chevalier, 1954), 451.

4. See, for example, Zygmunt Baumann, *Liquid Modernity* (Cambridge: Blackwell, 2000).

5. Dietrich Bonhoeffer, *Ethik*, ed. E. Bethge (Munich: Kaiser, 1966), 114f.

6. Ibid., 108.

7. Samuel Huffington, *The Clash of Civilizations and the Remaking of World's Order* (New York: Simon & Schuster, 1996).

8. See R. Duboux, *Métissage ou Barbarie* (Paris: L'Harmattan, 1994).

9. See A. Maalouf, *Les identités meurtrières* (Paris: Éditions Grasset, 1998).

10. Jacques Derrida, *Des tours de Babel*, in *Aut Aut* 189-90 (1982): 70.

A Protestant Perspective

Mercy Amba Oduyoye

I come to this conference totally vulnerable, feeling inadequate but expectant because I hope to leave here enriched and inspired to continue the quest for mutually empowering interreligious relations in the multireligious communities in which I participate daily. For the past twenty years I have intentionally tried to live among women of faith in Africa. I am also present because the planners saw fit to bring in a voice from the Protestant (Methodist) world to this gathering of Catholic theological ethicists. I am particularly grateful for this inclusion of a voice from another faith community.

To clarify the conference for myself, and in the process hopefully communicate my position, I want to look at the components of this consultation, beginning with the concept of ethics. Although one cannot say enough about the complexity of this constantly evolving global village, I will leave that to others. My focus will be on my immediate experience—the world of women in Africa—and more specifically on the experience of women in multireligious Ghana. Finally, I shall reflect briefly on the potential of interreligious dialogue for Ghana, for Africa, and for the global family.

My aim throughout is to raise some of the questions and issues that I struggle with in the hope that my colleagues here will provide fresh ways of looking at the challenges of ethics in an interreligious world. Archbishop Forte, Dr. Ma'arif, and I have been asked to state our views on the nature of dialogue on ethics in this global world.

The Nature of Ethics in the Globalized World

As a lay person in the pew struggling to conduct my life as a Christian, ethics denotes for me the rules of conduct governing "those who bear the name of Christ." The immediate question for me is, Are these rules the same for people of other faith communities? Can we discern commonalities or common grounds on which to have a conversation on ethics?

Is a roundtable of people of diverse faiths realistic? Can we agree on what is morally right and what is not? Whether we come to our concerns from the language of ethics or from those of morality we end up with the same questions. Can we agree on what ethical imperatives will portray us as truly human? You may find much of my reflection on ethics amateurish as I am not an ethicist. The ethical pro-

18

gram I lay before you is a mixture of social ethics and ethical imperatives I perceive arising out of Christian theology and, more specifically, theology articulated by contemporary Christian women theologians.

The globalized world, including nations like Ghana and Italy, is much more than the sum of its parts. Yet, as Ghana participates in this sum total, Ghanaians can see themselves as members and subjects in the globalized world. Not a new concept, globalization is at least two thousand years old. As far as I can determine, Christianity was the first religion that was determined to be global, claiming a mandate from its sacred scripture, which is also the source of its moral teaching. The *oikoumene* was Christianity's parish from the very beginning. Wherever humanity exists, Christianity claims a mandate to be present, bringing its carriers into conflict with peoples of other faiths. For centuries Christian missionaries have been pounding the surface of the earth with "beautiful feet," filling the ears of all humanity with a message that they claim is Good News—gospel—for all humanity.

While the Christian sacred scriptures are not found in the mother tongue of the founder (Aramaic), they do exist in Hebrew, Greek, Latin, Spanish, Arabic, Hindi, Korean, Mfantse, and many other languages. Where they do not exist in the mother tongue of believers, they are being translated. The airwaves also resonate with the Bible in many languages as part of Christianity's quest to be global. Other faiths that did not intentionally set out to be global have also become global as their followers have relocated throughout the world. As the world has become this large neighborhood, people of diverse faiths must learn to coexist. The globalized world is shaped not only by technology by also by the cultures, languages, and perceptions of people on the move. Because we live in a world of families and communities with varied values, cultures, and norms, our deliberations must be people centered.

Today, there is still a desire for national identity even while people strive to maintain life-enhancing international connections. Yet our globalized economy is so skewed as to produce a category of humanity labeled "the bottom billion" while others belong to a range of exclusive clubs. And while the many forms of media make people more aware of what is going on, they do not promote an ethic of the common good for either humanity or the rest of creation. Meanwhile, the many advances in science and technology tend to ignore the values of the multireligious world of human beings. And yet it becomes more and more evident that we must pay attention to the interreligious reality of the world if these advances are to be used to promote the well-being of the whole human community and the environment that sustains it.

In this globalized world, human interdependence increases by leaps and bounds. The Rev. Dr. Jay T. Rock, a Presbyterian pastor and theologian, said recently at a conference that there are no longer any problems that face humanity that can be addressed effectively by Christians alone or by any other religion acting on its own. He noted that "massive population movements have made almost all the major cities and sub-urban areas of the world religiously pluralistic."[1] This pluralism, he pointed out, "is no longer a passive plurality, but an active one in which each of the religious communities has begun . . . to assert their right . . . to participate fully in sociopolitical life on their own terms."[2] In most nations it is no longer "when in Rome do as the Romans." The practice now is to bring the way of life of Accra to Rome. And yet a Western woman from Los Angeles may have to conform to the dress code of Saudi Arabia or a Somali girl born in Canada may have to undergo genital mutilation.

Our cultural landscape has become more complicated, as have the norms for ethical decisions. The asymmetry in the way one culture accepts another culture calls out for dialogue. We must cultivate mutuality in our concern for and practice of liberative interreligious living. For me this means that members of diverse faith communities must come together to seek and to practice what makes for the flourishing of the human community. Via the air currents that we share, despite global intellectual resources, volcanic dust from Iceland can grind air travel to a halt and impoverish many in Africa. What more is there to say?

Africa's Faith Communities

A focus on religion generally tends to be abstract and to hold up well in theological debates, which is well and good and needed, as long as it is not transmuted into polemics. Theology, however, is needed to get to the roots of issues so that we can make a lasting impact. This is why I crave your indulgence to stay with the encounters of people of faith in order to make a few observations concerning the most visible faith communities in Africa.

In general, religion in Africa is presented as a triple heritage. The primal religious imagination of the indigenous peoples of Africa yielded an autonomous set of beliefs and practices that the academic world has structured and labeled African Traditional Religion (ATR). ATR is manifested in a variety of forms throughout the continent, and it remains the bedrock of traditional African cultures. It is so ingrained in the traditional worldview that some academics have gravitated to using the term "religio-culture," because many of the indigenous cultural mores and practices are faith based. This primal religion as it existed in northern and Nilotic Africa helped shape early Christianity long before it made its way to the West, and its ethos of consensus is still with us. But that is another story. The other two sources of religious belief, Christianity and Islam, do not need much preamble as they both made their debut in Africa in the early periods of their existence, leading some scholars to posit that both should be counted as "traditional" religions of Africa.[3]

In addition to this triple heritage, many other faith communities have representatives in Africa. They have arrived with immigrants, and some have made converts from among indigenous Africans. Today variations of Judaism, Hinduism, Buddhism, Confucianism, Bahai, and many other belief systems are present among us. The interaction of this variety of peoples of faith has made Africans extremely faith-conscious people. Everyday experiences, however, draw attention to the interaction among Christians, Muslims, and Traditionalists. As long as the factors of economy, politics, and hegemony are kept at bay, relationships among these peoples are generally cordial and respectful. Once economics, politics, and forms of hegemony encroach on communities, however, discord and even violence can result.

The presence of Western colonial hegemony in Africa privileged Christianity for most of the modern period, although in some places political expediency directed that Islam be left alone or privileged. In certain areas, as the traditional culture was undermined, so was its religion. And yet ceremonies still persist to transmit the traditional values. For example, several ethnic communities in Africa still maintain naming ceremonies for newborns during which the values of the community are rehearsed. Among the Akan of Ghana, the naming of the eight-day-old infant includes a ritual to distinguish two clear liquids by taste. The newborn can tell the difference between water and gin or water and Sprite or another soft drink. This follows the New Testament injunction to "let your nay be nay and your yea be yea" (Matt 5:37). While the goal of this ritual is to enhance relationships and the vision of the good life for the Akan is a life of integrity, they still belittle the presence of the female, preferring boys to girls.

Post-colonial claims for equity in the number of religious holidays on the national calendars in Ghana and Nigeria and occasional clashes between Traditionalists and Muslims or Traditionalists and Christians demonstrate that ATR is far from being superseded by Christianity. Islam is also alive and well and seeking a place in the sun. The religious kaleidoscope of Africa was very visible at the inauguration of the new South Africa. The variety of scriptures read, prayers said, and sacred poetry recited indicates the Africans' acceptance of religious pluralism. Similarly, in Ghana any independence-day celebration will open with prayers by cultic functionaries from the triple heritage. In sum, interreligious living is a daily reality in Africa. The triple heritage is present even in some nuclear families, and ordinarily Africans would share or at least respect one another's festivals.

Interreligious interactions hardly ever surface on the intellectual level of debating the substance of faith or the resulting ethics. Such dialogue belongs to the academy and to bodies created by churches. In Africa it is the Programme for Christian-Muslim Relations in Africa (PROCMURA) that stands for the will to enter into dialogue,[4] as both Muslim and Christian claims to hegemony exist in various African states. On the popular level, clashes have happened and continue to occur. Notions of interreligious dialogue in Africa will have to focus intensely on at least this triple manifestation of religion. Personally, I do not feel that "dialogue" accomplishes what is needed. After attending a most stimulating consultation on Christian-Muslim relations organized by Dr. John Azumah of the London School of Theology, I began to wonder if other faith communities are also deliberating these issues. It should be our Christian ethic of love of neighbor that makes us initiators of dialogue. In the world in which we live today it is time to actively seek and embrace people of other faiths who seek to walk the same road. The Parliament of World Religions, and similar organizations, might be such a forum for such interreligious discussions of ethics.[5]

Interreligious Dialogue

At a conference I attended, in his presentation entitled "Justice in the Dialogue of Religions," Prof. Dietrich Wiederkehr of Lucerne, Switzerland, made references to Hans Küng's Global Ethic Foundation, a project of ethical dialogue among the world religions.[6] I came away from the conference deeply impressed with the observation that these world religions were being brought together on the basis of ethical, social, and political convergences and invited to dialogue and commit to joining together to protect and promote basic ethical principles.

Dialogue, for me, has accrued to itself an image of adversarial communication in which one party is bound to lose or at best terminate in an unhappy compromise. Instead of dialogue, I would prefer a process that would lead to acknowledging the fact that we share a common heritage as human beings. Long discussions and deliberations are needed to reach a way to live in harmony with a dynamic and life-giving appropriation of our common heritage and our need to work together for the common good.

In Africa interreligious dialogue tends to be viewed as Christian-Muslim dialogue initiated by Christians to their own advantage. Globally, my experience of dialogue with people of other living faiths has been in the programs of the World Council of Churches (WCC),[7] which have included Jewish-Christian dialogue as well as Hindu-Christian, Christian-Buddhist, and other combinations. The WCC has sponsored events featuring many different faith communities that have demonstrated interest in working for harmonious coexistence. Similarly, many prominent representatives of other faith communities have been guest speakers on panels at events organized by the WCC.

Globally other interfaith conversations as well as multifaith associations and events, and the Parliament of World Religions exist to keep us mindful of our global religious diversity. How do these programs influence the ethics of our lives together as peoples of faith globally?

As far as Africa is concerned, the most significant gap has been in the conversation between Christians and followers of ATR. Personalities have been invited to specific events and some scanty publications exist in this area, but by and large there has been no concerted effort to increase understanding. Christians claim that ATR has no bona fide dialogue partners to offer. Periodically, however, the challenge to create a deliberate forum for undertaking Christian-ATR dialogue has been recognized. My sense is that if we moved from the image of dialogue among academics and scholars of religion to a conversation among practitioners, we would be more likely to find more conversation partners. This has been my experience in working with African women. As it is, not much happens because of the presumed absence of dialogue partners from the ATR side. (There is also an undisputed need for Muslim-ATR conversations in parts of Africa, but that lies beyond the present discussion.)

Restricting myself to the African sector of the globe, what I see is conversations among people of faith who claim to be directed by ATR, Christianity, and Islam. Sharing the same spaces, sometimes even the same rooms, there is an imperceptible osmosis of ideas, attitudes, and practices that derive from all three or even one, but are acknowledged by all. Ideally, what we seek is an informal, unannounced daily roundtable of people of faith looking one another in the face, speaking into the center, and listening from the center. None is on the periphery and none is deemed an outsider, for all are in the circle. The center of the circle is our common humanity and our faith in the ultimate good that faith inspires—the good being the divine, on which all our lives are anchored. All our names for the divine are accepted, as none is final, and all inspire us toward the good.

Structured conversations among people of faith need to have definite objectives. Among women of faith in Africa there exist conversations on issues of religion and culture and their impact on women's lives as well as women's appropriation of and impact on these factors. In this particular forum of theological ethics, I see our aim as seeking ways of bringing to the table the ethical issues confronting humanity globally. We come not just from Africa, but from Europe and Asia and Latin America and North America. What are the particular ethical concerns of people of faith, and how far and how fast can we walk together to create lifestyles that will engender the flourishing of humanity and the environment in which we have been placed?

I will now briefly sketch some issues and challenges of ethics as I understand them as an African woman of faith. I intend to observe and reflect on experience but will not offer analyses or recommendations. I deem it too early for such an undertaking.

Ethical Concerns

Those of us involved in these multifaith deliberations on ethical issues are expected to come to the table from a faith perspective and to go away enriched and empowered by our mutual sharing. A critical outcome, naturally, is the action that a particular faith-based partner will be ready to undertake.

Issues of fundamental ethics arising out of our common humanity find articulation in universal terms in the dictum "Do to others what you would like them to do to you." Put negatively, "Do not do to others what you would not like them to do to you." This basic advice is to be found in all religions and is enshrined in its negative form in my mother tongue as *Nea wompe se wode ye wo no mfa nnye wo yonko*.

Enshrined in the Judaeo-Christian Decalogue are ten injunctions. Apart from the first, which deals with monotheism, the rest may be accepted by all

to be fundamental ethics for communal living in all human societies. Issues of
fundamental ethics are also enshrined in the United Nations charter, the "Universal Declaration of Human Rights."[8] With many modifications coming from
the Africa charter and specific issues of application raised by women and others raised on behalf of children, as well as other modifications sought by other
communities, it is still the most commonly cited source of fundamental ethics.
Issues of choice, freedom, and responsibility are basic to our being human. So are
factors of personal worth and human dignity. It is generally agreed that individuals are valued in and of themselves and are to be accorded dignity and respect.
The equality of all persons—irrespective of race, color, creed, physical appearance, and nationality—is basic to generally accepted ethical norms. From this we
derive both social and personal ethics.

Adherence to these fundamental rights manifests itself in fields such as religious freedom, freedom of conscience, the right to private property, social responsibility toward the vulnerable, and so forth. Solidarity in the human community
is accepted as a virtue to be promoted. In the global community, wars are to be
discouraged, the environment is to be safeguarded, and economic justice is to be
promoted nationally, internationally, and globally. The common good also requires
an ethics of mutual responsibility and global interdependence. All issues of social
responsibility have to be worked out locally but also on a global level. Therefore,
the challenges of the persistent gap between rich and poor that often results from
unjust trade practices calls for concerted efforts toward its closure. This endemic
social factor has so exasperated one person as to suggest that there is "an international conspiracy against the poor." (And some would suggest that perhaps there is
a religious conspiracy against women.)

The need for a basic understanding of ethics that applies globally challenges
us to listen to women and the poor. Cooperation among multinational organizations, partnerships, and the complex levels of authority in governance all indicate
efforts that embrace the entire human community, including those without power
or voice. The task of social ethics is global and therefore has to be the domain of
communities of faith in conversation. Both fundamental ethics and social ethics
can also be stated in personal terms. From them we derive accepted codes that out-
law the trading of human beings or using persons to serve one's or another's selfish ends. Fundamental ethics guide us into seeking and maintaining the common
good, that which serves the good of all and not just that of a few individuals or
sections of communities. All human beings have the responsibility to participate in
generating the "stuff" of the common good so that the well-being of each member
of a community will be assured by the whole community as its members all guard
and promote the well-being of each member.

Among people of faith, personal ethics are paramount. The value of human
beings as whole and integrated entities created by God ensures that each is recognized as both a corporeal, sexual, and spiritual being. In faith communities,
however, bioethics and sexual ethics often loom large, overshadowing other ethical

concerns. Ethics is equated with morality, and morality is invariably associated with sexual ethics. Today, human sexuality has become a crucial talking point among Christians, and faith communities should actively accompany the faithful in their decision making regarding personal relationships and especially the meaning of marriage.

Personal ethics that often get short shrift because of the concentration on sexuality do need to be called to center stage by people of faith. We speak too easily of greed, bribery, cheating, and all manner of manifestations of the absence of personal integrity. Truth goes out the window when personal wealth in the business world is the issue. All these concerns require the attention of faith communities.

An Interreligious Task

A roundtable of people of various faith traditions represents the majority of the human population. In Africa, religion continues to hold sway among the general populace. People describe themselves as Christian, Muslim, or Traditionalist, or use some other religious identifier. Whatever term is used, religion is a major component of people's identity. Often it is said that since Traditional Religion is the bedrock of the traditional African culture, all who are formed by this culture are also in effect influenced by the beliefs of Traditional Religion. Our concern for ethics in Africa, therefore, cannot exclude the demands of ATR. Africa brings to the global conversation not only the African variants of global Christianity and global Islam, but also the specific ethics of the primal religion that Africa shares with various indigenous peoples. Areas of the world where the "major" religions have marginalized or even totally obliterated the autochthonous ones should not ignore the power of these primal religious imaginations.

African Christianity brings to the roundtable many ethical concerns of global Christianity. It is the nature of our global village that the private is political and the local soon becomes global. However, there are also ethical issues that are specific to Africa. A significant issue for us is that African women, whatever their religious persuasion, face ethical challenges related to the lack of gender equality and gender justice. Issues of equality and partnership, violence of all types, and double standards in sexual behavior affect women negatively. Teresa Okure has reminded us that "the virus of the (presumed) personal inferiority of women affects all religions globally."[9] Any roundtable of people of faith must examine this pressing issue.

When challenges such as HIV/AIDS confront the human community, they are dealt with through an ethic of fear and stigmatization, often buttressed by religious teachings, and Christians in Africa have used this approach to the pandemic. It took the reflections of an African woman to call attention to the neglect of the relationship between AIDS and poverty.[10] Positive ethical demands like love, kindness, tenderness, compassion, fidelity, and others were pushed to the back burner, and the onus was always on women to demonstrate these values. Faith communities need to implement measures globally against the instrumentalization of women's sexuality and the marginalization of the human rights of minors.

Christians must also bring environmental issues and the ethical demands that our faiths lay upon us to this global roundtable of people of faith. People of faith affirm that human beings do not own the cosmos. ATR, Christianity, and Islam in Africa all acknowledge the God of creation who has put humans on earth to tend the rest of creation and to represent the presence of God. We know what is required to fulfill this mandate. We have to arrive at a way of "covenanting for life" and a way to promote justice to the environment. The onus is on the communities of faith working together to champion the sanctity of creation.

In 2007 a global meeting of Christians in Accra produced a confession saying "justice is a matter of faith" and that it involves "economic and ecological justice ... [and] social, political and moral issues [that] are integral to faith in Jesus Christ and affect the integrity of the church."[11] It goes on to say that in order to be true to its foundations the church must stand "in solidarity with persons who are suffering and struggling" and should hear and respond "to the cries of people who suffer and to the woundedness of creation itself, over-consumed and undervalued by the current global economy."[12]

Women have tried to be the church by embracing an ethic of justice and care and by advancing compassion in all situations of estrangement and hurt. Such women may be found in all the faith communities as they comb their sacred texts and traditions to highlight the ethical demands that will make all of us truly human. Among the Akan of Ghana a person who has lost the attributes of respect, care, and compassion has in the eyes of the community lost his/her humanity. An abuser, we say, is one who has no fear of God; however, a human being is one who abuses neither the Creator nor the creatures.

As this forum seeks a way toward ethics and interreligious dialogue in the globalized world, we must not forget to listen to the voices of women and children and to indigenous spiritualities that are life affirming.

Notes

1. S. Wesley Ariarajah, "Wider Ecumenism—Some Theological Perspectives," as quoted in Jay T. Rock, "Is Christian Unity a Catalyst for Human Community?: Interfaith Relations and the Ecumenical Movement," a paper given at the Ecumenical Consultation called by the General Assembly Committee on Ecumenism, Louisville, Kentucky, September 27-29, 2007, 8 (Ecumenical & Interfaith News Network—PCUSA, http://www.eif-pcusa.org/WhoWeAre/documents/ecumenismandinterfaith-rock.pdf).

2. Ibid.

3. Thomas C. Oden, *How Africa Shaped the Christian Mind: Rediscovering the African Seedbed of Western Christianity* (Downers Grove, IL: InterVarsity Press, 2007).

4. For more information, see "Programme for Christian-Muslim Relations in Africa," http://www.procmura-prica.org/.

5. For more information, see "Council for a Parliament of the World Religions," http://www.parliamentofreligions.org/.

6. See "A Global Ethic Now!" Global Ethic Foundation, http://www.global-ethic-now.de/gen-eng/0a_was-ist-weltethos/0a-04-capitel-4/0a-04-00-die-stiftung.php.

7. See "Inter-Religious Dialogue and Cooperation," World Council of Churches, http://www.oikoumene.org/en/programmes/interreligiousdialogue.html.

8. The "Universal Declaration of Human Rights" is a charter accepted and promulgated by the United Nations on December 10, 1948. For a copy of the text, see "Universal Declaration of Human Rights," http://www.un.org/en/documents/udhr/index.shtml.

9. Teresa Okure, "Jesus in Nazareth (Luke 4:14-30): An Index to the Question of Poverty in Africa," paper given at the 13th Congress of the Pan African Association of Catholic Exegetes (PACE), Johannesburg, South Africa, September 2-8, 2007.

10. Ibid.

11. See "The Accra Confession," World Alliance of Reformed Churches, http://warc.jalb.de/warcajsp/side.jsp?news_id=1157&navi=45.

12. Ibid.

There was no space to say otherwise. If that was attempted, the Inquisition was the consequence. From this angle the Renaissance movement was a rebellion against the absolute religious position of the church at the expense of individual choice and freedom.

Sadly enough, however, this movement went too far by granting unlimited freedom to humanity. Thus, the concept of equilibrium in human life lost its religio-moral anchor dramatically, a condition that exists until the present day. The happy life defined by philosophers remains aloof from the reality of human expectation. I do not know how long this unbalanced phenomenon will endure, but to a very great degree leaders of religion have failed to offer a better alternative. Therefore, it is hoped that the leaders of interfaith dialogue will sincerely work hard to find a reasonable and workable solution to this modern dilemma. Unless and until that balanced solution is achieved, there is no reason to dream of living on a peaceful planet. It will not become a reality in the near future.

I would ask another question: "Do we really feel happy to live such an unbalanced worldly life in which the idea of justice and the spirit of human universal solidarity as taught by all religions have been non-existent for so long?" If one turns to the Qur'an on this matter, the answer will be clear and poetic: "The parable of those who take protectors other than God is the likeness of a spider which builds [for itself] a house; and verily, the weakest of houses is the spider's house, if they but knew" (Q 29:41). Muslims who claim to believe in God and life in the hereafter as the strongest spiritual anchor at the present time, in my personal observation, are part of those who inhabit the spider's web, but unfortunately the majority of them may not know it. In other words, that claim is nothing more than a false one without any organic connection with real life. This is an acute cultural crisis that has inflicted the Muslim mentality for a long time.

One person who keenly understood the Muslim cultural identity crisis was Muhammad Iqbal (1877-1938), a Pakistani poet-philosopher. In an imaginary dialogue with his spiritual teacher, Jalal al-Din Rumi (1207-1273), Persian mystic and poet, Iqbal asks Rumi,

> My lofty thoughts reach up the heavens;
> But on earth I am humiliated, frustrated, and agonized.
> I am unable to manage the affairs of this world,
> And I constantly face stumbling blocks in this path.
> Why are the affairs of the world beyond my control?
> Why is the learned in religion a fool in the affairs of the world?[5]

Rumi gives the following unpredictable yet logical answer:

> Anyone who [claims to be able to] walk on the heavens;
> Why should it be difficult for him to stalk on the earth?[6]

Through this sharp poetic statement, Iqbal warns Muslims to say *sayonara* (good-bye) to the false claim that completely contradicts their concrete reality of life.

I am afraid that modern civilization is also a spider's house, though its external facade looks spectacular and impressive. This soulless civilization or society, Eric Fromm writes, transforms humanity "into *Homo consumens*, the total consumer, whose only aim is to *have* more and to *use* more. This society produces many useless things, and to the same degree many useless people. Man, as a cog in the production machine, becomes a thing, and ceases to be human."[7] Meanwhile, as noted above, the Muslim world has long lost its creative and fresh mind to offer an alternative civilization to humankind. For centuries, the Muslims' historical burden in exist-ing as defeated communities has prevented them from saying "yes" to the challenge of the day. Hopefully the time will come when Muslims are aware of the historical role they should play in modern time, as their forefathers had done before.

Despite the mounting challenges we now face, there is, of course, always hope for the moral situation. Through serious and intensive interfaith dialogues to seek the truth and mutual understanding between believers and non-believers, I am sure that we will finally find the proper way to liberate ourselves from the prison of excessive anthropocentrism that has placed modern humanity in the cage of an uncertain future. For this reason, religious people should have the spiritual courage to openly criticize themselves. In order to put religions again in effective positions to establish justice for all, they should not let their minds and hearts be frozen. Human beings should be prepared to return to their authenticity as God's noble creatures, far above the position enjoyed by the angels. On this issue, the Qur'an makes an affirmative statement: "And indeed We have conferred dignity on the children of Adam, and We have carried them on land and sea, and have provided for them sustenance out of good things of life, and favored them far above most of Our creation" (Q 17:70).[8]

But this honorable status is conditional; it rests on human beings having sin-cere faith in God and doing good deeds. Otherwise, they will be reduced to the lowest of the low (Q 95:5). I believe these Qur'anic statements may be shared by other denominational communities, in both the West and the East. In the moral realm, our differences are actually minor. It is not impossible that one day we will be able to create a formula of a global ethic based on the moral teachings of different religions and ancient traditions, as initiated and pioneered recently, for instance, by Hans Küng and others since 1993.[9] Concerning the relations of religions and the idea of a new global ethics, Hans Küng is convinced that all religions agree on the following commitments:

1. Commitment to a culture of non-violence and respect for life: . . . "You shall not kill!" Or in positive terms: "Have respect for life!"
2. Commitment to a culture of solidarity and a just economic order: . . . "You shall not steal!" Or in positive terms: "Deal honestly and fairly!"

3. Commitment to a culture of tolerance and a life of truthfulness: . . . "You shall not lie!" Or in positive terms: "Speak and act truthfully!"
4. Commitment to a culture of equal rights and partnership between men and women: . . . "You should not commit sexual immorality!" Or in positive terms: "Respect and love one another!"[10]

Küng seems quite optimistic about the role of religions to save the future of human-kind, provided all religious people have tolerance, sincerity, and a commitment to the truth. They must act together as truth seekers.

We have already completed the last year of the first decade of the twenty-first century. Science and technology, particularly communication technology and military technology, have made tremendous progress, which our human ancestors could hardly have imagined. As regards morality, however, progress has been very slow. The Roman classical proverb coined by Plautus (d. 184 B.C.E.): *homo homini lupus* ("man is a wolf to [his fellow] man") has remained the rule of present history, while almost all religions, Islam included, act as passive observers and actors. Muslims in particular are still so preoccupied and exhausted by their internal conflicts and the tension between the progressive wing and fundamentalists that there is as yet no hint of reaching a relatively permanent reconciliation. Thus, historic Islam has more or less to bear the burden of its own destiny. Because of this, I feel it is not always easy to talk about what Islamic ethics can offer to the present fragile world, though its authentic teachings are rich on matters of the highest moral standards and ethical systems, as I indicated above.

In the present situation, Muslims on the whole still need more time to correct their internal weaknesses and shortcomings, theological and cultural, so that, provided with the sense of self-confidence, they can move strategically into the midst of contemporary history as their forefathers did in the past. In this connection, Muhammad Iqbal once made an interesting comparison between the role of a prophet and the role of a saint to change the course of human history. In a lecture entitled "The Spirit of Muslim Culture," Iqbal quoted and then commented on the statement by a Muslim saint, Abdul Quddus of Gangoh: "Muhammad of Arabia ascended the highest Heaven and returned. I swear by God that if I had reached that point, I should never have returned."[11] Iqbal comments:

In the whole range of Sufi literature it will be probably difficult to find words which, in a single sentence, disclose such an acute perception of the psychological difference between the prophetic and mystic type of consciousness. The mystic does not wish to return from the repose of "unitary experience"; and even when he does return, as he must, his return does not mean much for mankind at large. The prophet's return is creative. He returns to insert himself into the sweep of time with a view to control the forces of history, and thereby to create a fresh world of ideals. For the mystic the repose of "unitary experience" is something final; for the prophet it is the awakening, within him, of world-shaking psychological forces, calculated to completely transform the human world.[12]

It seems that most Muslims now are not the true disciples of a creative prophet who had the courage to change the course of history but are quite happy to follow blindly the passive life of a saint like Abdul Quddus. If that is the case, it will be difficult for Muslims to deal effectively with the challenges posed by the wave of an aggressive globalized world as part of modernity. But to let the global-ized world proceed unchecked, as we are witnessing today, will no doubt destroy all spiritual dimensions of human life that we badly need all the time, ancient as well as modern.

This real dilemma is not only a problem for Muslims, but also a problem for all *homo sapiens* or "wise humans," according to A. J. Toynbee's definition.[13] The qual-ity of *homo sapiens*, as Toynbee concludes, is far from the present face of modernity. "We have not earned this self-conferred title *homo sapiens*," wrote Toynbee. "We have shown little wisdom, so far, in controlling ourselves and in managing our rela-tions with each other. If we succeed in surviving the present technological revolu-tion, we may at last become *homo sapiens* in truth as well as in name."[14] Professor Toynbee was a contemporary thinker who, until the time of his death in 1975, was sharply critical of the development of Western secular modernity. He was eager to see a religious revolution. On this important issue, Toynbee made a convincing statement:

> For a true and lasting peace, a religious revolution is, I am sure, a *sine qua non*. By religion, as I hope I have made clear, I mean the overcoming of self-centeredness, in both individuals and communities, by getting into communion with the spiritual presence behind the universe and by bring-ing our wills into harmony with it. I think this is the only key to peace, but we are very far from picking up this key and using it, and, until we do, the survival of the human race will continue to be in doubt.[15]

Toynbee's skepticism on the negative side of modernity is well known, particularly for those who followed his personal bitter experience in the First World War dur-ing which many of his friends were sadly and dramatically killed.

Religion as a Perennial Demand:
Social Toleration and Its Challenges[16]

I fully agree with the belief that religion is a perennial demand of humankind at all times. I cannot imagine a world, for instance, void of the existence of the Transcendental Supreme Being who created and constantly controls the universe as if He Himself is not part of it. To believe in this dictum is not in the realm of "scientific probability," but it is completely in the realm of metaphysics. It is, you may say, "a metaphysical necessity," as Catholic philosopher Étienne Gilson has correctly put it.[17] For a believer, the creation of the universe without the Creator is perfectly absurd and palpably illogical. But, on the contrary, for a non-believer, or an atheist, belief in God is ridiculous because it cannot be scientifically confirmed and proven; the logic of this view is that any religious belief should be rejected outright.

In my view, the existence of two or three categories of humankind—if we include an agnostic in our discussion—is also a perennial problem that cannot be resolved satisfactorily until the end of the world. The Qur'an itself recognizes the rights of non-believers, or atheists, to coexist peacefully as human beings with believers, or theists. The Qur'an has again confirmed our argument: "And had your Lord willed, those on earth would have believed, all of them together. So, will you then, think that you could compel people to believe?"(Q 10:99). In another brief but condensed phrase, the Qur'an says, "There shall be no compulsion in matters of faith" (Q 2:256).

For centuries and to a very great degree, Muslim rulers, just or unjust, took the spirit of these verses not to force others to follow the faith of Islam. In other words, interfaith dialogue is possible not only between believers but also between believers and non-believers, or atheists, provided all participants respect one another equally. With this in mind, all human beings, regardless of their belief or unbelief, may contribute their talents to making this world richer, more secure, more just, and peaceful, since all have the right to do so. To move in this direction, all of us should strive for spiritual maturity, so that the principles of socioreligious toleration become actual.

Nobody has the right to monopolize this planet for the sake of his or her own worldly and pragmatic interests. All should have the right to make this world continue until the coming of the Day of Judgment as part of God's plan, which no one can anticipate. On the idea of the end of the world, Karl Jaspers has made a very moving and poetic statement:

> [T]he long ages of prehistory and the short span of history give rise to the question: Is history not a transitory phenomenon, in view of the hundreds of thousands of years of prehistory? At bottom, there is no other answer save the general proposition: that which has a beginning also has an end—even if it lasts for millions of years.[18]

Before that moment comes, according to the Qur'an, all human beings have sufficient opportunities to compete with one another in goodness, in fostering the act of peaceful coexistence among nations and religions, not in war and enmity. All nations have a noble obligation to prevent the world from falling into a civilizational *hara-kiri* (suicide), which means a total destruction of all the good that human beings have created with difficulty for centuries. In the words that are no less inspiring, Jaspers has written:

History itself becomes the road to the supra-historical. In the contempla-tion of the great—in the provinces of creation, action and thought—his-tory shines forth as the everlasting present. It no longer satisfies curiosity, but becomes an invigorating force. The great things of history, as objects of veneration, bind us to the matrix above all history.[19]

The problem we are facing now under the strong wave of modernity is that "the question of how" has exhausted our intellectual and spiritual energy and stamina by putting aside "the question of why," which is most relevant to the quest for peace and human understanding. How to make a nuclear bomb seems more important for the modern mind than the question of why we should do it. The question of how is purely technical, whereas the question of why is a theologico-philosophical one that may lead us to the realm beyond history. In this domain, the role of reli-gion not only becomes relevant; no other values can replace it.[20]

Notes

1. See the Qur'an (Q), chapter 21 (*al-Anbiyá*), verse 107.
2. Bertrand Russell, *The Prospects of Industrial Civilization* (London: Allen & Unwin, 1970), 80-81.
3. Ibid., 78-79.
4. See Gianni Vattimo, *The End of Modernity*, trans. Jon R. Snyder (Baltimore: Johns Hopkins University Press, 1991), 20.
5. See Fazlur Rahman, *Islam and Modernity: Transformation of an Intellectual Tradi-tion* (Chicago: University of Chicago Press, 1982), 58.
6. Ibid.
7. Eric Fromm, *The Revolution of Hope: Toward a Humanized Technology* (New York: Harper & Row, 1968), 38 (italics in original).
8. See also Muhammad Asad's translation of this verse in *The Message of the Qur'an* (Gibraltar: Dar al-Andalus, 1980), 430. Asad's Quranic exegesis is so far one of the best for the modern mind.
9. See Hans Küng, "Chicago Declaration of the Religions for a Global Ethics," Cen-ter for Global Ethics, http://globalethic.org/Center/kung.htm.
10. See "The Principles of a Global Ethics," Celebrating the Spirit: Toward a Global Ethic (Council for a Parliament of the World's Religions, 1993), http://www.conjure.com/CTS/principles.html.
11. Allama Muhammad Iqbal, *The Reconstruction of Religious Thought in Islam* (Lahore: Sh. Muhammad Ashraf, 1971), 124.
12. Ibid.
13. A. J. Toynbee, *Surviving the Future* (New York: Oxford University Press, 1973), 44.
14. Ibid.
15. Ibid., 66-67.
16. The source for this subtitle is partly taken from my paper "Ethical Inputs: The Role of Religions," presented at the International Seminar Organized by International

Catholic Movement for Intellectual and Cultural Affair-Pax Romana, Jogjakarta (Indonesia), July 20-22, 2009.

17. See the end of n. 20 in Étienne Gilson, *God and Philosophy* (New Haven, CT: Yale University Press, 1969), 141.

18. See Karl Jaspers, *The Origin and Goal of History*, trans. Michael Bullock (New Haven, CT: Yale University Press, 1968), 275-76.

19. Ibid.

20. Finally, allow me to express my deep and sincere gratitude to the organizers of this unforgettable conference, especially to Dr. James F. Keenan and his hard working and professional staff for inviting me to deliver a speech on this rare occasion that I will keep in my personal memory forever until the end of life.

Part II
THE PAST

INTRODUCTION

The second day of the conference was dedicated to the past. The many activities included a full plenary and a pair of parallel plenaries. The full plenary attended to the Council of Trent. The first parallel plenary considered the function of history

Fourteen Theses on the Legacy of Trent[1]

Paolo Prodi

I cannot attempt to present the history of the Council of Trent, nor explain why this little city on the border between the Italian and German territories was chosen as the site of the Council, nor relate the course of the Council's work in the twenty-five sessions from 1545 to 1563, nor speak about the setbacks that the conciliar debates caused to Western Christendom, which was already torn apart by the Reformation. I hope that you yourselves will be able to breathe in physically the atmosphere in which the bishops and theologians lived after they had reached the Council on horseback or on foot from the various regions of Western Europe.

I cannot even reply to the fundamental question of our meeting: What was the role of the Council of Trent in the birth of moral theology as an autonomous branch of theological thinking? All I can do is to follow Luther's example by propounding several theses. Yet I cannot set out ninety-five of them: I must stop at a much earlier point, after the fourteenth thesis. Every word that I speak requires at least another twenty words of explanation and documentation. But although these are necessary, I must omit them.[2]

Thesis 1. During the Middle Ages and up to the Reformation and the eve of the Council of Trent, theology was the science of what "is," while canon law (natural, divine, and positive) was the science of what "ought to be." There was no place for an autonomous science of ethics, but there were for preaching and for practical handbooks to help confessors and penitents.

Thesis 2. The modern state, as it was constructed at the beginning of the modern period, tended to invade the entire sphere of positive law. There was a transition from the pluralism of medieval legal frameworks (divine law, natural law, the law of the nations, civil and canon law) to the modern dualism between the conscience and the positive law of the state. In the ethical sphere, the religious crisis of the sixteenth century is the consequence of the decline of the regime of "Christendom." The response to this crisis moved in two different directions, though with many nuances within each. Faced with the dominion of the state, the new Protestant churches that were born of the Reformation affirmed (through the unique medium of scripture) the role of the individual conscience, while the Catholic Church con-

40

structed an autonomous normative and meta-juridical system that was no longer based on law but on ethics.[3]

Thesis 3. The Council of Trent is important for the birth of moral theology more in virtue of what it did not say than in virtue of what it did say. We all know that the Council did not succeed in repairing the fracture that had taken place in the body of Christendom, but we are less informed about the failure of the attempt to restore a regime of Christendom by subordinating those princes who remained Catholic to the authority of the Roman papacy. In the final sessions of 1562-1563, the Council was salvaged as an internal reform of the ecclesiastical body only by bowing to the opposition by the powers that had remained Catholic (especially Spain and France) and dropping the decree on the "reform of the princes." Chapter 20 of the reform decree of the twenty-fifth session is reduced to a simple exhortation to the Catholic princes to guarantee Christian discipline in their government. The entire body of Tridentine decrees contains no norm relative to morality, except in connection with the administration of the sacraments and ecclesiastical discipline.[4]

Thesis 4. It was not possible for the Tridentine church to lay down legal norms for social life. It undertook an enormous reconversion in order to develop control over peoples' behavior, no longer in the field of law, but now in the field of ethics. The church tended to transfer all its own jurisdiction into the internal forum, the forum of the conscience, constructing a complete alternative system of norms with the development of confession and the strengthening of the character of this sacrament as a tribunal, above all by means of practical and moral theology. The new *institutiones theologiae moralis*, a fruit of the Tridentine church, were the reply to modernity: a synthesis between theological reflection and the concrete life of society and history. This synthesis forms the basis both of university teaching and of praxis in daily life.[5]

Thesis 5. The central point of the religious arguments in the modern age has been power over peoples' consciences. On the one hand, the path of the evangelical and reformed churches was inevitably successful, thanks to an institutional and ideological alliance between state and church—an alliance destined to last until the state itself came of age in practical and ideological terms through the ideal of the nation-state generated by the French Revolution. On the other hand, the Roman Church attempted to construct a parallel sovereignty of a universal type. Since it was no longer able to remain competitive on the level of juridical ordinances, it pinned all its hopes on concordats with the states and on the control of peoples' consciences. This led not only to a separation between the domain of morality and that of positive state law but also to the definitive separation between moral theology and canon law. The latter survived only as a discipline concerning the ecclesiastical body and the external structures of the church.[6]

Thesis 6. It has been claimed that the seventeenth century can be called the age of the conscience. In the aftermath of the religious rupture and the birth of the territorial churches, the problem of the oath of fidelity and of the profession of faith became a basic issue of the political order. The dilemma between obedience to the laws of the state and adherence to one's own personal credo lay behind all the debate kindled throughout Europe, irrespective of the country or religious profession to which one belonged. As we shall see, while the forms may vary, a great part of intellectual and university life, extending far beyond the precincts of the theologians or the jurists, concerns this fundamental problem: What happens when the command of the prince and positive law clash with the principles of divine or natural law or with the dictates of the religion to which one belongs?[7]

Thesis 7. The hypothesis, therefore, was that after the religious rupture was consolidated, the path was open for a new type of dualism, no longer between different juridical orders but between positive law (of the state and also of the church) and the moral norm. The paths were different, just as the solutions were different. There were paths linked to the response of the Catholic Church, which tended to reinforce its magisterium and its jurisdiction over peoples' consciences. There were paths linked to the solutions mediated by the reformed churches, based on the relationship between the individual Christian and scripture. And there were paths taken by freethinkers who were impelled by the contradictions of the wars of religion and of the *cuius regio eius et religio* ("whose realm, his religion") to discover a subjective ethic.[8]

Thesis 8. The phenomenon that confronts us is therefore a reciprocal osmosis in which morality becomes more juridical and law becomes more moral. This leads to a process whereby sin is criminalized, and that which is illicit in civil or penal terms becomes subject to moral condemnation. Thomas Hobbes sees all disobedience to civil law as sin. In the Catholic Church, this leads to the birth of the "internal forum" in the modern sense, that is to say, separated from the civil and penal forum.[9]

Thesis 9. The construction of moral theology after Trent thus rested on two pillars. The first of these is the theoretical construction, namely, the coincidence between natural justice and ethics. Confronted by the growing monopoly of positive law promulgated by the state, the Roman Church maintained, through its brilliant school of thought *de iustitia et iure* ("on justice and law"), that it not only possessed the authority conferred by Christ to forgive sins but that it was also the sole true interpreter of the natural law that coincides with the moral law.[10]

Thesis 10. The second pillar is the science of individual cases that was developed concretely in the Tridentine praxis of confession and spiritual direction. This process is directly linked to the praxis of the sacrament of penance, which was invigorated by the Council of Trent and developed in the second half of the sixteenth century in the periodical meetings of the clergy in the deaneries of the dioceses and in the groups of priests who heard confessions in the cathedrals. These meetings discussed concrete problems of daily life, of sexuality, the family, and economic issues. All I want to do here is to say something banal: casuistry in the Tridentine church has its genesis in daily praxis, even if it is then transformed into academic disputations in casuistry that are abstract and indeed occasionally abstruse.[11]

Thesis 11. The extensive discussions that began in the moral theology of the seventeenth and eighteenth centuries at least until the great synthesis made by Alphonsus Liguori—discussions between rigorists and laxists, probabilists and probabiliorists, Jesuits and Jansenists—have obscured the underlying shared basis, namely, that throughout the entire modern period, thanks to the sheer hard work of moral theologians, the distinction between sin and crime was maintained. This distinction was fundamentally important for the life of the church. It also permitted the development of theories about basic human rights and modern constitutionalism, defending the primacy of the conscience over against positive legislation.[12]

Thesis 12. Changed circumstances in the second half of the twentieth century led to the collapse of the "Tridentine paradigm." One has the impression that at this turn of the century (or of the millennium) it is the pluralism of regulations and of fora that is collapsing. For the first time, we are confronted in the West with a "one-dimensional" norm and thus with one single forum, that of positive law and of the written norm, since all the other "judgment seats" that regulated almost the whole of our daily life until the present day have now lost their power. The positive "one-dimensional" norm that lacks any meta-juridical reference seems schizophrenic. On the one hand, it tends to invade all those spheres of society that were once the domain of ethics. On the other hand, it grows weak and indeed commits suicide as soon as it seeks to dominate peoples' consciences.[13]

Thesis 13. In the last fifty years, the general directives of the church's magisterium seem likewise to have marginalized the presence of sin as a relationship between the conscience and God. The very distinction between sin and crime seems to have largely disappeared, as we see in the considerable confusion in very recent years with regard to pedophilia and to the financial operations of the Roman curia. The ecclesiastical hierarchy appears to be insisting above all that it is necessary to obtain the transformation of sin itself into a crime that will be condemned by the political power (abortion, divorce, euthanasia) while relegating to second place the themes of the offense given to God and of one's personal salvation. And the instruments that are established, such as bioethical committees of every kind, often appear to be formulating a new set of norms of positive law rather than presenting afresh the theme of evil and salvation in the context of humankind today.[14]

Thesis 14. What we must do today is probably to "set out again" from Trent to propose the Christian dualism in new terms that are adapted to the new historical circumstances. The Tridentine paradigm has gone through its cycle of growth and decline, with successes and difficulties, with compromises and contradictions. Paradoxically—though not too paradoxically—we can affirm that the appeals to Trent that resound every day in church polemics end up by impoverishing historically the great attempt at reform and of adaptation to the modern period that was carried out in the past by the Council of Trent.

Notes

1. This essay was translated into English by Brian McNeil.
2. See P. Prodi, *Una storia della giustizia: Dal pluralismo dei fori al moderno dualismo tra coscienza e diritto* (Bologna: Il Mulino, 2000); P. Prodi, *Settimo non rubare: Furto e mercato nella storia dell'Occidente* (Bologna: Il Mulino, 2009); *Il paradigma tridentino: Un' epoca della storia della Chiesa* (Brescia: Morcelliana, 2010); and P. Prodi, "L'istituto della penitenza: nodi storici," in *Collana Chiesa e Storia*, 1: *La penitenza: dottrina, controversie e prassi tra medioeve e età moderna*, ed. L. Mezzadri and M. Tagliaferri (Franzione Pian di Porto: Tau Editrice, 2011): 15-68.
3. For all these aspects, I refer the reader to P. Prodi and W. Reinhard, eds., *Il concilio di Trento e il moderno* (Bologna: Il Mulino, 1996), and to the writings of E.-W. Böckenförde, especially "Zum Verhältnis von Kirche und moderner Welt: Aufriss eines Problems," in *Studien zum Beginn der modernen Welt*, ed. R. Kosellek (Stuttgart: Klett-Cotta, 1977), 154-77.
4. I limit my references here to collective research in which I myself took part: P. Prodi and J. Johanek, eds., *Strutture ecclesiastische in Italia e in Germania prima della Riforma* (Bologna: Il Mulino, 1984); H. Kellenbenz and P. Prodi, eds., *Fisco, religione, stato nell'età confessionale* (Bologna: Il Mulino, 1989); H. G. Koenigsberger, "The Unity of the Church and the Reformation," now in his book *Politicians and Virtuosi: Essays in Early Modern History* (London: Hambleton Continuum, 1986); Hubert Jedin and Paolo Prodi, eds., *Il concilio di Trento come crocevia della politica europea* (Bologna: Il Mulino, 1979); Hubert Jedin, *Geschichte des Konzils von Trient, 1: Der Kampf um das Konzil* (Freiburg: Herder, 1949); and P. Prodi, *Il sacramento del potere* (Bologna: Il Mulino, 1992), 314-17.
5. See P. Prodi, "Note sulla genesi del diritto nella chiesa post-tridentina," in *La Legge e il Vangelo* (Brescia: Paideia, 1972), 191-223; P. Prodi, "Il concilio di Trento e il diritto canonico," in *Il concilio di Trento alla vigilia del terzo millennio*, ed. G. Alberigo and I. Rogger (Brescia: Morcelliana, 1997), 267-85; and M. Turrini, *La conscienza e le leggi* (Bologna: Il Mulino, 1991), 245-99, on the obligation in conscience of human laws and in particular of penal and tax laws.
6. See A. Lauro, *Il cardinale Giovan Battista de Luca: Diritto e riforme nello Stato della Chiesa* (Naples: Joven, 1991), 78-99. On the figure of De Luca in general, see the article by A. Mazzacane in *Dizionario Biografico degli Italiani* 32 (1986): 529-36; A. Mazzacane, "Jus commune: Gesetzgebung und Interpretation der 'höchsten Gerichtshöfe' im Werk des De Luca," in *Gesetz und Gesetzgebung im Europa der frühen Neuzeit*, ed. B. Dölemeyer and D. Klippel (Berlin: Duncker & Humblot, 1998), 71-80; P. Zagorin, *Ways of Lying: Dissimulation, Persecution and Conformity in Early Modern Europe* (Cambridge, MA: Harvard University Press, 1990), 220; J. Delumeau, "S. Alfonso dottore della fiducia," in *Alfonso M. de Liguori e la società civile del suo tempo*, vol. 1, ed. P. Gianantonio (Florence: L. S. Olschki, 1990), 206-18; and G. M. Viscardi, "Confessione: il tormento e l'estasi," *Ricerche di storia sociale e religiosa* 24 (1995): 23-50. In this perspective, I find particularly interesting the relationship between Liguori and the reforming minister Tanucci. See G. De Rosa, "Sant'Alfonso de' Liguori e Bernardo Tucci," in his *Tempo religioso e tempo storico: Saggi e note di storia sociale e religiosa dal medioevo all'età contemporanea* (Rome: Edizioni di Storia e Letteratura, 1987), 205-26. In view of the immense bibliography on Alphonsus Liguori, I mention only recent studies that emphasize the problem of his legal education: F. Chiovaro, "S. Alfonso Maria De Liguori. Ritratto di un moralista," *Spicilegium Historicum*

Congregationis SSmi Redemptoris 45 (1997): 121-53; and P. Perlingeri, *Alfonso de Liguori giurista: La priorità della giustizia e dell'equità sulla lettera delle legge* (Naples: Edizioni Scientifiche Italiane, 1988). These essays can also be found in P. Gianantonio, ed., *Alfonso M. de Liguori e la civiltà letteraria del Settecento* (Florence: L. S. Olschki, 1999). For a synthesis of his thought, see L. Vereecke, *De Guillaume d'Ockham à Saint Alphonse de Liguori* (Rome: Collegium S. Alfonsi de Urbe, 1986), 553-94. Let me mention only one of the hundreds of manuals that were written following in the footsteps of Alphonsus Liguori: J. P. Gury, *Compendium theologiae moralis ex genuina doctrina S. Alphonsi Mariae De Ligorio* (Milan: Oliva, 1857).

7. See P. Legendre, "L'inscription du droit canon dans la théologie: Remarques sur la Seconde Scholastique," in *Proceedings of the V International Congress of Medieval Canon Law* (Vatican City: Biblioteca Apostolica Vaticana, 1980), 443-54; and P. Legendre, *Leçons I. La 901e conclusion: Études sur le théâtre de la Raison* (Paris: Fayard, 1998).

8. See M. Bergamo, *L'anatomia dell'anima: Da François de Sales à Fénélon* (Bologna: Il Mulino, 1991); M. De Certeau, "Du système religieux à l'éthique des Lumières (17e-18es): la formalité des pratiques," in *La Società religiosa nell'età moderna*. Atti del Convegno di studi Cappacio-Paestum, 18-21 maggio 1972 (Naples: Guida Editori, 1973), 447-509; and B. Clavero, "Delito y pecado: Nocion y escala de transgresiones," in *Sexo barroco y otras transgresiones premodernas*, ed. F. Tomás y Valiente et al. (Madrid: Alianza, 1990), 57-89 (all the essays in this volume are relevant to our present concern).

9. For a thorough analysis of the various opinions and theories, see G. Saraceni, *Riflessioni sul foro interno nel quadro generale della giurisdizione della Chiesa* (Padua: CEDAM, 1961); A. Mostalza Rodriguez, "Forum internum—forum externum (Entorno a la naturaleza juridical del fuero interno)," *Rivista española de Derecho Canonico* 23 (1967): 253-331; A. Mostalza Rodriguez, "De foro interno iuxta canonistas posttridentinos," in *Acta conventus internationalis canonistarum* (Rome, May 20-25, 1968) (Vatican City: Typis Polyglottis Vaticanis, 1970), 269-94; M. Turrini, *La coscienza e le leggi*; and I. Von Döllinger and F. H. Reusch, *Geschichte der Moralstreitigkeiten in der römisch-katholischen Kirche seit dem 16. Jahrhundert*, 2 vols. (Nördlingen: C. H. Beck, 1889). For an overview and bibliographical information, see J. Theiner, *Die Entwicklung der Moraltheologie zur eigenständigen Disziplin* (Regensburg: F. Pustet, 1970); J. Mahoney, *The Making of Moral Theology: A Study of the Roman Catholic Tradition* (Oxford: Oxford University Press, 1987). See, for example, J. Gründel, "Vom Gesetz der Freiheit," in *Abschied von Trient* (Regensburg: F. Pustet, 1969), 27-38; J.-M. Aubert, "Morale et casuistique," *Recherches de science religieuse* 68 (1970): 167-204; G. Angelozzi, "L'insegnamento dei casi di coscienza nella pratica educativa della Compagnia di Gesù," in *La ratio studiorum: modelli culturali e pratiche educative dei Gesuiti in Italia tra Cinque e Seicento*, ed. G. P. Brizzi (Rome: Bulzoni Editore, 1981), 121-62; G. Angelozzi, "Interpretazioni della penitenza sacramentale in età moderna," *Religioni e società* 1 (1986): 73-87; and Vereecke, *De Guillaume d'Ockham*, 495-508.

10. See G. Ambrosetti, *Il diritto natural della riforma cattolica: Una giustificazione storica del sistema di Suarez* (Milan: Giuffrè, 1951); G. Ambrosetti, *Diritto naturale Cristiano: Profili di metodo, di storia e di teoria*, 2nd ed. (Milan: Giuffrè, 1985); G. M. Chiodi, *Legge naturale e legge positiva nella filosofia politica di T. Hobbes* (Milan: Giuffrè, 1970), 190; L. Vereecke, *Conscience morale et loi humaine selon Gabriel Vazquez S.J.* (Tournai: Desclée, 1957); and J.-F. Courtine, "Théologie morale et conception du politique chez Suarez," in *Les jésuites à l'âge baroque (1540-1640)*, ed. L. Giard and L. de Vaucelles (Grenoble: Jérôme Millon, 1996), 261-78.

11. For a general history of casuistry in moral theology, see A. R. Jonsen and S. Toulmin, *The Abuse of Casuistry: A History of Moral Reasoning* (Berkeley: University of California Press, 1988); S. Burgio, *Teologia barocca: Il Probabilismo in Sicilia nell'epoca di Filippo IV* (Catania: Società di Storia Patria, 1988); P. J. Holmes, ed., *Elizabethan Casuistry* (London: Catholic Record Society, 1981); P. J. Holmes, *Resistance and Compromise: The Political Thought of the Elizabethan Catholics* (Cambridge: Cambridge University Press, 1982); L. Gallagher, *Medusa's Gaze: Casuistry and Conscience in the Renaissance* (Stanford, CA: Stanford University Press, 1991); and M. L. Brown, *Donne and the Politics of Conscience in Early Modern England* (Leiden: E. J. Brill, 1955). The essays in E. Leites, ed., *Conscience and Casuistry in Early Modern Europe* (Cambridge: Cambridge University Press, 1988), are fundamental in this field. See also P. Zagorin, *Ways of Lying*. For the role played by this problem in the history of moral theology and a basic bibliography, see A. Bondolfi, "'Non dire falsa testimonianza': Alcuni rilievi storici sul preteso carattere di assolutezza dell' ottavo (non) comandamento," in *Verità e veracità: Atti del XVI congresso nazionale ATISM*, ed. B. Marra (Naples: ATISM, 1995), 41-55; M. Foucault, *Histoire de la sexualité*, vol. 1: *La volonté de savoir* (Paris: Gallimard, 1976); J. Barrientos García, *Un siglo de moral economica en Salamanca, 1526-1629* (Salamanca: Ediciones Universidad de Salamanca, 1985); M. Bianchini, "I fattori della distribuzione (1350-1850)," in *Storia dell'economia italiana*, vol. 2, ed. R. Romano (Turin: Einaudi, 1992), especially 194-95; B. Neveu, *L'erreur et son juge: Remarques sur les censures doctrinales à l'époque moderne* (Naples: Bibliopolis, 1993); B. Neveu, *Érudition et religion au XVIIe et XVIIIe siècles* (Paris: A. Michel, 1994); D. Pastine, *Juan Caramuel: Probabilismo ed encyclopedia* (Florence: La Nuova Italia, 1975); and P. Pissavino, ed., *Le meraviglie del probabile: Juan Caramuel 1606-1682*. Atti del convegno internazionale di studi, October 29-31, 1982 (Vigevano: Comune di Vigevano, 1990), with essays by D. Pastine, M. Turrini, J. R. Armogathe, P. Pissavino, and others.

12. See L. Kolakowski, *Chrétiens sans Eglise: La conscience religieuse et le lien confessionnel au XVIIe siècle* (Paris: Gallimard, 1969); R. Taveneaux, *Jansénisme et Réforme catholique* (Nancy: Presses Universitaires de Nancy, 1992); P. Valadier, *Éloge de la conscience* (Paris: Seuil, 1994); W. J. Bouwsma, "The Two Faces of Humanism: Stoicism and Augustinism in Renaissance Thought," in *Itinerarium Italicum*, ed. H. A. Obermann and T. A. Brady (Leiden: E. J. Brill, 1975), 3-60; D. Taranto, "Una politica senza diritto: Pascal e la giustizia," in *Individualismo, Assolutismo, Democrazia*, ed. V. Dini and D. Taranto (Naples: ESI, 1992), 195-209; P. Cariou, *Pascal et la casuistique* (Paris: PUF, 1993), especially 75-77; B. Pascal, *Pensées*, no. 294, in B. Pascal, *Œuvres complètes*, vol. 1, ed. M. Le Guern (Paris: Gallimard, 1998); V. Dini, "Prudenza, giustizia e obbedienza nella constitutione della ragion di Stato in Spagna e in Francia: Assaggi di lettura e prospettive di ricerca," in *Aristotelismo e ragion di Stato* (Florence: L. S. Olschki, 1995), 249-71; C. Maire, *De la cause de Dieu à la cause de la nation: Le jansénisme au XVIIIe siècle* (Paris: Gallimard, 1998); and D. Bertrand, *La politique de Saint Ignace de Loyola* (Paris: L' analyse sociale, 1985), especially 162-71. However, we still lack an adequate political history of the Society of Jesus in the sixteenth century. See P. Cariou, *Les idéalités casuistique: Aux origines de la psychanalyse* (Paris: PUF, 1992); and R. Briggs, "The Science of Sin: Jacques de Sante-Beuvre and his *Cas de conscience*," in *Religious Change in Europe 1650-1914: Essays for J. McManners*, ed. N. Aston (Oxford: Oxford University Press, 1997), 23-40. For a specific experience in Italy in the same period, see E. Stumpo, "Alle origini della psicanalisi? Il *Diario spirituale* di Filippo Baldinucci e la direzione spirituale nell'Italia moderna," introduction to F. Baldinucci, *Diario spirituale* (Florence: Le Lettere, 1995). See also M. Villey,

La formation de la pensée juridique moderne (Paris: PUF, 2003); and C. Dolcini, "Pensiero politico medievale e nichilismo contemporaneo: Riflessioni sul problema dello stato e dell'unità di Italia," 3rd series, *Studi medievali* 38 (1997): 397-421. A final example is very erudite, but it appears to me to belong to this category of "genealogical" studies: A. S. Brett, *Liberty, Right and Nature: Individual Right in Later Scholastic Thought* (Cambridge: Cambridge University Press, 1997).

13. See G. Stratenwerth, "Quanto è importante la giustizia?" *Materiali per una storia della cultura giuridica* 25 (1995): 413; this essay was first published in Fritjof Haft et al., eds., *Strafgereichtigkeit: Festschrift für Arthur Kaufmann* (Heidelberg: C. F. Muller, 1993), 353-62. In many of his writings, Arthur Kaufmann initiated reflection on the ethical responsibilities of law in the postmodern era. See most recently his *Rechtsphilosophie in der Nach-Neuzeit*, 2nd ed. (Heidelberg: Decker and Müller, 1992).

14. A paper delivered at a congress at the Catholic University of Milan in April 1997 draws an interesting conclusion: "It was characteristic of penance in the West that it was regarded as an analogy to a judicial and penal action. Penance was called the 'tribunal of penance.' The confessor was seen as a judge, and the works of penance as punishment and expiation. This analogy disappears with the reform by Paul VI, since the image of judicial action is replaced by the image of therapy. The confessor is seen as a doctor who must make a diagnosis and prescribe a therapy. . . . I believe that the abandonment of the penal character that happened through the reform of Paul VI was a very significant turning point in the history of Western penance." See E. Mazza, "Il rito della riconciliazione dei penitenti, tra espiazione penale e reintegrazione sociale," in *Colpa e pena? La teologia di fronte alla questione criminale*, ed. A. Acerbi and L. Eusebi (Milan: Vita e Pensiero, 1998), 97-126. For a deeper perspective on the postconciliar period and further information, see J. Ramos Regidor, *Il sacramento della penitenza: Riflessione teologica, biblico-pastorale alla luce del Vaticano II* (Turin: Elledici, 1979); P. Arendt, *Busssakrament und Einzelbeichte: Die tridentinischen Lehraussagen über das Sündenbekenntnis und ihre Verbindlichkeit für die Reform des Busssakramentes* (Freiburg: Herder, 1981); P. Prodi, "Cristianesimo e giustizia, peccato e delitto nella tradizione occidentale," *Daimon* 4 (2004): 81-95 (this entire fascicle is devoted to the theme of justice in the laws of the monotheistic religions); and M. Ventura, *Pena e penitenza nel diritto canonico postconciliare* (Naples: ESI, 1996).

The Council of Trent
in the African Experience

Laurenti Magesa

Trent and the Consolidation of Grand Narratives

Certainly the most enduring general legacy that the Council of Trent (1545-1563) bequeathed to the global Catholic Church was its institutionalization of "grand narratives" or, in other words, uniform pedagogical systems worldwide as a tool for evangelization. This affected in a special way the territories and peoples of the southern hemisphere (Africa, Asia, and South America), until recently generally referred to in Catholic circles as "mission territories." Missionary work to these geographical areas of the world in its present form in the Catholic Church began in earnest after this grand meeting of bishops and theologians at Trent.

Grand narratives are universalizing stories. They are born of the human tendency to generalize what is particular and local, to make one's own experience of reality applicable to everyone or to the majority of people. This happens particularly in the social and cultural domains. In practice, this human inclination serves the often-unacknowledged urge for power and domination of some over others. Whether they are explicitly aware of it or not, few persons or groups are entirely immune from this instinctive trait. All too often it is rationalized and justified in many ways, but it can be rightly understood from one of two perspectives, and oftentimes from both together: chauvinism and/or altruism.

The chauvinistic tendency is blatant. It is expressed in terms of some perceived or felt superiority of one person or group over the *different* other or others. This is the basis of racism, tribalism, sexism, class distinctions, and religious fundamentalism. Eventually, all of these attitudes lead to some form of violence, whether psychological or social.

The other inclination, more subtle in appearance but no less fundamentally prejudiced and destructive of human dignity, is often cast in seemingly gracious intentions "to do good," or altruism. It arises from the assumed conviction that one or one's group possesses a "higher" or "better" level of cultural or ethical values than the other and that one has therefore the duty to force them upon the other. These approaches do appear different, but they are connected in that they contain fundamental aspects of each other. Chief among these is the disregard for and even disrespect of the values inherent in the social and ethical vision of the other.

48

This form of grand narratives must be distinguished from the deep sense of those other, equally universalizing narratives that are implied in documents and efforts such as the United Nations Universal Declaration of Human Rights (UDHR).[1] Many attempts similar to the UDHR, aiming at actualizing the dignity of human persons globally, exist today. The difference between them and other grand stories lies in the fact that instead of differentiating between "us" and "them," they concentrate on what is common between or among "us." Differentiation invariably includes concomitant notions of superiority and inferiority, of one side offering largesse and the other simply receiving. The struggle for human rights, on the contrary, focuses on what unites us as human beings. There is a difference of attitude in the two approaches that defines and dictates fundamental practical conceptions of human relationships. Whereas chauvinistic and frequently so-called charitable grand stories are prone to objectifying the other, in struggles for human rights, for instance, everyone is a subject, bound and acting together for the same objective. Objectification suppresses self-actualization, while acknowledged subjectivity greatly enhances it.

Although we do not usually apply the expression "grand narratives" in its negative sense to the Catholic or Christian churches (or to most religious activity of conversion in general), all proselytizing activity invariably operates more or less out of this context, either deliberately or unconsciously. Jesus' final commission in the Gospel of Matthew to his disciples to "Go . . . make disciples of all nations, baptizing them . . . [and] teaching them to observe all that I have commanded you" (Matt 28:19-20) is an instance of one of the grandest of narratives in human religious history. Christianity has adhered to this mandate for two millennia now, correctly understanding it as its reason for existence. The Second Vatican Council (1962-1665) affirms it by defining the church as "the universal sacrament of salvation." It further describes the church's "one sole purpose" to consist in the realization of "the kingdom of God" and "the salvation of the human race" through Christ.[2] We may, of course, today call this a form of globalization. Yet, contrary to chauvinistic globalization trends, Christians must understand this mandate of Jesus to be not alienating but life-giving. This is how Jesus intended it, to be "good news" of human communion in freedom. It respects the identity and integrity of different peoples and cultures while at the same time elevating all of them toward the wisdom that only God can give.

However, the practical application of this commission, the foundation stone of the historical Christian Church and its endeavor to impart divine wisdom, is what is historically contentious for us, especially since Trent. Many African and Africanist theologians have pointed this out.[3] How has Catholic or Christian evangelization been done in Africa? The grand story that most Christian evangelizers have presented to Africa can generally be placed in the chauvinistic camp as a narrative of superiority. Its central motif has been "to bring light to darkness, to subdue the savage and to elicit the nobility, to change the primitive to the civilized, to show the way to the truth."[4]

While we have heard this criticism concerning the old approaches to evangelization many times before, it must not be forgotten that it remains operative in many significant ways and cases up to the present day.[5] In the absence of a conscious, deliberate, genuine, and comprehensive pursuit of dialogue between and among cultures and religions, these notions of superiority and inferiority, including their concomitant attitudes and practices, remain operative in their underlying motivations wherever Christian mission is carried out, with only minor differences of degree here and there.[6]

The main point in all this is that some of these methods of evangelization are not merely procedural but clearly ethical issues. As F. Joseph writes, "those who came to convert, took and left the innocent with nothing but their insides to haunt them."[7] When evangelization becomes a question of domination and expropriation of the humanity and dignity of the converts, it must be seen in moral terms. Further, when evangelization turns into a matter of alienating converts from themselves, it must be interpreted from an ethical perspective. In Africa, expropriation of native culture from the indigenes was usually the missionary assumption, goal, and working plan. This is common knowledge: "What they . . . [the converts] had, and were born with, was wrong, bad, evil, of the devil. What they were to acquire in exchange for giving up their traditions and culture was to save them from fire and brimstone, from hell and the wrath to come."[8]

Quite the opposite of human dignity was demanded of converts by this approach. What, for missionary evangelization, "was the acquirement of righteousness, poverty, meekness, [was] the [converts'] ability to keep turning the other cheek. It was not to whip anybody from the temple. It was not to sack thieves and protect themselves against the invasion of outsiders."[9] Virtuous teaching would, however, have suggested the other side of the picture—the necessity of the converts' self-identity and worth as equally children of God, created in God's image and likeness. This latter is, beyond all doubt, the central message of the gospel and, consequently, the reason for evangelization.

The Socioreligious Context of the Council of Trent

To appreciate the historical and current situation of the Catholic Church in Africa, it is useful to revisit briefly the socioreligious context within which the Council of Trent took place. When Pope Pius III convened the world's bishops for this Council,[10] it was for a specific aim: to confront head on an extraordinary situation in the church in Europe, namely, the Protestant Reformation. The Reformation was a movement initiated by the German Augustinian friar Martin Luther. Thus, today Luther stands as a central figure of both the experiences of the Protestant Reformation and the Council of Trent. Almost three decades earlier, in 1517, he had published his "Ninety-five Theses," which were essentially statements describing what he saw as major abuses in the current theology and pastoral practice of the Catholic Church. In his theses Luther distanced his thought from some of what he saw as serious theological, doctrinal, structural, and pastoral errors in the teaching of the Roman Church of the day. These errors, according to him, contravened the basic principles of scripture. He was to elaborate on many of these issues later in his numerous sermons and writings. Luther's stand triggered the activities of many other Reformers in sympathy with him all across Europe. This is one side of the picture.

The other side is that, perhaps predictably given the times and circumstances, the Roman church authorities grew increasingly inflexible and defensive in the face of these challenges. They became intolerant toward the theological arguments and demands of the Reformers, even where the latter might have been right in what they argued and proposed. Positions gradually hardened, with neither side ready or willing to listen to the other. The mutual suspicion and antagonism arising from this situation culminated in the Reformers' formal break with Roman church authorities. The Protestant Reformation grew into a full-blown movement. By the time the Council of Trent convened thirty years later, notes historian of the church's councils Norman P. Tanner, "the Reformation had spread far and wide and the wounds within the church proved too deep to heal."[11]

The major concerns of the Council of Trent were therefore doctrinal and structural. The Tridentine agenda was exclusively determined as a rebuttal of the claims of the Protestant Reformation about the sacraments and the authority of the clergy in the church, especially the episcopate. Thus, the description usually given to the Council of Trent as the Catholic- or Counter-Reformation is accurate. Trent was an effort to fortify an institution that saw itself under siege in its doctrine, structures, life, and discipline. In particular, Trent intended to reassert once more the authority of the bishops in the church, specifically, the power of the papacy, obviously conceived in pre-Reformation forms, over the entire church. This, plus papal claims to any temporal power, was the contention that many of the Reformers were challenging.

Though now considered in predominantly spiritual and ecclesial terms, the question of the authority of the pope was taken up and completed three centuries later by the First Vatican Council (1869-1870) in its contentious teaching on papal infallibility. According to its Dogmatic Constitution *Pastor aeternus* of July 18, 1870, Vatican I affirmed that the pope possesses "full and supreme power of jurisdiction over the whole church." Probably still having in mind the Reformers' objections, as well as the Enlightenment and Modernist movements, Vatican I condemned anyone who held contrary views. *Pastor aeternus* insisted in unequivocal language and medieval mentality that the pope's power and authority over the universal church are "absolute," "ordinary," and "immediate."[12]

On this question, the Constitution argued that it based itself on "the tradition received from the beginning of the Christian faith," saying,

> [W]e teach and define as a divinely revealed dogma that when the Roman Pontiff speaks *ex cathedra*, that is, when, in the exercise of his office as

Notes

1. See "Universal Declaration of Human Rights," United Nations, http://www. un.org/en/ documents/ udhr/index.shtml.

2. *Gaudium et spes* (Pastoral Constitution of the Church in the Modern World), 45. See Documents of the Second Vatican Council, http://www.vatican.va.

3. For example, see F. Eboussi Boulaga, *Christianity without Fetishes: An African Critique and Recapture of Christianity* (Maryknoll, NY: Orbis Books, 1984); Kwesi A. Dickson, *Uncompleted Mission: Christianity and Exclusivism* (Nairobi: Acton, 2000); Walbert Buhlmann, *The Missions on Trial: Addis Ababa 1980, A Moral for the Future from the Archives of Today* (London: St. Paul Publications, 1978); Cyprian Tirumanywa, *Christian Religion on Trial: The Good News Is Justice and Peace for All on Earth* (Dar es Salaam: Dar es Salaam University Press, 1991); and Paul Gifford, *Christianity: To Save or Enslave?* (Harare: EDICESA, 1990).

4. F. Joseph, Prologue to Muthoni Likimani, *They Shall Be Chastised* (Nairobi: Kenya Literature Bureau, 1974), iv.

5. See Paul Gifford, *Ghana's New Christianity: Pentecostalism in a Globalising African Economy* (London: Hurst, 2004).

6. For the imperative of dialogue, see Laurenti Magesa, *African Religion in the Dialogue Debate: From Intolerance to Coexistence* (Vienna: LIT Verlag, 2010); and Frans Wijsen and Peter Nissen, eds., *"Mission Is a Must": Intercultural Theology and the Mission of the Church* (New York: Rodopi, 2002).

7. F. Joseph, Epilogue to *They Shall Be Chastised*, 232.

8. Ibid.

9. Ibid.

10. The assembly of bishops began to sit on December 13, 1545, and ended on December 4, 1563.

11. Norman P. Tanner, *The Councils of the Church: A Short History* (New York: Crossroad, 2001), 77.

12. *Pastor aeternus* (The Dogmatic Constitution from Vatican I), 3:9. See "The Dogmatic Constitution from Vatican I—'*Pastor aeternus*,'" Fisheaters, http://www.fisheaters. com/pastoraeternus.html.

13. *Pastor aeternus,* 4:9.

14. See John Baur, *2000 Years of Christianity in Africa: An African Church History* (Nairobi: Paulines Publications Africa, 1994); and Elizabeth Isichei, *A History of Christianity in Africa: From Antiquity to the Present* (Grand Rapids, MI: Eerdmans, 1995).

15. Adrian Hastings, *Church and Mission in Modern Africa* (London: Burns & Oates, 1967), 239.

16. Ibid., 239 n. 1.

17. Anecdote related several times orally to the author by Fr. Michael C. Kirwen, M.M., who was working at the time at Masonga Catholic Church, Diocese of Musoma, in northwestern Tanzania. Catholic and Mennonite missionaries were then rather crudely competing for converts in the area by vilifying one another's faith.

18. Aylward Shorter, *Toward a Theology of Inculturation* (Maryknoll, NY: Orbis Books, 1988), 256.

19. See *Ecclesia in Africa* (Post-Synodal Exhortation of the Holy Father John Paul II), (Nairobi: Paulines Publications Africa, 1995), 63.

20. See "Report by Mons. Sithembele Anton Sipuka, Bishop of Umtatah (South Africa)," http://storico.radiovaticana.org/en3/storico/2009-10/326592_report_by_mons _sithembele_anton_sipuka_bishop_of_umtata_south_africa.html.

21. *Syllabus Errorum* (The Syllabus of Errors Condemned by Pope Pius IX), 15, 77, 78. See "The Syllabus of Errors Condemned by Pope Pius IX," Papal Encyclicals Online, http://www.dailycatholic.org/syllbus1.htm.

22. Tanner, *The Councils of the Church*, 77.

LIVING WITH LOSSES: THE CRISIS IN THE "CHRISTIAN WEST"

Regina Ammicht-Quinn

The "Christian Occident" Is Drifting

We are used to looking at church councils as points of origin for doctrines, rules, and norms that shape the church and the character of theology to come. And we do so with a certain pride. We—as non-historians—sometimes overlook the fact that councils such as Trent are first of all reactions: reactions to uncertainties when people who by nomination or vocation are in charge and feel the ground shifting under their feet. Councils are more often than not reactions to an identity crisis of church and theology. Theological innovation, and that is council history, too, emerges from people who are exposing themselves to these shifting grounds and not trying to overcome them by wishful thinking, talk, or prayer.

The ground was certainly shifting in 1545. In the light of this almost-binary structure of uncertainty and innovation (which of course can fold back into itself and lead to new uncertainties), let me explore this heritage of uncertainties and innovations, especially the uncertainties of the Christian West. The fathers of the Council of Trent were as well—despite the queerness of the image—midwives of this "Christian Occident."[1]

The year 2010 was the year of strong movements of the earth—from Haiti to Guatemala to Iceland, from the oil spill in the Gulf of Mexico to Indonesia. But perhaps the Christian Occident is drifting even more so. Looking back at Trent, we see how perceptions of religion have changed and are still changing. In 1982, almost thirty years ago, Niklas Luhmann told us that there was a significant change in the perception of religion: whereas previously disbelief or unbelief was a private matter, belief had become a private matter.[2] Are we still on the same page?

No, and yes. Faith and theology are also public. Yet the Christian West, which so far has prided itself in being and having the real thing—the real faith, the real tradition, the real theology—struggles with its self-definition. In the public sphere, there is a societal but also aesthetic, almost ornamental, character of faith and religion. It is often visible when at crucial points in their lives people turn to religion as affirmation or decoration, as ground or background for the ultimate heights and depths in their lives. It is also visible where popular consumer culture is a grateful recipient of religious symbol systems that have fluidly drifted into other contexts:

brand names of beauty products seem to be generated by advertising companies not with Google but with prayer books and catechisms on the home pages of their PCs. My two personal favorites are an aftershave called "Eternity for Men," on the one hand, and a perfume called "Vive Maria—Almost Innocent," on the other. The latter has the following product description: "The slightly waisted flask alludes to the female figure; the lid is a stylized crown with fifteen indentations referring to the Feast of Assumption on August 15."

While there is still some truth in Luhmann's statement, it is not clear-cut—if it ever was. Part of public disbelief is very private, and part of private belief is very public. This changing landscape of the "Christian West" is connected with strong emotions, with two of the strongest being pride and shame. Let me explore this very briefly on two levels.

Matters of Shame: Loss of Identities

On a first level, questions of self-identification in the Christian West are adopted by politics: Who is allowed to be part of "us"? These are, of course, questions of immigration and questions about which role Islam and European Muslims should play and about what space and visibility are allowed to them. In this context, the idea of the Christian Occident functions mostly as a (more cultural than religious) demarcation line. It expresses itself through a "we vs. them" rhetoric, notwithstanding the fact that this concept is based on an illusion: what seems in retrospect a happy and homogeneous religious past. Christianity seems to guarantee a long-term memory as well as the actuality of culture and cultural identity; questions of faith and moral responsibilities retire to the cheaper back seats of this discourse. There are discussions about church steeples that have to be higher than minarets, discussions of social and educational problems as problems of a certain religion, and discourses of identities and losses of identities.

An interesting example is Switzerland, where in November 2009 a popular vote led to the ban of minarets. No more building permissions would be granted. The rural, alpine, and not exactly minaret-plastered areas, not the culturally diverse urban regions, voted especially in favor of the ban. This is a matter of shame. Anxieties blind people in such a way that facts, responsibilities, and histories lose their impact. It is a matter of shame that Christian thought is publicly instrumentalized while the insistence on "our values" is highly selective. Do "we," unlike Muslims, not discriminate against women and homosexuals? The popular vote in Switzerland is part of the tectonic drift that unsettles lives and institutions.

Matters of Shame: Loss of Face

After the crisis in the United States and Ireland, in January 2010 the huge problem of sexual violence in the church engulfed Germany and other European countries. After one Jesuit school in Berlin publicly accounted for its own history, a wave of formerly hidden knowledge overwhelmed the public sphere. With very

Matters of Shame: Loss of the Body

Shame is considered a consequence of one's losing face. The loss of face the church is experiencing now, however, can be seen as a consequence of another loss: the loss of the body. There are many discourses, doctrines, and documents on the loss of the body in the history of theology, many of them foundational to moral theology.[7] An image and a story will describe my point. The image is that of St. John's head on a platter, and the story is that of Herod.

Since the thirteenth century, especially in southern Germany and Austria, *Johannesschüsseln,* or "St. John's platters," have been an important part of religious art.[8] Typically, the platter holds St. John's head, sometimes with peacefully closed eyes, sometimes with eyes that are closing. Some of them are reliefs, and others are full sculptures in which the dying head lifts itself from the platter. These St. John's platters are themselves transitional objects, three-dimensional objects that are released into space[9] and "situated between the narrative and the relic,"[10] between signs and symbols, between the verity of the word and the concreteness of the object, between what is present in representations and what is present in the body. The *Johannesschüsseln* are used like relics against headaches and head colds and thrown into the ocean to detect drowned bodies.[11] There are cultural affinities between the head depicted on the *Johannesschüsssheln* and the head of Medusa and also between the *Johannesschüsseln* and the ritual of headhunting, one of humankind's oldest rituals.

The underlying story is the story of a nameless girl (Mark 6:17-29; Matt 14:1-12), daughter of a woman named Herodias, the illegitimate wife of Herod. At the celebration of his birthday the girl dances so beautifully that Herod vows to grant her any wish she might have, even if it were half of his empire. The girl—and we might imagine her confused by this barely concealed incestuous and pedophilic desire—asks her mother what to wish. The mother tells her to demand the head of John the Baptist, because it had been John who had accused Herod of adultery when he took Herodias, his brother's wife, as his own. "And immediately the king sent an executioner, and commanded his head to be brought: and he went and beheaded him in the prison, and brought his head in a charger, and gave it to the damsel, and the damsel gave it to the mother" (Mark 6:27f., KJV).

This story is the origin of all those pictures we know—both still and moving, talking, singing in the history of art and music, theater, and opera. All those pictures show the metamorphosis of the nameless girl into the seductive Salome (whose name is mentioned in another context by Flavius Josephus). Salome's *décolleté,* emphasizing the connection between head and body, leads, without much digression, to the *decollatio,* the decapitation, and the head is in one way or another served at the feast: a suggestion of anthropophagy and at the same time a reference to and travesty of the Eucharist.

The platter functions as a picture frame: the *Johannesschüssel* becomes a special *Andachtsbild,* or devotional picture, that does not return but absorbs our gaze.

Thus, the image evokes less *compassio* than *consumptio*—a multileveled absorption. The frame provides the face with the intensity and potency of a *vera icon*[12]—a very special *vera icon* in which the underlying narrative shows what is violently missing: the rest of John.

As those *Johannesschüsseln* give us a perspective on the story of John and Herod, we see a stylized and simplified confrontation. There is, on Herod's side, a headless, (lower) body-driven desire. On John's side is the bodiless moral superiority, visible in the visage. On one side is the pure bodiless face; on the other, the spiritless lower body. With Freud, who connected decapitation and castration,[13] the situation becomes complicated: the worship of the decapitated, who in fact is castrated, functions as symbolic castration of Herod. At the same time, John's decapitation can be seen as liberation—liberation from the body and its desire. John has already reached a state where he meets Christ: face to face. The St. John's platter is, however, beneath the silent salvation, ear-splittingly violent.

St. John's platters are part of an occidental history of ideas that is written not only in (Neoplatonic) doctrines, but also on our bodies. It can be deciphered on both surfaces. Where does this leave us when the body is, as Foucault says, the "zero point" of experience,[14] the place in our own coordinate system where our experiences intersect? In a majority of historical and contemporary religious and spiritual experiences the body plays no role, or only a negative one: then the body is a very foreign body, *Körper als Fremd-Körper*. The reason is not only that the body does not keep what we feel is promised in that it is falling sick, aging, dying. The reason is also to be sought in this occidental history of ideas.

Art conspired through history with Herod and with "Salome" in giving flesh and beauty, emotion, and presence to that which is on another (moralistic) level despised, condemned, and preferably eliminated: the impure body with its needs, its desires, its appetites. The matter of shame is the shameful body.

Christian tradition, however, is multileveled and many voiced. There are images and imaginations of bodies that are openly erotic, and these are not only the images of Eve and Salome, Mary from Magdala, or the whore of Babylon, images that depict the erotic body to defame the person. These are also images that show the instantaneous and powerful encounter between the human body and the sacred, an encounter that is shown as relevant for salvation: Mary baring and offering her breasts, the mystics receiving Christ as lover, and many more.

Yet the mainstream tradition, at least in theological reflection, tends to concentrate on the human head, the human face. It is the countenance, what in German is called *Angesicht*, the *Antlitz*, that represents humanity and is seen as the initial point of ethics, because the *Angesicht* of the other demands to be seen, to be appraised, and to be protected, as in the widely adopted ethical approach by Lévinas.

The overwhelming metaphor of the *Angesicht* in Christian ethics is problematic. It perpetuates a valuation where the body is not only divided but fragmented and has pure and impure, good and bad, acceptable and unacceptable parts. The somewhat-tame intellectual notion of an "anthropological dualism" reveals its brutal undercurrent with John the Baptist's head on a platter: the body violently hacked apart with the *Angesicht* thus representing its wholeness and holiness.

People living a pious and concrete bodily life in this pretext are precariously balancing on the crevice that opens up in their self-perception.

The images of Herod, Salome, and John, which are all hidden in the St. John's platters are double-faced, perhaps multifaced, because they—as do myths—stylize extreme antitheses and reunite them on an aesthetic level. They can take an epistemic lead that has consequences for thinking and practicing theology. This epistemic lead puts a spotlight, for example, on the end of the third century (roughly the same time when Plotinus, who was ashamed to be in the body, stopped caring for his body, which included cleaning it[15]). Origen states, "God created the present world and he chained the soul to the body for punishment."[16] He thus not only teaches of the gap between body and soul, matter and immateriality, but of an active state of war between the two with frequent surprise attacks: ascetic attacks on the body by the soul and ecstatic attacks on the soul by the body. The victory is an uncertain one, not finally decided until death. For the soul is imprisoned in the body.

In this tradition, one among others although influential, the body of the priest is less "body" than other bodies. Only on a secondary level does this allude to celibacy. It is first a body that is in a singular and powerful way part of the collective body of the church, staged in neat rows and squares. It has to be a body that fits. It gets dangerous when its needs and necessities do not fit in squares, hierarchies, or representations, and it gets quiet. Quiet, because the collective body covers the individual body. And dangerous, because violence toward oneself or toward other persons is not a necessary but an obvious result from a history of violence that pervades the history of Christianity, a violence that tries to slowly diminish and eventually put to death the individual body's needs, desires, and appetites. With the lifelessness of the individual body, the dying of the collective body of the church sets in.

We all know that sexual violence is by no means mono-causal. Each case has its history, its mindsets, its vulnerabilities, its fantasies, its sorrows, and its brutalities. But we cannot and are not allowed to ignore that there are not only psychological or pedagogical reasons but also theological ones.

We are familiar with the crevice that opens up in a perpetrator's self-perception, and it is horrifying. It is part of a theology that made the shift from a body that bears stigmata (as a remembrance of suffering) to the body that *is a stigma*. And it is part of a theology where abuse is condemned as a "grave sin" and listed in the same breath with the other grave sin of the "concelebration of the Eucharistic sacrifice . . . with ministers of ecclesial communities which do not have apostolic succession," as noted in the documents on *gravioribus delictis* 2001 and 2010.[17]

Living with Losses

How should we live with these losses that mark the crisis in the Christian West? Theological innovation, as we learn from council history, is only possible through people who expose themselves to the shifting grounds they are living on. In this sense, the topics of immigration and secularization, of the shifting land-scape in the (former?) "Christian" West and the topics of sexual violence in the church are connected. Both cases shake or shatter Christian identities. What used to be "normal" or "natural" is no longer so. This is true on the political level with the questions of secularization and the immigration of people who seem to be as religious and pious as we once were, only within the wrong religion. It also holds on the political level of church policy, with questions of faith interwoven with vio-lence and of trust and of "God's defeat in his church."

In both cases it is necessary to act, to establish rules and regulations regardless of the strong emotional and power-related need to maintain pride in what is con-sidered a glorious past. We need rules and regulations against the discrimination of religious minorities in Western countries, and we need rules and regulations against the covering of the individual body by the collective body. We need to rec-ognize that the insistence on the Occident's singular religious identity is a mistake with most serious consequences. We need to recognize that (theologically) ignor-ing and despising and thus eventually losing the body while not educating and cul-tivating its needs is a mistake with most serious consequences. But, eventually, we need to learn to live with shame.

Shame has a bad reputation, philosophically and otherwise. In discourse and daily lives it is perhaps the most hidden emotion. Shame's bad reputation results from its connection to sexuality on the one hand and from anthropological claims on the other. In different contexts both Margaret Mead[18] and later Ruth Benedict[19] construct the clear polarity between "shame" and "guilt," considering "guilt" more valuable and "higher," because only the ability to feel guilt constitutes the moral individual. Shame is the emotion of children and non-Western societies where shaming as an external sanction forms a person's conduct.

This clear polarity has to be challenged;[20] it only (and effectively) hides the role shame has for all societies and all individual lives. Shame is always double-faced. It can be destructive: shaming others because of their otherness is a strong social means of allocating power and recognition. At the same time, a completely shameless person or a shameless society is a social and moral nightmare. Shame is also constructive in that it shapes identities and societies by insisting that there are situations where guilt "does not go far enough,"[21] where shame is called for. Shame is not primarily about what I have done, but about who I am. The most basic defini-tion is that guilt is about things, and shame is about persons.

New Testament texts include a complex structure of acceptance and rejection of shame. Those who are put to shame, the poor, the sick, the morally dubious, are, more often than not cast as role models, in the center of symbolic actions and parables. The story of the passion of Christ, from the crown of thorns to the vinegar sponge, is a series of shaming rituals. And the first Jews who believed in Christ as the Messiah rejected the shame that was put onto them. "I am not ashamed of the gospel of Christ," says Paul (Rom 1:16, KJV), and the letter to the Hebrews attributes this rejection of shame to Christ and God: Christ is not ashamed to call them "brothers" (Heb 2:11), and God is not ashamed to be called their God.

Christianity, similar to all liberation movements we know, started with the rejection of shame and transformed shame into pride. Looking back at the Council of Trent and at conciliary structures of uncertainty and innovation, the simple process from uncertainty to innovation has become extremely complicated. Even if, as in the case of sexual violence, we succeed in creating rules and norms that actually make sense, the shame put on the church and Christianity cannot be turned into pride. As long as church officials and representatives, in accordance with or contrary to their own rhetoric, reject this shame and try to maintain pride—even if it is only visual, not verbal, pride, we all continue to feel the ground moving beneath our feet, as volcanic ash burns people and pollutes the air and oil spills into a formerly beautiful sea.

To work through the scandal of sexual violence in religious contexts is a necessary but not sufficient condition for overcoming the crisis in the Christian West. And there are other fundamental reasons for shame in church structures and practices, structures and practices that are separated from life and separated from faith and thus damage life and faith.

The Australian historian of culture Elspeth Probyn[22] said with regard to the colonial past of her country that shame might be a continuing part of the every public sphere in the country. And she asks, "Would that be a bad thing?" Shame keeps us humble, aware, and involved. The possibility is real: God can be defeated in God's own church. This reason for shame can and must shape our identities. But before we solve our identity crisis, we have to accept that it exists. Accepting the crisis is not the solution, but nearly five centuries since moral theology was "invented" at the Council of Trent, it could be a beginning.

Notes

1. I use this expression to state my fear that especially for Europe it is—not still but again—not so much the global South that is recognized as counterpart but some kind of idealized and despised "Orient."

2. Niklas Luhmann, *Funktion der Religion* (Frankfurt am Main: Suhrkamp, 1982), 239.

3. Rainer Bucher, "Body of Power and Body Power: The Situation of the Church and God's Defeat," in "The Structural Betrayal of Trust," ed. Regina Ammicht-Quinn, Hille Haker, and Maureen Junker-Kenny, special issue, *Concilium* 3 (2004): 120-29; 129.

4. Pope Benedict XVI, Homily at the Holy Mass for the Conclusion of the Year of the Priests, June 11, 2010, http://www.vatican.va/.

5. Pope Benedict XVI, Homily at the Eucharistic Celebration, Westminster Abbey, September 18, 2010, http://www.vatican.va/.

6. Ibid.

7. Regina Ammicht-Quinn, *Körper—Religion—Sexualität: Theologische Reflexion zur Ethik der Geschlechter*, 3rd ed. (Mainz: Grünewald, 2004).

8. Barbara Baert, "A Head on a Platter: The *Johannesschüssel* or the Image of the Mediator and the Precursor," *Antwerp Royal Museum Annual* (2003): 8-41.

9. Ibid., 39.

10. Ibid., 16.

11. Paul Satori, "Johannes der Täufer," *Handwörterbuch des deutschen Aberglaubens*, vol. 4 (Berlin: De Gruyter, 1932).

12. Baert, "A Head on a Platter," 17ff.

13. See the 1922 essay "Medusa's Head," in Sigmund Freud, *Sexuality and the Psychology of Love* (New York: Simon & Schuster, 1997).

14. Michel Foucault, *Die Heterotopien: Der utopische Körper* (Frankfurt: Suhrkamp, 2005), 34.

15. Wilhelm Weischedel, *Die philosophische Hintertreppe* (Munich: Nymphenburger Verlagshaus, 1974), 82.

16. Origen, *De Principiis: Bücher von den Prinzipien*, ed. Herwig Görgemanns and Heinrich Karp (Darmstadt: Wissenschaftliche Buchgesellschaft, 1976), 1: 8.

17. *Normae de gravioribus delictis*, 2.1. See "Normae de gravioribus delictis," CatholicCulture.org, http://www.catholicculture.org/culture/library/view.cfm?recnum=9353#normae.

18. Margaret Mead, "Interpretive Statement," in *Cooperation and Competition among Primitive Peoples*, ed. Margaret Mead (New York: McGraw-Hill, 1937), 493-505.

19. Ruth Benedict, *The Chrysanthemum and the Sword: Patterns of Japanese Culture* (London: Routledge & Kegan Paul, 1967).

20. Sighard Neckel, *Status und Scham: Zur symbolischen Reproduktion sozialer Ungleichheit* (New York: Campus, 2001); and Regina Ammicht-Quinn, "Das Andere der Vollkommenheit: Stigma und Scham," in *Vollkommenheit: Archäologie der literarischen Kommunikation X*, ed. Aleida Assmann and Jan Assmann (Munich: Fink, 2010), 41-52.

21. Barbara Ehrenreich, *Nickeled and Dimed: On (not) Getting By in America* (New York: Metropolitan Books, 2001), 220.

22. Elspeth Probyn, *Blush: Faces of Shame* (Minneapolis: University of Minnesota Press, 2005), 105.

CRITICALLY DIFFERENTIATING THE PAST: HISTORY AND ETHICS[1]

Alberto Bondolfi

I have been interested in the theme of this session throughout my entire scholarly work in both Catholic and Protestant theological faculties, since this is a theme that ought to interest every form of ethical reflection of a theological type, even if we must immediately and readily admit that this theme is not specifically theological but is equally relevant to ethical and philosophical reflection.

Before we go into the merits of this question, I would like to draw the reader's attention to a preliminary observation. What is the state of historiography in the specific field of theological ethics? It is easy to lose our bearings, given the sheer abundance of recent publications,[2] which makes it difficult to formulate a nuanced judgment.

The State of the Art

For various reasons, interest in the positions taken by moral theologians in the course of history has certainly increased in the last decades. Many questions that are currently being asked display analogies to those proposed in past centuries. Historical research intends, at least in some cases, to help us see more intensely and precisely what happened in the past in order to make us more sensitive in our perception of the challenges of the present day.

We immediately notice some tendencies in historiography that merit our critical attention. Above all, we can observe that so-called secular historians are sometimes more interested than professional moral theologians in some of the historical developments in moral theology and that they study these on a more serious academic level.[3] Of course, it must be admitted, in exoneration of my colleagues (and obviously of myself as well), that it is not easy for one who has specialized in theological ethics to undertake wide-reaching historical research, because academic work of this kind implies a knowledge of methodologies and of sources that cannot easily be acquired through classical studies in philosophy and/or theology.

This argument, however, neither explains nor justifies the late arrival of many contemporary moral theologians on the scene of historical research that touches directly on their own specific themes. It is indeed true that one needs knowledge of the general field of historiography in order to carry out historical research that meets appropriate standards, but it is equally true that historical research on ethical themes, and more specifically of ethical-theological themes, presupposes a solid theological culture.

Many "secular" historians today display a theological culture of this kind. Their work thus contributes to a better knowledge of our own ethical-theological tradition and thereby stimulates us to pay more attention to historical research, both in the context of our own specific research and in our teaching and research institutions.

A Variety of Paths for Investigation

When we reconstruct some significant paths of moral theological research or investigate in depth the historical aspect of some of the key themes of our academic discipline, we are obliged to pose a variety of questions that are not reducible to one single methodology. In this short essay, I wish to present four areas for historical investigation into moral theological matters. We begin with the basic issue of the facticity of the phenomena and culminate with the area that is most closely linked to theory and to systematic reflection.

History Is Concerned with Facts

One who studies history intends above all to reconstruct facts, events, or concrete situations that have no necessary correlation to ethical doctrines. However, this affirmation on my part does not imply that such events are irrelevant to our discipline and to its history, since an event can possess a symbolic meaning. Such meaning may already be inherent in it when it occurs, or it may be acquired subsequently, thanks to the influence it has had on the understanding of the generations who have handed it on and interpreted it anew.

Let me offer some examples. The proclamation of the Jubilee in 1300 and publication of the bull *Unam sanctam* by Boniface VIII had a rich significance for our understanding of the political ethics inspired by Western Christianity—a significance that goes beyond the contents of the written documents.[4] It is perfectly true that this bull contains elements of an ecclesiology and of a social and political ethics, but the event of the proclamation of the Jubilee and its ritualization, to which the iconography of the period also bears witness, gives the doctrinal positions defended by Boniface VIII a vivid context in life that transcends the affirmations contained in the document itself.

To take another example, when the Dominican Antonio de Montesinos cast doubt on the morality of the conquest of the new American lands in the sermon he preached on December 21, 1511, a Sunday in Advent, something happened of which Montesinos was not fully aware, namely, there was a paradigm shift in the understanding of how non-Christian and Christian peoples should live together. The "fact" of the sermon of Montesinos then became an element of doctrinal discourse in Bartolomé de Las Casas, who is our only source for the reconstruction of this exemplary event.[5] Later doctrinal developments, which we find above all in the works of the theologians of Salamanca, will bestow both theoretical and systematic dignity on the intuitions of the preacher Montesinos, but it is the fact of his Advent sermon that will take on a special exemplarity in view of everything that followed it. In other words, facts are not simply "brute facts." Under certain conditions, they can become elements of theoretical reflection and of a paradigm change in the way moral demands are understood.

History Is Also Concerned with Praxis

Historical research also seeks to proceed from individual events to analyze the practices that become established, sometimes by means of extremely complicated processes, in a given period. Moral theology ought to have a very lively interest in the historical reconstruction of praxis, because it claims that its systematic reflection allows it to affirm or deny the legitimacy of individual practices on the basis of rational considerations and for genuinely theological reasons.

Practices have a historical existence, since they can vary in their concrete manifestations and in their motivations or moral justifications. In general, fundamental moral reflection finds it difficult to follow these metamorphoses, but after a delay that I would call "physiological," moral reflection adapts its own lines of argument for or against the individual practices, in keeping with the changes that happen precisely on the level of these practices themselves.

Two examples can illustrate what I mean. The praxis of matrimony has been consistently accompanied by a moral theological reflection on its meaning, its modalities, and its rules. Moral theological reflection has been obliged to accept the changes that have taken place in the practices that are linked to this institution, even if it has done so only very slowly. Some normative elements of matrimonial praxis have appeared constant (for example, its unicity and indissolubility), but a very acute historical analysis demonstrates today how elements of discontinuity have found their way into matrimony despite the apparent consistency of the practices. For example, recent historical investigation of the praxis of divorce in the church in the first centuries has brought to light practices that were less consistent than moral theologians were inclined to believe and affirm until a few decades ago.[6] It seems, therefore, that the institution of matrimony manifests permanence over the course of time, but the permanence of the name cannot hide the diversity of practices. A critical study of the juridical sources could and should lead to a renewal of the historiography that is present in theological moral investigations. These tend in general to read the history of the institution of matrimony as an ever-more-conscious "discovery" of the specific character of Christian marriage. Such research is somewhat too "optimistic" and does not take account of the twists and turns that have occurred over time or of their structural causes, whether within or outside theology itself.

The historical analysis of the praxis of lending at interest, or of oath-taking, shows even more strongly than in the case of matrimony the striking discontinuities, and sometimes indeed the inconsistencies, that characterize the evolution of practices in Western Christianity. Even the reference to the biblical text, which appears particularly clear in the case of oath-taking and its prohibition, undergoes metamorphoses that are rather blatant. Today's theologian or moral theologian cannot ignore these if he or she wishes to present anew in a credible manner a contemporary systematic reflection on the same problem.[7]

History Is Also Concerned with Doctrines

Historical research is also concerned with a stratum that lies much deeper than that revealed by the analysis of ethically relevant practices. It also analyzes the changes in the doctrinal discourses employed to legitimate precisely these changing practices. Historiography is thus also interested in doctrines and in their changes across time and space.

We must acknowledge that specialists in moral theology also pay preferential attention to this area.[8] It is in fact possible, and not at all difficult, for any scholar in this field to analyze the evolution of doctrines by working on the available written sources, and it is relatively easy to establish lines of dependence on earlier authors or on individual currents of thought. Behind this apparent easiness, however, significant difficulties lie hidden. I mention only a few here, which I myself have encountered in the rare historical explorations that I have undertaken in the years of my academic activity.

Sometimes doctrinal changes are almost imperceptible, and it seems possible to interpret them as continuities in a tradition of thought in which they seem to alter only a few secondary details. But these small signs sometimes conceal a genuine paradigm shift that sheds a completely new light on a question. This is because there is a tendency in the theological milieu to emphasize the continuity of the message across the centuries; in other words, even radical changes are sometimes manifested in a very discreet way by means of the addition of an adjective or a carefully worded specification, not by a new systematic presentation of everything that one has studied.

Let me give a concrete illustration. A modern reader of the *Relecciones* of Francisco de Vitoria on the doctrine of a just war or the treatise by Cardinal Cajetan on almsgiving will have the impression of reading an almost mechanical reproduction of the positions taken by Thomas Aquinas on these two normative questions. It is only a more critical reading that considers the circumstances linked to the composition of these texts that will reveal a qualitative change in the examination of the two problems, that of war and that of the redistribution of goods. These circumstances included a society—the sixteenth century—that had changed in very many respects from the society of the thirteenth century. Even if the vocabulary and the categories appear not to have changed, these two theologians do in fact introduce a qualitative leap into reflection on these matters. Their reflections bring them into the sphere of the early modern age, despite the fact that the problem is still being formulated in the language of the medieval context.[9]

History Is Also Concerned with Mentalities

In order to grasp these paradigm shifts within an apparent continuity in the argumentation, we must perhaps bear in mind the fact that history is not concerned only with doctrinal changes, but also with mentalities. This category, put forward by the celebrated historiographical "Annales" school, constitutes the deepest stratum of the river of history.[10] If I may employ a metaphor coined by a celebrated historian of this school, we may say that in the deepest stratum the water seems not to move, whereas it flows very rapidly in the more superficial strata, those of the history of events. This variation in speed in the different strata applies also, and indeed primarily, to moral convictions.

Historical research in the ethical-theological domain must also be concerned with the change of mentalities in its own field of research. Within the various Christian theologies, one can observe different mentalities at work in the approach to biblical texts, and one can see how different mentalities perceive and approach the same set of phenomena. Also needed is an authentically ecumenical historiography when looking at facts and doctrines of the past in order to grasp their specific roots and the polemical significance that they possessed in the past but need not necessarily possess today. I take my example, inevitably enough, from the city where this congress is taking place, namely, the progress that has been made by both Catholic and Protestant historians in our understanding of the Tridentine document on justification. The recent common Declaration on Justification[11] would not have been possible without the patient work by many historians who have helped us to see the texts of the Council of Trent not as an insurmountable obstacle to a common understanding of the Pauline doctrine of justification by faith but as a partial understanding that was due to the circumstances of time and place in the sixteenth century.

Here too, we may certainly speak of a paradigm shift, even when the terminology appears to remain unchanged. Other examples also seem to illustrate this intuition, for example, the category of "sacrifice" as a characterization of the Eucharist, or that of "merit" in the specifically ethical domain.

Specialists in moral theology who seek to integrate the results of historical research that examines mentalities into genuinely theological reflection must possess great intellectual and interpretative abilities. This fact goes some way toward explaining the rather "meager" reception of this historiography in the literature of moral theological in recent decades. For example, there is a need to integrate into the treatises of moral theology the abundant historical and anthropological literature on sexuality, matrimony, and the family; such a work of reception would entail numerous difficulties. The task is immense, and it is probably impossible for one single author to undertake it alone.

Conclusion

If we are to comprehend and to change the present and to give an argumentative consistency to the systematic reflection that is carried out in the field of theological ethics, a critical and differentiated exploration of the past in its various stratifications is indispensable. Historical research proves indispensable for systematic research, if the latter wants to have both an argumentative consistency and an adequate perception of the objects it is examining and criticizing.

The past does not offer us magical formulas for managing the present, but it helps us to understand better what lies before our eyes, to see the remote and the proximate causes, to establish the conditions required for a possible change, and to offer an adequate legitimation of such changes.

Historical research also preserves us from "leaping into the void" of a future that lacks proper foundations because it is merely the fruit of our imagination, rather than of a well-documented historical explanation. A well-ordered exercise of historical memory and a methodical examination of the sources are a better aid to understanding the true elements of continuity that must be preserved (because they are inherent in the "Tradition") and the elements that must be abandoned because they are contingent (and are the object of individual "traditions"). This means that historical research, far from constituting a brake on the future of our discipline, is in fact a specific and indispensable stimulus.

If this is to happen, however, internal renewal is necessary, leading to better access to historical work. Let me formulate some requirements, which I submit to readers for critical analysis and discussion.

First, in recent years, the Internet has greatly facilitated access to sources, but further progress is still both possible and necessary. Above all, we must eliminate the inequalities between rich and poor countries with regard to access to historical documentation. The patristic sources and the works of the Protestant reformers have been accessible on Web sites for a number of years now, but this access has to be paid for, and only universities in rich countries can afford a continuing subscription to these sources. Accordingly, theology too displays the so-called digital divide that separates the world into two parts, the high-income countries and the countries that have little purchasing power.[12] The principle of open access to which many European and northern countries subscribe must be applied consistently, so that scholars in developing countries will have equal access to historical sources, permitting serious research work even in those places without substantial libraries.[13]

Second, the sources themselves must be expanded, because it is necessary to discuss critically the selection that has been made over the course of time. Many sources that are incorrectly regarded as "secondary" or even "irrelevant" must be made available to scholars who wish to interpret them critically. This task is particularly difficult because the presence of some themes or positions that we find extremely interesting with regard to the historical period in which they are formulated may be more or less objectively representative of the collective perception that existed in one particular historical epoch.

The most representative example that immediately comes to mind is the history of women.[14] There can be no doubt that feminist historiography has correctly highlighted the problematical aspects of historical certainties that were regarded until very recently as indisputable. Methodological prudence, however, shows us that although new interpretive keys are required for the reading of historical phenomena that have been interpreted in a "masculine" manner, this does not necessarily imply that such phenomena have themselves become "different." The change of the key employed in reading these phenomena gives visibility to events and intellectual products that had remained in the shadow up to the present day. But the objectivity of the facts that occurred and of the reflections that were put forward nevertheless remains unchanged.

Third, students of moral theology must be encouraged to engage in historical research in order to benefit anew from that systematic reflection. This investment may not seem useful at first sight, but it will certainly bear fruit in the medium and long term. The investments in "doing history" in the past continue to bear fruit in the present as well. Here, we may recall the "Migne phenomenon" in France, which not only renewed patristic studies in the nineteenth century but also laid the foundations for innovative initiatives in the twentieth century such as the *Sources chrétiennes* collection. We must therefore hope that the first years of our own century may see the birth—aided by informatics and telematics—of new historiographical initiatives in the moral theological field that can lay the foundations for new initiatives in the future. I am speaking in the city of Trento, where it is natural to hope that many documents that as yet lie undisturbed in various archives may be made widely accessible, helping us to understand better the multiple causes that led to the confessional rupture of the sixteenth century.

Finally, let me mention what may be the greatest challenge facing all who practice theological ethics. Our position in relation to philosophical ethics seems to have become particularly fragile. No doubt, many other considerations of a theoretical and systematic character are required in order to explain this fragility; but I believe that good historical research, undertaken in common by scholars in the fields of philosophy, theology, and "secular history," would do much to "solidify" our discipline. Historical research of this kind could and should illustrate the continuous contacts that moral theology has had with moral thinking in the field of philosophy. These contacts often had the character of conflict and of apologetics, but occasionally there was also a genuine will to understand each other and to engage in a mutual dialogue.

Debates in very recent times, especially in the field of bioethics, have shown that there is a lack of common philosophical reflection. This has led to misunderstandings that were avoidable, objectively speaking, but that were also inherent in a lack of will to understand each other. In this specific field, historical research that employs critical instruments and is free of preconceptions could demonstrate the complexity of some of the problematic questions, such as abortion.[15]

In other words, it is only through more intensive communication with philosophical reflection in the ethical field that we will succeed in correcting the relevant historiography, opening it up to new themes and to more critical research. The archives and the sources seem not to change with the passing of time, but the questions one may put to these sources are in reality inexhaustible. This means that they must be opened up to the intelligent curiosity of both present and future generations.

Notes

1. English translation by Brian McNeil.

2. For an initial overview, see R. Gerardi, *Storia della morale: Interpretazioni teologiche dell'esperienza Cristiana: Periodi e correnti, autori e opera* (Bologna: EDB, 2003).

3. Many historians could be cited here, but I mention only some of those who have written in Italian. In this specific area, there is a great abundance of high-level academic studies. See Paolo Prodi, *Settimo non rubare: Furto e mercato nella storia dell'Occidente* (Bologna: Il Mulino, 2009); P. Prodi, *Una storia della giustizia: Dal pluralismo dei fori al moderno dualismo tra coscienza e diritto* (Bologna: Il Mulino, 2000); P. Prodi, *Il sacramento del potere: Il giuramento politico nella storia costitutionale dell'Occidente* (Bologna: Il Mulino, 1992); A. Prosperi, *Tribunali della coscienza: Inquisitori, confessori, missionari* (Turin: Einaudi, 2009); and A. Prosperi, *Dare l'anima* (Turin: Einaudi, 2005). We should also note the attention paid today by both "secular" historians and specialists in moral theology to the phenomenon of casuistry as it was cultivated in both Catholic and Protestant theology from the sixteenth to the eighteenth century. Among the many publications in this field, see R. Schüssler, *Moral im Zweifel*, 2 vols. (Paderborn: Mentis, 2003); S. Boarini, *Introduction à la casuistique* (Paris: L'Harmattan, 2007); and P. Hurtubise, *La casuistique dans tous ses états* (Montreal: Novalis, 2005).

4. This is easily demonstrated by a critical historical reconstruction of this event. See A. Paravicini-Bagliani, *Bonifacio VIII* (Turin: Einaudi, 2003).

5. For a detailed study that illustrates this brief account, see A. Bondolfi, "La théologie morale espagnole face au défi de la découverte du 'nouveau monde,'" *Freiburger Zeitschrift für Philosophie und Theologie* 39 (1992): 314-31. Although an immense amount of scholarly work has been devoted to the problem of the conquest, we seldom find studies that draw a direct link between the "brute facts" and the theoretical reflection that follows upon these facts. For a synthesis of moral theological thinking of that period and cultural sphere, see J. Belda Plans, *La escuela de Salamanca* (Madrid: Biblioteca de Autores Cristianos, 2000); M. A. Pena Gonzales, *La escuela de Salamanca* (Madrid: Biblioteca de Autores Cristianos, 2009).

6. I refer the reader to a study now regarded as a classic, which I believe confirms what I have written here: J. Gaudemet, *Le marriage en Occident: Les mœurs et le droit* (Paris: Cerf, 1987).

7. See the research by Paolo Prodi on this specific historical topic (n. 2 above).

8. See, for example, the various approaches taken by Louis Vereeke, *De Guillaume d'Ockham à Saint Alphonse de Liguori: Etudes d'histoire de la théologie morale moderne 1300-1787* (Rome: Alfonsianum, 1986); Giuseppe Angelini, *Teologia morale fondamentale: Tradiziione, scrittura e teoria* (Milan: Glossa, 1999); Giuseppe Angelini and Ambrogio Valsecchi, *Disegno storico della teologia morale* (Bologna: EDB, 1972); and Giuseppe Angelini and Silvano Macchi, eds., *La teologia del Novecento* (Milan: Glossa, 2000).

9. For the teaching on almsgiving, I refer to my article "Elemosina" in *Nuovo dizionario di teologia morale*, ed. Francesco Compagnoni, Giorgio Piana, and Salvatore Privitera (Milan: Paoline, 1990), and to my own research: A. Bondolfi, *Helfen und Strafen* (Munster: LIT, 1997).

10. For an introduction to the debate among historians about the stratification of historical reality, see R. Rauzduel, *Sociologie historique des "Annales"* (Paris: Lettres du monde, 1999); C. A. Aguirre Rojas, *Die "Schule" der Annales: Gestern, heute, morgen* (Leipzig: Peipziger Universitätsverlag, 2004); A. Burguière, *L'école des Annales: Une histoire intellectuelle* (Paris: Jacob, 2004); and A. Rüth, *Erzählte Geschichte: Narrative Strukturen in der französischen Annales-Geschichtsschreibung* (Berlin: de Gruyter, 2005).

11. See the Lutheran World Federation and the Roman Catholic Church, *Joint Declaration on the Doctrine of Justification* (Grand Rapids, MI: Eerdmans, 2000).

12. On this subject, see the research by N. Zillien, *Digitale Ungleichheit: Neue Technologien und alte Ungleichheiten in der Informations- und Wissensgesellschaft* (Wiesbaden: Verlag für Sozialwissenschaften, 2006).

13. For an initial analysis of this problem, see Roberto Caso, ed., *Pubblicazioni scientifiche, diritti d'autore e Open Access*, Atti del Convegno tenuto presso la Facoltà di Giurisprudenza di Trento, June 20, 2008 (Trent: Università degli Studi di Trento, 2009). This text can be accessed at University of Trento eprints, http://eprints.biblio.unitn.it/ archive/00001589/. Roberto Caso published version 1.0 (February 2009) with a license: Creative Commons Attribuzione-Non commerciale-Non opera derivate 2.5 Italia (CC BY-NC-ND 2.5). This permits the non-commercial use of this work, provided that the attribution to the author is always mentioned. For more information, see Creative Commons, http://creativecommons.org/licenses/by-nc-nd/2.5/it.

14. For an initial approach, see the five-volume work edited by G. Duby, M. Perrot, et al., *History of Women in the West* (Cambridge, MA: Harvard University Press, 2000).

15. See the historical research by P. Sardi, undertaken with the desire to demonstrate the continuity of a doctrine, but which also illustrates the discontinuities: *L'aborto ieri e oggi* (Brescia: Paideia, 1975).

Moral Theology and History: A Peculiar Relationship[1]

Diego Alonso-Lasheras

In a 1959 discussion of theological unity Yves Congar said that there were two moral risks, especially after the sixteenth century when casuistic discussion began to take precedence over the moral side of theological science in the manuals for confessors. The first risk was forgetting the vital and organic nature of morality as a part of theology, reducing it to a discipline of norms. The second was to treat morality as a completely human project, forgetting its theological nature as discourse about a God who speaks to us in Christ, sanctifying us and calling us to live as the people of the covenant.[2]

At the urging of Vatican II in *Optatam totius*, the subsequent development of moral theology was largely based on the doctrine of Holy Scripture and on a return to the sources.[3] This movement, which both inspired and was inspired by the Council, led to a better understanding of the history of moral theology,[4] partly averting the risks of which Congar warned. Certainly today's moral theology is much more than a discipline of norms. But historians of moral theology still have a big task ahead of them. The call to return to the sources has received more attention in dogmatic and ascetical theology than in moral theology. In the task ahead, I believe Congar's warnings still apply to the way we moral theologians approach the history of our field. In particular we should remember its theological nature, which places moral theology in a special perspective. Whenever we study our sources, we dare not forget that this is more than an academic exercise; we are coming into communion with a historic moment in the One Church.

The Special *Theo*logical Perspective in Studying the History of Moral Theology

There are many reasons for studying the history of a discipline. In the case of moral theology, one reason—often left unspoken—is to historically legitimate one's own position. This approach to history often incurs the first risk that Congar mentioned: legalism, or the reduction of morality to a science of norms. The historian treats the monuments of moral theology[5] as a jurist studies jurisprudence, to support the reasoning of earlier verdicts. We look to history for some recognized author who defends a position, if not the same, at least similar or analogous to ours.

This approach, legitimate in the field of law, ignores the special *theo*logical perspective that must be considered even while studying the history of our discipline: the relationship of moral theology to its history is different from that of biology or philosophy, because studying the history of moral theology is a theological act.

For a Catholic moral theologian, the study of history is more than an academic exercise of following hermeneutical approaches to a text in accordance with its historical context or the meaning of the words and terms it contains. Studying the history of moral theology is an act of faith seeking understanding. It is an act of faith, not only because every theological exercise presupposes a faith seeking understanding, but because studying history in general, and the historical sources of moral theology in particular, is most meaningful when it is done from a confessional belief in the unity of the church.

A historian of philosophy does not try to enter into communion with Aristotle, but instead to understand the meaning of his texts by using all the available hermeneutical methods. In contrast, moral theologians should approach our texts not only with a knowledge of the original languages, the history of the period, the author, and the problems discussed in the text. All that is part of the rigor that the practice of moral theology needs and requires. In addition, however, moral theologians studying the traditional texts should be aware that in the last analysis we are entering into contact and communion with the One Church, in which the Spirit of the Lord is made manifest. In interpreting the traditional texts we must always follow the hermeneutical rules—but we must never forget that to touch the tradition is not only to stir up the river in search of the gold nuggets that time has left there; it is also a privileged opportunity for contact, for communion, with the life of the church where the Spirit lives.[6]

This does not mean that every text we study is an inspired text or that all texts have the same value. But if, as *Dei verbum* says, it is true that "the Church, in her teaching, life and worship, perpetuates and hands on to all generations all that she herself is, all that she believes,"[7] then our encounter with the most important monuments of the history of moral theology enables us to be in touch with the "deposit of meaning" of the experience lived and read in the light of the Christian faith, within the church. This is both a historical experience and a moral experience.

Contact with this experience enables us to live more deeply what we believe and to understand more clearly the type of life that the Christian faith offers. In the traditional texts, in the history of moral theology—the fathers of the church, the scholastics, the councils, the pronouncements of the church—we encounter the revelation lived, understood, formulated, and handed on as a way of life, as a norm of action. For that reason we should approach the history of moral theology as part of a tradition greater than we are, an unbroken tradition, a tradition that is a history shared not only with our contemporaries but with all who form part of the body of Christ, a theological reality that transcends time.[8]

When we see this relationship between history and moral theology as theological, as moral theologians in touch with history, with our own history, we will then make an effort to know it in depth and to find in it new ways of expressing what we have received. Moral theologians who do this are able to enter into relationship with culture and society in order to transform and enrich them, because it is a creative tradition that we have received. We can become "radically traditional,"[9] which does not mean merely repeating and perpetuating old formulas—for these may mean something very different in new social contexts—nor innovating for the sake of novelty, which entails the grave risk of simply following a passing fashion.

Suggested Criteria for Being Radically Traditional

To be radically traditional is a challenge that any moral theologian may find disconcerting. It is not easy to study our history, to enter in contact with it and reformulate it in ways that renew the church and transform and enrich the society in which we live. For that reason it is important to establish some criteria that will avoid the risks of mere repetition and adaptation to passing fashions.

In the second part of his work *Vrai et fausse réforme dans l'église* (*True and False Reform in the Church*), Yves Congar explores four conditions needed for a reformation without a schism: (1) the primacy of charity and pastoral concern; (2) remaining in communion with the whole; (3) showing patient respect when things go slowly; and (4) seeing renewal as a return to traditional principles rather than a mechanical introduction of something new.[10] Although Congar's work is in the field of ecclesiology rather than moral theology, I believe that these criteria can be usefully reinterpreted and applied to the task of being radically traditional.

The Primacy of Charity and Pastoral Concern

In studying and reformulating the history of moral theology, we must take care to seek the renewal of the church and not something that is simply new. We begin with the church as an existing reality—not as something to be discovered or remade but as a reality present to me, the focus of my work. Therefore, charity and pastoral concern must be my first priority.

With charity and pastoral concern as the first priority, we can avoid an "intellectual Donatism" that seeks the perfection of our reasoning at the cost of whatever contributes to fullness of life for Christians. We can study our history and reinterpret its best fruits for the sake of our imperfect brothers and sisters who live in a church that is holy but not perfect.

Maurice Pontet points out a difference between Augustine's speculative and polemical treatises and his sermons, and he affirms that the holy bishop of Hippo was unconsciously instructed and guided by his listeners.[11] Knowledge and contact with the pastoral reality of the church—which may be mediated in different ways—is a fundamental step toward a correct reading of moral theology that situates it in the here and now of our own world. Excessive intellectualism, always a danger for those who live in the academic world, may turn us away from communion toward a reading and presentation of history that lead away from the pastoral concerns of the people of God.

An important part of the success—if we can call it that—of the Council of Trent is that it did not concern itself only with dogma and doctrine. This was partly because of the struggle with the reformers, but Trent was also a deeply pastoral council, recognizing that the evils afflicting the church were more pastoral than doctrinal. This is clear from the fact that along with doctrinal decrees, it also issued decrees of reformation, pastoral decrees such as a residential obligation for bishops and the creation of seminaries.

Remaining in Unity with the Whole

According to Congar, the conditions of the Holy Spirit's work are essentially communitarian.[12] Our first criterion was a warning against the constant danger of intellectualism in the academic world; it is also important to guard against the danger of individualism. The study of the history of theology is demanding; it requires preparation in languages and history, a broad knowledge of philosophy and theology, and a willingness to enter into *formae mentis* that are different from ours. Such a demanding discipline can be carried out only by spending many hours over one's books in the solitude of a library or an office. But we must never forget that the study of the history of moral theology should always be a collective task, something I do with others, even from the solitude of my place of study. If we can stay in unity with the whole, then the corrections and additions needed in any historical pursuit will not come from a special act or effort. Such corrections and additions will come through the force and impulse of the communion that helps to shape our work and softens its sharp edges.

We never possess the whole truth except in unity with the whole church, from the apostles to those who will come after us. If we believe this, if we are able to live it in our work as moral theologians and in the study of its history, then even when our affirmations seem unilateral or ambivalent they can be interpreted positively, precisely because of our union with the whole. This union is not only with the apostles, although it certainly includes them. As Congar says, it is not "a pure obedience to the determinations of authority, since the name of the Church does not refer only to the hierarchy in isolation from the body of the faithful."[13]

The true movements of reform that have occurred in the church were marked by a return to the sources and also by a strong dimension of life together and of work in cooperative relationships. It is difficult to study, know, and develop the received tradition apart from a community context. We cannot enter into communion with the One Church of another time—the *proprium* of the study of its history by moral theology—unless we are already in communion with the One Church in our own here and now. This can happen only through a community that seeks to live as brothers and sisters and that mediates our belonging to the church.

Traditionally, since moral theology was cultivated by the clergy, this common and brotherly life was almost automatic; moral theologians grew, developed, and bore fruit within a religious order or in the heart of a diocesan parish. The advent of lay teachers and scholars of moral theology has led to new forms of life in common. One example of this is the Congress on "Catholic Theological Ethics in the World Church," held in Trento in July 2010, that has contributed to an international exchange of ideas among Catholic ethicists and to the exploration of new forms of common life in the future.[14] Another interesting initiative is the annual meeting of "New Wine, New Wineskins," held every year at Notre Dame University in connection with the feast of St. Alfonso Maria de Liguori. In addition to the academic exchange that occurs at these meetings, there is also an appreciation for the informal spaces they provide that encourage the experience of study as a common task. These new forms of life together grow out of the need for union with the whole, and they are increasingly important in view of the critical and urgent problems we face today.

Patience and Respect in the Face of Delay

Congar says that although the reform and renewal of the church have sometimes come from the hierarchy—think of the Gregorian reform that freed the church from interference and submission to the power of the emperor, kings, and feudal lords—on the whole, "the initiative usually comes not from the center but the periphery, from below rather than above."[15] At the same time, if a proposal is not approved by those in the church with the charism of authority, it is of little use; it does not breathe life into the people of God, and it may lead to absurd theological and pastoral wars. Obedience to the Spirit—which is needed for communion with the church today as in other times—is fundamentally marked by a tension that must be accepted as part of our dedication to the study of moral theology and its history.

It does not take great intellectual effort to discover that things are not working right in an institution. But to discover how to improve them with what we have been given, what we have received, what we have—and not what we wish we had—how to improve, expand, and develop what we have: that does require a great effort of intellect and patience!

In relation to patience and to the primacy of charity and pastoral concern, I would like to highlight Congar's advice against prematurely seeking the approval of the hierarchy. He says that sometimes the hierarchy of the church takes a position that says in effect, "Do it, but don't ask to have it approved as a specific proposition."[16] The hierarchy is aware that many of the practices and doctrines that are common in the church today began at the margin—within the church but at the margin—and that they received ecclesiastical approval only after they had been tested, after their sharp edges had been softened, after they had met the test of time, patience, and pastoral practice. We should not ask the magisterium of the church to do more—or less—than it can, and the development that comes from tradition and its renewal will be accepted only after repeated testing.

In this sense the pursuit of truth obliges us to follow uncharted paths without asking for explicit approval in advance, to make a way through the no man's land in the kingdom of truth that separates commonly accepted truth from the borderlands of error. We cannot fail to explore that *terra incognita* that belongs to the field of truth. That would be a poor service to the truth that the church proclaims. It is a delicate exercise, because it requires the patience and humility to accept that in communion with the whole, we are stepping into a truth not yet shared by all, and we must avoid crossing the line into error.

This patience is possible only in the presence of the two conditions just discussed—the primacy of charity and pastoral concern, and union with the whole—because that is the only way to resist the temptation to see ourselves as sole possessors of the truth, abandoned by the church.

Renewal as the Result of a Return to the Principle of Tradition,
Not by a Mechanical Adaptation to Introduce Something "New"

Congar faults modernism for accepting the eighteenth-century principle of the perfectibility of Christianity rather than its development; that is, its progressive transformation through external influences rather than as an expression of the best that is within it. Dialogue with the surrounding world must lead the church to accept the elements of truth that it contains, but the principle of renewal must be found in the church herself, in what she is and lives, in the charisms that the Spirit gives in every age.

Tradition does not mean a routine and mere return to the past. Historians of moral theology must avoid this defect. To turn to history with loyal and affectionate respect means respect for its permanent and valid forms and critical, intelligent respect for its transitory forms. It means to be moved by "more than what the church has said, but by the Spirit that inspired the Church to speak then and that tries to speak to us about our contemporary problems."[17] To avoid a mechanical adaptation, we need a real life community that follows the words of St. Paul: "Do not quench the Spirit. Do not despise the words of prophets, but test everything; hold fast to what is good; abstain from every form of evil" (1 Thess 5:19-22, NRSV).

Conclusion

The task may seem huge, almost impossible, if we see it as a task for one person, but not if we see it as the work of a whole generation. In this sense, every generation is charged with renewing the church—not with innovating—and it can do so only by getting in touch with its sources and developing them in order to hand them on to the next generation as something alive, not as a dead corpus of doctrines. To make contact with the history of moral theology is a theological act that allows the moral theologian to receive the vital fluid in order to express the eternal newness of the gospel. I think this is not an easy task. It takes academic rigor and living faith, an ability to "be converted" in our own intellectual convictions, and an ability to enter into communion with the One Church—letting the One Church judge our work to see if we have rightly expressed the perennial newness that we find in history.

Notes

1. This essay has been translated into English by Margaret D. Wilde.

2. Yves Congar, *La foi et la théologie* (Tournai: Desclée, 1962), 181. Congar says at the beginning that the book was written in 1958-59, but it did not receive the *Imprimi potest* until 1962.

3. *Optatam totius* (Decree on Priestly Training), 16.

4. See the useful discussion by James F. Keenan in *History of Catholic Moral Theology in the Twentieth Century: From Confessing Sins to Liberating Consciences* (New York: Continuum, 2010).

5. By "monument" I mean "a scientific, artistic or literary work that is memorable for its exceptional merit." See Real Academia de la Lengua, Diccionario de la Lengua Española, http://buscon.rae.es/draeI/SrvltConsulta?TIPO_BUS=3&LEMA=monumento.

6. I think James F. Keenan means something like this when he says about his course on twentieth-century moral theology: "When I taught the course I was mindful of introducing my students not only to the works that shaped the century but more importantly to the persons" (Keenan, *History of Catholic Moral Theology*, vii).

7. *Dei verbum* (Dogmatic Constitution on Divine Revelation), 8.

8. This part of my reflection is inspired by Ottavio De Bertolis, "Libro III del principatus politicus di F. Suarez: il potere del Pontefici Romano sui re temporali," in *Periodica de re canonica* 97, no. 4 (2008): 673-75.

9. This phrase comes from Paul Murray, "Faith, Theology and the Secular Cloister," *The Tablet*, 29 (2010): 12-14, which has enriched my reflection.

10. Yves Congar, *Vrai et fausse réforme dans l'église* (Paris: Edition du Cerf, 1969), 209-317. The following pages of my reflection are largely based on this text from Congar. I have chosen ideas that can be "translated" for use in studying the history of moral theology.

11. Maurice Pontet, *L'exégèse de saint Augustin prédicateur* (Paris: Aubier, 1945), 511, quoted in Yves Congar, *Vrai et fausse réforme dans l'église*, 233.

12. Congar, *Vrai et fausse réforme dans l'église*, 241.

13. Ibid., 249.

14. See James F. Keenan, ed., *Catholic Theological Ethics in the World Church: The Plenary Papers from the First Cross-cultural Conference on Catholic Theological Ethics* (New York: Continuum, 2007).

15. Yves Congar, *Vrai et fausse réforme dans l'église*, 251.

16. Ibid., 292.

17. Ibid., 304.

Historical Building Blocks for a Consistent Relational and Sexual Ethics

Roger Burggraeve

In order to realize a loyal and critical interaction between history and theological ethics in a concrete way, I suggest we direct our attention to the current problem of the "deviant behavior" or "irregular lifestyle" of many Christians on the intimate relational level. We cannot deny the widespread phenomenon, even among Christians, of premarital sexuality, pre- and non-marital cohabitation, and civil remarriage after divorce. And aside from these heterosexual behaviors, neither can we close our eyes to the relationships and manners of cohabitation (leading up to civil marriage) of Christian homosexual men and women. The question is, how can we deal ethically with these behaviors that, as far as the church's view is concerned, must be labelled as morally "illicit"? For such an "ethics of the illicit," can we find paradigms in the history of the church and in moral theology that can help us move forward?

The Paradigm of "Deculpabilization"

The church has always been aware of morally "deviant" behavior, precisely because she has developed an explicit and extensive view of all things sinful, especially in the pastoral context of the practice of the confession of sins. No further explanation is needed on how the Council of Trent (1545-1563) played a decisive role in this regard. In its resistance against the individualistic mentality of the Renaissance and the Reformation and their preference for the personal judgment of conscience, the Council put all emphasis on the objectivity of correct actions and their corresponding moral rules and norms, and in line with that the clearly delineated transgressions and sins that were the subject of confession.

The traditional approach to human behavior, as we find today among others in the 1995 *Catechism of the Catholic Church*,[1] consists of the distinction between "objective good or bad" and "subjectively excusable." People do deeds that objectively speaking, according to the moral order or norm, are illicit, while subjectively they should not be held guilty on the basis of their psychoaffective incapacity or their social conditioning. Freedom makes the human person responsible and accountable for one's deeds "to the extent that they are voluntary."[2] The church is very much aware, however, of the ethical fragility of concrete persons, in the sense that the "imputability and responsibility for an action can be diminished or even nullified by ignorance, inadvertence, duress, fear, habit, inordinate attachments, and other psychological or social factors."[3]

Even the above-mentioned intimate relational behaviors are susceptible to psychoaffective and social conditioning that reduce or annul their freedom. Youngsters and young adults who choose premarital sexual relations and unmarried cohabitation are—certainly in Western societies—under great social pressure: these behaviors indeed have become so "obvious" and "normal" that they have been elevated to the new "social norm." If one desires to be accepted in one's own social environment and circle of friends, then one should at best—then one *must*—act in a "socially correct" manner, in other words, following the social mainstream. As far as unmarried cohabitation as the basis for forming of a family is concerned, a similar and growing social obviousness applies.

The same goes for remarriage after divorce. For divorcees to remain alone and unmarried is neither obvious socially or personally. On the basis of their actual family situation—if there are any children among other things—*and* on the basis of the existential fear of loneliness and the often strong need for intimacy, divorcees are under internal and social pressure to enter into a new relationship. They find themselves incapable of going through life alone.

Homosexuality is also in the church's thinking the subject of deculpabilization. For most gays and lesbians it is psychologically and affectively impossible to maintain the church's moral norm of "living in abstinence." Hence, "their culpability will be pledged with prudence,"[4] and they "must be accepted with respect, compassion, and sensitivity."[5]

An honest evaluation of the paradigm of deculpabilization cannot overlook its abiding value. It is a form of humility that acknowledges that our human freedom is neither almighty nor heroic—even though perhaps we do dream of heroism. However sovereign and unassailable in essence our will may seem to be, it is at the same time marked by a permanent violability. This realistic awareness of human fragility helps in not burdening people more heavily than they can bear and what their personality or character, their capacity for free choice and responsible actions, allow. The rise and the development of the human sciences (psychology, social sciences, and all sorts of human behavioral sciences) as well as of empirically scientific orientated endocrinology, neurobiology, sociobiology, and evolutionary psychology have only increased awareness of the boundaries of free and responsible human action.

It is an incontestable fact of pastoral practice that in concrete circumstances, it is occasionally necessary to "excuse" people and thus relieve them of a responsibility that actually cannot be tailor-made for them, since they are not really—not yet or no longer—capable of it. This realistic deculpabilization likewise helps people in ridding themselves of destructive guilt feelings. Furthermore, the paradox of such "moral unburdening" is that it can help tap new forces of growth. People can be so burdened by accusation and guilt that they blame themselves and even begin to hate themselves, while actually they are the victims of particular psychosocial conditionings, even though objectively, according to Christian moral prescriptions, they have acted wrongly. Thus, they can rediscover faith and trust in themselves in order to stand upright and once again take up their existence responsibly and positively.

The paradigm of deculpabilization, however, also has its limits. Deculpabilization can indeed go so far that it ends up in "de-ethicization," or, in other words, a quasi-mechanistic approach to human behavior that removes all possibilities for free self-determination and responsibility. In this regard, the paradigm of deculpabilization evokes only a negative image of the moral subject. An inadvertent consequence of exaggerated deculpabilization is that one pays no attention to the real, albeit limited, ethical possibilities of growth of concrete people.

In ethical guidance, therefore, we must stubbornly keep on presupposing that in the person and his or her life story "traces" of moral accountability can be tapped. Conversations with homosexuals indicate that "understanding based on deculpabilization" is at the very least ambiguous. Some stated quite clearly that they had no need of compassion from the church. They do not want to be considered as *minus habentes* or as morally inferior, weak, immature, or indigent persons. They experience compassion as a form of infantilization, which they actually find more serious than a strict objective doctrinaire condemnation of their homosexual behavior as such. They feel insulted and violated in their dignity as moral persons who do not so much as accept their own sexual condition "in resignation" as a handicap or a "flaw." On the contrary, they want to gain recognition for being morally capable of developing their orientation as a positive life choice.

This critique on the paradigm of deculpabilization is also applicable to other so-called deviant forms of intimate relationships. Heterosexuals who enter into pre-, non-, or postmarital intimate relationships and cohabitation equally do not feel at all helped by a form of condescending pity that covers up their flaws with regard to moral maturity with the "mantle of love." They do not ask for understanding but for respect for the uniqueness, the possibilities, and the challenges of their condition, situation, or choice.

The Paradigm of the "Law of Gradualness"

A more positive view of the moral subject can be found in the paradigm of the "law of gradualness," as it was launched and introduced by John Paul II in the apostolic exhortation on the family, *Familiaris consortio* (1981).[6] The synod document interprets the "law of gradualness" as the "step by step and unceasing progress" of married couples in their moral life, namely, in substantiating better and better their relational and familial vocation in and through their concrete choices regarding responsible parenthood.[7] The concept of gradualness rests on the conviction that the human person is a historical being: "Man, who has been called to live God's wise and loving design in a responsible manner, is an historical being who day by day builds himself up through his many free decisions; and so he knows, loves and accomplishes moral good by stages of growth."[8] The psychological sciences have familiarized us with the development of the person on bodily, psychological, and affective levels as well as on moral and spiritual levels.[9]

Gradualness, however, does not stand on its own. It concerns an orientated growth. *Familiaris consortio* presents a necessary path toward growth.[10] This growth must be directed toward a goal, namely, the realization of the moral law. Hence, through the already-mentioned quote from John Paul II and by making use of a play on words, the warning immediately follows that the law of gradualness "cannot be identified with 'gradualness of the law.'"[11] Even though it is accepted that in concrete circumstances in time and space, and in personal, social, and cultural contexts, people will not act in harmony with the norm or the desirable, they are still faced with the task to act in the direction of the normative good. Although people here and now do not succeed in realizing the norm effectively, as a consequence of their internal (personal) or external (contextual) circumstances, they still are faced with the task of striving at least for the realization of the law. This presupposes that they acknowledge the church's ethical norms, even though they do not yet comply with them. In turn, this implies the awareness that "conversion," namely, the will and the attempt to turn away from one's present deviant behavior, is necessary as a condition for turning toward the desirable behavior.

Now, the question is which goal for growth is aimed at by *Familiaris consortio*. A careful reading of the text demonstrates how gradualness and growth are directly related with the theme of birth control as an expression of responsible parenthood.[12] According to the church, since *Humanae vitae* (1968) only the use of a natural method of birth control is permissible. The law of gradualness proceeds from the fact that while many Christians de facto act differently, at the same time the church tries to stimulate them to evolve and to grow in the direction of what the church upholds; during this process, there must be awareness that this change will not be smooth and easy and that quite a number of people shall perhaps never reach the upheld norm. Taking into account the possibilities and limits of married couples in the context of their relationship, the church judges their deviant behavior mildly as provisional, on condition that the persons involved acknowledge their behavior as provisional and also create the necessary conditions in order to be able to live up to the norm in the future.

With regard to deviant intimate relational behaviors, the church moral law is clear, namely, the commandment on premarital abstinence, the prohibition on preconjugal and non-conjugal cohabitation, and the norm of abstinence both for homosexuals as well as for those who divorce. Even though there is an understanding that persons and couples may not comply or succeed in complying with the church moral norm, they are still faced with the task to grow toward the acceptance and realization of that norm. Notwithstanding the fact that the law of gradualness is a morality of intention and good will rather than of consequences, the law itself indeed does not tolerate any concession or nuance with regard to the goal to be attained.

This leads to a discord. No matter how promising the idea of the law of gradualness may be, the possibilities of its applicability are strongly constrained by the way in which the idea of the moral law itself is filled in. This is clearly apparent from the complete version of the comment of John Paul II already cited: "What is known as 'the law of gradualness' or step by step advance cannot be identified with 'gradualness of the law,' *as if there were different degrees or forms of precept in God's law for different individuals and situations.*"[13] What is striking in this comment is an utterly rigid, static, and even simplified view of the moral law. Remarkable, almost shocking, is the unnuanced identification of the human moral law with the divine law in the conviction that "the moral order reveals and sets forth the plan of God the Creator."[14] The third paradigm will nuance the relationship between both.

Moreover, the gradualness paradigm, in line with the traditional deculpabilization paradigm, employs an act-oriented view of human behavior. The broadening of this view will be discussed in the fourth part of this essay.

Paradigm of *Epikeia*

A third model that we can draw from our tradition is that of *epikeia* ("equity").[15] In and through its dynamic and differentiated view of the moral law, it also offers the possibility of approaching deviant intimate relational behavior in a more nuanced fashion.

Originally *epikeia* was seen, especially by Aristotle, as a reasonable manner of dealing with positive social laws. What is unique to social rules and laws is that they are never formulated for one situation but always for the community as a whole. In other words, laws have a general formulation and validity on the basis of the intention of the lawmaker, who by so doing intends to promote the general well-being of the community. The application of these laws, however, takes place in changing circumstances, so much so that—precisely on the basis of their universal form—they are simply no longer adequately applicable to all new situations. Precisely for that reason, the virtue of *epikeia* is needed, which, on the basis of reason and in respect for the general interest as the intention of the law, surpasses the imperfection of the law by deviating from the law or applying it in a better way. In line with Aristotle, Thomas Aquinas was of the opinion that *epikeia* is part of the virtue of justice and that this equity is necessary in order to fulfil the law, meaning to realize the true intention—the *bonum commune* (general well-being)—of the law in changing circumstances and contexts.

Under the impulse of Thomas Aquinas and Francisco Suarez, and later of Alphonsus de Liguori, the conviction arose in moral theology that *epikeia* was not only applicable to social laws but also to moral rules of action. According to the Thomistic tradition, the moral "natural law" (*lex naturae*) within human history is an expression of the divine "eternal law" (*lex aeterna*), although neither is equated with the other. Thomas accepted the mediation of human experience and development, as these were expressed gradually among others in the *mores* or "moral values of peoples." That is also why a distinction is made between different levels of reasoning and legislative draftings.

For speculative reason, we have the evident fundamental principle that one must strive for and do the good and one must avoid evil. Practical reason then formulates the *principia primaria*, namely, the universal norms of conviction that strictly apply justice, honesty, faithfulness, and chastity, which in the Christian faith tradition are brought to a unity in *agape*. Subsequently we have the *principia secundaria*, namely, the concrete norms of action that in a descriptive way formulate prescriptions or prohibitions on specific domains of life: no violence, no appropriating of someone else's possessions, no speaking untruths or giving false witness, the returning of borrowed or deposited goods, and so forth. Since these norms are formulated in a general and abstract manner, outside any context or conflict of values, they apply "only in most cases" (*valent ut in pluribus*).[16] This "non-absolute" applicability applies a fortiori to rules of action even farther removed from the fundamental principles than the secondary rules of action. There are, therefore, distinct levels in the moral law.

It is precisely this nuanced view of the moral law that makes *epikeia* possible. It is necessary for the concrete application of the generally formulated norms of actions in particular circumstances, and also to resolve conflicts between norms of action. *Epikeia* is also applicable on the level of sexuality and relationships. We find a strong example already in Alphonsus de Liguori, an advocate of a merciful equiprobabilism (balancing between the laxism of probabilism and the rigorism of probabiliorism or tutiorism). He finds, on the one hand, in line with what the church and other moral theologians traditionally state, that the disruption of sexual intercourse goes against the moral law. On the other hand, he states that, in case of a conflict of values, a married couple can find recourse in a permissible manner in *coitus interruptus* on condition that a just reason (*iusta causa*) exists.

Epikeia is likewise applicable to the intimate relational behaviors cited at the beginning of this essay in the presupposition that the moral law remains valid and thus that the deviance remains exceptional. A couple can be of the opinion that in their singular situation they may deviate from the prohibition on premarital sexuality and cohabitation. Or gay men and lesbians who accept the church's view of homosexuality can on the basis of *epikeia* come to the conclusion that in their situation they have a just reason not to maintain the church norm of abstinence and still enter into an intimate relationship. Or married couples, who share the church's view of indissolubility, can judge that in their case divorce is acceptable, or even more humane than remaining together. Or they come to the judgment of conscience that it is better for them to remarry civilly or enter into a new lifetime relationship than remain alone.[17]

In the present moral doctrine of the church, as we find it synthetically in the *Catechism,* the moral *epikeia* is strikingly absent. Is it a form of memory loss, or of repression, in fear that the valuing of *epikeia* would lead to laxism and situationism, namely, to personal preferences that aim to legitimate every possible behavior? A good understanding of *epikeia* that is in service of the spirit of the law does not in any way have to lead to relativism and arbitrariness. It is a virtue that gives expression to respect for Christians as ethical adult persons who are capable of arriving at an "informed judgment of conscience" and who have the intention of substantiating the moral law as qualitatively as possible.[18]

There is a disadvantage, however, to the *epikeia* model. It still employs an act-oriented view of human behavior.

A Plea for a Consistent Relational and Sexual Ethics

For that reason, we need a broader concept of human action. The urgency hereof is likewise apparent from an aspect of the above-mentioned deviant intimate relational behaviors that remained until now in the background. Those behaviors are still qualified by church ethics as illicit, namely, as heavy sins of impurity, lewdness, and concubinage.[19] Over and against that view stand more and more Christians—certainly in the West, but also elsewhere—who no longer consider those behaviors immoral but, on the contrary, acceptable and at times even desirable. In other words, these are not only about deviant "facts" but about facts that express "lived convictions,"[20] thus about behaviors that ensue from deviant views. That is why it is more correct to label the above-mentioned behaviors not only as "deviant" but also as "heterodox," precisely because they contrast with the "orthodox" church view.

These heterodox "lived convictions" mean that the three cited paradigms are no longer applicable for a good number of Christians. Those who choose premarital sexuality, pre- and non-conjugal cohabitation, homosexual or lesbian relationships, or remarriage or cohabitation after divorce do not desire any deculpabilization of their deviant behavior (paradigm 1), precisely because they perform their behavior with full awareness and conviction as adult and mature persons. That is also why they are not inclined to reject their choice or behavior and grow in the direction of the church moral norms, as paradigm 2 suggests. Much less is their choice reduced to a case of *epikeia* (paradigm 3). In heterodox intimate relational behavior, an acceptance in principle of the norm is already out of the question; one is after all dedicated to a very different conviction.

If the church and moral theology desire that their view of love and sexuality would still be heard by believers at the base, another paradigm is needed that takes seriously the new convictions that are lived out and that acknowledges the quality of the corresponding behaviors. With that, yet another aspect of the new lived-out convictions is important. They presuppose after all a different concept of human behavior than the act-oriented model already cited. Partners experience certain relational choices and sexual behaviors not as acts in themselves but as part of a comprehensive way of life that furthermore unfolds itself as a process of growth. Hence our plea for the concept of "life form" wherein the distinct options, acts, behaviors, and styles of interaction are not only integrated but also derive from it their meaning and value. Therefore, this concerns a *qualitative* life form that realizes and approaches meaningfulness, and that has a direct link with the Christian striving for perfection: the progressive appropriation, knowledge, and experience of love in its fullness in the distinct domains of life.

On the intimate relational level, the Christian tradition gives preference to the life form of marriage as the basis for the family. To do justice to the heterodox behaviors mentioned above, we suggest an "enduring relationship of love" as a life form that is mirrored, on the one hand, in marital love understood integrally and that broadens, on the other hand, this love into an intimate life relationship based on free and informed consent, exclusiveness and reciprocity, equality in difference, non-violence and authentic intimacy, and creative fidelity.

On the basis of this concept of an "enduring relationship of love," it is possible to develop a consistent relational and sexual ethics that is applicable not only to marriage but also to deviant and heterodox intimate relationships. For this consistent ethics we find inspiration in that great heritage from our Judeo Christian tradition, namely, the Ten Commandments. All Christians are faced with the appeal to develop their life relationships as humanely as possible, however deviant and heterodox they may be with regard to heterosexual conjugal love. For that purpose, the four behavioral norms of the second table of the Ten Commandments can offer an inspiring framework.

"Thou shall not kill" states that no dignified intimate relationship is possible when partners inflict violence in whatever form on each other. "Thou shall not steal" means that partners should not reduce the other to oneself, nor should they dissolve their mutual differences in fusionality, which is likewise a form of violence. "You shall not lie" makes it clear that a loving intimate relationship cannot be based on dishonesty and untruthfulness. And "You shall not commit adultery" forbids sexual, and also other forms of, infidelity. And since these are not commandments but prohibitions that only indicate the bottom line or the conditions for love without establishing the qualitative content of that love,[21] the creative freedom of the partners is challenged to develop for themselves the fullness of love and find inspiration in the experiences and examples of others.

The first prohibition challenges couples to search for forms that express respect and that promote life for each one individually and for both of them together. The second prohibition requires a culture of difference, so that the partners acknowledge each other's irreducible uniqueness and develop it into a form of enriching commonality. The third prohibition summons partners to build up creatively a reliable and honest way of relating to each other that will engender trust. The prohibition against adultery stimulates partners to develop a "culture of creative trust," including a qualitative erotic companionship, in such a way that their partnership existentially becomes enduring.

Conclusion

In conclusion, a consistent sexual and relational ethics should in no way lead to the equalization or levelling of all intimate relational and cohabitation life forms with marriage. Without denying the essential differences, the qualitative similarities are likewise acknowledged. That is why a Christian ethics that also wants to be pastoral is faced with the challenge not only to develop orientations and rules for those who experience marriage according to the "Catholic book" but likewise for those who enter into a different form of intimate, enduring relationship. No other relational ethics is valid for heterosexuals and homosexuals, just as no distinct relational ethics exists for those who live in premarital, marital, non- or postmarital cohabitation. And surprisingly, it is the ancient text of the Ten Commandments that inspires us to draw out the new from the old (see Matt 13:52).

Notes

1. *Catechism of the Catholic Church* (New York: Image Books, 1995).
2. Ibid., 1734.
3. Ibid., 1735.
4. *Persona Humana* (Declaration on Certain Questions Concerning Sexual Ethics), 8.
5. *Catechism of the Catholic Church*, 2358.
6. See Alain You, *La loi de la gradualité: Une nouveauté en morale?* (Paris: Lethielleux, 1991).
7. *Familiaris consortio* (On the Role of the Christian Family in the Modern World), 34.
8. Ibid.
9. Aristide Fumagalli, "The Parameter of Temporality and Its Importance for Moral Theology," in *Formation and the Person: Essays on Theory and Practice*, ed. Alessandro Manenti, Stefano Guarinelli, and Hans Zollner (Leuven: Peeters, 2007), 141-56.
10. *Familiaris consortio*, 9.
11. Ibid., 34.
12. Ibid.
13. Ibid.
14. Ibid.
15. Günter Virt, *Epikie—Verantwortlicher Umgang mit Normen: Eine historisch-systematische Untersuchung zu Aristoteles, Thomas von Aquin und Franz Suarez* (Mainz: Grünewald, 1983); and Günter Virt, *Damit Menschsein Zukunft hat: Theologische Ethik im Einsatz für eine humane Gesellschaft* (Würzburg: Echter, 2007), 42-55. For further discussion, see Josef Fuchs, *Für eine menschliche Moral: Grundfragen der theologischen Ethik. Band II: Ethische Konkretisierungen* (Freiburg: Herder, 1989), 178-93; and John Mahoney, *The Making of Moral Theology: A Study of the Roman Catholic Tradition* (Oxford: Clarendon, 1989), 224-45.

16. Some formulations of norms do not allow for any exceptions, just as, for example, the prohibition on rape, incest, (pedophiliac) sexual abuse, murder, genocide, and so on. But in these formulations descriptive terms are no longer used (cf. to kill, to speak untruth, to amputate) and instead synthetic terms are substituted that ethically qualify a certain act as irresponsible or immoral: murder, lying, mutilation, and so forth. This is then no longer about acts in themselves but about acts *in toto*: the intention, the act itself, the circumstances, the result.

17. See Günter Virt, "Epikie in der Geschiedenenpastoral," *Theologisch-praktische Quartalschrift* 142 (1994): 368-71.

18. See James F. Keenan, "Roger Burggraeve's Ethics of Growth in Context," in *Responsibility, God and Society: Theological Ethics in Dialogue*, ed. Johan De Tavernier, Paul Schotsmans, Joseph Selling, and Johan Verstraeten (Dudley, MA: Peeters, 2008), 287-304.

19. *Catechism of the Catholic Church*, 2351-56.

20. Wilhelm Korff, "Empirical Social Study and Ethics," *Concilium* 36 (1968): 15-17.

21. See the 1993 encyclical *Veritatis splendor* (The Splendor of Truth), 13.

Trent: The Historical Contribution and the Voices that Went Unheard[1]

Antônio Moser

"Trent" is one of those words that, at first mention, provokes contradictory feelings in Christian circles. In one sense, we could say that there is an ambivalence about Trent, not so much about the Tridentine texts in themselves as about the reasons that lead to contrasting hermeneutics.

Some see the Council of Trent not only as the longest but also as one of the most important councils in church history. It saved from ruin a church that was drowning in one of the deepest crises in its history. Thanks to the precision of the theological-pastoral and disciplinary contents of its decrees and to their verbal expression, Trent established for succeeding generations a sign that must not be forgotten or lost. It is of vital importance today not only to reread Trent, but also to excavate many of its treasures that have been buried over the course of the following centuries and especially in more recent times. This theological, pastoral, and disciplinary salvage work deserves serious consideration today, especially in the moral sphere where the church proceeds with uncertain steps and exercises virtually no influence on the direction taken by the secularized world, and indeed by an ever-growing number of Christians who call themselves by this name even when they ignore the directives of the official church. For it is a fact that more and more Catholic Christians live like the rest of the world and independently establish their own norms.

Others see the Council of Trent as a synonym for a kind of fossilization. At the time, the church was incapable of grasping the power of historical movements and of listening to the aspirations and prophetic voices of that period, voices that had been raised for a long time and had become more vehement in the sixteenth century. For those who follow this negative reading, Trent lost a historic opportunity to encounter the gospel with the most legitimate tradition of the apostolic and patristic age, and with the best elements of medieval scholasticism. It also missed the opportunity to let itself be questioned by the values that came to light among the people of the so-called New World, which had just been discovered. And there is more to be said. Thanks to a concatenation of historical circumstances and to the spirit that came to characterize the Second Vatican Council, Trent continues to be a kind of shadow that has never ceased to oppress the church and that appears even more dense and uncomfortable in our own days.

The Tridentine spirit continues to be the main obstacle that prevents the church from discovering its own self. In both theological and pastoral terms, we are moving backward in a measured but unmistakable return to the "great discipline."[2] The fact that the Tridentine spirit is still active and powerful can be seen in the negative reaction to the new ecclesial praxis that was generated by the basic ecclesial communities and that simultaneously found expression in a new way of doing theology that became known as the "theology of liberation." All this has led to a moribund church that is neither dying nor alive. It is distant both from the world and from its own deepest identity and is steadily losing its place in history. This means that Trent cannot be regarded as anything other than a sad episode in the life of the church, with negative repercussions on society as well. Trent ought to be forever banished to the archives.

As often happens in similar cases where different and contrasting hermeneutics are possible, it might perhaps be opportune and more honest to take a less radical and exclusive approach to Trent. This would mean recognizing the unfortunate fact that many aspirations and voices from the Council of Trent have not been adequately heard from then to the present. At the same time, this more irenic approach would mean recognizing that Trent left deep and positive furrows in the past and that it can help us in various ways to find more definite paths, encouraging us to develop a spirit of welcome for what is new without losing our Catholic and Christian identity. This could give new vigor to the church, which is going through a period that presents many difficulties.

At the same time, it would be possible for us to offer an indispensable contribution to today's world, because we were all enlightened and nourished by the gospel of life. For methodological reasons, our first step will be a reading that is closer to those who see the positive side of Trent. In the second section, we shall read the Council alongside those who regard it as a disaster. In the third section, we shall attempt a "rereading" in which moderation predominates.

Grasping the Ambivalence of the Hermeneutics: Some Presuppositions

The existence of at least three possible systems of hermeneutics suggests that we should set out (even if only briefly) some of their presuppositions, since none of them is wholly unfounded. First of all, we must mention the difficult process involved in holding the Council itself. We shall then look at the complex religious and social context of the texts. Finally, in order to understand the ambivalence of the possible interpretations, we cannot forget the basic underlying conceptions, both theological and pastoral. The important point in this first step is to perceive the complexity of each of these presuppositions. This means that the same facts and arguments can be given a place in any of these readings, depending on the perspective and the social and ecclesial background of the one who analyzes the facts.

A Difficult Gestation—but with Good Results

Everyone is familiar with the difficulties that were encountered after the Council of Trent was convoked. After its announcement, its convocation was delayed for twenty-five years and then was interrupted twice. It began in December 1545, with the presence of only four cardinals, four archbishops, and twenty-one bishops. It is significant that none of these came from the German province that had already been gravely shaken by the movement launched by Martin Luther. It was only at the end that the representative voice of the church was heard by means of 217 fathers from fifteen nations. If we bear in mind that, formally speaking, the sessions took place in the course of only three of the eighteen years covered by the Council, we can only marvel at the extent and the profundity of what it undertook.[3]

We may safely say that no urgent question was neglected and that the Council looked at all the theological, pastoral, and disciplinary fields. At the same time, we must certainly affirm that, given the turbulent ecclesial, political, and social situation, Trent displayed an extraordinary effectiveness in its use of time and, indeed, from every perspective. Its effects were steady rather than immediate, and it is perhaps for this reason that it left such deep furrows. The Tridentine decrees were the principal point of reference for all internal reform and evangelizing action of the church and served as the source of canon law for four centuries until the promulgation of the Codex in 1917. Thanks to these decrees, the Council had a profound impact, even in a society that was torn by great tension and was falling apart.[4]

We shall see this more clearly if we bear in mind the contexts that underlie the texts. This also helps to explain the theological and pastoral positions that constituted the central features of both the Reformation and the Counter-Reformation. Rediscovering the context of the texts will bring out more clearly certain fixed points, both within the church and in its external activities, that continue down through the centuries and are in some sense necessary today.

The Context of the Texts

It is simply impossible to present in a few words the richness of all the documents and decrees issued by Trent. Nor is this necessary for the perspective that interests us, namely, that of the "voices that went unheard." But in order to locate better the context of the texts, it is useful to mention some essential points in each of the three phases. The first phase (1545-47) defined the data considered essential with regard to scripture and tradition as sources of the faith. In connection with the sacraments, especially baptism and confirmation, original sin and the paths of justification were presented. During the second phase (1551-52), when the Eucharist was presented as the sacrament that manifests and confirms the communion of all the faithful, the question of conciliarism arose, and this in turn led to the question of the primacy of the bishop of Rome. The third phase (1561-63) resulted in the measures of the so-called Counter-Reformation that were intended to confront the theses of Luther and other critics. At the same time, the foundations were laid for the broad and deep reform of the church itself.

The principal traces of the historical context emerge between the lines. Without these traces, Trent cannot be adequately understood. Once again, let me briefly describe the climate that predominated at that time. First and foremost, the history of the Council of Trent cannot be read in a monolithic manner, detached from everything else. We are often told that the church and society formed a unity at that time, but we must not overlook the plurality of the situation or the natural historical cultural differences between one region and another. Besides this, every period of history is a process with a "before," a "now," and an "after," and all of these are characterized by nuances and tensions.[5]

The "before" of Trent points back to the humanism of the Renaissance that opened up broad horizons in every sense, but that also became the starting point of modernity. What we call "modernity" entails a series of challenges, especially for a church that had hitherto been the possessor of almost all power and almost all knowledge. The "before" also recalls the era of the navigators who had just discovered new lands and new peoples. Each new land had its own distinctive character, but all of them were very different from the small world of Europe. It was very difficult to grasp fully what this meant, bearing in mind not only the difficulties inherent in communications, but precisely the shock of something new. Some found the New World fascinating, but others found it strange and threatening, an area that must be conquered.

The "now" and the "after" pose a large number of new questions with regard to the initial contacts with various peoples and as a result of the economic, political, and social changes that were generated by such contacts. If we look at central Europe, the obvious background is the Protestant Reformation with its various aspects and its numerous divisions, both religious and political-social—we have a picture of a whole series of tensions that were subsequently translated into genuine wars of religion, though with other historical and cultural components. Europe as a whole continued to proclaim its hegemonic role even after it confronted the new civilizations that came to light as they emerged from immense oceans that had never been crossed before, yet it sensed that all its anthropological, religious, and ethical conceptions had been destabilized. This complex and confused situation demanded a high level of lucidity and the courage to take a clear position, a position that naturally provoked various and diverging reactions.[6]

Theology and Pastoral Work: A Picture of Decadence

To speak of the theological climate in the centuries that preceded Trent means considering scholasticism in all its splendor. Important universities were founded

in many places, and true luminaries kept alive not only the celebrated and polemical "disputations" but above all the flame of a vibrant faith. Philosophy and theology developed in a harmony that favored a harmonious image of the church, of the
world, and of society. In this context, the various schools, each producing great
intellectual figures, nourished in one way or another the faith of the faithful, even
of the great masses who received little education and were not capable of understanding the discussions in the universities (which were not always conducted with
the same degree of depth and clarity).[7]

Trent was a genuine necessity in a period dominated by the so-called low scholasticism (with all that this term implies). In the early Middle Ages, there was harmony between reason and faith, but in the centuries that immediately preceded
the Council of Trent, it was above all reason that acquired a stronger position as a
science capable of answering on its own the great questions of personal and social
life. This breach between reason and theology created favorable conditions for the
emergence of the modern age, with all this implied in both theological and
pastoral terms. The professorships of the great masters were gradually taken over
by the pupils of their pupils, and only very few of these reached the level of the
masters.

Above all, in the more specific field of morality, both the great intuitions that
found a good theological expression in the Thomistic school and the less perceptive
intuitions of the Franciscan school ended up in a diluted form in the *summas* for
confessors, which were increasingly detached from systematic theology and sacred
scripture. Even at that date, a meticulous casuistry was beginning to mold a cold
legalism that, instead of encouraging the Christians, intimidated those who were
in search of spirituality. This tendency was perfected as Trent evolved. The combination of a lack of theological depth and the great moral corruption and scanty
intellectual abilities that were typical of the clergy made it impossible to put into
practice any kind of pastoral work that would have been better structured and
more effective. This entire situation demanded a true reform that would restruc-
ture both church and society. And that is precisely what Trent attempted to do.[8]

The Historical Contribution and
the Voices That Went Unheard

When we speak of "voices that went unheard," we refer once more to an
ambivalent situation. Some voices remained unheard in the sense that they were
not received and assimilated by the Council itself; others were lost in the course of
time, thanks to innumerable factors, both religious and sociocultural. In the eyes
of the supporters of Trent, the problems lie only in the insufficient reception of the
Tridentine message and in the destructive attitude of the followers of Luther, Calvin, Wycliffe, Zwingli, and the other heretics who succeeded in influencing both
their own age and succeeding epochs.

In the eyes of the critics of the Council, the church simply rejected the signs of the times that were manifested in the theological, spiritual, mystical, and social aspirations, because it did not know how to welcome them.

Which Persons Were Unjustly Declared Heretics?

In order to comprehend adequately the persons who played an important role in specific historical periods or spheres, we must get to know them more closely. Above all, we must locate them in their historical context. No one incarnates a great historical revolution on his or her own. It is also true, however, that no great historical turning point would have arrived if there had not been a powerful guide who was capable of incarnating the profoundest aspirations of that historical moment. This means, on the one hand, that when we speak of "voices that went unheard," we cannot limit ourselves to only a few persons; on the other hand, however, we cannot overlook these persons.

Among many others, the first of these is Martin Luther,[9] a religious with a deep spirituality and great idealism but at the same time a man ready to confront every obstacle that his aspirations encountered and accept full responsibility for all his actions. In addition to the personal problems and the dramas of conscience that wracked his personality, Martin Luther dreamed of a church that would be stripped of its wealth and its powerful position and would place the vernacular Bible in the hands of the people of God. This church would abandon an idealistic conception of the human being and accept a more realistic anthropology that saw the human being as one corrupted by sin (beginning with original sin), but also as one who humbly seeks not self-justification but the justification that comes from divine mercy.

We can say something similar about John Wycliffe, Girolamo Savonarola, Ulrich Zwingli, Jean Calvin, and many others in different places who played prominent roles in that historical period and were in some measure contemporaries of Luther. All of them started out as fervent men who were inspired by the Bible and sought to lead a life more in keeping with the gospel. Nevertheless, they were so disgusted by the general corruption of the church that they took radical positions that led to a breach. In various places and with different nuances, they ended up clinging to *sola gratia*, *sola scriptura*, and *sola fides*. In other words, without abandoning their aspirations that were deeply rooted in the soil of the gospel, they broke with a certain type of ecclesiastical structure, not only abandoning the official church but energetically opposing it.

Despite what has sometimes been said, it appears that none of them—with the exception of Henry VIII of England, from whom Anglicanism has its origin— broke with the church in order to justify personal decisions. This means that the priests did not abandon the official church or found churches of their own in order to justify their rejection of celibacy. Rather, this rejection took place at a second stage and as a kind of protest against the hypocrisy that was so prevalent among both the higher and the lower clergy with regard to celibacy and other matters. It was only at a second stage that the reformers included the abolition of celibacy among their demands.

Not Only Revolts, but Also the Search for Something New

The social background of these aspirations included revolts in the countryside and in the city, which led to a weakening of feudalism. These revolts were generated by an increasingly unbearable situation of harsh poverty and oppression. Epidemics of plague and wars only intensified the climate of revolt. At stake was the sheer survival of a multitude of wretched persons who were completely under the dominion of an aristocracy that was decadent, arrogant, and overbearing. But it was undeniably the discoveries of the new lands and of their unimaginable wealth that gave birth not only to a new conception of the distribution of goods, but above all to a new understanding and division of society. This generated a favorable climate for deeper breaches that to a greater or lesser extent consolidated new positions in the religious and moral sphere.

From the thirteenth century onward, the driving force of the aspirations that were genuinely in keeping with the gospel, as well as the aspirations manifested in the many movements that dreamed of a reform of morals in the clergy and the laity, had taken concrete form in the so-called mendicant orders.[10] But among those who launched a revolt against the church and what it represented, there were many who were looking for renewal and change and who hoped in vain for theological and pastoral support.

Although the historical splits were profound, a more attentive reading often reveals a whole series of nuances and the coexistence of a variety of tendencies in one and the same epoch, and indeed within one and the same current of thought. This is how we must read the fourteenth, fifteenth, and sixteenth centuries if we want to understand what happened at the Council of Trent. Of course, one may underline the intellectual, theological, and moral decadence or the revolts that had a similarly generalized character, but one must not forget that these same centuries were also marked by a Renaissance spirit and by deep theological, spiritual, mystical, and social aspirations.

In the same way, the background to these spiritual aspirations is to be found in the preceding centuries. We note the deterioration of the authority of the popes, which culminates in the so-called Western Schism of 1378. The loss of papal authority is accompanied by an attenuation of the authority of the bishops and of the higher and lower clergy. In the case of the higher clergy, the loss of authority is due not only to their moral decadence but also to the choices they made, which were dictated by their aristocracy and their wealth rather than by religious and spiritual preoccupations. Worldliness ruled. In the case of the lower clergy, in addition to the well-known problems with regard to celibacy, their poverty and their poor intellectual formation made it impossible for them to exercise the ministry in an adequate manner. Therefore, we may truly say that Trent was faced with a decadent church. More and more people felt the urgent need for a reform *in capite et in membris*.[11]

The Discoveries of Lands and Peoples without the Assimilation of the Richness of the Different Cultures

At the time of the Council of Trent, the discoveries of new lands and new peoples were still recent events. Bearing in mind the slowness of communications and of historical processes, it is clear that the Council could not immediately realize the multifaceted richness of the new cultures. Intellectual honesty thus obliges us to turn a critical eye on the period after the Council, rather than on the Council itself. It faced a broad spectrum of challenges that were shaking the Old World, and it was impossible to assess adequately the new challenges from across the Atlantic.

Although there are nuances in the reaction of the evangelizers to the process of consolidation of the conquests, we must recognize that they were slow to propose an interpretation that underlined the values inherent in the autochthonous cultures. Instead, they laid particular emphasis on the so-called barbarism of the native inhabitants. And it is precisely thanks to this impoverished and distorted vision of reality that it was ultimately possible to ask whether or not the indigenous peoples were truly human. These questions and distorted interpretations may have helped to justify not only the absolute condemnation of indigenous customs, but also the enslavement and even the definitive elimination of the natives themselves.[12]

There were few voices—such as Antonio Vieira and Bartolomé de Las Casas—and few concrete initiatives that permitted a process of inculturated evangelization. This basic scenario took shape and was consolidated in the course of the eighteenth century when the process of "Romanization" began to suppress the relatively few initiatives that allowed a more adequate comprehension of the cultural values.[13] In this way, liturgical standardization, accompanied by the imposition of a moral regime full of legalistic casuistry that accentuated the awareness of guilt and the loss of self-esteem, introduced to the New World the poorest part of the theological and ecclesial conception of Trent. This only served to make it more difficult to see and to read the signs of God in time and in history.

Voices That Return to Speak to Us Today

As we have indicated, these voices and these aspirations in favor of new times for the church and for society remained unheard. Some scholars argue that this happened because the conciliar fathers lacked the sensitivity that would have allowed them to perceive the values of the "modern age" that was coming into existence and the new winds that were blowing from all directions. Instead of welcoming these voices and these aspirations that were so thoroughly in accordance with the gospel—even if they were sometimes accompanied by a radicalized interpretation—the Council not only lost a unique historic opportunity to respond correctly to the signs of the times but excluded for centuries the possibility that this might happen in the future. We must ask whether this opportunity was indeed lost forever. Can we perhaps retrieve it in some way?

An Inadequate and Violent Response to Profound Aspirations

The climate of tension, radicalism, and revolt certainly led the conciliar fathers to take up radical doctrinal, theological, and disciplinary positions. The rigidity with which the canons were formulated left no space for nuances. These canons were categorical: they contained the truth and the whole truth. Anyone who did not accept the doctrine and the norms formulated in this doctrine was simply considered to be a heretic and was excommunicated. The number of the anathemas is symptomatic, and it is worthwhile to mention some of the relevant areas: justification—33 anathemas; sacrament of penance—15; sacraments in general—13; matrimony—12; baptism—14; Eucharist—11; celebration of the Eucharist—9; sacrament of orders—8; anointing of the sick—4; total: 119. One may attempt to offer a kinder interpretation of the word "anathema," but it is impossible to avoid the clear impression of a spirit that is moved by the intransigent absolutism of one who is incapable of accepting new challenges and of distinguishing nuances.

The historical context described above, which reveals a situation that was extremely serious and difficult, obviously explains in a certain sense the need for clear and precise formulations. Ultimately, it was a question of safeguarding the doctrinal patrimony and the good customs of the church. On the other hand, however, it is precisely the historical context and the difficulties involved in interpreting the aspirations of the time that ought to have led to decisions that took the form of appeals rather than of condemnations. It is true that there were attempts at dialogue, especially with Luther, but in fact the aspirations, the fundamental concerns, and the central points of the reformers' positions did not cease to constitute a deep challenge to a church that had shown itself unable to separate the wheat from the chaff. Later developments, with the creation of the Index of Prohibited Books and the consolidation of the inquisitorial spirit, which was transformed into one of the saddest institutions in church history, only confirmed that instead of pursuing reconciliation, Trent had made the divisions worse—with disastrous consequences in every area.

The Merits and the Enduring Teachings of Trent

We have already mentioned the numerous merits of the Council of Trent. Although the texts and decrees can be interpreted in various ways, it cannot be denied that Trent did what it could and that it achieved much. First and foremost, it had the courage to tackle a situation that was extraordinarily complex. In the midst of political, social, and theological tensions and by reflecting on the way of life of a society that lacked points of reference, the conciliar fathers arrived at a consensus on all the doctrinal and disciplinary points that were fundamental to the life of the church. In this way, the Council demonstrated that it is possible to tackle crises, no matter how large they may be, and that this courage is possible only to one who truly believes that, in the final analysis, the church is always guided by Jesus Christ. Trent was an act of faith and hope. As an anonymous note found in the University Library in Bologna states, one who studies this council in depth is entitled to affirm that one knows all the councils of the past, since we find here a synthesis of all the others.[14]

With regard to the practical measures that were intended to put matters in order within the church—a church in a state of generalized decadence that affected both the high-hierarchical authorities and the simple faithful—we must emphasize the disciplinary measures[15] that guided pastoral praxis and that led to the creation of seminaries and a commitment to the task of clergy formation. These measures were a direct attack on two great manifestations of the decadence of the higher and the lower clergy, namely, their dissolute lifestyle and their ignorance.

Trent may not have achieved all that it wanted, but it opened a new stage in the history of the church. It suffices here to recall the catechism and the immense endeavors that were undertaken to evangelize indigenous peoples. It is clear that the missionaries were not always capable of making the transition to an inculturated evangelization in the sense that we understand this term today. We should note, however, the heroic endeavors both in the Old World and in the New. The missionary spirit acquired fresh vigor. Unfortunately, it was not always the most positive elements that were transmitted.

In What Sense Can We Say That a Retrieval of History Is Necessary?

As we have seen, many precious voices were lost, either because of the complexity of the situations we have described or because the church was perhaps not yet sufficiently mature to welcome and to discern what the Second Vatican Council was to call the "signs of the times." Many voices remained unheard, but we must ask whether it is advisable and perhaps even necessary to retrieve them for the present day. Of course, it is true that the context is completely different. It is possible, nonetheless, that the basic aspirations of people five centuries ago may be similar to those of today, despite all the evolutions and revolutions that have characterized the intervening centuries and that make such a claim appear unlikely.[16]

My reply lies implicitly between the lines of these reflections, but I should like to conclude by making three points. The first refers to the courage involved in tackling situations of crisis. It suffices to recall shocking and very recent events that have sullied the image of the church in order to realize the relevance of this point. A second point concerns the need to pay attention to paradoxical situations that may at first sight seem shocking but can turn out to contain values if they are analyzed with greater care. One example is the progress made in the spheres of biogenetics and biotechnologies. We must be careful not to get out of step with history.

Finally, a third point concerns the greater participation of all the faithful in what we might call the priestly ministry of the baptized. This means in specific terms that the hierarchy and the clergy in general must be closer to the people of God, and that more of the non-ordained must be prepared for a whole series of ministries, including above all that of evangelization. Good theological training—beginning with the formation of the clergy—will greatly increase the evangelizing power of all the baptized.

Notes

1. English translation by Brian McNeil.

2. See Paolo Sarpi, *Istoria del Concilio Tridentino* (London: Appersso G. Billio, 1619); and J. B. Libânio, *A volta à grande disciplina: Reflexão teológico-pastoral sobre a atual conjuntura da Igreja* (São Paulo: Loyola, 1983).

3. Giacomo Martina, *La chiesa nell'età della riforma* (Brescia: Morcelliana, 1983), 173-89.

4. See Giuseppe Alberigo, *Storie dei concilii ecumenici* (Brescia: Queriniana, 1990).

5. See Hubert Jedin, *Kleine Konziliengeschichte: Die Konzilien im Rahmen der Kirchengeschichte* (Freiburg: Herder, 1960).

6. Jean Delumeau, *Il cattolicesimo dal XVI al XVIII secolo* (Milan: Mursia, 1983), 33-58.

7. See Hubert Jedin, *Geschichte des Konzils von Trient*, vols. 3-4 (Freiburg: Herder, 1970, 1975).

8. Louis Vereecke, "Théologie morale et magistère avant et après le Concile de Trente," *Revue d'éthique et de théologie morale* 177 (1991): 7-22, at 13-17.

9. See Jedin, *Geschichte des Konzils von Trient*, vol. 2 (Freiburg: Herder, 1957).

10. See Marie-Dominique Chenu, *La théologie au XIIe siècle* (Paris: Vrin, 1969).

11. See Jedin, *Geschichte des Konzils von Trient*, vol. 4.

12. See Riolando Azzi, *A crise da cristandade e o projeto liberal* (São Paulo: Paulinas, 1991); and Riolando Azzi, *O altar unido ao trono: Um projeto conservador* (São Paulo: Paulinas, 1992).

13. See Pedro Ribeiro de Oliveira, "Catolicismo popular e romanização do catolicismo brasiliero," *Revista Eclesiástica Brasileira* 141 (March 1977): 131-41.

14. See Luigi Carcereri, *Il Concilio di Trento dalla traslazione a Bologna alla sospensione*, vol. 3 (Collana: Biblioteca Storica Bolognese, 1910).

15. See Pio Paschini, *Il Catechismo Romano del Concilio di Trento: Sue origini e sua prima diffusione* (Rome: Pontificio Seminario Romano, 1923); also Paschini, *Cinquecento Romano e riforma cattolica* (Rome: Facultas Theologica Pontificii Athenaei Lateranensis, 1958), 39-91.

16. See Giuseppe Alberigo, "Prospettive nuove sul concilio di Trento," *Critica storica* 5 (1966): 267-82.

THE MISSING VOICES OF WOMEN

Anne Nasimiyu-Wasike

World history and church history present accounts of those individuals who have contributed to science, economics, sociology, religion, and politics, among other disciplines. A few of these persons are named and remembered, but there are others whose names are not mentioned and are barely remembered, yet their input could have been relevant. The unnamed and unremembered individuals are referred to as missing voices. Every cultural setting has its missing voices, depending on the social structure that governs the life of the people. Perhaps the largest numbers of missing voices throughout history have been the voices of women.

Patriarchal societies, for example, are marked by the rule of the father, and by legal, social, economic, and political systems that validate and enforce the sovereignty of male heads over dependent persons.[1] The status of women in patriarchal societies is therefore one of subordination, without legal standing in their own right. This has often meant that the subjugation of women includes patrilineal systems wherein the generational lineage of children is traced from the father; male children are favored over female children; wives' sexuality and reproductive capacity belong to their husbands; the dominion of the husband over his wife goes as far as his right to beat her; and the right of daughters or widows to inherit property is severely restricted and if they do inherit property, it is administered by a male relative or guardian.[2]

In addition, such societies have nearly always limited women's contributions traditionally to household skills and minimal literacy. According to current global population statistics, there are one billion poor people in the world, and three-fifths of them are women and children. There are 960 million illiterate adults in the world, and two-thirds of them are women. Of the 130 million children not attending school in the world, 70 percent are girls.[3]

Children and the elderly are other large groups of persons whose voices are missing in standard history accounts. This essay will focus on women's history in both religious and secular traditions in the world and on women in traditional African societies, and primarily those in Kenya. Finally, drawing upon experience in Kenya, it will consider briefly the plight and silence of elderly persons as missing voices.

The Missing Voices of Women in the Bible

Long before the Bible was written, it was lived and experienced by real people, leading real lives. As Bridget Meehan asserts, the stories of Sarah, Rebecca, Martha, and many others reflect not only a particular time and place, but they also deliver strong messages that reverberate across the generations that challenge and empower women in their daily lives.[4] In addition to these extraordinary women, there are other women present in the Bible who are voiceless and often even nameless. For example, in the narrative of 2 Samuel 3:7, Rizpah is silent, but her later actions and presence challenge even King David (2 Sam 21:8-11); as a result, transformation takes place and new life emerges.[5]

There are also a number of women in the New Testament whose names are not given—for example, the Canaanite woman who asks Jesus to heal her daughter (Matt 15:21-28) and the woman who was healed of the hemorrhages she had suffered for twelve years (Mark 5:21-34). As portrayed in the New Testament, Jesus was very sensitive to women in his teaching. He used examples from the experiences of both women and men, giving some voice to each. He bore the message of liberation for all, especially the marginalized and disadvantaged. He treated men and women as equal children of God.[6] Yet even in the Bible, too many women's voices remain missing, and the question of their absence is perhaps more urgent precisely because of the witness of Jesus.

Lynn Bundesen argues helpfully that the absence of many women characters in the Bible does not in any way demonstrate that women were incompetent voices for God to use.[7] Their absence is, rather, a function of the patriarchal cultures that influenced the writing of the Bible. But despite the patriarchal cultural setting of the New Testament, Jesus is portrayed as having a revolutionary attitude toward women. And although in some of Paul's letters (for example, 1 Cor 11:2-16), Paul accepts the culture-bound relationship between men and women as that of superior over inferior, he nonetheless provides glimpses of his belief in the equality of women and men before God, if not before one another. Some critics maintain that Paul had a "sit-down-and-shut-up!" attitude toward women. Nevertheless, it is Paul who has given us the following significant text in Galatians: "There is no longer Jew or Greek, there is no longer slave or free, there is no longer male and female; for all of you are one in Christ Jesus" (Gal 3:28, NRSV).

However, we must pursue the historical situation in which the Bible was written. Patriarchy indeed prevailed. Women were viewed as lesser beings than men. Secular records tell us that women lacked not only political rights in biblical times, they also lacked credibility in the public domain. According to the historian Flavius Josephus, whose writings are contemporary with the New Testament, the practice of the exclusion of women in the Jewish government as legal witness went something like this: "But let not a single witness be credited, but three, or two at the least, and those such whose testimony is confirmed by their good lives. But let not the testimony of women be admitted, on account of the levity and boldness of the sex."[8]

Nonetheless, biblical scholars of both the First and Second Testaments argue that there are many instances where women played an important part in God's plan even when seen through the lens of male writers.[9] For example, Miriam, prophetess and leader along with Moses and Aaron, focused her ministry on the women of Israel (Exod 15:20-21). Deborah, also a prophetess, became a national judge in Israel (Judg 4:4; 5:7). The prophetess Huldah was consulted by Josiah's chief men for her opinion (2 Kgs 22:14-20). Jael, a noted woman of respect, was a living indictment to the weakness of Barak and other men in Israel (Judg 4:9), and it was Abigail (1 Sam 25) who persuaded David not to kill Nabal. In addition to the roles of particular women, it is notable that in the Decalogue, the fourth commandment implies a requirement of equality in honor to mother and father. Still, in the ninth commandment the woman is relegated to the level of the oxen and donkeys (Exod 20:2-18); she is no more than a part of the property owned by the man.

Interpretations of the Bible allow an understanding of the Bible's central message, but it is easily obscured by biblical stories that appear to approve of the degradation of women[10] and by the silence imposed upon women by the majority of the writers of biblical texts. The Bible, we can presume, would have been quite different had it been written by women.

Women as Missing Voices in Church History

The dominant culture in any given society dictates the roles of persons and the structures for relationships. Over the centuries, the voices of the common people have been lost, often because they were illiterate and no one bothered to discover and record their daily experiences. History provides accounts of wealthy and accomplished men and extraordinary women but leaves out many others who have contributed equally to the community. What accounts there are of women in history suffer from the general underestimation and undervaluation of women both economically and socially. It is not that women were unable in the past to express themselves or were inactive, but their lives remain hidden in many historical interpretations. Today, however, scholars are attempting to retrieve a more accurate account of women's roles in the past. A brief look at the status of women in the Middle Ages (in the West) is illuminating in this regard.

Historian John Mundy laments that women in the Middle Ages were valued as economic commodities.[11] Women were perceived as functionaries for childbearing and manual labor. Their status was sometimes equated with that of children. The conditions of their lives were often extremely harsh. They were coerced into marriages where they were subject not only to the authority of their husbands but to beatings as a means to control their subservience. Their safety frequently depended on their ability to please their husbands and to bear sons. Women died at younger ages than men—if not in childbirth then from the heavy physical labor they had to undertake, or opportunistic diseases to which they were vulnerable because of the conditions of their work.

Still, there is some reason to believe that if we could hear the voices of women down through the ages, we would learn not only of their burdens but of their strengths, not only of their total subordination but of their productive roles. Since women were not even counted in a national census most of the time, their very existence was silenced and hidden for the future. Nonetheless, historians today are finding evidence that at least some women in the Middle Ages were credited with being pillars of the economy and of society as a whole, as well as pillars of virtue in the family.[12]

We have seen, however, that in the medieval West, if a woman were to survive she generally had to be submissive and patient. This is the major reason that the voices of women were silent in the traditional Western world and in the world where patriarchy was or is the system of life. Women were subordinate to men not because they deserved to be so but because of the cultural orientation of the time.

This is not the place to trace in depth the role and status of women in church or secular history or in societies and cultures worldwide. Suffice it to say that stories analogous to those within biblical history or medieval history have continued to persist in one form or another until the present time wherever patriarchy has been the dominant model for human relationships. But I turn now to the past and the present in traditional African societies.

Missing Voices in African Traditional History

The story of missing voices in Africa is not unlike this story in other times and places. The voice of women is largely missing. Although there have been both patriarchal and matriarchal societies in traditional Africa, it is the minority that are matriarchal, and even in these societies—where lineage is marked maternally— it was and is the men in the mother's family that make the decisions affecting the family. As to the majority of African traditional societies, they are patriarchal, and nearly every aspect of life is given a male interpretation. In most African communities, women are viewed as part of the property owned by the patriarch, and they have no voice in the social, political, or economic affairs of the community.[13] By and large, African women are voiceless members of the community and are grouped with children.[14]

In addition to the absence of women's voices in the larger community and the home, the African indigenous sociocultural context is one in which violence against women is supported by African religio-cultural practices.[15] Domestic violence is today a factor that increases the vulnerability of women to infection with HIV. Even when women are not subjected to physical violence, African scholars note that culture is universally used by most men in order to maintain power over women and to justify misogyny. There is in Africa a general perception that men are superior and women inferior, although paradoxically, women are perceived as nicer than men, more morally upright than men.[16] The persistent inequality of power, however, leads to internalized oppression, whereby women believe the judgment of their inferiority and behave accordingly.[17] They are willing to settle for less in life, even to accept abuse.[18]

African women scholars, however, have embarked on writing the stories of African women who have contributed to the development of African history and whose voices have nonetheless heretofore been silent—women like Ma Katilili Wa Mensa of Kenya, who organized Giriama resistance against colonial intervention.[19] One of these authors, Macere Mugo, reflecting on the historical accounts of the struggle for freedom in Kenya, sadly remarks that the heroines of African history have been neglected.[20] She tells the story of Mary Muthoni Nyanjiru, who, demanding the release of Harry Thuku, the leader of the freedom fighters, was shot dead for opposing the colonial powers. Another strong and brave African woman, Mary Muthoni Maingi, proved that women were part of the struggle for liberation of the Kenyan peoples when she moved the crowds into action. Her voice was not silent, although she subsequently died with twenty-one others who were shot by the colonial forces.[21]

The Ignored Voices of Women in Kenya

The treatment of and attitude toward women in some parts of Kenya are no better than that of women in the medieval West or in other parts of Africa and the world. Despite clauses in the African Union constitution, and despite the World Organization against Torture (OMCT), based in Geneva,[22] women in Kenya still live in the valley of darkness under the brutality of their male counterparts. Even though Kenya has a large coalition of non-governmental organizations striving for the rights of women, women still experience all forms of cruel, inhuman, and degrading treatment or punishment. The voices of women, regardless of their relevance, have been the most ignored voices in Kenya. Today, however, their silencing is becoming visible since the local and international media include stories of women in rural and urban areas of Kenya who are brutalized daily.

Other Missing Voices in Kenya

Equality and respect for all are important in any society because they bring about stability, harmony, and development. Each person should be viewed as an important part of the social, economic, political, religious, and psychic development of any society. It is unjust to marginalize some members of the community and thereby dismiss the importance of their voices. It is illogical to emphasize collective responsibility in national development and yet ignore the collective voice of the people. For instance, the Kenyan government has emphasized the importance of all peoples' participation in voting for civil leadership, yet after the elections leaders have rendered voiceless many of those who voted them into office.

Missing Voices of the Elderly

Old age is often perceived as an unavoidable, undesirable, problem-ridden phase of life that everyone is compelled to live. But perception of old age in this way is actually a recently misplaced phenomenon, certainly in Kenya. In Kenya's past, when life was simpler and certain values were clearer, those who reached old age held an enviable place in society and community; they could relax and enjoy their twilight years secure in the knowledge that they still commanded attention, respect, and affection. Although they were well past their prime, all that they had given their lives for was still important—and so were they as persons.

Today, however, older persons in Kenya are among the most neglected members of the society. Neglect, abuse, and marginalization of the elderly cause them to die earlier from opportunistic illnesses, and their bodies are often rendered more feeble and more vulnerable than they would otherwise be. The aged population in Kenya is left without medical, financial, or even spiritual attention by the very people they raised and cared for. Basic human needs are poorly addressed by both the government and the members of their immediate families. Easily forgotten is the fact that in their productive years the elderly contributed to the existing resources that generate income for the current young and working generation.

A research study carried out in eight countries—Argentina, Austria, Brazil, Canada, India, Kenya, Lebanon, and Sweden—revealed remarkable similarities across the participating countries in three areas.[23] First, elderly persons commonly experience neglect, isolation, abandonment, and social exclusion. Second, they encounter abuse of their human, legal, and medical rights. And third, they are subjected to deprivation of choice, decision making, status, finances, and respect. The survey investigated crime records, reports in journals, and social welfare records, and carried out individual in-depth interviews with aged persons in these countries. The survey's findings are not difficult to corroborate, at least not in Kenya.

Countering the problems that beset an aging population requires above all that the voice of the elderly be activated and heard. But this voice is largely missing. The elderly in Kenya, for example, are not even made aware of the existence of organizations that can speak for them. The organizations do exist, however— organizations such as the World Health Organization (WHO) Department of Chronic Diseases and Health Promotion, the WHO Department of Violence and Injuries Prevention, the International Network for the Prevention of Elder Abuse (INPEA), Help Age International, and partners from academic institutions in a range of countries.[24]

All human beings, young and old, are social beings. Elderly persons in Kenya, for example, suffer loneliness. Many are left in rural homes, while their children work in towns. Some children who go to towns in search of work do not have permanent jobs that will support travel for regular visits with parents. The elderly lack the company of their own children, their grandchildren, and their age mates. Their socioeconomic dilemma subjects them to anxiety, fear of the unknown, and doubts about their own health. This further weakens their physical and mental health, making them feel that they are insignificant and deserve to die.

In some medical centers in Kenya, some health workers judge care for the elderly as a waste of scarce resources, a judgment that translates into serious forms of abuse, neglect, and exploitation. On the other hand, Kenyan hospitals commonly experience pervasive corruption and conflicts of interests. Elderly persons may be overcharged, and they are often vulnerable to the moods and impulse of the medical staff.[25] Because of such widespread mistreatment and corruption the elderly often avoid hospitals and resort to traditional medicine healers. They are then prey to some fraudulent men and women who pose as medicine healers only to take advantage of the people, fleecing them of their meager resources. And most appalling of all, some elderly persons—especially women in some parts of Kenya—are accused of practicing witchcraft and are executed by being burned alive.

Conclusion

The orthodox history in major textbooks is the reflection of the dominant culture of a given society. The voices of marginalized peoples are generally considered unimportant unless they are extraordinary individuals. Women have been the most marginalized in all patriarchal societies, and their voices have been silenced, ignored, and taken for granted. Marginalized people everywhere have to claim their rights, speak up, organize, protest, and bring about an all-inclusive society that takes everybody seriously. Since all people are made in the image and likeness of God, it is important that all voices are equally considered so that all contribute to the history of humanity. It is essential that the stories that the mothers of tomorrow tell their children are not those of suffering, injustice, and inequality but of harmonious equal personhood and equal discipleship of women and men.

Although traditional Africa revered and venerated its elderly, this too has drastically changed for the worse. Today elderly people face neglect, isolation, abandonment, deprivation, and violation of their rights. There is a distinct need to educate society and awaken its awareness about the elderly, and the elderly need to be acquainted with their rights and the services available to them in society. Any society should empower its elderly to exercise their rights and advocate for their own interests. Intergenerational relationships should be encouraged so that the young generation respects the old generation and that together they can create positive relationships.[26]

Notes

1. Rosemary Radford Reuther, *Reading towards a Feminist Theology* (Boston: Beacon, 1996), 205.
2. Ibid.
3. Elizabeth Abel, ed., *Writing and Sexual Difference* (Brighton, UK: Harvester, 2002).

4. See Bridget Mary Meehan, *Praying with Women of the Bible* (Liguori, MO: Liguori, 1998).

5. Nyambura Njoroge, "Spirituality of Resistance and Transformation," in *Liberating Eschatology: Essays in Honor of Letty M. Russell* (Louisville, KY: Westminster John Knox, 1999), 66-82.

6. Anne Nasimiyu-Wasike, "Christology and an African Woman's Experience," in *Jesus in African Christianity: Experimentation and Diversity in African Christology*, ed. J. N. K. Mugambi and Laurenti Magesa (Nairobi: Initiatives, 1989), 126.

7. See Lynne Bundesen, *Woman's Guide to the Bible* (New York: Crossroad, 1993).

8. S. N. Emswiler, *The Ongoing Journey: Women and the Bible* (New York: Women's Division of the United Methodist Church, 1977), 144.

9. See Rosanne Gartner, *Meet Bathsheba: Dramatic Portraits of Biblical Women* (Valley Forge, PA: Judson, 2000).

10. See Megan McKenna, *Not Counting Women and Children: Neglected Stories from the Bible* (Maryknoll, NY: Orbis Books, 1994).

11. See John H. Mundy, *Europe in the High Middle Ages* (London: Longman, 1980), 207-23.

12. See Carlo M. Cipolla, ed., *The Fontana Economic History of Europe* (Glasgow: William Collins Son, 1981), 44-45, 59, 200, 234, 250, 266.

13. John S. Akama and Robert Maxon, eds., *Ethnography of the Gusii of Western Kenya: A Vanishing Cultural Heritage* (New York: Edwin Mellen, 2006).

14. See J. Fedler and Z. Tanzer, "A World in Denial: International Perspectives on Violence against Women," in *Reclaiming Women's Spaces: New Perspectives on Violence against Women and Sheltering in South Africa*, ed. Y. J. Park, J. Fedler, and Z. Dangor (Johannesburg: Nisaa Institute for Women's Development, 2000).

15. Audrey Mullender and Rebecca Morley, eds., *Children Living with Domestic Violence* (London: Whiting and Birch, 1994).

16. See John Archer and Barbara Lloyd, *Sex and Gender*, 2nd ed. (London: Cambridge University Press, 2002).

17. See Anne E. Hunter and Carie Forden, *Readings in the Psychology of Gender: Exploring Our Differences and Commonalities* (Boston: Allyn & Bacon, 2002).

18. See Harold I. Kaplan and Benjamin J. Saddock, *Synopsis of Psychiatry: Behavioural Sciences/Clinical Psychiatry*, 5th ed. (London: William & Wilkins, 1988).

19. See Cynthia Brantley, *The Giriama and Colonial Resistance in Kenya, 1800-1920* (Los Angeles: University of California Press, 1981), 144.

20. Micere Mugo, "The Role of Women in the Struggle for Freedom," in *The Participation of Women in Kenya Society*, ed. Achola Pala, Thelma Awori, and Abigail Krystal (Nairobi: Kenya Literature Bureau, 1978), 213.

21. Although Mary Muthoni Maingi mobilized the African people and dared the African men to fight for their independence and the colonialists to set Harry Thuku free, one is saddened to find that in the few historical accounts this brave woman is just mentioned in passing.

22. See *Violence against Women and Children* (Geneva: World Organization against Torture, 2008); available at http://www.omct.org/files/2005/09/3070/alt_report_on_violence_against_women_children_kenya.pdf.

23. See World Health Organization, *Missing Persons: Views of Older Persons on Elder Abuse* (Geneva: World Health Organization: INPEA 2002). This report can be accessed at http://whqlibdoc.who.int/hq/ 2002/WHO_NMH_VIP_02.1.pdf.

24. Information about these organizations can be found at "Chronic Diseases and Health Promotion," World Health Organization, http://www.who.int/chp/en/; "Violence and Injury Prevention and Disability (VIP)," World Health Organization, http://www.who.int/violence _injury_prevention/en/; International Network for the Prevention of Elder Abuse, http://www.inpea.net/; and Help Age International, http://www.helpage.org/.

25. World Health Organization, *Missing Persons*, 17.

THE SYSTEMIC ERASURE OF THE BLACK/DARK-SKINNED BODY IN CATHOLIC ETHICS

Bryan Massingale

One of the questions I address in my scholarly work is this: *What would Catholic theological ethics look like if it took the "Black Experience" seriously as a dialogue partner?* To raise the question, however, is to signal the reality of absence, erasure, and "missing" voices. The question is necessary only because the "Black Experience"—the collective story of African American survival and achievement in a hostile, exploitative, and racist environment—and the bodies who are the subjects of this experience have been all too often rendered invisible and therefore "missing" in U.S. Catholic ethical reflection.[1]

The Historical Omission of Racism and Racial Justice

An example illustrates this invisibility, which, I contend, amounts to a systemic erasure. In 1948, the eminent U.S. moral theologian Gerald Kelly considered the question of whether the Sunday Mass obligation ceased for a Negro who was excluded from the local "white church."[2] Kelly judged that such racial discrimination was "unjust, impious, and scandalous." He also expressed regret at the harm given to "the Negro's spirit" and sense of church membership. Nonetheless, Kelly concluded that such discrimination within the church "does not of itself excuse him from hearing Mass. That question must be solved on the basis of the difficulty of getting to another church."

He did reiterate that white Catholics were duty bound to extend ordinary courtesy and respect to black people, noting that the refusal to do so was "a sin against charity."[3] Note, however, that white Catholics were not duty bound to protest against the social evil of racial segregation itself, whether in society or in the church. Nor was there any expressed obligation for Catholics to engage proactively in the struggle to change this sinful situation. Nor was there but the most fleeting attention given to the perspective of the dark-skinned victim of such ecclesial exclusion.

A review of the two major professional journals of U.S. Catholic theological ethicists—namely, the authoritative "Notes on Moral Theology" published by *Theological Studies* (1940-96) and *The Proceedings of the Catholic Theological Society of America* (1946-96)—confirms the stark and glaring omission of the issue of white racism. U.S. Catholic moral theology's past reveals embarrassing omissions whereby theological ethicists were seemingly oblivious to the major social movements occurring around them (such as the Civil Rights and Black Power Movements of the 1960s). One searches these journals in vain for in-depth analyses or reflections on the reality of racism or race relations. The Civil Rights Movement, the catalyst for some of the most epochal social transformations in U.S. history and a paradigm for many other justice struggles globally, passed unnoticed by U.S. Catholic ethicists who were consumed by other matters—specifically, the controversies surrounding the morality of artificial contraception. Indeed, if one depended solely on these sources for one's knowledge of the period, one would never know of Martin Luther King Jr.'s life, contributions, or even his death because Catholic moralists of that time scarcely averted to him.[4]

Thus, one noted scholar, in reflecting on the omission of racial justice in U.S. Catholic ethical reflection, concluded:

> Historically it is impossible to deny that from the end of the Civil War until modern times, an almost universal silence regarding the moral issues involved in segregation blanketed the ecclesiastical scene. The American hierarchy and theologians have remained mute, and this at a time when ... enforced segregation was growing and extending more and more into all areas of life.[5]

Not Only a "Historical" Omission

The observation that the muting of the Black Experience and the overlooking of ethical attention to the reality of racism is not, unfortunately, a matter of past history has been more recently confirmed. In October of 2008, a conference was held at the Catholic Theological Union and DePaul University in Chicago to explore the task of "Building a Catholic Social Theology for the Americas." As part of the closing panel charged with noting the conference's achievements and remaining tasks, I observed the omission of any consideration of race. For example, although the conference participants examined and lamented the poverty revealed in the United States through the Hurricane Katrina event, they never averted to race as a decisive factor in how this tragedy unfolded.[6]

The assembled scholars also lamented the difficulty of elaborating a common social theology for the Americas—both North and South—given our differing histories and origins. But such an observation ignored our shared history of racism and slavery—undergone by both African and indigenous peoples—which not only marks both of our continents but also has been decisive in the formation of Latino/a identity. *La raza*—the *mestizo/mestizaje* reality of Latin America—would not exist without the racial mixing that stemmed from the deep wounding and often unacknowledged pain of slavery and economic exploitation. Race-based enslavement, colonialism, and conquest are common histories that are foundational not only for the Americas but for Western culture as well. These cannot be adequately understood without a forthright and in-depth engagement with racial injustice and a naming of white supremacy.

The Erasure of the Black Embodied Voice

Moreover, when the dark bodies of African Americans did appear in Catholic ethical discourse, they were as the objects of white sympathy, charity, and assistance. (I use the word "object" deliberately.) Though the leading moralists of the 1950s agreed that racial segregation was unjust, the solution advocated was to encourage whites to yield or concede rights to blacks, rather than encourage African Americans to press for what was their due.[7] Catholic moral discourse treated black people as *objects* of white study, analysis, and charity—and rarely deemed them as *subjects* capable of independent action or creative initiative. There was no acknowledgment of black *agency*; black people are usually acted upon and seldom the actors in U.S. Catholic moral discourse.[8] Their voice and agency are muted, absent, erased—and at the same time opposed, feared, and resisted.[9] Such practices and attitudes could not but render Catholic ethical reflection in matters of race inadequate and impoverished, if not absolutely erroneous.

This "underside" of history revealed in the erasure and distortion of the Black Experience in Catholic ethical reflection is well expressed by David Tracy:

> There is an underside to all the talk about history in modern religion and theology. That underside is revealed in the shocking silence in most theologies of historical consciousness and historicity alike on the evil rampant in history, the sufferings of whole peoples, the destruction of nature itself. ... [It is] a history without any sense of the radical interruptions of actual history, without a memory of historical suffering, especially the suffering caused by the pervasive systemic unconscious distortions in our history—sexism, racism, classism, antisemitism, homophobia, Eurocentrism.[10]

Why the Evasion of the Black Body?

Yet we must deepen our inquiry into this "shocking silence . . . on the suffering of whole peoples," and particularly of black- and darker-skinned peoples, on the part of Catholic theological ethics by raising the question of *why*. Why, despite the "turn to the subject" and the embrace of historical consciousness, did U.S. Catholic theological ethicists *not* attend to the blatant and endemic racism of American society? Why was the most pressing moral issue of the 1960s artificial contraception and not the Civil Rights Movement or the racial violence of 1967 and 1968 that tore apart that nation's cities and has enduring consequences today? Why was, and why still is, the "radical interruption" of the black body continually overlooked, ignored, and thus erased?

There are multiple reasons for this state of affairs. M. Shawn Copeland suggests that one reason may be that the black body is what she calls a "structural embarrassment,"[11] that is, an uncomfortable reminder of the invisible ghosts of enslavement, colonization, and racial supremacy—that is, the "unjust enrichment" through exploited labor[12]—that haunt and hover over our histories. Another reason for the avoidance of the black body in Catholic theological and ethical discourse is that a forthright engagement with it would bring to the surface the deep complicity and collusion of Western Christianity in the suffering, abuse, and horror that attended European and American colonial expansion.[13] Yet perhaps the most profound reason for avoiding the black body is that challenging its invisibility would entail making white bodies visible as "white," that is, as sites of conferred racial dominance and privilege.

Marking white theologians as "white" means naming and facing the deforming effects of culture on the consciousness of North American and European theological ethicists. It means facing not only the possibility but indeed the probability that Catholic ethicists of the past (and too often in the present), being (de)formed by the systemic distortion of Western racism, did not and could not have regarded persons of African descent as numbered among the "subjects" to whom they should "turn."[14]

This probability is neither idle nor speculative. Social scientists have uncovered the reality of what they call "racially selective sympathy and indifference," that is, "the *unconscious* failure to extend to a minority the same recognition of humanity, and hence the same sympathy and care, given as a matter of course to one's own group."[15] It is important to underscore, however, that this "selective indifference" is not necessarily a matter of conscious decision or intentional willing. It results, rather, from the unnoted effects of socialization in a culture of racism and the corrosive impact of a racialized ethos on one's identity and consciousness.

As the historian Taylor Branch notes, "almost as color defines vision itself, race shapes the culture eye—what we do and do not notice, the reach of empathy and the alignment of response."[16] And because of such social conditioning, certain lives become easier to ignore or, put another way, certain bodies have a higher claim upon a community's energy and concern, even among Catholic theological ethicists.[17]

Thus, a forthright engagement with the black body in Catholic theological ethics would demand making white ethicists visible as "white" and confront the challenges this poses for personal integrity in a compromised social system. These challenges are neither uncomplicated nor easily faced.

Systemic Erasure and Compromised Ethical Reflection

However, the "missing" voices of our darker sisters and brothers are significant not only for the personal integrity of Catholic moral theologians but also for the integrity and adequacy of Catholic ethical reflection. Because of this silencing and invisibility, there are not only voices that have not been heard, there are moral questions that have not been asked by Catholic theological ethicists of previous generations, such as the following: "What does it mean to be a disciple of Jesus in a racist society?"; "In a world where 'black' is an illegitimate or inferior mode of being human, what are the social implications of believing that Black Americans are made in the image of God?"; "How are persons of African descent to live ethically in a society that denies, questions, or attacks our humanity?"; "How do we tell those whom society ignores, fears, and disdains that they are sons and daughters of God?" Not averting to such questions in a society of endemic racism makes one's ethical project not only inadequate and incomplete, it also strains credibility.[18]

Moreover, the invisibility of black bodies and darker voices masks methodological deficiencies in Catholic ethical reflection. I highlight, for example, Catholic moral theology's understanding of sin and moral culpability. Its primary focus on obvious acts of conscious and voluntary racial malice blinds us to the deeper and more sinister social evil that afflicts us. The issue is that we are tacitly ensnared in and malformed by a web of evil that we cannot yet even satisfactorily name.

In a recent work, I expressed this concern thus: "Because of the covert nature of racism's transmission, its meanings are internalized without awareness of the source and judged to be . . . normative."[19] That is, one's sense of right and wrong, one's grasp of morality, one's very conscience, become blunted and twisted by one's socialization in a culture of racism. One cannot become aware of the absence or omission of certain voices or perspectives if one believes that such omissions are "normal" and the way things ought to be.

This is not a matter of mere culpable ignorance. Nor do I believe that the issue can be satisfactorily resolved through an appeal to what the tradition calls "invincible ignorance." Such appeals can somewhat deal with individual culpability, but do not attend to the deeper web of injustice that is truly "evil" but for which Catholic theological ethicists have not developed a precise way of naming, nor the church a proper forum for repentance and reconciliation.[20]

Nor does an appeal to "social" or "structural" sin suffice. For I am trying to call our attention to "the underlying set of cultural meanings . . . that are (re)inscribed in social customs, institutional policies and political processes."[21] Social or structural sin addresses the latter—that is, how social institutions and structures are the causes of unjust suffering—but not the former, namely, the underlying set of cultural meanings and symbols that social institutions reflect. Culture animates the social order, and our moral theology has not yet developed the tools for examining, much less naming, this layer of human-caused evil. Merely calling the "culture of racism" an accumulation of many acts of personal sin (*pace* the *Catechism of the Catholic Church*) fails to do justice to the enormity of entrenched cultural evil and its deleterious impacts. There is a "radical evil" at work in human history that the predominant understanding of sin as a voluntary and conscious act can neither address nor redress—and indeed compounds.

Thus, the systemic erasure of the black- and darker-skinned body in Catholic theological ethics not only implicates the personal integrity of Catholic ethicists, but also compromises our ability to adequately reflect on the challenges of moral living in a multicultural and multiracial world. Taking the Black Experience and darker bodies as serious dialogue partners is a daunting challenge that promises to have profound, necessary, and yet perhaps unknown effects on the discipline of Catholic theological ethics and its practitioners.

Lament as a Way Forward

What, then, are we to do in the face of the weight of history and the complicity of Catholic theological ethics in the silencing of the suffering of peoples? It is tempting to offer a series of concrete proposals that, if followed, would lead Catholic ethicists into an intellectual "promised land." But I have become more convinced that racism engages us viscerally at a "gut" level that cannot be addressed solely through rational discussion. I have become more aware of the limits of discursive or intellectual practices alone. Thus, I believe that we Catholic ethicists need to *lament* the ambiguity and distortions of our history and their tragically deforming effects on ourselves. We need to lament, mourn, and grieve our history.[22]

The scriptures remind us that lamentation is an expression of complaint, grief, and hope rooted in a "trust against trust" that God hears the cry of the afflicted and will respond compassionately to their need. Lamenting holds together both sorrow and hope in ways that defy easy rational understanding. Laments honestly name and forthrightly acknowledge painfully wrenching circumstances, and yet proclaim that in the midst of the pain there is another word to be heard from God—a message of compassion and deliverance. Lament thus facilitates the emergence of something new, whether a changed consciousness or a renewed engagement with external events. It is indeed a paradox of protest and praise that leads to new life.

For example, consider the African American spiritual "Nobody Knows the Trouble I've Seen."[23] Composed by an unknown black enslaved man whose family was rent asunder by being sold to different slave masters, the song piercingly relates that no one could possibly comprehend or "know my sorrow." Yet, the singer ends his lament on an unexpected, even incomprehensible note: "Nobody knows the trouble I've seen. Glory Hallelujah!" Through the practice of honest and forthright protest, the singer finds the strength to bear and endure unspeakable loss and harsh circumstances. History afflicts but does not crush him.

I offer such lament as a possibility for Catholic theological ethicists. Lament has the power to challenge the entrenched cultural beliefs that legitimate racial privilege. It engages a level of human consciousness deeper than logical reason. Lamenting can propel us to new levels of truth seeking and risk taking as we grieve our past history and strive to create an ethical discourse that is more reflective of the universality of our Catholic faith.

Nearing the limits of time and space for this reflection, I conclude on this note: The systemic erasure of dark-skinned bodies and the silencing of black voices in our history are not of concern only for an adequate account of the past. For, as the U.S. novelist William Faulkner noted, "The past is not dead, it is not even past."[24] Race-based enslavement, conquest, and colonialism are common foundational experiences—the "original sins" that link the Americas, Africa, Europe, and Asia. We cannot, then, give an adequate account of present controversies and moral responsibilities—much less develop a Catholic theological ethics for a world church—if we fail to attend to the voices of the dark bodies that hover over and haunt our histories despite our embarrassed silence and studied neglect.

Notes

1. James Cone, the pioneer of black American liberation theology, defines the "Black Experience" thus: "The black experience [in the United States] is the atmosphere in which blacks live. It is the totality of black existence in a white world . . . in a system of white racism. . . . The black experience, however, is more than simply encountering white insanity. It also means blacks making decisions about themselves. . . . It is the experience of carving out an existence in a society that says that you do not belong." See James Cone, *A Black Theology of Liberation*, 2nd ed. (Maryknoll, NY: Orbis Books, 1986), 24-25.

2. Readers from outside the U.S. context need to recall that ironclad racial segregation was the official legal and social policy of the United States from 1896 to 1965. Justified under the fiction of providing white and non-white peoples "separate but equal" educational, social, and economic opportunities, this racial segregation was a means of advancing white supremacy in political, social, and economic matters. Such racial exclusion was, unfortunately, a reality in the U.S. Catholic Church as well. Black men and women were all but excluded from participation in the priesthood and religious life. Catholic parishes were often designated as "white only" or "black only"—especially but not solely in the southern United States. For a seminal study detailing the Catholic Church's collusion and complicity in U.S. racialized evil, see Cyprian Davis, *The History of Black Catholics in the United States* (New York: Crossroad, 1992).

3. Gerald Kelly, "Notes on Moral Theology," *Theological Studies* 8 (1947): 112-14. I present this article because it illustrates the standard treatment that racism received when it was considered by U.S. Catholic theological ethicists. One should also appreciate that, while it is easy to be critical and even dismissive of the limitations of this approach, at least the ethicists of the 1940s adverted to the topic. After 1963, the topic of racial justice all but disappears from *Theological Studies'* annual moral survey until the late 1990s.

4. I detail this sad legacy in Bryan Massingale, "The African American Experience and U.S. Roman Catholic Ethics: 'Strangers and Aliens No Longer'?" in *Black and Catholic: The Challenge and Gift of Black Folk: Contributions of African American Experience and World View to Catholic Theology*, ed. Jamie T. Phelps (Milwaukee, WI: Marquette University Press, 1997), 79-101.

5. Joseph T. Leonard, "Current Theological Questions in Race Relations," *Catholic Theological Society of America Proceedings* [hereafter, *CTSA Proceedings*] 19 (1964): 82.

6. For the signal impact of U.S. racism in the response to the plight of Hurricane Katrina's victims, see Bryan Massingale, "The Scandal of Poverty: 'Cultured Indifference'

and the Option for the Poor Post-Katrina," *Journal of Religion and Society*, Supplement Series 4 (2008): 55-72; and Bryan Massingale, "About Katrina: Catastrophe Exposes U.S. Race Reality," *National Catholic Reporter* 43, no. 18 (2007): 10-13.

7. Citing the eminent U.S. moralist John Ford, "[T]he doctrine of Christ inculcates more insistently that we must *give* rights to commutative justice; nowhere does Christ encourage us to *fight* for what is our due. It would be better for theologians and priests generally to preach to whites that they should give rights due to the Negroes, rather than urge the Negroes to press for the rights that are their due. Otherwise we might be encouraging fights and violence." See C. Luke Salm, "Moral Aspects of Segregation in Education—Digest of the Discussion," *CTSA Proceedings* 13 (1958): 61; emphasis in the original.

8. As noted above, there was very little examination or treatment of the black-led Civil Rights Movement in U.S. Catholic theological ethics. Indeed, in previous work, I detail the suspicion of black initiative and the pervasive white paternalism that typifies the U.S. Catholic engagement with racism. See my *Racial Justice and the Catholic Church* (Maryknoll, NY: Orbis Books, 2010), chap. 2.

9. John LaFarge, S.J., a preeminent advocate for racial justice in the mid-twentieth century, nonetheless was suspicious of and opposed to African American agency and leadership in the quest for racial justice. See David W. Southern, *John LaFarge and the Limits of Catholic Interracialism 1911-1963* (Baton Rouge: Louisiana State University Press, 1996).

10. David Tracy, "Evil, Suffering, and Hope: The Search for New Forms of Contemporary Theodicy," *CTSA Proceedings* 50 (1995): 29.

11. M. Shawn Copeland, *Enfleshing Freedom: Body, Race, and Being* (Minneapolis, MN: Fortress Press, 2009), 3.

12. Joe R. Feagin, *Systemic Racism: A Theory of Oppression* (New York: Routledge, 2006), 18.

13. In the U.S. context, Malcolm X is perhaps the sharpest critic of the collusion of Western Christianity in the racial oppression of dark bodies. I treat his thought in *"Vox Victimarum Vox Dei:* Malcolm X as Neglected 'Classic' for Catholic Theological Reflection," *CTSA Proceedings* 65 (2010): 63-88.

14. Bryan Massingale, "The African American Experience and U.S. Roman Catholic Ethics," 79-101.

15. Charles R. Lawrence III, "The Id, the Ego, and Equal Protection: Reckoning with Unconscious Racism," *Stanford Law Review* 39 (1987): 317-88, at n. 135.

16. Taylor Branch, *Parting the Waters: America in the King Years, 1954-63* (New York: Simon & Schuster, 1989), cited in Haki R. Madhubuti, *Black Men: Obsolete, Single, Dangerous?* (Chicago: Third World Press, 1990), 264. Madhubuti further declares, "The white response to the majority of the world's people, who are not white, is indeed grounded in race. More than any other factor in the Eurocentric context, *race* defines, categorizes, tracks, destroys and redefines cultures."

17. I explore the realities of "unconscious racism" and "racially selective sympathy and indifference" in my *Racial Justice and the Catholic Church*, 26-33. I note, however, yet another reason for the invisibility of the black body as "black" in Catholic moral discourse, namely, the myth of—or even aspiration to—so called "colorblindness." As the celebrated novelist Toni Morrison explains in another context, "One likely reason for the paucity of critical materials on this large and compelling subject is that, in matters of race, silence and evasion have historically ruled literary discourse. . . . It is further complicated by the fact that the habit of ignoring race is understood to be a graceful, even generous, liberal

gesture. To notice it is to recognize an already discredited difference. To enforce invisibility through silence is to allow the black body a shadowless participation in the dominant cultural body." See Toni Morrison, *Playing in the Dark: Whiteness and the Literary Imagination* (New York: Vintage Books, 1993). This official "color blindness" marks the public policies of many countries, including France and Uruguay, where race-based social and economic disparities among social groups are officially "erased" through a refusal to collect the data that would reveal them. The problem with "color blindness," no matter how well intentioned, is that in a sociocultural context where skin-color difference plays a significant and even decisive role, not to attend to this difference in practice preserves and defends entrenched social privilege.

18. Bryan Massingale, *Racial Justice and the Catholic Church,* 160-61.

19. Bryan Massingale, "Author's Response: Review Symposium on *Racial Justice and the Catholic Church,*" *Horizons* 37 (2010): 138-42.

20. David Tracy, for example, states that naming social evils such as racism as "sin" may not be doing justice to the depth and pervasiveness of the evil we confront through an encounter with the systemically silenced and erased. Rather, we need a more radical doctrine of sin—and grace—to do justice to the enormity of entrenched evil present in our history and in the present. See his discussion in *Plurality and Ambiguity: Hermeneutics, Religion, and Hope* (Chicago: University of Chicago Press, 1994), 74-75.

21. Laurie Cassidy, "Review Symposium: *Racial Justice and the Catholic Church,*" *Horizons* 37 (2010): 127-28.

22. I treat the practice of lament and its significance for racial-justice praxis in more detail in *Racial Justice and the Catholic Church,* 104-14. The reader is directed there for a more in-depth discussion.

23. Bruno Chenu, *The Trouble I've Seen: The Big Book of Negro Spirituals,* trans. Eugene V. Leplante (Valley Forge, PA: Judson, 2003), 265; and John Lovell Jr., *Black Song: The Forge and the Flame* (New York: Paragon, 1972), 122.

24. Cited in Tracy, *Plurality and Ambiguity,* 36.

Part III
The Present

Introduction

On the third day we discussed the present, focusing on three matters: first, a plenary on moral reasoning, and then a pair of parallel plenaries on political ethics and health issues.

On moral reasoning, Belgian Éric Gaziaux offers a splendid synthesis of moral reasoning in light of the debate from the 1970s between autonomous ethics in the context of faith and an ethics of faith. Positing them not as antithetical but as differences of emphasis, Gaziaux sees the first as based more on a theology of creation and the other more on a theology of redemption. His resolution of the debate provides a good foundation for contemporary theological ethics and naturally moves to the second essay.

Then, Margaret Farley from the United States illuminates the meaning of moral discernment, whether done individually or together, by exploring three key human experiences that make moral discernment both possible and necessary: moral obligation, free choice, and love. In proposing a distinctively African approach to moral reasoning, Congolese Bénézet Bujo looks at a fundamental understanding of African anthropology that is relationally three dimensional with the community, the ancestors, and those yet to be born. In that "self-understanding" the moving toward normative morality proceeds through a cosmologically conscious communal discourse (or "palaver") ethics.

On political ethics, the Australian Redemptorist Brian Johnstone offers to make sense of contemporary interpretations of the just war tradition by retrieving the thought of Thomas Aquinas. In particular, he raises questions about invoking the "tradition" and the so-called *prima facie* claim against using violence. He steers the reader to Aquinas and the just war argument, while highlighting charity, underlining its primacy and priority, in working with justice to promote civic concord.

Mexican theologian Miguel Ángel Sánchez Carlos provides a ground-breaking essay by arguing that urban life goes unobserved in the work of contemporary Catholic theological ethicists and in the writings of the contemporary magisterium. He argues that the Council of Trent was the last council of the era of Christendom, which has now been replaced by the urban phenomenon that undermines any notion of the objectively ethical, both by its massive anonymity and by its support for an indifferent autonomy.

From Zimbabwe, David Kaulemu offers an astute comment on the role of the laity in the promotion and "consistent application" of Catholic social teaching. With a focus on southern Africa, he challenges the episcopacy to recognize the de facto exercise of ecclesial authority by lay leaders in their use and development of these social teachings.

On health care, Brazil's Leo Pessini presents an international overview of challenges to health care but then enters into a Latin American context to engage the principles of justice and equity as central to the future needs of health care. From India, Pushpa Joseph looks at gender and sex differentials in Indian health care and highlights a broad set of challenges and contradictions facing Indian women today. From Kenya, Margaret Ogola looks at the world of HIV/AIDS both internationally and locally. As a health-care worker for twenty-five years in the field of HIV/AIDS in Nairobi, she offers a view of today's challenges for serodiscordant couples, specifically regarding reinfection, the particular barriers facing women in such relationships, and finally the issue of the ethical legitimacy of condoms as part of the solution for preventing a spouse from becoming infected by one's partner. It is a moving and compelling presentation.

IN WHAT SENSE
IS MORAL THEOLOGY RATIONAL?[1]

Éric Gaziaux

I begin my discussion of the role of moral reasoning in contemporary theology by sketching the historical background from the Second Vatican Council up to the present, highlighting the status of rationality in the debate between autonomous morality and faith ethics. I shall then examine some characteristics of rationality that operate in moral reasoning.

Historical Background

The Second Vatican Council marked the end of post-Tridentine moral theology and the disappearance of the old casuistic moral theology.[2] Although the Council texts do not contain "a structured exposition of Christian moral theology," they nevertheless contain "indisputable 'openings'" with regard to moral theology.[3] This was confirmed by the postconciliar debate between autonomous morality in the Christian context and faith ethics. The central question here concerned the rationality of Christian behavior.

In their desire to make Christian morality plausible in a secularized context, the proponents of autonomous morality emphasized the importance of an up-to-date interpretation of natural law. They attempted to extend the paths opened up by texts such as *Gaudium et spes*.[4] Alfons Auer, the father of autonomous morality, regards ethics as communicable because it is based on human reason. The moral reasoning that Auer employs operates not so much on the level of abstract speculation as on that of reflection on human experiences that reveal the paths of success and failure.

Morality no longer consists in submission to a theonomous ordinance that is laid down in advance, nor in an abstract deduction of duties that are generated by natural law and detached from history. Rather, morality consists in revealing the duties that are inherent in human existence, and these are discovered by grasping what it means to be a human person. This rationality depends on the human sciences and aims at anthropological integration. It leads to a normative intervention on the part of ethics—something that is never easy and is always a matter of discussion.[5]

Other theologians expound autonomous morality from different perspectives, but the basic line is always trust in the human reason with regard to the definition of ethics (which is regarded as a common good of the human race) accompanied by the rejection of a categorical morality that would be accessible only to believers. Autonomous morality concerns primarily the level of a person's intention or motivations.

The trend that proposes a specifically Christian morality (or faith ethics) in the Catholic Church, affirming the existence of a morality proper to Christians, is a reaction against precisely this claim of autonomous ethics. The encyclical *Veritatis splendor* (1993) attempted to put an end to the debate by recalling the intrinsic link between freedom and truth, the authority of Christ and of the church's magisterium in moral matters, and the existence of intrinsically evil actions and of moral norms that admit no exceptions.

There is a renewed interest today in the discussion of autonomy and thus in the rationality and freedom of ethics, thanks to the emergence of "communitarian" trends. This in turn leads to a renewed interest in the concept of moral reasoning in theology. Communitarianism is a reaction against the project of autonomous morality, claiming that this obscures the link between religion and ethics.

Alasdair MacIntyre addressed a number of criticisms of the morality generated by the Enlightenment.[6] Similarly, Stanley Hauerwas severely criticizes the use that moral theology makes of natural law and the project that is inherent in autonomous morality in a Christian context. Hauerwas holds that morality involves more than rational criteria of evaluation. It depends primarily on the way in which the community and the narratives that it bears shape each individual. There is thus no universal ethics; the task is to rehabilitate the particularity of peoples' convictions in the face of a universality that Hauerwas regards as destructive of identity and inclined to violence. He accuses autonomous morality of emphasizing the continuity between Christians and their culture rather than the discontinuity. He opposes the absolutism of a deductive discourse based on universal principles and concentrates on the narrative approach, thereby incurring the risk of positing an antithesis between rationality and narrativity.[7]

This debate thus reveals two different concepts of rationality and of moral reasoning, one that is centered more on the continuity between Christian morality and the secularized world and one that sees more of a breach. One concept depends more on a theology of creation and the other more on a theology of redemption. Although autonomous morality may seem to give a privileged position to rationality rather than to particular narrative traditions and a categorical specificity of behavior, it nevertheless intends to safeguard the freedom and responsibility of the moral agent.

Communitarian morality is correct to criticize a rationality that is "empty" and detached from history. But although it underlines the rootedness of the subject in a community of life and of meaning, does it not risk too quickly eliminating the role of rationality—which is also the sign of the freedom of the human being? We must therefore ask how we are to conceive of a rationality in ethics that takes account of the demands of reason and of the specific rootedness of the moral subject.

Openings

A Rationality That Is Historical and Dynamic

It is clear that both the concept proposed by autonomous morality and the criticism of a certain kind of rationality by "communitarian ethics" refute the idea of absolute reason. Reason exists only as something real and historical. It can be exercised only on the data it receives and not independently of these data. In the context of moral reasoning, therefore, it is the task of reason to classify, to evaluate, and to clarify these data, and to impose order on them. This is certainly the nucleus of moral reasoning. Accordingly, moral reason always lives in a form of dependence, in what we might call a heteronomy, on the traditions of thought and of life that it has not bestowed upon itself but on which it must reflect and work.

Allied to rationality, autonomy means basically that the ultimate principles that determine action and moral reasoning cannot be individual arbitrariness or blind authoritarianism. To act on one's momentary impulses with no other reason than one's immediate inclinations is to behave with just as little morality as one who submits blindly to tradition or social custom or authority simply because these *are* tradition, social custom, or authority. Autonomy is not opposed to tradition or to community, but to submission to arbitrariness.

The necessary endeavor to rehabilitate ethical historical reason does not consist in positing an antithesis between reason and tradition but by drawing on both experience and tradition to discover what is ethically "livable," bearing in mind what is technically realizable and what is worthy of the human being. Ethical norms are transmitted historically and are open to critical reexamination by reason. In this perspective, ethical reasoning consists in discussing ethical experiences and the moral tradition, employing arguments to examine these, and opening them up from the hollow space of their particularity into a potential universality (and hence communicability).

To appeal to reason in ethics does not mean appealing to a sort of substance that floats above historical and contingent realities and from which one can simply deduce norms and values. On the contrary. To refer to reason and promote a morality founded on rationality points to a way of living, commits one to a societal praxis and signals a way of resolving problems, of indicating a discipline, and of unmasking idols. Practical reason thus has the critical function of investigating "the dissimulated mechanisms of distortions through which the legitimate objectifications of the communitarian bond become intolerable alienations."[8]

A Critical Rationality

A dynamic rationality holds that a decision can be called rational and reasonable only if it has passed through the fire of discussion, critical confrontation, and openness to other points of view. This also applies to moral theology. Accordingly, there cannot

> exist mysterious norms of ethical action making an intimate demand that is not positively comprehensible and clearly identifiable. . . . Moral norms make objective demands, and it is essential that their content be intelligible. Intelligibility in what is to be done is a constitutive element of responsible behavior among human beings.[9]

This conception leads to two consequences for theology. The first involves taking seriously the rationality of *human* ethics to such a degree that

> on the ethical and moral level, the biblical faith adds nothing to the predicates "good" and "obligatory" when these are applied to action. The biblical *agape* comes from an *economy of the gift* that has a meta-ethical character. This leads me to affirm that a Christian morality does not exist, except on the level of the history of mentalities. There is only a common morality . . . that the biblical faith puts into a new *perspective*, where love is linked to the "naming of God."[10]

The second consequence is the requirement that we unmask the tendency to self-absolutization in human morality or rationality. "Faith's act of listening presupposes that one renounces self sufficiency; and this means that it presupposes knowledge of the Cross. But this mortification is far from annihilating reason. On the contrary, it makes reason cross over the threshold into its true dwelling place by means of the audacity of a transgression."[11]

Henri Bouillard states clearly what this means in theological terms:

> Strictly speaking, God does not command. He establishes the basis of what we call a "commandment," that is, the requirement of coherence in human conduct. . . .[12]
>
> Moral consciousness is the transcendental condition of Christian ethics. . . .[13]
>
> The existence of God is certainly the basis of the absoluteness of duty. . . . But it is the human being who asks the ethical question and discerns the answer (even when one is guided by the light of revelation). In doing so, one acts not as a sinner, but as a creature. . . .[14]
>
> Christian ethics has thus a double source. Its inspiration comes from faith, and its definition comes from the moral consciousness. . . .[15]

One who justifies theological theses by means of a reflection of this kind, that is to say, a philosophical reflection, is not self-condemned to subordinate the Word of God to the judgment of human reason. All one is doing is to recall that what one says about the Word of God is not identical to this Word; and one must refrain from presenting as a divine precept an obligation that one has arbitrarily deduced from the Word of God. Since the Word of God is addressed to the human being in view of his or her salvation, one may not prescribe in the name of God anything that cannot be justified from the perspective of the human being. At the same time, the human being has an innate openness to inspiration from the Gospel, and the theologian reminds us of this. From this double perspective, we must reflect both on the requirements and on the opening of moral consciousness.[16]

Rationality as a Search for Meaning

Rationality thus presents itself as a search for meaning. An ethic that is motivated by a rationality of this kind seeks to define "the coherence of intersubjective relationships" and to promote the intersubjective recognition of the human person.[17] An imperative can be moral only if it expresses the logic of intersubjectivity and of freedom, for otherwise, it would support arbitrariness, and obedience would be akin to slavery. When this rationality is at work, it does not aim to eliminate people's convictions in the name of omnipotent reason. Rather, it invites these convictions to accept examination by means of arguments. The strongest conviction demands recourse to arguments—where it risks being refuted. Rational argumentation is thus seen as a critical voice that operates within the convictions that it seeks not to eliminate but rather to bring into the rank of "well-weighed convictions" in an equilibrium that is the outcome of reflection, as John Rawls affirms.[18] This leads to a moral judgment that is the fruit of a debate, a dialogue, a sharing of convictions, and not the fruit of a rational deduction based on a priori principles.

A close interaction between theory and practice is necessary, since

> theory does not flow from praxis, nor is it simply a replica of praxis. It systematizes praxis and rectifies it, while theory itself is at the same time rectified and developed through its realization in praxis. Theory is the guide of praxis. Praxis is the incessantly renewed critique of theory. In other words, the only way to comprehend theory is to get it involved in praxis; but praxis *on its own* can never demonstrate the validity of theory.[19]

In the context of this interaction between theory and praxis, between conviction and argumentation, the reference to rationality in ethics is akin to the search for the constitutive meaning of human existence and action. But this meaning or significance does not so much designate *that which is*—the *per se* of a practice, its essence, its nature. Rather, it designates the network of connections and relationships and the structuring of these connections and relationships that constitute a given practice.

What then becomes *significant* is the *gap*, the *difference* between the elements of a practice and this practice itself, taken in the variety of cultural situations in which it occurs. This means that speaking of humanly meaningful praxis never amounts to eliminating the differences. On the contrary, it means recognizing them and clarifying this network of connections and relationships. It means supplying the conditions for the production of the practice, for its empirical genesis. It means unmasking the legitimations this practice bestows on itself, the self-criticism and the criticism by others that it demands, and the transcendence it implies. . . . It follows that an ethical practice does not become comprehensible or open the door to a relevant evaluation unless it is given its place in the complex network of the elements that it includes and in the historical substance in which it is rooted.[20]

When we speak of praxis that is humanly meaningful, we must include one aspect of praxis that is generated by the summons and the demand, the overtaking and the transcending—in short, by an ethical life that is associated with the idea of vocation. "Human existence is called to" a life in accordance with reason. "It is in such a life that it can find its meaning, and the realization of this form of life is also the realization of the humanity of the human person. The decision taken in favor of reason is the acceptance of the vocation that defines the human person."[21]

Ethical rationality is thus intimately linked to the hope for meaning. "It is the hope for this meaning that, remote from all legalism, allows in each individual instance the rational being to run the risk of a moral choice that is not arbitrary."[22] But precisely what this vocation demands remains largely undefined. This is why the appeal to reason must be considered in terms of a process and not in terms of ready-made answers.

A Christian ethic inspired by this way of understanding reason works in keeping with the model of relationship and responsibility, rather than simply with the model of "particularity and universality" or "deontology and teleology." This model commits us to pay attention to the communitarian and relational reality of our existence—God's salvation comes to us through the community of the people of God—and makes it possible both to avoid the cult of excessive particularism or of sterile universality and to overcome the exaggerated antithesis between the teleological and deontological models. At the same time, it preserves creativity by describing this as a limited creativity in a multirelational context.

A Rationality That Contains a Significant Gap

The concept of rationality in process leads us to recognize the fallibility and the vulnerability of rational ethics, as a well as a gap that lies between what is and what ought to be. This gap opens up the space for action and for the moral praxis of discernment. In this sense, we can say that a rational ethics is a dynamic ethics that is in a perpetual state of being realized. This rationality seeks to understand itself "not only in what it accomplishes in terms of its operation or in conceptual terms, but also in what precedes it and prepares the way for it, and also in its relationship to the horizon that reveals to it the future when it will be fully established."[23] It thus leads us to recognize a distance between de facto praxis and what ought to be the case, and this is why ethics is sometimes structured in the form of a duty or an imperative. This gap between what is and what ought to be is the precise space for action and for moral praxis. Ethics must reduce this gap. At the same time, ethics can never be identified with the observance of the law itself.

The recognition of this gap means recognizing the fragility of the ethical will. A holy will or an infallible reason would no longer need any law or imperative. Ethics "limps" as it walks, as Merleau-Ponty said; it can grasp things well, but it can also grasp things badly. An ethics that recognizes the distance that both separates and unites what is and what ought to be gives human freedom a space for imagination and for creativity. It also opens onto the hermeneutical dimension of ethics that is in search of worlds in which we can live together. The law is constitutive of the realization and the flowering of liberty, but liberty itself is both under the law and above the law. Once we have grasped this, we see that ethical behavior must be free behavior.

A Rationality Influenced by Theology

Theologically speaking, the recognition of this rationality is based on belief in creation and on the responsibility of faith itself. Reason affirms that nothing that is human is foreign to it; but it cannot compel faith to consider what it says, since that is the responsibility of faith itself, and a decision is needed. Fundamentalism can be "understood as a conception of religious commitment that makes this commitment radically autonomous in relation to every claim made by rationality to pronounce a verdict on what is true or morally just." It risks giving the impression that the dimension of belief is incompatible with the dimension of rationality.[24]

But reason belongs to the universe that God created and that bears witness to the power of God and to God. Since it belongs to the work of creation, reason belongs to the constitution of the world and is indeed the principal presupposition of the very heart of revelation, namely, God's intervention in history and the coming of salvation in Jesus Christ. The work of creation is continued in the work of redemption, in which it is taken up anew and given its place as the foundation on which the work of redemption rests. And we must not underestimate the fact that what is proclaimed in the preaching of Jesus Christ takes the form of "a ratification of the dimension of reason."[25]

To affirm human freedom in this way means showing how God's revelation itself presupposes an autonomous philosophy, or the consistency of the human being. The act of the God who opens and reveals Godself can be the act of free love only for one who comprehends oneself, is self-possessed, and commits oneself in an autonomous manner. Revelation does not suppress the autonomy of the human spirit. On the contrary, the human spirit requires this autonomy, because revelation is gratuitous. If revelation were to suppress autonomy, it would suppress the human spirit; but in doing so revelation would suppress itself. Freedom expresses a radical dependence and is based on passivity, since the human being receives the possibility of freedom as a gift that is related to creation. On the other hand, this same freedom proclaims a solid independence, since the human being must personally keep open the path along which this freedom can be realized.

Faith is thus led to recognize reason in its own powers: faith recognizes its own critical creativity and its positive meaning in the work of salvation.

> On the other hand, since faith is the assent to the work of salvation or (to use a different term) to the construction of the "kingdom of God," it is in itself a light that shows us the presence of this kingdom in the signs of the kingdom that are given to us. It brings enlightenment only by receiving in its own power the power of the natural light that is operative in the work of reason. This is why faith is in itself an appeal to the understanding.[26]

Faith is not only commitment and decision. It also demands a double clarity: the clarity of the critical labor that seeks to come ever closer to what is said in the word of proclamation, and the clarity of the process of hope that is the expectation of knowledge through vision.

Ethical rationality in this dynamic tension between "creation and redemption" thus tends to show how moral behavior is the expression of our response to this destiny. But when we have said this, we have certainly not said everything, since there is more to the human being in this sense than morality. When faith looks at morality, it emphasizes that ethics must be liberated from its claim to be itself the source and the goal of existence. Faith is what Dietrich Bonhoeffer called *das Vorletze*, "the penultimate reality."[27] The theological perspective, the perspective of the relationship to God and before God, both relativizes and intensifies ethics. It relativizes ethics because this is not the ultimate criterion of our existence (which consists of more than morality); at the same time, it intensifies ethics because our existence takes on new significance as the place where our relationship to a God who is creator and redeemer is verified.

This intersection between theology and ethics—between a theology that finds its source and its goal in God and an ethics that is regarded as permeated by this theological movement—allows us to envisage human and Christian freedom as a liberty that is in accord with hope.[28] At the same time, it does justice to a Christian morality that is constituted by the autonomy of ethics (in the sense of the rationality that is employed in it) and to an orthopraxy that is inspired by faith.[29] The Christ of the cross unmasks the folly of the human being—a folly that can find one of its major expressions in ethics—at the resurrection, which is the victory of a logic of life over the lethal logic of sin. The transition that Christ brings about here reveals that the temporal dimension in which our conduct and our ethics are located can become the meaningful history of a freedom in which grace bestows itself mysteriously.

Notes

1. English translation by Brian McNeil.
2. See, for example, Philippe Delhaye, "L'apport de Vatican II à la théologie morale," *Concilium* 75 (1972): 57-64.
3. Jean-Louis Brugues, *Précis de théologie morale générale*, vol. 1: *Méthodologie* (Paris: Mame, 1994), 155.
4. I have discussed this in the following books and articles: Éric Gaziaux, *Morale de la foi et morale autonome: Confrontation entre P. Delhaye et J. Fuchs* (Louvain: University Press, 1995); Gaziaux, *L'autonomie en morale: Au croisement de la philosophie et de la théologie* (Louvain: University Press, 1998); Gaziaux, "Morale 'autonome' et éthique 'communautarienne': Quels rapports pour quelle éthique chrétienne?" in *Les communautés chrétiennes et la formation morale des sujets*, ed. Philippe Bordeyne and Alain Thomasset (Paris: Cerf, 2008), 193-215; and Gaziaux, "Le statut de la raison en éthique et le thème de l'autonomie," in *Introduction à l'éthique: Penser, croire, agir*, ed. Jean-Daniel Causse and Denis Müller (Geneva: Labor et Fides, 2009), 69-93. The second part of the present paper draws on the last-mentioned work.
5. See Alfons Auer, *Autonome Moral und christlicher Glaube*, 2nd ed. (Düsseldorf: Patmos, 1989), and my presentation in *L'autonomie en morale* and "Morale 'autonome'" (n. 3 above).
6. See Alasdair MacIntyre, *After Virtue* (Notre Dame, IN: University of Notre Dame Press, 1981).
7. See Stanley Hauerwas, *The Peaceable Kingdom: A Primer in Christian Ethics* (Notre Dame, IN: University of Notre Dame Press, 1983).
8. Paul Ricoeur, *Du texte à l'action: Essais d'herméneutique*, vol. 2 (Paris: Seuil, 1968), 258; see also Martin Honecker, *Einführung in die theologische Ethik: Grundlagen und Grundbegriffe* (Berlin: W. de Gruyter, 1990), 201.
9. Franz Böckle, *Fundamentalmoral*, 5th ed. (Munich: Kösel, 1991), 293-94.
10. Paul Ricoeur, *Soi-même comme un autre* (Paris: Seuil, 1990), 37.
11. Stanislas Breton, *Le Verbe et la Croix* (Paris: Desclée, 1981), 28.
12. See Henri Bouillard, *Karl Barth: Parole de Dieu et existence humaine*, vol. 2 (Paris: Aubier, 1957), 233-34.
13. Ibid., 234.
14. Ibid., 235.
15. Ibid., 238.
16. Ibid., 241.
17. Ibid., 233.
18. See P. Ricoeur, *Soi-même comme un autre*, 335, with reference to J. Rawls, *A Theory of Justice* (Cambridge, MA: Harvard University Press, 1971).
19. Saul Karsz, *Théorie et politique: Louis Althusser* (Paris: Fayard, 1954), 51.

20. René Simon, *Pour une éthique commune: Réflexions philosophiques et éclairages théologiques (1970-2000): Textes réunis par Éric Gaziaux et Denis Müller* (Paris: Cerf, 2004), 24-25.

21. Jean Ladrière, *Sens et vérité en théologie: L'articulation du sens*, vol. 3 (Paris: Cerf, 2004), 178.

22. Bouillard, *Karl Barth*, 258.

23. Ladrière, *Sens et vérité*, 183.

24. Ibid., 186-87.

25. See J. Ladrière, *Sens et vérité en théologie,* 3: 187.

26. Ibid..

27. D. Bonhoeffer, *Ethique*, trans. L. Jeanneret (Geneva: Labor et Fides, 1997), 97.

28. See Paul Ricoeur, "La liberté selon l'espérance," in *Le conflit des interpretations: Essais d'herméneutique* (Paris: Seuil, 1969), 393-415.

29. See Dietmar Mieth, "Autonomie: Emploi du terme en morale chrétienne fonda-mentale," in *Autonomie: Dimensions éthiques de la liberté*, ed. Carlos Josaphat Pinto de Oliveira (Paris: Cerf, 1978), 85-103; and Dieter Mieth, "Theologie und Ethik: Das unter-scheidend Christliche," in *Grundbegriffe der christlichen Ethik*, ed. Jean-Pierre Wils and Dietmar Mieth (Paderborn: F. Schöning, 1992), 209-24.

A Framework for Moral Discernment

Margaret A. Farley

I have argued elsewhere for the need for communal moral discernment in the church, based on the fact that all human knowledge is partial and the conviction that every human person is responsible to seek moral insight, but not alone.[1] This means that not only official church leaders, and not only theological ethicists, but all members of the church have a task of moral discernment in their own life situations and in the larger context of a believing and acting church. Church leaders have an important responsibility to discern and to teach, which implies also a responsibility to listen and to learn. The same is true of theological ethicists whose particular vocation is to aid the church and the world in moral discernment. But all co-believers also have a role in communal discernment—listening, learning, and contributing to the search for moral wisdom in and for the church.

My aim in this essay is to illuminate the meaning of moral discernment, whoever is engaged in it and however it is done, individually or together. I do this, however, not by delineating methods for discernment but by exploring three key human experiences that make moral discernment both possible and necessary. These are the experiences of moral obligation, free choice, and love.

The Experience of Moral Obligation

We speak readily of morally "binding" rules, of morally "binding" obligations within relationships, and of "obligatory" courses of action. We reason about the grounds of a moral obligation, its gravity, and the possibility of its release. These ways of speaking imply that we do not simply *know* that we are morally obliged in certain ways, but we *experience* being morally obliged. Acknowledgment of such experience runs throughout Western moral philosophy and theology, but few attempts have been made to understand how the experience itself arises. Exceptions may be found in Plato's "apprehend-ability" of truth,[2] Augustine's "my love is my weight,"[3] and Thomas Aquinas's implicit assumption that principles of the natural moral law "break through into human consciousness" (my language, not his), imprinting passively but awakening actively as we "speak" the received law of our being to ourselves.[4] Quite different exceptions appear in David Hume's theory of moral "sentiments" as an inbuilt affective trigger for the experience of moral obligation,[5] and in Immanuel Kant's description of "awe" before the law as well as the transformation of the will by categorical imperatives.[6]

Still, there is relatively little accumulated insight, or even interest, in how it is that we experience moral obligation.[7] To reflect on this question we must turn more carefully to the experience itself—that of others and our own. We have classic examples in the narrative histories of some individuals' lives—such as Martin Luther's "Here I stand," or Nelson Mandela's visibly persistent struggle against the horrors of apartheid, or the story of Joan of Arc's "I will not deny the voices I have heard." We have other examples in the lives of persons we know—parents caring for their children, children caring for their elderly parents, friends dedicating their lives to the demands of solidarity with the poor, writers evincing intellectual honesty even at a cost to their professional careers. In the community of theological ethicists we have examples such as Josef Fuchs, who refused to back down from his new insight (gained by listening to the experience of others) regarding the moral permissibility of the use of contraceptives. Almost everyone can recall experiences of their own, dramatic or mundane, of a clear moral obligation that cannot be denied, even if it can be refused.

Not everyone, of course, experiences moral obligation in the same way. A particular experience is shaped by a particular claim, by what generates it, and by the level of capacity in the individual to recognize it. We may experience it in a command of God, or through a whole way of believing and living shaped by the following of Jesus Christ, or in an encounter with a human person in grave need, or in the new claims of an unfolding great love, or through insight into the sheer logic of a moral principle that grasps our assent in a concrete context. Depending upon circumstances, personal history, a deeply ingrained perspective on the world, or on a particular event in the world, people can experience moral obligations that are at odds with the experiences of others. In a given situation, for example, one person can experience an obligation to oppose violent action, and another can experience an obligation to engage in it. Or, in the face of particular moral issues, we may not only disagree regarding policies of, for example, stem cell research, same-sex marriage, or capital punishment; our disagreement may be based in profoundly different experiences of moral obligation. These possibilities show something of the need for moral discernment, but also the need for at least initial respect for diversity in moral perceptions and sensibilities. Such diversity of conscience, we might say, does not ineluctably yield relativism, but it may—for many reasons—yield genuine pluralism.

Sometimes an experience of moral obligation precedes and prompts moral discernment. Whatever occasions or generates the experience, it frequently must be probed—to ascertain its authenticity, to understand its content, to discern its gravity, to deliberate about how we shall or shall not respond. Sometimes the experience of moral obligation does not come first but last in a search to understand what ought to be done or left undone, or what kind of person we ought to try to be; when this is the case, moral discernment leads to and yields an experience of moral obligation.

But what constitutes any experience insofar as it can be called an experience of "moral" obligation? It can, I think, be described in terms of five elements:[8] (1) It is an experience of a *claim* made upon us, a demand made of us. But (2) the claim itself is experienced as *addressed to our freedom*. Even if we theorize that there is no such thing as human freedom of choice, we experience this kind of claim as one to which we can respond or not.[9] (3) As a moral claim, it is experienced as, perceived as, *unconditional*.[10] It is not a matter of "if I want to avoid punishment, I ought to do X" or even "if I want to get to heaven, I ought to do X," but simply (though with reasons) "I ought to do X."

In a particular situation where the obligation is in tension with a competing claim, it may or may not continue to be experienced as unconditional. For example, a parent experiences an unconditional claim to love and care for each of her or his children, yet circumstances (special need or possibility) may be such that priority ought, at a given time and in a particular way, be given to one of them. This latter claim may, then, become the unconditional one at the center of a particular experience of moral obligation. In addition (4), the claim must at least appear to be *justifiable*, and hence legitimate. If upon reflection or the gaining of more information, I conclude that the claim is not able to be justified—that it is a false claim, or unfair, or a matter of my runaway superego, or a claim that is relativized because it is overridden by a competing claim—then it ceases to be experienced as a "moral" claim. For example, I may experience a moral obligation to participate in what I judge to be a just war, yet as I actually take part in this war, I discover that it has no moral legitimacy; in this case, my experience of moral obligation evaporates, or perhaps it modulates into an experience of obligation not to abandon my comrades, or it changes into a perceived claim to oppose the war.

(5) Finally, a moral claim is experienced as both an *obligating demand* and a *liberating appeal*. It is not just a felt requirement to sustain oneself as innocent. It is a liberating appeal because, even when a response to it appears extremely difficult, it is nonetheless experienced not as an alien imposition but a way of being "true to myself." Yet it is not thereby simply a desire of mine (although it may be in accord with at least some of my desires); rather, it appears as "larger" than myself or my own desires. It demands something *of* me. It is a form of command and even a call.

What this kind of description of the experience of moral obligation provides is a glimpse into what is at stake in the moral life—the springs of motivation and action, the determination of what one will be as well as do, the meaning of one's life. It also illuminates the utter significance of moral discernment in the exploration and identification of genuine moral obligation. Within the limits of this essay, the description I have offered remains but a thumbnail sketch of key elements in an experience of moral obligation. To clarify it further would require at least two additional considerations: first, distinguishing moral obligation (or claim or ought) from other kinds of obligations and oughts—such as intellectual, pragmatic, and aesthetic oughts; and, second, bringing this description of moral experience into relation with theories of moral development (like those of Lawrence Kohlberg,

Carol Gilligan, or Søren Kierkegaard, for that matter[11]). The key to a distinctive understanding of "moral" obligation lies primarily in the unconditionality of the claim and in a thorough explication of each of the other experiential elements that characterize it. While this analysis needs to be done, it is impossible to do here.

The usefulness of theories of moral development is evident in the light they shed on grounds and degrees of moral obligation. The experience of a small child is not likely to include the kind of experience of moral ought that I have just described. Although the term "moral" for behavior and its motivations is frequently used in developmental theories at every stage, most of the stages more accurately describe a capability for pragmatic obligations—obligations based on fear of punishment or desire for approval or gain. The kind of experience of moral obligation I have tried to describe seems to appear only in the mature stages of moral development. What this means for moral discernment is no doubt important, but it is another analysis that cannot be done here.

Free Choice

In pursuit of insight into the significance of moral discernment I now attempt another thumbnail sketch of a second profoundly important human experience: free choice. Free choice is a capability and an action whose power is the power of self-determination. It appears in many ways in human life, but perhaps nowhere more significantly than (as we have seen) as the determiner of response to a moral claim within the core of the experience of moral obligation. It is, of course, not an instrument in the "machine" of the human person, but the human person herself as moral agent, or at least potential moral agent. It is not my aim here to demonstrate that we possess a capacity for free choice but to explore what at least seems to be our experience of it. As Samuel Johnson is supposed to have said, "All theory is against freedom of the will; all experience for it."[12] A vantage point for this exploration emerges if we consider the question, "What do we choose when we choose?"[13] To follow this question leads us once again to levels within the human self that are central to the meaning of our lives.

Commonly we think that what we choose (when we make a free choice) is a particular thing or person or path or commitment. We choose among alternatives—as in choosing, for example, coffee or tea, this job or that, this form of relaxation or that. And while it is true that we can choose among certain states of affairs, or among objects such as specific persons or things, free choice does not really mean anything unless our choice is of an action of our own in relation to one or another competing option. Nothing "happens," nothing is effected or even attempted, in relation to coffee or tea unless we choose to drink (or buy or make or sell) coffee or tea; nothing "happens" in choices regarding persons unless we choose to companion (or befriend, or assist, or love, or use, and so on) this person or another; nothing is effectuated in relation to alternative potential jobs unless we choose to accept an offer of (or interview for or prepare for) one job in preference to another. Without choice of an action of our own (internal or external) in relation to competing alternatives, there is no choice at all. To recognize this, within the experience of free choice, is to discover a complex structure of affections and judgments that are part of what we choose when we choose.

If every choice is a choice of an action of our own, not just any sort of action even of our own can be an option for choice. There is important evidence that, for example, for an action to be a "viable" option, it must be an action in the present and an action that at least appears to us to be possible. Our choices surely can affect our future actions, but they do so through actions in the present—actions such as commitment, resolution, promise making, planning, preparing. And we do sometimes choose actions that appear impossible for us, but we do so by choosing to "try" to do them—if "trying" seems possible even though we expect ultimately to fail.

More significantly, the only kind of action that is a candidate for our choice is an action that in some way we want or desire to do. This seems to fly in the face of our at least occasional experiences of choosing to do something that we do not really want to do. But of course our affections and judgments may be ambivalent, ambiguous, erratic, seemingly tangled in complex ways. From some point of view we can want and yet not want to choose a particular action. We have competing desires for competing alternative actions in relation to competing objects of choice.

Yet, we cannot choose an action to which we are in every way indifferent or totally averse. A somewhat trivial example can reveal this: Suppose I have in hand a piece of cake, and I am hesitant about what to do with it. I can choose to eat it, or to keep it for another time, or to give it away to a friend, or even to bury it in the ground. I desire to eat it, since I am hungry; I also desire to save it for my evening snack when I anticipate being even more hungry; and I may desire to give it to my friend who is hungrier than I. It is unlikely, however, that I have any desire at all to bury it in the ground. If this is the case, then only the first three options are "live" options; the fourth cannot be chosen by me because there is no desire already within me to do it.

In a more serious example, suppose I am confronted with alternative possibilities for action in relation to a situation where personal safety is at stake—where my security competes with my love for a friend who is in need. My alternatives are to stand firm in a painful and dangerous situation or to run away from it. I want, desire, to stand firm (because, let us say, I see this as my duty, or because the friend whom I love needs me to do so), and I also want, desire, to run away from the situation (because I am afraid for my life, or because I know that my life is important for someone else). Both of these desired ways of acting are real alternatives for choice. But if I am so frightened that I have no desire to be courageous (if, that is, I am so overwhelmed by fear, or I have so little concern for the other in danger that the option of doing my duty or being faithful to my friend has no appeal whatsoever in the concrete moment), then there is no desired alternative and no possibility for present choice.[14]

Desire is therefore a qualifier of alternative actions to be chosen (and the mode of desire can vary—from, for example, desire for personal pleasure, to desire for a friend's well-being, to desire to be responsible in the use of a good, to desire to do God's will). Insofar as this is an accurate description of elements in our experience of choosing, something even more important emerges. Just as choice is never merely of things or persons but rather of the free agent's own actions (in regard to things, persons, states of affairs), so free choice is, more inwardly, concerned with the free agent's own spontaneous desires for these actions—desires that spring from and express a disposition of his or her being. To repeat, then, actions to be taken are alternatives for free choice only inasmuch as they are actually desired (in one way or another). Therefore, when we choose (among alternatives) an action of our own that is desired by us, we actually choose not only the action but the desire. While the desired actions to be taken are, prior to choice, only possibilities; the desires for these actions are, prior to choice, already actual. Choice is, essentially though partially, the ratification of one desire and the renunciation, or at least deferral, of the other(s).

There is, however, more to what we choose than this. One reason why this is so is that no desire is self-explanatory. We have long recognized the sorts of factors that unconsciously shape the personal history of each individual—the biological, genetic, societal, familial, environmental, psychological, and neurological factors that give rise to and shape our desires. But there is another way in which desires are not self-explanatory—not because of their past etiology but because of their present dependence on a root form of affectivity of which we can be consciously aware. Desire is an affective tendency, an inclination, that rises out of a more fundamental affective activity. We may desire one thing for the sake of another, in a long chain of desires, each rising out of the one before it (as in: I desire X because I desire Y because I desire Z). Even so, the whole chain is not self-explanatory; its intelligibility comes finally from a more radical affective activity, the affective activity that we call love.[15] This means that choice is not only of alternative possible actions and of the desires that have these actions as their objects. Free choice is most profoundly a choice between or among the at least implicitly conscious sources of our desires—that is, our loves.[16]

As should be obvious by now, the affections of human desire and love have a cognitive element within them. They are shaped by reasons. We can come to understand them (more or less), assess them, evaluate them, identify with them, or deny them. Free choice, then, has as its object not only an external action (and its object), but complex desires, loves, reasons, evaluations, judgments, and even *moral* judgments along with the very criteria by which such judgments are made. All of these are, or can be, presented to our freedom for ratification, deferral, or denial, and for issuance (or not) into the action to which they lead. This is why free choice is determinative of ourselves, in the deep regions of our being. This is why moral discernment is utterly important in the service of what we do and who we become—individually and together.

Love

Love is the third central human experience that is important to our understanding of the function of moral discernment. There are many definitions of love, some aiming to be normative, some descriptive. As with the experiences of moral obligation and of free choice, we can explore the experience of love—seeking in it, too, consistent constitutive elements. I draw here on the descriptive analysis of the experience of love provided by Jules J. Toner, S.J.[17]

According to Toner, human love is first of all a *response* to what is lovable—to the value, the being, the beauty, or usefulness of whatever is loved. This response is itself unitive; love is a *union* between lover and loved—even if the lover is unknown to the loved. The beloved is in the one loving, and the lover is in the one loved. But love is responsive and unitive precisely as an *affective affirmation* of what is loved. These elements in the experience of human love are constitutive of all kinds of human loves—whether for things or persons, for means or ends, for love of self or other-centered love.

Although human love is a responsive, unitive, affective affirmation of what is loved, we know that there are good loves and bad, wise loves and foolish, just loves and unjust. Love can be mistaken or distorted in its response to and affirmation of the beloved. If, for example, a mother loves her child when he is thirty in exactly the same way she loved him when he was three, her love and deeds of love are in some sense mistaken and may be harmful. If an owner of a factory loves his employees in the same way he loves his shining equipment, he loves them inadequately, even falsely—since they are persons, not machines. It begins to be clear, then, that the criterion, the norm for right and good and adequate love, is the concrete reality of the beloved—of whatever or whoever is loved. Just as knowledge can be true in terms of accuracy and adequacy, or it can be marred by ignorance, mistakes, and even lies, so love can be true and just, or it can be distorted, mistaken, even a lie.[18]

If the norm of a just and true love is the concrete reality of the beloved, everything will depend on how we interpret this reality. The reality to be interpreted encompasses both personal and nonpersonal beings—and the complex realities of their relationships, histories, contexts, actions, capabilities, *teloi*. Such interpretation is at the heart of moral discernment, which is in the service of moral obligation, free choice, love and desire, and action. In such discernment we need to know not only where to look—that is, to concrete realities and the forms of right love in relationships with ourselves, our neighbors near and far, the world and universe around us, and with God. We need also the methods and sources that illuminate what we see—whether contextual analysis, historical-critical examination, principles and narratives, and whether through the lenses of scripture, communal wisdom, the many disciplines of human study and knowledge, or the experience of particular persons or groups. We need explicitly to anchor and expand what we have seen regarding moral obligation, free choice, love and desire, and action within a theological perspective. For the fullest meaning of what I have been suggesting in this essay cannot be probed apart from our understandings and beliefs about God, human persons, the universe, creation and redemption, grace and salvation, and the ultimate integration of our loves in relation to what we love above all.

Moral discernment that reaches all the way to our own loves, desires, judgments, and experiences of moral obligation reaches ultimately thereby to the objects of our loves, desires, judgments, and experiences of moral obligation. It is part of the process of our relational self-determination—part, therefore, of the process of becoming who we are, centered within and beyond ourselves. I began this essay by asserting the importance of communal as well as individual moral discernment. I have come only to the threshold of such a shared task.

Notes

1. Margaret A. Farley, "Ethics, Ecclesiology, and the Grace of Self-Doubt," in *A Call to Fidelity: On the Moral Theology of Charles E. Curran*, ed. James J. Walter, Timothy E. O'Connell, and Thomas A. Shannon (Washington, DC: Georgetown University Press, 2002), 55-75.

2. Plato, *Republic* 6, as interpreted by Susan F. Parsons, "Concerning Natural Law: The Turn in American Aquinas Scholarship," in *Contemplating Aquinas: On the Varieties of Interpretation*, ed. Fergus Kerr (Notre Dame, IN: University of Notre Dame Press, 2003), 166-67.

3. Augustine, *Confessions* 9.9.

4. Aquinas, *Summa Theologiae* I-II, q. 90, a. 1, ad 1, q. 91, a. 2.

5. David Hume, *Treatise of Human Nature*, ed. L.A. Selby-Bigge (Oxford: Clarendon, 1968), III.2.5.

6. Immanuel Kant, *Critique of Practical Reason*, pt. I, bk. I, chap. 3; *Groundwork of the Metaphysics of Morals*, chaps. 1 and 2.

7. Important theological insights, however, can be found in, for example, Gerard Gilleman, *The Primacy of Charity in Moral Theology* (Westminster, MD: Newman, 1959), 13-14, 253-79; and Klaus Demmer, *Living the Truth: A Theory of Action*, trans. Brian McNeil (Washington, DC: Georgetown University Press, 2010), 118-25. For a philosophical description, see Maurice Mandelbaum, *The Phenomenology of Moral Experience* (Glencoe, IL: Free Press, 1955), 46-51.

8. I do not claim complete originality in this descriptive analysis. Parts of it can be found in some form in other theories. A primary influence on my own efforts to articulate this is from ideas shared with me by the late Jules J. Toner—ideas that remained unpublished at the time of his death.

9. Of course, if the claim is profound enough, and sufficiently in accord with who we are, our freedom may already be shaped in a way that, like Luther, we can say not only "Here I stand," but, "I can do no other." In this case, I would argue that the whole of the response is marked by freedom—previous free choices, and now a condition of the self that is often referred to as "liberty of spirit." It is also possible that we experience moral obligation in a situation where it seems we are not free to respond positively to it (as in an addict's helplessness in the face of a recognized obligation to discontinue certain activities). This element in the experience of moral obligation needs careful nuancing, therefore; but our general experiences signal its virtually universal presence.

10. To say that the claim is unconditional does not mean that there are no conditions that must characterize a situation out of which the claim is generated. Nor does it mean that the claim is necessarily absolute. Here again there are important nuances to identify were this a longer essay.

11. See, for example, Lawrence Kohlberg, *The Philosophy of Moral Development* (New York: Harper & Row, 1981); and Carol Gilligan, *In a Different Voice* (Cambridge, MA: Harvard University Press, 1982); and the countless publications of both of these authors since the 1980s. As for Kierkegaard, see his treatment of aesthetic, ethical, and religious stages in such major texts as *Either/Or, Concluding Unscientific Postscript to Philosophical Fragments*, and *Philosophical Fragments*.

12. James Boswell, *Life of Samuel Johnson*, ed. John Wilson Croker (Boston: Carter Hendee, 1832), 169.

13. For a previous effort on my part to analyze the experience of free choice, see Margaret Farley, *Personal Commitments: Beginning, Keeping, Changing* (San Francisco: Harper & Row, 1986), 25-29.

14. To understand how choice is possible or impossible in more complex situations than this, see the analysis I offer in an earlier essay, "Freedom and Desire," in *The Papers of the Henry Luce III Fellows in Theology*, vol. 3, ed. Matthew Zyniewicz (Atlanta: Scholars Press, 1999), 57-73.

15. For a fuller analysis of this, see Farley, "Freedom and Desire," 68-69.

16. To return to the examples I described earlier, we might say, "I desire to eat or keep my cake because I desire to satisfy my hunger"; we do not say, "I desire to satisfy my hunger because I desire myself"; we say, "I desire to satisfy my hunger because I love myself."

17. Jules J. Toner, *The Experience of Love* (Washington, DC: Corpus Books, 1968), reprinted in Jules J. Toner, *Love and Friendship* (Milwaukee, WI: Marquette University Press, 2003), 13-175. Anyone familiar with Toner's careful analysis will recognize how constrained by space is my rendering of it—in the barest of outlines. This constraint means, also, that I unfortunately offer as assertions what Jules Toner substantiates by persuasive analysis and argument.

18. For further analysis of these claims, see Margaret Farley, *Just Love: A Framework for Christian Sexual Ethics* (New York: Continuum, 2006), chap. 5.

Reasoning and Methodology in African Ethics[1]

Bénézet Bujo

We are familiar with the debate in ethics about the universality of norms and the planetary ethos as this is conceived by a theologian such as Hans Küng. This question is important when we compare the concept of ethics that is the fruit of Western philosophy with the concept that is found in a different cultural sphere. This was the main problem when missionary Christianity encountered the practices in sub-Saharan Africa and elsewhere, and it is far from being resolved. The teaching of the magisterium and the movement of globalization show that it still resonates today. In order to be a Christian, must one have peace, live as a democrat, and so on, and conform to the dictates of a certain kind of Christianity that has a specific cultural situation or to a philosophy based on a contextual background that is different in time and space? The following reflections seek to attempt to answer these questions.

What Is the Basis of African Ethics?

The only way to grasp the basic question about African moral behavior is to refer to anthropology, which is, so to speak, the driving force in everything. We can say that everything gravitates around life and that life is articulated in the community, including the community with God, and without forgetting the cosmic unity.

The Three-Dimensional Community as the Place Where the Person Is Constituted

Before going further, it is appropriate to underline that the community in Black Africa always has a threefold dimension, namely, the living, the dead, and the not-yet-born. And everything ultimately reposes in God, who is the very matrix of the community that is understood in this way. I need not speak at length about this affirmation concerning the place of God in the life of Africans, since, despite some opinions that cannot be taken seriously, the existence of a supreme being on whom everything depends must be considered an obvious fact for most African peoples.[2] Rather, I want to show how African ethics, although it may not always explicitly mention God, is articulated in daily living. It is in this context that I have mentioned the three-dimensional conception of community.

The essential and typical characteristic of this community is the life that is preserved and is increased by means of interpersonal relationships. First of all, the members of the partial community of the living can survive only through the mutual strengthening of one another's lives. This means that one exists only thanks to the others; or better, that one becomes a "human person" thanks to the others. The Sotho in southern Africa express this idea when they say *Motho ke motho ka batho ba babang,* or *Umuntu ngu muntu nga Bantu.*[3] The Barundi emphasize *Umuntu ni uwundi* ("The human person is constituted by the other"). In Congo-Kinshasa, one would speak here of *bisoïté,* a French word derived from the Lingala word *biso* ("us"). In a similar way, we have French nouns derived from Kiswahili: *sisi-logie* and *mimi-logie,* from *sisi* ("us") and *mimi* ("me/I"). This amounts to the affirmation that the "me/I" (*mimi*) includes the "us" (*sisi*) and vice versa.

All these African expressions affirm that in order to exist one must belong to a community where one feels accepted and where one also accepts the others and shares in their integral development. In other words, the person is not defined in Africa by means of the Cartesian principle of *cogito ergo sum,* which is based on intellectual performance. The determinative factor is the "bundle" of relatedness: "I am related, and that is why I exist by means of the others, that the others exist by means of me, and that ultimately we exist by means of one another."

Relatedness here is meant not only in terms of blood relationships (for example, membership in an ethnic group, a clan, or a family). In Africa, one can become a relative without having a purely biological origin in common. The various alliances (for example, the pact of blood, the initiation group, and so forth) are constitutive elements of this kind of relatedness. Ultimately, if the African ideal is thought through in a consistent manner, the bundle of relatedness is not limited to the groups that I have just mentioned. It includes the entire human race. This is what the Baluba of Kasayi in the Democratic Republic of Congo emphasize when they speak of *Muntu-wa-Bende-wa-Mulopo,* that is to say, "Every human being is of *Bende,* and he is of *Mulopo.*" *Bende* is the first human being, and *Mulopo* is God. As an ethnic conception, this principle means that one must always endeavor to discover and promote a reflection of God in each person one meets, without for a moment taking into account his or her origin in a family, a clan, an ethnic group, or a race.[4]

The same idea can be seen in the Banyarwanda when they speak of *Ubupfura,* the fundamental quality that ought to characterize every person. This "nobility of the heart" is an ideal toward which every member of the community should strive in order to enrich the others. In Burundi, people prefer to speak of *Ubushingantahe.* This complements *Ubupfura* magnificently, since both ideas refer to a state of being so thoroughly humane (*Ubumuntu/ubuntu/bumuntu*) that one makes oneself all things to all persons.[5] Besides this, the word *ubumuntu/ubuntu* or *bumuntu* is very widespread in many ethnic groups in Black Africa.

As I have indicated, its ultimate affirmation is always that a community can enjoy a life worthy of the name only if each member makes the other another "himself/herself." We can state this more concretely: One must give life to the other in such a way that each one gives birth to the other. This reciprocal act of giving birth is constituted by everything that I do to help the other to develop, so that he or she may increase in life on every level. In this way, after the biological birth of a child, the parents continue the work of giving birth—just as the child, through its acts of *ubumuntu*, gives birth to its own parents, brothers, sisters, and so on.[6]

Interpersonal relationships are not limited to the earthly community, which is only one part of the whole. The living in this world are in continuous interaction with the dead, whom John S. Mbiti calls "the living-dead."[7] Communion with the dead is realized permanently in acts of anamnesis aimed at increasing the life in the two "partial" communities, since in order to be happy and to continue to grow in their personalities, the dead need the support of those members of their family who are still in this world. It is thus appropriate to surround them with respect and affection, remembering their heroic actions and the place of their burial, offering them the first fruits of our harvests, or associating them in all our family celebrations.[8]

Likewise, the living in this world depend for the growth of their personality on the support of their dead. It is thanks to the intervention of the dead that "those on earth" can lead a healthy life without accidents, sickness, famine, or other harm. Families will no longer be afflicted with sterility. Descendants will be guaranteed forever. Here, too, we must emphasize the act of perpetually giving birth, which goes from the living to the dead and returns from the dead to the living.

Ultimately, however, the living and the dead can survive only thanks to the not-yet-born. This term does not necessarily refer to children in their mother's womb. The "not-yet-born" are all those children who even before their biological presence in the mother's womb[9] already constitute the hope of the living and the dead, thanks to their future potential, and who exist in the thought of God before they exist in this world.

The living and the dead know that it is these children who will have to continue to ensure their growth in life later on and to contribute to the process whereby their personal being will never cease to come into existence. This means that the not-yet-born are not neutral beings with a future potential. Rather, they are already included in the bundle of relationships both of the dead and of the living. Accordingly, African rationality sees them already as persons to whom we must hand on a new and welcoming world. It does not see the not-yet-born children as simply passive "recipients" of life. In their turn, they contribute through their presence and their future mission to give the dead and the living a hope of survival, and this is why they are eminently active builders of the future and the common good of humanity. The living can survive only thanks to these children who will one day be their worthy successors. The anamnesis that keeps the "living-dead" alive and continually makes them persons will be possible only thanks to this world of the not-yet-born, who give birth to their own predecessors so that these may have a new life.

As Anita Zocchi Fischer has noted,[10] this African conception of the three-dimensional community is situated on the level of contributive justice (*iustitia contributiva*). Scholars are beginning to grasp the importance of this factor in social and cultural development today. Every member of the community must get involved in the task of maintaining and increasing the most important common good, which is precisely life in all its ramifications and its variety.

The Role of the Cosmos in the Process of the Constitution of the Person

Although this point has not been extensively developed in African ethics, the cosmos plays an extremely important role in safeguarding the identity of the human person. In the world, the human being and the rest of creation live in a relationship so intimate that what happens to the one simultaneously concerns the other. In this sense, the human being is not only a part of the cosmos; we can also say that the human being is the "resumé" of the totality. Engelbert Mveng emphasized this more strongly than any theologian before him.[11] There is a vital flow between the human being and the cosmos, so that there is a genuine solidarity in creation that ultimately binds everything to the Supreme Being, who is God.

Many stories and legends illustrate this fact. Those who have been present at traditional healings have noted that the medical practitioner sometimes administers the medicine together with minerals, pieces of dry wood, animal bones, and so on, which must be applied to the patient. A superficial observer, or one who knows nothing of these practices, will doubtless find them irrational. But for African rationality, these natural elements, although they are apparently impersonal and inanimate, are paradoxically full of life and communicate the abundance of this life. The fact of touching a natural element or of smelling the scent of a plant creates harmony with the entire cosmos and reestablishes health in the holistic sense. Accordingly, the human being is not in the universe in order to exploit nature or to demonstrate to nature a superiority that is due to reason. Rather, the human being seeks to be an ally of nature and an ally who can exist only if everything survives. And it is in this context that the adage "I am related, therefore we exist" (*cognatus sum ergo sumus*) is proved true. The human being and the elements in the cosmos are not isolated atoms. They live in a continuous interaction, thanks to which they survive.

In many traditional milieus people are aware even today that certain forests or certain species of trees are protected. Certain mountains or portions of the territory are supposed to be sacred, and taboos are sometimes invoked in order to preserve them from abuse. But the fundamental idea is to save the creation, which is vitally important for the human being. Among the Bahema in the northeast of the Democratic Republic of Congo, for example, we find the ficus, a tree that invites respect because it incarnates the anamnetic idea. In this sense, it is a tree that is primarily reserved for planting on tombs, in order to represent the continuing life of the dead. It is therefore forbidden to vandalize it. It is planted on a tomb and thus incorporates the person who is at rest in this place.

What we have said about the Bahema applies equally to some other ethnic groups such as the Gikuyu and Maasai in Kenya, for whom certain trees are sacred or symbolize the presence of God. The leaves of other trees are employed to express forgiveness.[12]

This understanding of the elements of the cosmos seems to be rather widespread across Africa. Another example is the ethnic group of the Achewa in Malawi. In the Achewa tradition, the virgin forest is a place where life teems. But this sacred forest not only generates life for the plants, the insects, and the animals, it also concerns the life of the human being, and this is why traditionally the chief has a sacrificial hut in the forest where he offers gifts in the name of all the people and prays for rain, fertility, and the strengthening of all life. This means that the forest is in fact the place where God gives life to human beings just as much as to animals and plants.[13] The traditional Achewa chief is very attentive to the fact that if the forest is not preserved, there cannot be any rain nor any animals or plants, and that this would at the same time mean the end of human beings on earth.

The cosmic unity appears here without any ambiguity. The African consciousness of this finds expression in various rites. I have mentioned some when I spoke about medicine, and even clearer examples can be found in liturgical celebrations, which often take on a cosmic character. Elements of nature such as skins, furs, and teeth of animals, feathers of birds or of chickens, plants, minerals, and so on are always employed in these liturgies. The earth itself is also involved, even if only by means of kaolin or other kinds of clay that the participants smear on their bodies.[14]

A rapid overview of African tradition with regard to the cosmic dimension displays a tremendous dynamism, and this influences the spirituality and ethics of creation. The cosmic unity that is present in the African conception recalls the teaching of Saint Paul that the creation eagerly awaits the revealing of the children of God (Rom 8:19-22). The creation groans together with us, and like us, it awaits redemption. It is often the human being who destroys the harmony in nature and subjects it to slavery, without reflecting that through this action one contributes to one's own destruction.[15]

The reader will doubtless ask at this point whether the modern African still cultivates this conception of nature. The first thing that must be said is that it is not so certain that the modern African lacks all appreciation of the tradition of the ancestors. We know that many so-called modern African intellectuals have a weakness for the practices of their tradition, which seems to accompany them in a latent and patient manner (to borrow the expression coined by G. Bukasa Tulu Kia Mpansu, a sociologist from the Democratic Republic of Congo).[16] A recent study has confirmed the view that even today Africans are profoundly permeated by the invisible world that influences both their Christian faith and their social, economic, and political behavior.[17]

The last African Synod (October 2009) points eloquently in the same direction when it notes the recrudescence of belief in sorcery in almost the whole of sub-

Saharan Africa. When they speak of this phenomenon, the synod fathers call it a "scourge" from which Africans must be set free.[18] All these facts warn us against a hasty judgment that would dissuade us from continuing to pay any attention to the African tradition on the pretext that this has already been swallowed up by modernity. But even if it were true that Africans no longer remember the cultural richness of their ancestors, should this prevent us today from recalling it and adopting positive elements from this richness in order to receive fresh vigor as we take up the challenge posed by some deviations in our own society, which is in contact with other cultures that are not necessarily beneficial in every respect?

We must ask why Africans ought to be initiated into Western traditions that are more foreign to their own roots, while one deprives them of something that is closer to them and that they can more easily assimilate. It is at this level that the same synod proposes that "[t]raditional African religion and its cultures should be the object of in-depth academic studies culminating in diplomas in the Catholic universities in Africa and the faculties of the Pontifical Universities in Rome."[19] When Africans receive a solid formation in their tradition and are well informed about both the positive and the negative elements in their culture, they will be capable of living their own identity and of developing an ethic that will not be an import from somewhere else, without any relationship to the soil in which the Africans are deeply planted.

To take one example: In the field of ecological ethics, Africa would benefit from the adoption of the same respect for nature that the ancestors practiced, and this could also be a universal contribution to the protection of the creation.

At this point, we must ask how Africans who are not content with the status quo in their tradition elaborate ethical norms.

The Elaboration of Norms and the Moral Life

Given that the community and interpersonal relationships are of capital importance for the moral behavior of Africans, it is completely normal and logical that the constitution and the elaboration of norms should take place in the same framework. Two elements stand out in this context. First of all, we must emphasize the place of the spoken word in this community and its impact on interpersonal relationships. Second, we must ask how this word functions within the community in such a way that the moral behavior of each member contributes to the promotion of the common good in the African sense of this term, that is to say, encourages life in its three-dimensional character (the living, the dead, and the not-yet-born). This involves the whole cluster of problems connected with *palaver* as a community discourse that is concerned with constituting, discussing, and justifying norms and accompanying the individuals in the concrete application of the words that are the basis of moral behavior. This will help us to see a little more clearly the difference from some Western ethical theories that often seem to see an antithesis between individual responsibility and freedom on the one hand, and the intervention of the community on the other. The latter is often interpreted as the oppression of the individual, who is a person with inalienable rights.[20]

The Function of the Word in African Ethics

African anthropocentrism (which does not exclude theocentrism) is based on interpersonal relationships that in turn presuppose communication between the various members who make up the community. It is incontrovertible that one of the essential elements of communication is the word. It is the word that founds the community and maintains its cohesion—although it can also destroy the community. In Africa, the word is powerful in the biblical sense of this term, since it produces the effect it is meant to have (see Isa 55:10-11). The West could say *scripta manent verba volant* ("written things remain, words fly away"), but words do not fly away in Africa.

Indeed, words can be even more powerful than a written text. This makes it very important to uncover the full meaning of hearing; we cannot be content with a culture of visualization. And this is why traditional Africa attached great importance to the way people speak. This was something to be learned in the company of the sages, and this again means that in order to acquire this skill, one must become a better hearer. Hearing is not simply attentiveness. Rather, one must eat the word, chewing it well and digesting it. In some traditions, it was normal—as is still the case in certain places—for an aged person to invite a younger person to share a meal or a drink. While the younger one ate or drank, the host began to relate all the wisdom of the clan. The child or the younger person was thus eating and drinking the word, that is to say, the wisdom, together with the food and drink. In order to become wisdom, this word had to be chewed well and digested well. And this is possible only if one continues to keep company with the sages who are skilled in the art of letting wisdom penetrate the flesh and blood of others.

It is thus thanks to the company of the sages that one acquires the necessary instruments that can form the conscience. The word is always eaten and drunk with a view to the service of the community. In order to create relationships with others, and not to do harm to them, it must reemerge from within. Accordingly, it must not be privatized. It is destined to give birth to other lives, so that one can move on from the stage of the monad to that of the dyad, the triad, and the crowd.[21] In order to achieve this goal, the orator must always ask whether his or her word is a correct interpretation of the word of the sages, since it has power only on the basis of the foundational word of the ancestor who is supposed to have bequeathed the word of life and not the word of death. Only an exercise of this kind is capable of promoting reconciliation, justice, and peace in the human community.

This brief sketch of the role of the spoken word in Africa suffices to show the responsibility borne in Black Africa by the media of communication such as radio and television. It is easy to abuse the word when one perceives it as "power," thereby subjecting an entire people to oneself. This often happens in the political arena, where some of those who have responsibility for the nation make use of the means of oral communication to manipulate opinions, especially in illiterate milieus where the word that is transmitted by radio has an indisputable authority. The authors of this word do not in any way take account of the people, who suppose that what is said by the chief reflects the common good that the ancestors willed. It is true that the word pronounced by our political leaders today does not lack a reference to a higher order. But this no longer has the assent of true ancestors. Rather, it is backed by false ancestors who have now become great international powers in the world. This is a word deprived of its traditional dimension of anamnesis, which always activates the life-giving remembrance of the ancients and the ancestors.[22]

In connection with this central function of the word, let me once again emphasize the place occupied by hearing in the African tradition. The modern means of communication such as television and the Internet make their impact today by means of images. One has the impression that the culture of deafness is spreading, yielding ground to a culture where it is the visual that counts. People no longer have the time to listen, and it is usually only through images that a fact becomes credible. But just as Saint Paul spoke of "faith from hearing" (Rom 10:17, in Greek as *pistis ex akoēs*; in Latin, *fides ex auditu*), so the African can speak of "wisdom from hearing" (*sophia ex akoēs*, or *sapientia ex auditu*). Otherwise, we end up with a superficial culture in which people do not listen to one another and dialogue becomes impossible. However, hearing alone does not suffice.

As I have said, hearing can truly bear fruit only to the extent that everything one hears is well chewed and digested. And this work cannot be done in private. It comes to perfection in, with, and for the community. This is why the palaver (*lo, baraza, gacaca*) is necessary.

Masticating and Digesting the Word in Community

African ethics does not hold that the validity of ethical norms and their application are a responsibility that lies upon the "atomized" individual alone. It is possible that an isolated individual has badly chewed and badly digested the word that he or she has received. This makes the palaver the ideal place for testing the effectiveness of the word and ensuring that it contributes not to the destruction but to the building up of the community. In this context, the word is examined anew, so that if it has been badly masticated and insufficiently digested, it can be chewed and digested afresh in the mouth and stomach of the community. This is the time for the "rumination" in common of the word that has been heard; for although each individual is by definition a "ruminant" of the word, not every individual is always capable of performing this difficult task. The palaver must find out whether the wisdom contained in the word has been well assimilated, so that it can serve to knit together the interpersonal relationships that make life in the community grow.

There are various kinds of palaver: therapeutic, familial, suprafamilial, and administrative. Within each genre, one can draw a distinction between the irenic and the antagonistic palaver, depending on whether or not a conflict is involved. In general, the palaver is the ideal place for the elaboration, the justification, and the establishing of ethical norms.

The object of a palaver can be very varied, since the center of everything is the life that must be allowed to grow in its totality. In its concern for ethical norms, therefore, the palaver aims at the promotion of the human person in a holistic manner, taking account of moral, spiritual, and physical well-being. Since the ethic based on the palaver is primarily interested in life, and not in abstract principles, it is above all sapiential.

Unlike the discourse ethics of Jürgen Habermas and Karl-Otto Apel, for example,[23] the palaver is not content with purely rational arguments. In the procedural ethics envisaged by these two authors, one can enter into discussion only with persons who are capable of arguing rationally. This is not the case with the palaver, which is not limited to specialists who are thoroughly at home in intellectual life and alone can grasp rational nuances.

Gestures, symbols, proverbs, chants, and so on can play an important role in the course of a palaver. We may therefore say that the palaver includes all the members of the community and that it implies the intervention of the ancestors, who belong to the invisible world. Indeed, a palaver is genuinely effective and promotes the common good only if it also includes, at least implicitly, the not-yet-born, since decisions must be taken in view of a better world in the future for the coming generation, which at present is waiting to take the place of the living (who tomorrow will belong to the invisible world). The inclusion of the ancestors and of the not-yet-born in the process of the palaver means that we must mention the place of the cosmos. The decisions taken by the community must be in harmony with the whole of nature, since the human being—who is a microcosm within the macrocosm, to use a fine expression coined by Mveng[24]—can realize himself or herself truly only in association with this cosmos.

This procedure of the palaver brings us back to what we have said about the African understanding of contributive justice. Participation in the form of the palaver is a process that involves each individual member. Each one is invited to make a contribution that helps the community to find a good solution to ensure the increase of life, which is the highest common good. This is never a question of only receiving or only giving. Everyone is involved in the interaction between giving and receiving. One who participates actively in elucidating the problems that are being debated endeavors to propose paths that can make the solution easier for the others, while at the same time allowing oneself to be instructed and enlightened by these others. In this way, he or she in turn benefits from the interlocutors, who make it easier to reach a better understanding and decision.

This conception of contributive justice also concerns the dead and the not-yet-born, since African rationality does not perceive them as beings who are passive in the course of the palaver. The community of the dead is explicitly consulted and must make its own contribution, so that the living may be able to live in peace and harmony—thereby ensuring the survival of the dead. Although the not-yet-born are not invoked explicitly, their contribution cannot be forgotten, since they are located at a profound level in the relational bundle and therefore activate the community's hope for a better future. In this way, they prompt the living and the dead to make the right decisions and thus ensure that life will not be interrupted. Ultimately, this means that the not-yet-born are not merely beings with a future potential for whom one does everything without receiving anything in return. Rather, they themselves share in the preparation of their future by influencing the process and the decisions of the palaver.

These remarks about contributive justice reveal another important difference with regard to discourse ethics. The discussion in the palaver is not only interested in establishing or justifying the principles of ethical behavior in a formalistic manner. Ethics based on the palaver is equally interested in the substance of the norms. In other words, it is not only content with establishing the correctness of the principles; it is also concerned with the concrete application of these norms. The existing norms, which are often based on the words and gestures of the ancestors and the ancients, are called into question in the course of the palaver. The community expresses doubt about their applicability and their efficacy with regard to the increase of life.

Once this doubt has been removed, the community is not content with formulating a new principle. It also accompanies the individuals in the application and realization of the norm that has been found. In this, it differs from communitarian thinking, which rightly protests against the atomization of the individual but does not think that the community ought to intervene in the concrete application of moral principles by individuals. The community makes a profound imprint on the individual, but the decision that is taken in moral conduct is individual. African ethics takes a different path, because it sees the community not only as a reality that makes a profound imprint on the individual but as a reality that must accompany him or her in, before, during, and after the decision that is taken with regard to something that is seen as vital for everyone.

This observation brings us to the problem of liberty, which we cannot discuss here.[25] The essential point can be summarized as follows. We have seen that the fundamental conception in Black Africa is not only that one becomes a person thanks to interpersonal relationships but that persons give birth to each other in order that life may be strong and intense. This also involves liberty, since one is not free on one's own. One becomes free "thanks to," "with," and "for" the others. Accordingly, the individual's mission is to give birth to the liberty of the others, just as their task is to give birth to the liberty of the individual. It is in this interaction that people give birth to one another and make the community free. The "I" cannot call itself free as long as the "we" is not set free, and vice versa. The individual must be with the community, so that all may be with each one. This also means that liberty does not only consist in "being free from." At the same time, it means "being free thanks to, for, and with." In the African perspective, liberty thus includes a contributive dimension that is not only receptive or self-centered but is participatory and is concerned for the life of the living, the dead, and the not-yet-born.

Conclusion

The African rationality that I have attempted to present raises a number of questions with regard to classical Western ethics, which is based on a different way of doing philosophy. One example is the Western ethical discourse that is based on the natural law, whereas African ethics puts the community and interpersonal relationships in the center. Unlike Western Catholic theology, it knows no separation between the natural and the supernatural or between the sacred and the profane. God's creation is one. And it is as one totality that it manifests God and returns to him. We can see the difference such a concept makes in the model of the relationships between church and state. The meaning is not that one must practice a religious fundamentalism, but rather that one must propose a model where genuine human life as willed by God exists only in the unity of the human person. It is the task of the traditional palaver to work out how this should be formulated in concrete terms.

I should also mention the teaching about the individual conscience as the ultimate authority. According to the logic of the palaver, this cannot mean the absolutizing of the individual's will. The word that is eaten and forms the conscience must confront other opinions and must enter the mouth and the stomach of the community in order that its innocence may be tested. This procedure eliminates fundamentalist tendencies that, following the example of ethics, could subjugate the community to a kind of dictatorship.

Once this is said, I must immediately add that African ethics with its own rationality is not impermeable in relation to other models. On the contrary, it knows universally accessible principles that one can unhesitatingly call universal. Here it suffices to recall the Luba principle of *Muntu-wa-Bende-wa-Mulopo* noted above; and we know that many African proverbs offer us a teaching that is not limited to one group or region, but encompasses the whole of humanity. Faithful to its praxis of the palaver, African rationality wants to be a partner for other rationalities, in order that the human race may be enriched by a patient and fraternal dialogue and can thus reflect the diversities that the Creator has bestowed on it.

Notes

1. English translation by Brian McNeil.
2. I refer the reader here to what I have written elsewhere: Bénézet Bujo, *Die ethische Dimension der Gemeinschaft: Das afrikanische Modell im Nord-Süd-Dialog* (Freiburg:

Universitätsverlag, 1993), 21-23; B. Bujo, *Introduction à la théologie africaine* (Fribourg: Academic Press, 2008), 128-30.

3. See the commentary by Musa W. Dube, "'I Am Because We Are': Giving Primacy to African Indigenous Values in HIV/AIDS Prevention," in *African Ethics: An Anthology of Comparative and Applied Ethics*, ed. M. F. Murove (Scottsville, South Africa: University of KwaZulu Natal Press, 2009), 188-217, at 212.

4. On this subject, see the study by Tshiamalenga-Ntumba, "Afrikanische Philosophie: Zum originären Vertrauen des afrikanischen Menschen," in *Eglise et droits de la société africaine*, ed. A. Mutombo-Mwana and E.-R. Mbaya (Mbujimayi: Cilowa, 1995), 109-20.

5. For a very illuminating study of these concepts, see I. Consolateur, "La conception du pouvoir traditionnel dans la sagesse rwandaise: Tradition et foi chrétienne pour un monde meilleur" (licentiate dissertation, University of Freiburg, 2007), 45-55; M. A. Niyirora, "Pour une éducation à la paix au Rwanda: Une réflexion morale et catéchétique" (licentiate dissertation, University of Freiburg, 2009), 59-61.

6. See M. Kayoya, *Sur les traces de mon père* (Bujumbura, Burundi: Presses Lavigerie, 1971), 26f. See the more detailed elaboration of this concept in B. Bujo, "Für eine Spiritualität des Lebens in Schwarzafrika," in *Christliches Ethos und Lebenskultur*, ed. G. Augustin et al. (Paderborn: Bonifatius Druckere, 2009), 625-35.

7. See J. S. Mbiti, *African Religions and Philosophy* (London: Heinemann, 1992), 25f., 50, 53.

8. On this question of the relationship between the dead and the living, see B. Bujo, "Esquisse d'une eschatologie africaine et chrétienne," in Bujo, *Introduction à la théologie africaine*, 120-26.

9. This is why expressions such as "unborn" or "not born" are not precise in African theology. It is preferable to bring out the dynamic aspect of the community, with its future potential, by a term such as "not-yet-born."

10. See A. Zocchi Fischer, "Beteiligungsgerechtigkeit als Struktur- und Verhaltensnorm: Rechte und Pflichten angesichts von Marginalisierung und Exklusion" (Ph.D. diss., University of Freiburg, 2009), 294-310.

11. E. Mveng, *L'Afrique dans l'Eglise: Paroles d'un croyant* (Paris: L'Harmattan, 1985), 12f.

12. On this subject, see especially S. K. Gitau, *The Environmental Crisis: A Challenge for African Christianity* (Nairobi: Acton, 2000). See also P. N. Wachege, *Jesus Christ Our Muthamaki (Ideal Elder): An African Christological Study Based on the Agikuyu Understanding of Elder* (Nairobi: Phoenix Publishers, 1992), 48-55.

13. See B. Bujo, "Ökologie und ethische Verantwortung aus afrikanischer Perspektive," in B. Bujo, *Die ethische Dimension der Gemeinschaft*, 197-214, at 199-200.

14. See Mufuta-Kabemba, "L'art dans la célébration cosmique," in *Méditations africaines du sacré: Célébrations créatrices et langage religieux*, Proceedings of the Third International Symposium of CERA, Kinshasa, February 16-22, 1986 (Kinshasa, Congo: FTC Publishing, 1987), 193-207, at 203-5. See also Mudiji-Malamba-Gilombe, "Liturgie cosmique et langage religieux: Pour une conciliation universelle par la prière liturgique," in Proceedings of the Third International Symposium of CERA, Kinshasa, February 16-22, 1986 (Kinshasa, Congo: FTC Publishing, 1987), 241-49, at 245-49.

15. For an exegetical commentary, see, for example, U. Wilckens, *Der Brief an die Römer*, vol. 2, Evangelisch-katholischer Kommentar zum Neuen Testament 6 (Zurich:

Benzinger, 1980), 156: A. Ganoczy, *Aus seiner Fülle haben wir alle empfangen: Grundriss der Gnadenlehre* (Dusseldorf: Patmos, 1989), 77-79.

16. See Buakasa T. K. M., "L'impact de la religion africaine sur l'Afrique d'aujourd'hui: Latence et patience," in *Religions africaines et Christianisme*, International Symposium of Kinshasa, January 9-14, 1978 (Kinshasa: FTC Publishing, 1979), 20-32.

17. See G. ter Haar, *How God Became African: African Spirituality and Western Secular Thought* (Philadelphia: University of Pennsylvania Press, 2009). See also the article by B. Bujo, "Ce que l'on pourrait attendre du Deuxième Synod pour l'Afrique," *Hekima Review* 41 (2009): 19-29.

18. See "Synode des Evêques: Liste finale des propositions," *Synodus Episcoporum Bulletin*, Bureau de Presse, proposition 13. This text can be accessed at http://eucharistiemisericor.free.fr/fichier_livres/091208_propositions_synode.pdf.

19. Ibid.

20. We cannot discuss the details of this question here. See B. Bujo, *Wider den Universalanspruch westlicher Moral: Grundlagen afrikanischer Ethik*, Questiones disputatae 182 (Freiburg: Herder, 2000), 70-104. The English translation of this work is *Foundations of an African Ethic* (New York: Herder & Herder, 2001), 75-106. See also B. Bujo, *Die ethische Dimension der Gemeinschaft*, 53-82.

21. For these terms, see E. Mveng, *L'art d'Afrique noire: Liturgie cosmique et langage religieux* (Paris: Mame, 1964), 75-85; E. Mveng, "Essai d'anthropologie négro-africaine," *Bulletin de Théologie Africaine* 1 (1979): 229-39.

22. See B. Bujo, *Die ethische Dimension der Gemeinschaft*, 65f.

23. See J. Habermas, *Moralbewusstsein und kommunikatives Handeln* (Frankfurt: Suhrkamp, 1983); K.-O. Apel, *Diskurs und Verantwortung: Das Problem des Übergangs zur postkonventionellen Moral* (Frankfurt: Suhrkamp, 1988). For a commentary, see B. Bujo, *Wider den Universalanspruch westlicher Moral*, 82-104 (*Foundations of an African Ethic*, 54-71).

24. E. Mveng, "Essai d'anthropologie négro-africaine," 234.

25. See the following earlier studies: B. Bujo, *Wider den Universalanspruch westlicher Moral*, 149-81 (*Foundations of an African Ethic*, 107-30); and B. Bujo, *Introduction à la théologie africaine*, 141-45.

THE PRESUMPTION
AGAINST WAR AND VIOLENCE

Brian V. Johnstone

"The presumption against war," invoked by the U.S. bishops in their pastoral letter *The Challenge of Peace* (May 3, 1983),[1] became a staple in Catholic literature on the themes of war and peace.[2] This is related to a "common concern to avoid violence,"[3] from which, it is said, arise both just war doctrine and pacifism. As I understand the argument, the presumption against violence is more fundamental; the presumption against war is a specification of the presumption against violence.

My contention is that the notions of the "presumption against violence" and the "presumption against war," taken by themselves, are not helpful contributions to the development of the just war tradition. But my argument does not entail accepting the critique of these notions as put forward by George Weigel and James Johnson.[4] The most well-known reply to Weigel's thesis is that of the Archbishop of Canterbury, Rowan Williams.[5] Williams, however, still employs the terms "presumption against violence," and "*prima facie* duties" which, as I will seek to show, are inadequately grounded.

My first criticism is that Weigel, while appealing to "the classic tradition,"[6] does not explain what constitutes "tradition." Nor does he explain why tradition should be morally binding, why this particular tradition is morally binding, how the content of the tradition is selected, who selects that content, on what criteria the selection is made, or who decides whether new developments can be accepted in the tradition. In fact, it is Weigel himself who decides on the answers to these questions. The just war tradition may not be subordinated to the ends of a "statecraft," as Weigel contends; this is an arbitrary narrowing of the tradition.

Paul Griffiths's main criticism is that Weigel does not explain where the burden of proof lies.[7] Griffiths argues, rightly in my view, that for the Catholic tradition on just war, the burden of proof lies with those who would seek to justify war. According to Griffiths, in the logic of the just war doctrine, the tests required by that doctrine have to be satisfied before the presumption against war can be overcome. I agree that the burden of proof is the key. But there is a need to explain why the burden is located in the way it is. Further, the tests of the just war doctrine have to be passed if the war is to be justified, but why are these tests required in the first place, and why does the passing of these tests morally justify a war? These points are likewise not explained. To provide such an explanation we need a more fundamental moral framework. I hope to provide a sketch of such a framework.

Tradition, as I am using it here, means more than Alasdair MacIntyre's argument across time about the goods of the tradition.[8] The word here means a teleological, or goal-oriented process that is ordered by the intentions to which the community is committed and embodied in the practices that express their intentions.[9] We are concerned here with the Catholic tradition. A first question is, "Which constitutes the fundamental intentions of this tradition, justice or love?" Weigel's position seems to presume the primacy of justice, and furthermore he seems to envision justice as primarily concerned with the violation of justice in respect to a particular nation. Instead, I would argue that justice is not primary; the primacy belongs to charity, which requires justice in order to protect the basic relations of charity between individuals, groups, and nations.

Unless justice is given this universal range by charity, justice is in danger of becoming the justification of the wars of a particular state for the purposes of the particular state. We could recall here the comment made by Leroy Walters that all the theologians whose theories he discussed ended up justifying the wars of their own nations.[10]

There is the further question of the interpretation of Thomas Aquinas, in particular, of *Summa Theologiae*, II-II, q. 40, a. 1, to which both sides of the debate appeal.[11] Herbert McCabe interprets St. Thomas as follows. In modern usage the word "charity" often conveys the idea of individual kindness manifested in giving help to the needy, and this makes it hard for us to appreciate the central place St. Thomas gives charity in his thinking about war and peace. Charity here means political charity. Thomas adopts and expands Aristotle's political notion of *philia* (*amicitia*, or friendship) as his model for the *caritas* that is the foundation of the community of the human family as not merely creatures but children of God. The city state or *polis*, for Aristotle, had its basis in *philia*. This means not so much friendship in our modern sense but "companionship with trust."[12] In St. Thomas's enlarged conception, political charity means companionship in a shared project to create together not merely a *polis* but an inclusive human family.[13]

This element of charity was preserved in the subsequent development of the tradition among others by Francisco Suarez (d. 1617),[14] and even by Hugo Grotius (d. 1645).[15] Subsequently, however, it was lost sight of, even in standard "Catholic" accounts of the doctrine, and the narrow concept of justice between nations became the guiding criterion for the interpretation of the just war doctrine. I would suggest that in the Catholic tradition charity has primacy and that charity as friendship or "companionship with trust" guides social relationships.

In the political sphere, however, we need a further notion to express the combined working of charity with justice; this notion is "civic concord." As Gregory Reichberg notes, we occasionally find Aquinas drawing out practical implications from the view that civic concord results more formally from *caritas* than from *justitia*.[16] Love of friendship cannot adequately shape the complex relationships of human society nor deal with the conflicts that inevitably arise. To deal with these features of human society, charity requires justice in order to protect the more fundamental relationships of friendship. Justice then requires us to establish the social, legal, and political structures that are necessary to sustain, foster, and protect the more fundamental relationships of friendship. I am defending here a view of the relationship between charity and justice. According to this view, justice is not fundamental nor is it "perfected" by charity. Rather, charity is fundamental and charity requires justice, both the virtue of justice and those social, political, and legal structures that embody justice. Charity without justice would be ineffectual and inadequate to promote, historically, the development of the whole human family.

In constructing the moral framework I have identified four structures:

1. the historical goal-oriented tradition directed toward unifying the whole human family;
2. the dynamism within that tradition that is charity, expressed as universally extended companionship with trust;
3. charity, working with justice, to promote civic concord; and
4. civic concord, guided by universal charity, extended to concord between nations.

I now come to the more particular level of determining where the burden of proof lies and how the traditional tests are to be applied. In this context I will argue that there is a difficulty with the "presumption against violence."[17] James Childress argued that "[B]ecause it is *prima facie* wrong to injure or kill others, such acts demand justification." In just war theory the function of the various criteria is to provide this justification or, as Childress also puts it, to "overrule" the *prima facie* obligation. What is meant by *prima facie* duties?

The notion of *prima facie* duties was clarified if not inaugurated in W. D. Ross's *The Right and the Good*. Ross proposed that there are many "morally significant relations" in which we live. Each of these relations is the foundation of a *prima facie* duty, which is "more or less incumbent" on us, "according to the circumstances of the case."[18] In a particular situation, I may form the "considered opinion" that one of these duties is more incumbent on me than another. This being so, "I am bound to think that to do the *prima facie* duty is my duty *sans phrase* in the situation." The ethical theory here would seem to be some kind of intuitionism. I consider both concepts—the "presumption against violence" and that of "*prima facie* duties"—at least as explained by Ross and Childress, as unsatisfactory.

I propose that it is only within a tradition that we can explain the grounds for a presumption of this kind and provide a framework to explain how a presumption may be reasonably overcome. As used here, the concept of tradition has three levels. First, it refers to a basic intention, guided by charity working with justice, to seek the goal of a united human family. Second, it refers to the historical embodiment of this intention in the practice of the community of the church pursuing this end through engagement with the existing social and political structures. Third, it refers to the particular sub-tradition that has come to be called the "just war" tradition. The function of this theory was to provide a framework for assessing whether war or particular wars could or could not be considered as a coherent expression of the higher level intentions that guided the tradition.

It is in this framework that we can meaningfully ask questions about the practice of war. Those persons who are committed to the tradition, that is, who order their personal intentions according to the intentions of the tradition, have to inquire whether the practice of war can be an embodiment of those intentions. It would appear that war cannot be accepted as such, since war entails the killing of human persons and tears apart the human family. Because the basic intentions are directed to the promotion of peace, the burden of proof falls on those who would argue that war is not contrary to these intentions but can be shown to be ordered to the goals of those intentions. The question then is, can the practice of war be ordered and limited in such a way that it can embody the intentions that guide those who have committed themselves to this tradition?

The tests provided by the just war theory were proposed as guides to answering this question. The first test is whether the intention that guides those engaged in a particular war is coherent with the basic intentions of the tradition; the requirement was that this intention be directed to "peace." This, I argue, does not only mean peace between adversarial nations but overall peace, what I have called the unity of the human family. This is what "right intention" means.[19]

We then move from the intention to promote unity, that is, from the sphere of charity, to the sphere of justice, that is, the structures that promote and protect the historical project aimed ultimately at the unity of the human family. Here we raise questions about social and political structures. Again, following the logic of our basic intentions, we inquire whether there has been a violation of social and political structures such that a nation, including our own and those of other nations, can no longer fulfill its task of protecting and promoting peace. If there has been such a violation, then justice, guided by our basic intentions, may require us to intervene so as to counter the violation. This could mean resisting armed aggression against our own nation or against other nations or groups by armed force. This is the question of "just cause."

Next comes the question of proper authority. Only a person or group with the capacity to order the forceful activities of the community, normally the nation, according to the basic intentions of the tradition, that is to peace, may initiate the war. The capacity to order the activities of the community resides in the first place with the members of that community. But the effective ordering will usually be the task of someone who has been designated to lead the community. Such a person will normally be one who has been designated by a just process to order the activities of the community or nation, according to its intentions—that is, a political leader.

Only those forceful actions that repel the aggression, either by counter-attack or by removing the capacity of the aggressor to attack, can be recognized as being coherent with the intentions of the tradition. Such an action could then be judged to be proportionate to the due ends as established within the tradition. Note that what is required is that the act be proportioned to the particular end of repelling a particular act of aggression and so enabling the nation or community under attack to resume its contribution to the unity of the human family. Only in this way can the act of armed resistance be proportioned to the primary end of the community and of the tradition—that is, peace. The proportion here is the proportion of the act to its end and *not* the "proportion" between the harmful effects and the beneficial effects of an act of war.[20]

If the notion of a presumption against violence and war is not viable, what then could provide a shared vision within the one tradition for just war thinkers and pacifists? I suggest that they might agree that they are both committed to a fundamental intention, in charity, to seek the universal family of humankind, but that they differ as to the kind of historical process that could embody that intention. Just war theorists argue that war can be so ordered and limited that it could, at least in theory, be the embodiment of that fundamental intention. Pacifists are convinced that it cannot. Just war theorists would have to recognize the role of pacifists within the tradition in compelling them to scrutinize carefully that theory. The pacifist rejection of all war is both a witness to the condition of peace that would be the most coherent historical expression of the fundamental intention of the tradition. Its presence in the tradition is also a continuous reminder that all claims that some form of war can be a coherent expression of that intention are historically conditioned and imperfect.

Notes

1. See *The Challenge of Peace—God's Promise and Our Response: A Pastoral Letter on War and Peace by the National Conference of Catholic Bishops* (Washington, DC: United States Catholic Conference, 1983), 93.

2. Lisa Sowle Cahill, *Love Your Enemies: Discipleship, Pacifism, and Just War Theory* (Minneapolis, MN: Fortress Press, 1994), 3. See also Richard B. Miller, "Aquinas and the Presumption against Killing and War," *Journal of Religion* 82, no. 2 (2002): 173-204.

3. Cahill, *Love Your Enemies*, 1.

4. For a recent presentation of Weigel's views, see George Weigel, "The Just War Tradition," National Review Online, December 12, 2009, http://article.nationalreview.com/417745/the-just-war-tradition/george-weigel. For a critique, see Christ Eberle, "The 'Presumption against War': Eberle Critiques Weigel," Mirror of Justice: A Blog Dedicated to the Development of Catholic Legal Theory, December 15, 2009, http://mirrorofjustice.blogs.com/mirrorofjustice/2009/12/the-presumption-against-war-eberle-critiques-weigel.html.

5. Rowan William and George Weigel, "War and Statecraft: An Exchange," *First Things* 141 (March 2004): 14-28, at 15.

6. See Miller, "Aquinas and the Presumption against Killing and War."

7. George Weigel, "Just War: An Exchange. Debate with Paul J. Griffiths," *First Things* 122 (April 2002): 31-36.

8. See Alasdair Macintyre, *After Virtue*, 3rd ed. (Notre Dame, IN: University of Notre Dame Press, 2007), 222. The full definition is: "A living definition then is an historically extended, socially embodied argument, and an argument precisely in part about the goods which constitute that tradition."

9. Brian V. Johnstone, "Moral Experience in the Test of History," *Église et Théologie* 16 (1985): 319-38; Brian V. Johnstone, "Can Tradition Be a Source of Moral Truth? A Reply to Karl-Wilhelm Merks," *Studia Moralia* (1999): 431-51; Brian V. Johnstone, "¿Qué es la tradición?" in *La ética cristiana hoy: Horizontes de sentido: Homenaje a Marciano Vidal*, ed. Miguel Rubio, Vicente Garcia, and Vicente Gómez Mier (Madrid: Instituto Superior de Ciencias Morales, 2000); and Brian V. Johnstone, "The Argument from Tradition in Roman Catholic (Moral) Theology," *Irish Theological Quarterly* 69 (2004): 139-55.

10. Leroy Walters, "Historical Applications of the Just War Theory: Four Case Studies in Normative Ethics," in *Love and Society: Essays in the Ethics of Paul Ramsey*, ed. James Johnson and David Smith (Missoula, MT: Scholars Press, 1974), 136. The authors in question are Francisco de Vitoria (d. 1546), Hugo Grotius (1645), Balthazar Ayala (1548), Alberico Gentili (d. 1608), and Paulus Vladimiri (d. 1435). In a historical study of the application of the doctrine to particular situations by some of its "classic" proponents, Leroy Walters notes that these authors developed their versions of the doctrine, in significant part, to defend the war policies of their own countries. He writes: "The past theorist's preponderant use of just war thought as an apologetic instrument can be viewed as a warning—a caution against the possibility of self deception in moral reasoning when matters of crucial importance to one's own nation are at stake." Thus, where an application of the "just war doctrine" functions as an apologia for the war policies of a particular nation, a "hermeneutic of suspicion" is in order. The arguments in favor of war must be scrutinized with care.

11. Thomas Aquinas, *Summa Theologiae* II-II, q. 40. a. 1 deals with the question of whether it is always sinful to wage war.

12. Herbert McCabe, "Manuals and Rule Books," in *Understanding Veritatis Splendor*, ed. John Wilkins (London: SPCK, 1994), 64.

13. Perhaps this is reading too much into St. Thomas. An interpretation of the Catholic tradition as directed to the forming of one human family is to be found in Joseph Joblin, *L'église et la guerre: Conscience, violence, pouvoir* (Paris: Desclée de Brouwer, 1988), 300.

14. Francisco Suarez, S.J., *De caritate*, disp. 13, sec. 1. See *Omnia Opera*, vol. 12 (Paris: Vivès, 1858), 737.

15. Timothy M. Renick, "Charity Lost: The Secularization of the Principle of Double Effect in the Just-War Tradition," *The Thomist* 58 (1994): 458.

16. Gregory Reichberg, "Is There a 'Presumption against War' in Aquinas's Ethics?" *The Thomist* 66, no. 3 (2002): 335.

17. James E. Childress, "Just-War Theories," *Theological Studies* 39 (1978): 427-45.

18. W. D. Ross, *The Right and the Good* (Indianapolis, IN: Hackett, 1988), 19.

19. We ought to recognize that a particular nation has a right to continue to exist and to live in peace, because only as such can it effectively participate in the shared process toward the unity of the whole human family and so fulfill its purpose. We ourselves are

justified in committing our allegiance to a particular nation because we are committed to making a contribution to that unity of the whole human family and this particular nation is such that it can make such a contribution. To adhere to a particular nation solely because it protects us would not seem to be a just reason.

20. For the notion of an act being proportioned to its end, see Aquinas, *Summa Theologiae* II-II, q. 64, a. 7.

Urban Life, Urban Ethics[1]

Miguel Ángel Sánchez Carlos

Ethics and the City

Urban life or urban ethics—that is, the meaning and orientation of all human behavior under the effects of the diverse factors that make up the social phenomenon we call the city—is a relatively new theme in both the sociocultural arena and Christian ethics. I believe that a reflection on that theme requires consideration of the specific characteristics of what we call the urban way of life.[2]

The modern city is diverse: one of its main characteristics is cultural diversity, which can be traced to the evolution of the mercantile city in the late eleventh century, when human beings began to develop a distinctively urban identity. In this medieval urban identity we find the seed of what is now called civil ethics: the dispositions that regulated social, cultural, and commercial life (such as the Charter of Arras in 1194, which permitted an outsider to become a resident protected by the law of the city after living there for a year and a day without opposition) were gradually separated from the religious or cultural factors that governed human society.[3]

But this diversity has always been affected by the interests of social class or ideological factors. Diversity was rejected by the liberal bourgeoisie, which was white, male, and Christian; it became prevalent only in the late twentieth century, mainly in Europe and the United States through the new concepts of the "public realm" and "civil ethics."[4] The cultural dimension of this diversity, the subject of this reflection, is one of many elements that have emerged in modern cities.

What I have said suggests that the city is an ambiguous phenomenon: it is the laboratory of a vibrant culture, but it excludes all those who do not share in that vibrancy. This ambiguity is a permanent feature in the history of cities. In Latin America, for example, the development of Spanish cities was associated with political power and excluded the first peoples who lived there—the indigenous groups who were relegated to rural life, to "otherness," were excluded from the public space. There was a brief exception during the wars of independence, when the rural was momentarily incorporated into the urban picture.[5] The same thing was happening in Europe, and in the mid-nineteenth century Latin American cities entered that public space by copying European urban development in the new world. As an ethical consequence of the urbanization process, they too created their own symbolic universes and recreated their own urban patterns, putting their own stamp on individualism and competition between individual and collective interests.[6]

The Modern Secular City

For our purposes it seems useful to consider what the Fifth General Conference of the Latin American bishops noted in the document of Aparecida: that "large cities are laboratories of this complex and many-sided contemporary culture,"[7] and that "complex socioeconomic, cultural, political, and religious transformations are taking place in the urban world, and they impact all dimensions of life."[8] Thus, large cities are the great cultural laboratory of our time, the real and symbolic place in which groups and movements take flesh and project a diversity of ethical values. We might call cities the great Areopagus of modern culture.[9]

It is worth noting that we are not simply identifying urban ethics with civil ethics. Urban ethics can be considered a prior condition of civil ethics, since it is not primarily a reflection on the basic or minimum criteria governing the behavior of a contemporary society; rather, urban ethics is the committed practice of social subjects, individual or collective, who live and promote a meaningful life amid the contradictions caused by the broken promises of the city. The Latin American city "promises" progress, education, and enjoyment, but only a social minority achieves those objectives.

Among these ethical subjects are social organizations that work for representative or participatory democracy: women's groups struggling against domestic violence or supporting migrants on their way to the United States; collectives that defend and promote the rights of vulnerable groups such as street children or sex workers; small business enterprises that resist the hegemonic logic of the neoliberal marketplace; and groups that work to reweave the social fabric in cities torn apart by violent crime, drug trafficking, and government corruption, such as Chihuahua, Ciudad Juárez, Nuevo Laredo, or Monterrey, in Mexico.

These ethical subjects are practicing what we might call "social ecumenism."[10] They bring together women and men, religious or not, who defend the meaningful life as an indispensable value in making a humanly habitable common home, or *ecumene*. This form of urban ethics can be classified as Christian ethics and, by extension, linked to the recently developed concept of civil ethics.

One important aspect of this description is that "urban culture is hybrid, dynamic and changeable, for it brings together many forms, values and ways of life, and affects many different collectivities."[11] This phenomenon poses a real challenge to Christian ethics because, as the Aparecida document points out, "Christians today are no longer at the forefront of cultural production, but rather they receive its influence and impacts."[12]

In other words, given the hybrid and pluralistic—though not undifferentiated—condition of urban life, clearly there is no viable alternative to collaboration in setting out and formulating a pluralist ethic in which the most important issues, in our judgment, are not about the moral redemption of urban society or the establishment of moral norms and codes to improve it. These would be unsatisfying and practically impossible tasks today. Rather, we should seriously question the quality of life in our cities and look for ways to collaborate with others who from different mystical and logical perspectives are working to build more humane cities, especially for the impoverished or excluded majorities around them.

I am thinking of city dwellers who, in ethical terms, are generally autonomous and secularized. They do not reject norms as such, but they do not uncritically accept a normativity imposed by others on the basis of religious revelation or moral authority. Normativity must be justified by rational arguments that make it clear and convincing.

The Perspective of Christian Ethics and Urban Pluralism

In my view an ethical commitment to urban life entails two fundamental requirements. First, since the city is "a symbolic territory in constant construction and expansion, which exceeds the physical limits of what is traditionally called a city,"[13] we need to analyze its rituals and symbolic expressions, both confessional and secular.[14] In this sense, urban ritual, a hybrid of the religious and secular, connects human beings with some form of transcendence and enables them to reorder the environment or create a cosmos within the chaos of the city. This gives new meaning to their existence and establishes or strengthens their group identity, which has generally been limited by different levels of social or cultural exclusion.[15]

We also need to analyze the "invisible cities" and the ethical and Christian values they express. In this context, the invisible cities are made up of homogeneous urban groups that live or work in dispersion around the large city. Their homogeneity is determined by the way they respond to the diverse stimuli of urban life, including time, work, leisure, divinity, and culture, among others.[16] Thus, in any large city there are multiple cities that we need to approach and understand through expressions that are not readily perceived, such as their imaginaries or their ritual or symbolic manifestations. Otherwise we will not fully grasp their reality.[17]

A more complete approach to the city as a phenomenon is through the urban imaginary, that is, through an understanding of the mental ways in which people apprehend the city, conceive of themselves within it, and construct it with their existence. The most common way to perceive the people's urban imaginary is through their rituals and symbolic expressions; religiosity, both secular and confessional, plays an important part in this environment. Thus, "urbanization is much more than living in cities."[18] Technology makes it increasingly unnecessary to go into the city in person, since we can carry out virtual "encounters" with people or groups through on-line chat sessions and have access to administrative, bureaucratic, and financial services through the Internet.

We must understand that in reality or imagination, the modern city seems to epitomize dimensions that once could only be experienced through religion, such as omniscience, omnipotence, or ubiquity. Now these dimensions have also

become part of the secularization process, depriving the religions of their monopoly on transcendence.

The second fundamental requirement of an ethical commitment to urban life
is to remember that ethical pluralism does not come only from social interaction
(coexistence) in civil peace among different groups in a single society.[19] One key element of modern pluralism is what Peter Berger calls "cognitive contamination,"[20] a
process that invites subjects to open up their worldview by seeing that other worldviews beside their own also contain positive elements or truths. In this way certainties and convictions acquire a very personal value, and people can see a relationship
between their own and those of others. It then becomes possible to keep in mind
different conceptions of the world. This process generally leads urban subjects to
a more or less constant reordering of different beliefs, values, and ways of life. Of
course this social process has always existed in human nature, but, as Berger says,
"cities have constituted a propitious place for it to happen."[21]

Thus, just as urbanization means more than creating cities, pluralism is more
than the result of physical interaction among people. It is primarily a mental phenomenon resulting from contact, or contagion, among different cultures and worldviews.
People do not even have to leave home, thanks to social communication media. In the
same way that the city generates different forms or mental models for perceiving and
conceiving of the urban reality, it also generates modes of behavior that break down
consensual understandings or social norms and create new ones over time.

The Need for Change

All this implies, especially for Catholic ethics, a need to change from the
monistic moral paradigm of premodernity to the cultural context of the modern
city that is dominated by the autonomous subjectivity of the individual. In today's
secular world, the religious foundations on which the church's ethical teachings
were based have eroded, and the church will need to make its ethical project understandable and reasonable in order to communicate it to people who do not share
the same faith. The rejection or fear of pluralism makes it impossible to collaborate
in the ethical strengthening of today's society.[22] In this way the city may become a
cultural arena of ethical chaos or anomie, resulting from what Marciano Vidal calls
"the loss of an ethical home" or "the corrosion of moral self-esteem."[23]

At the same time we need to keep a balanced view of ethical pluralism. While
it does not always depend on the opinion of the majority, we should not formulate
or establish an ethic without considering the viewpoint of the population and the
ways it is changing.

We often say that ethics are not based on consensus, but consensus does play
a partial role in real life. This is clear from a comparison between the everyday
customs of a few years ago and those of today. Take the example of courtship. In
much of Latin America fifty years ago it was unacceptable to see a young woman
sitting in her boyfriend's lap on the bus or a couple kissing passionately in public.

While there has been no new ethical convention on courtship practices that would give rise to that change, in everyday life there has been a change of views, based on changed ways of judging behavior. Of course, as we have said, not all behaviors are acceptable because the majority practices them, but we also cannot conceptualize an ethics *behind the back* of popular practices, especially in the modern city. There is also a kind of *natural selection* in behavioral practices.

We have seen that urban imaginaries are diverse and have many meanings; this means that our approach to them, especially from an ethical viewpoint, must be theoretically and practically concrete, flexible, and multidisciplinary. This is a great challenge to Christian ethics, since it has generally been hard for Christianity to accept such pluralism—let alone to respond to it in carrying out our mission in the context of urban reality.[24]

The modern city makes available a great deal of information and communication, especially of ideas and lifestyles, which opens up a wide range of choices for life and behavior. The variety of lifestyles is part of the richness of the city, but it can also lead to the extreme of thinking that lifestyles are a matter of personal choice and nobody else's business. That in turn often leads to an absolute indifference among city dwellers. In the field of ethics, this is reflected in a variety of behaviors, behavioral values, and ways of thinking about values.

Just as there is ambiguity between the richness of urban ways of life and the indifference caused by both "massification" and individualism, there is also a lack of concern for humanizing the city. This can lead to anomie, to disinterest in living by the ethical norms that govern our life together and, in some cases, to acceptance by default of the law of the strongest. Usually it is not that ethical norms are lacking, but that people live as if there were none. That is, pluralism may not serve as a seedbed for diverse ethical options but rather lead to fragmentation and ethical disintegration. Without becoming overly pessimistic, we should keep this side of the ambiguity in mind as we think about ethics in cities.

Catholic Dissent: A Silent Schism?

The ethical pluralism of the world's megacities does not exist only in secular urban culture. We Catholics are city dwellers too; we live and experience the same pluralism in our life choices within the church, sometimes with great difficulty. Although obviously all human beings are conditioned by their sociocultural context, we need to repeat that urban Christians are no exception. Indeed, modern Christianity does not exist apart from the life that Christians live from day to day, in this case often in the context of a city. Of course there is always a transcendent, mystical dimension, a spirituality, a doctrine, but these have to be embedded in the everyday life of people as part of their sense of orientation to life and its choices. Otherwise Christianity is reduced to an object of study in the history of doctrines or ideas. My point here is that just as city dwellers live in the context of great ethical pluralism, urban Christians live the same pluralism and develop different values in accordance with their worldviews.

In the case of Mexico, it is well known that the majority of Catholics differ significantly from the official ethical positions of the Catholic hierarchy, especially on specific issues of sexuality and the ethics of life. According to opinion surveys among Mexican Catholics:[25]

> 73% approve of the use of contraceptive methods in some or all situations
> 52% approve of premarital sexual relations in some or all situations
> 53% approve of homosexuality in some or all situations
> 62% approve of divorce in some or all situations
> 72% approve of remarriage by divorced persons
> 32% approve of abortion in some situations

And between 42% and 59% of Catholics believe that the opinion of priests has little or no influence on their decisions regarding the issues listed above.

I cite this opinion sample not to support the ethical validation of these specific viewpoints but to point out that although Catholicism is the majority religion in Mexico City and is a predominantly traditional religion, Catholics accept urban pluralism as natural despite the difference between its opinions and practices and the pronouncements of the ecclesiastical hierarchy.

This survey coincides with another recent opinion survey among Catholics in Mexico City, shown below:[26]

Percentage Acceptance of Official Church Positions with Respect to:

	Fully Accept	Partly Accept	Fully Reject	Don't Care
Political preferences or opinions	7.5	39	25	27.8
Scientific theories and essays	8.1	42.3	24.8	24.8
Economic and social theories	10.6	49.2	17.8	22.4
The arts	24.7	41.5	12.3	21.5
Literature, film, entertainment	16.7	43.9	20.1	19.3
Family life	46	34.9	10.1	8.7
Sexual life	15.8	39.2	28.4	16.4

As the study shows, the official positions of the Catholic Church are not accepted as a package. For Catholics in Mexico City, there is a separation of spheres, with total dissent on the most controversial and most private aspects (political preferences or opinions and sexuality). It appears that the prevalent pluralism of modern urban societies is also prevalent within the Catholic Church. The study also shows the need for further development of the *sensus fidelium* and the ecclesial role in moral issues as themes for Christian ethics.[27]

All this is cause for concern about the possibility of an ethical schism within Catholicism. This would be a silent schism, since faithful Catholics who disagree with the official ethics do not speak out publicly but simply make their own choices, without considering the official positions of the ecclesiastical magisterium. We may also ask if this is not a sign of a practical pluralism within Catholicism, similar to the pluralism of today's urban society.

Urban Christian Ethics and Social Commitment

Along with the ambivalence of urban reality, cities—especially cities in the developing nations—are a place of great social and cultural asymmetries that lead to impoverishment and exclusion, which cause the destruction of the social fabric. Magnificent residential, business, and commercial zones, which are really small fenced-in cities protected by barbed wire and private guards, display a scandalous opulence in comparison with the larger neighborhoods around them that provide almost no urban services. These asymmetries express the social exclusion that afflicts a majority of the urban population. Enormous problems of insecurity, unemployment, and underemployment destroy the social fabric, making interaction difficult among the inhabitants. Interpersonal aggressiveness erupts in the daily rush to work, both in automobile traffic and on public transportation. These situations gradually disrupt and sometimes destroy the social fabric.

In this lived experience of chaos and urban conflict, obviously the great majority of city dwellers are denied the three vital promises of the megacity: fullness of life, upward mobility, and recreation. This asymmetrical reality, caused by political and economic structures that we cannot begin to analyze here, has turned the city into a pressure cooker, and people naturally find different escape outlets. Either they will adopt an attitude of solidarity that leads to liberating initiatives from a grassroots perspective, or they will find a false refuge that makes the problem worse, such as crime, alcohol, or drugs.[28]

Conclusions

The points covered in this essay can be summarized as follows:

It is important not to see the city as an object to be studied or dealt with but as something that we have created and that creates us in turn. That is, we should grasp it as the creation of today's Christians, who give it life and help to shape it in their own way.[29] There are a number of different theological or *theologal* ways of looking at the city.

We need to understand that the days of Christendom are over and will not return, that today's city presents a challenge and opportunity to reshape the meaning of Christian ethics. According to the historical theologian Evangelista Vilanova, the fathers of the Council of Trent—the last council of Christendom— refused to cross the boundaries that religion had drawn around the sacred sphere and failed to focus their attention and their exhortations on the emergence of a new human being and a new society in the midst of the economic, social, and cultural changes that were taking place.[30] Sometimes it seems as if a majority of the ecclesiastical magisterium and the Catholic hierarchy cannot read the signs of the times in today's emerging urban culture and thus cannot relate to it or approach it either theologically or pastorally.

Another key aspect is to encourage, in the context of a healthy pluralism, the development of a civil ethic by urban subjects themselves. This is one of the alternatives that the modern city both offers and requires of us. For this purpose we can learn from the currents already moving within Christian and Catholic ethics, despite the tensions that this situation may provoke.

Finally, let us remember that the fundamental and achievable purpose of Christian ethics in the urban context is not the moral redemption of the city nor a return to the cities of Christendom but rather that we collaborate in rebuilding our ethical home in our own uniquely Christian way; that is, to build or rebuild more humane—and thus more Christian—cities.

Notes

1. Translated into English by Margaret D. Wilde.

2. We begin by considering that within their anthropological makeup all human beings have the ability to orient their existence around a project that they gradually discover and acquire. Christian revelation, with the person and mission of Jesus Christ as its paradigm, appears as an invitation that enlightens, accompanies, and strengthens that project. See Edouardo López Azpitarte, *Hacia una nueva visión de la ética cristiana* (Santander: Sal Terrae, 2003), 14.

3. Livingston Crawford and Pamela Flores, "América Latina: La Ciudad Negada," *Investigación y Desarrollo* 14, no. 1 (2006): 226-39, at 228.

4. Ibid.

5. Ibid., 230.

6. Ibid., 232.

7. *Document of Aparecida*, no. 509. See *Aparecida, Concluding Document: Fifth General Conference of the Bishops of Latin America and the Caribbean, May 13-31, 2007* (Washington, DC: USCCB, 2008). This document can be accessed at http://www.rcpos.org/ v2.0/downloads /Concluding %20Document%20CELAM%20Aparecida.pdf.

8. Ibid., no. 511.

9. Ibid., no. 491. The city has also been rightly called "a symbolic/institutional space of pluralism, mobility and syncretism, whose plausibility has undoubtedly been a modern phenomenon." See J. Legorreta, "La ciudad latinoamericana: Aproximaciones sociológicas," in *10 palabras claves sobre pastoral urbana*, ed. J. Legorreta (Estella: Verbo Divino, 2007), 20.

10. Social ecumenism can also be understood as macroecumenism, which goes beyond the religious or creedal factor and seeks to work with others to build a common home for meaningful life on earth. See M. A. Sánchez, "Macroecumenismo-ecumenismo," in *Cien palabras claves para evangelizar la ciudad* (Mexico City: Dabar, 2004), 53-54.

11. Ibid., 58.

12. *Document of Aparecida*, no. 509.

13. See A. Silva, "Ciudades imaginadas: Sevilla," Seminario taller imaginarios urbanos: Hecho Público (Workshop seminar on Urban Imaginary: Made Public), UNIA arteypensamiento, http://uayp06.tripod.com/mundo/mundo02/proy_1_imag.htm.

14. Soccer games (*futbol*) are an example: "Like it or not, *futbol* offers surrogate experiences that go beyond everyday life, providing ways to solve everyday problems. [Another aspect] of great importance: *futbol* offers models of behavior and social relations associated with a set of values, emotions, and we might also say, new popular heroes." See Andrés Fábregas, *Lo sagrado del rebaño: El futbol como integrador de identidades* (Mexico City: El Colegio de Jalisco, 2001), 24.

15. Benjamin Bravo, "Rito," in *Cien palabras claves para evangelizar la ciudad*, 85-86.

16. Benjamin Bravo, "Ciudad Invisible," in *Cien palabras claves para evangelizar la ciudad*, 19-20.

17. "Sometimes cities replace other cities on the same soil and under the same name, emerging and dying without knowing one another, with no communication between them." See I. Calvino, *Las ciudades invisibles* (Madrid: Siruela, 1999), 43.

18. A. Silva, "Ciudades imaginadas: Sevilla," http://uayp06.tripod.com/mundo/mundo02/proy_1_imag.htm.

19. Peter Berger, "La secularización y el pluralismo," in *Una gloria lejana: La búsqueda de la fe en época de credulidad* (Barcelona: Herder, 1994), 53.

20. Ibid., 56.

21. Ibid., 55.

22. Azpitarte, *Hacia una nueva visión de la ética cristiana*, 72-73.

23. Marciano Vidal, *Moral de actitudes*, vol. 1: *Moral fundamental* (Madrid: Editorial PS, 1990), 45-49.

24. See Conference of Mexican Bishops, *Del encuentro con Jesucristo a la solidaridad con todos* (Mexico City: CEM, 2002), nos. 174-75.

25. See the survey conducted by Ipsos Bimsa, "Encuesta de opinion pública sobre el aborto 2006" (Public Opinion Survey on Abortion, 2006) (Mexico City: Ipsos Bimsa, 2006). Note that this survey was requested and published by a private firm of traditional Catholic tendency. Although it should be compared with more progressive sources, it shows that even the most traditional Catholics recognize the phenomenon of ethical pluralism within Catholicism.

26. José Legorreta, *Identidades eclesiales en disputa: Aproximación "socioteológica" a los habitantes de la ciudad de México* (Mexico City: Universidad Iberoamericana, 2006), 90-94.

27. See B. Sesboüé, "El *sensus fidelium* en moral: Un ejemplo: El préstamo con interés," in *El magisterio a examen: Autoridad, verdad y libertad en la Iglesia* (Bilbao: Mensajero, 2004).

28. Dolores Villagómez et al., "Fenomenología de la urbe," in *La ciudad: Desafío a la evangelización* (Mexico City: Dabar, 2002), 65-100.

29. One interesting approach to the city as a theological or *theologal* place is found in J. Libanio, "La experiencia urbana como lugar teologal," in *10 palabras claves sobre pastoral urbana*, 217-56.

30. Evangelista Vilanova, *Historia de la teología cristiana*, vol. 2 (Barcelona: Herder, 1989), 565.

CATHOLIC SOCIAL TEACHING AT A CROSSROAD

David Kaulemu

I look at Catholic social teaching from the point of view of a committed lay Catholic who has worked *in* the church, *for* the church, and *with* the church. If it makes sense at all for a Christian to work *outside* the church, I have done that too. Inspired by the church's teaching on social justice, I have had exciting times working in, for, with, and outside the church, meeting extremely gifted and committed lay Christians, especially Catholics. There have also been some challenging and discouraging times.

The work of the lay faithful is not usually taken seriously in "official" Catholic Church structures unless it is a result of instructions from priests and bishops; if not, it is not regarded as part of the work of the church. As the *Decree on the Apostolate of the Laity* clarifies, "But no enterprise must lay claim to the name 'Catholic' if it has not the approval of legitimate ecclesiastical authority."[1] Describing "Catholic Action," the Vatican II fathers further explained this point as follows: "The laity, whether coming of their own accord or in response to an invitation to action and direct cooperation with the hierarchical apostolate, act under the superior direction of the hierarchy, which can authorise this cooperation, besides, with an explicit mandate."[2]

Lay Catholics always have to work hard to prove that their intentions are one with the church. They are not trusted to the point of being recognized as legitimate church representatives even in areas in which priests, bishops, and other church "officials" cannot work. In other words, the lay faithful on their own are not church "officials" and therefore do not automatically represent the church even when they do what they do from the inspiration of the church's social teaching, gospel values, and the church's traditions.

But as more and more lay faithful become more socially conscious and active in using Catholic social teaching and understanding the church traditions, are we getting to a point where the laity will demand their right to be "official" church representatives? This is especially so in the context where more and more church "officials" have been found to be misrepresenting the values, traditions, and institutions of the church.

Several cases seem to point in this direction. For example, Catholic social teaching is specifically meant to inspire the faithful and others who are usually referred to as "people of good will" to work in specific ways in the social sphere. Pope John Paul II encouraged "the training of the lay faithful so that they will fully exercise their role of inspiring the temporal order—political, cultural, economic and social—with Christian principles, which is the specific task of the laity's vocation in the world."[3] When lay people follow this encouragement fully, they are sometimes discouraged by officials of the church who drag their feet and are reluctant to let the "official" church institutions engage the temporal order and oppose the lay people who expect the church to do so.

We have reached a stage where some lay faithful have started to push "officials" of the church to inspire the temporal order with Christian principles. In Kenya, Zimbabwe, and other countries, the lay faithful have struggled to encourage their respective Catholic bishops' conferences to support the impoverished populations and make public statements against social injustice and bad governance.

Pope John Paul II emphasized that

> formation is of primary importance. People who have never had the chance to learn cannot really know the truths of faith nor can they perform actions which they have never been taught. For this reason "the whole community needs to be trained, motivated and empowered for evangelisation, each according to his or her specific role within the church." This includes bishops, priests, members of institutes of consecrated life and societies of apostolic life, members of secular institutes and all the lay faithful.[4]

The question, however, is who trains whom? Can the laity train the church fathers on social issues and social justice? If so, how? What are the procedures? Can the church hierarchy accept given insights that inspire the social order with Christian principles? We seem to be moving in this direction. Yet we still have a long way to go. It is frustrating and discouraging to the lay faithful to be inspired by Catholic social teaching and yet receive no recognition or support by "official" church structures.

Catholic social teaching is therefore ambivalent about the status and contribution of the lay faithful in the church and in the world at large. The Second Vatican Council acknowledged how the church can profit from the world.

> Nowadays when things change so rapidly and thought patterns differ so widely, the Church needs to step up this exchange (between the church and people in the world) by calling upon the help of people who are living in the world, who are experts in its organisations and its forms of training, and who understand its mentality, in the case of believers and non-believers alike.[5]

This "stepping up" is needed more today than in the past. Yet the knowledge, experiences, professions, and expertise of the Catholic laity are still largely regarded as irrelevant to Catholic social teaching and its growth. Sometimes church "officials" actively resist insights and reflections of the lay faithful that could deepen the church's teaching. Catholic bishops' conferences have sometimes taken up positions on issues with little consultation with the laity. In some countries, Catholics are frustrated by their bishops' conferences, as they seem at least to condone if not to be complicit with bad national governance, corruption, and social injustice. In Zimbabwe, some Catholics helped to form Christian Alliance, a group of concerned Christians pushing for a more vocal and politically active church in Zimbabwe.[6]

In general, however, most Catholic lay faithful still make little connection with their faith commitments and their private and professional lives. It does seem to be safer that way. Catholic politicians, businesspeople, and civil servants, for example, do not normally see their activities as linked to their faith commitments. The documents describing the church's social teaching still feel too abstract, too general, and too far removed from the more specific social, political, and economic realities of the lay faithful. In situations where these documents and statements try to be close to peoples' lives, they seem to be far removed from people's "joy and hope, [their] grief and anguish."[7]

The church's social teachings seem to be paradoxically either too restrictive and insensitive to peoples' thoughts and feelings or too distant and abstract. For example, in personal sexual conduct, the church's teaching seems keen to follow and direct the laity even in their bedrooms, in hospital wards, and on the street. This is justified by the gospel values of respect for life, respect for the dignity of the human person, and love. Yet the same values must inspire us to protect all human beings from being killed by hunger, political processes, economic exploitation, cultural oppression, and social cruelty.

To be consistent, shouldn't the church's teaching be following Catholic politicians, businesspeople, and professionals into state houses, boardrooms, and battlefronts? Why are cruel and corrupt dictators and economic exploiters accepted as part of the fraternity of Catholics, while weak women and men caught up in complex social and cultural relationships are barred from receiving the Holy Sacrament because they are deemed evil? In the name of preserving the sanctity of marriage, many women and children have been abused to the point of social dysfunction and death. The politically and economically powerful men and women who create conditions that condemn weak people to violence, suffering, and death are generally treated with respect by the "official" church hierarchy. And those who need its support are rejected and condemned.

I recently attended an international conference on Pope Benedict's *Caritas in veritate* in the context of Africa. This conference brought together lay and religious people working in Catholic Church structures on issues of justice and peace in Africa. Lay people had deep experiences of the social issues bedevilling the continent—social, political, economic, and religious. Yet, in the end, the issue that turned out to be the critical area of concern was that of abortion. Through some insidious direction from a German professor who claimed to be safeguarding Catholic social teaching, the participants were moved to produce a statement that submerged their social priorities under the church's response to the issue of abortion.[8]

Poverty in Africa is a matter of life and death—more so than the issue of abortion. In most African societies, abortion is not a matter of freedom of choice. It is, essentially, one of the social consequences of poverty. Our responses to the challenges of poverty in Africa must inform how we deal with the challenges of abortion—not the other way round.

In Kenya, the "official" Catholic Church did not seem to take seriously the lay peoples' experiences of social and political life when it asked them to reject a negotiated 2010 draft of the national constitution. Yet many committed Catholics felt that the draft had captured the bulk of their aspirations at that time in their national history. Here, the issue of abortion influenced the "official" church's position. The majority of Kenyan lay people knew that if they followed the recommendations of the official Kenyan Catholic Church to vote against the draft constitution, the church itself would not be in a position to deliver to them a better and more just Kenya. By voting in support of the draft constitution in spite of the "official" church recommendation, do the Catholic lay faithful gain more confidence in actively interpreting Catholic social teaching and engaging "official" church positions?

For a time since Zimbabwean political independence in 1980, the Catholic Church in Zimbabwe considered it more important to work with the government of the day than to be in solidarity with the marginalized and impoverished citizens. Even when more than twenty thousand of its citizens were massacred in Midlands and Matabeleland in the mid 1980s,[9] and even while its own Commission for Justice and Peace had all the evidence of the massacre, the Catholic Bishops' Conference still maintained that it was better to keep discussions at the level of principles. Whatever reasons were offered for the relative silence, it is difficult to believe that the official church is consistent in its concern for the sanctity of life and that the lay peoples' views are regarded with equal respect.

Catholic Social Teaching at Three Levels

Catholic social teaching has worked at three different levels. It has been understood as dealing with and teaching *general values and principles*. These are the gospel values and principles of the dignity of persons, common good, solidarity, participation, and so on. This level of general principles restrains the church from making specific policy choices but allows it to teach on the general nature of integral development, stewardship of creation, good governance, the responsibilities of citizens, and the nature of public virtue. Many pastoral letters remain on this level: they have generally condemned injustice but hesitated to identify it in the concrete world; they have defined social evil but refused to name names. This is why corruption, injustice, poverty, and disease have continued to thrive side by side with the church's condemnation of them. In places where the church has raised its voice to condemn evil in general, such condemnation has not necessarily affected those social and political evils.

In Zimbabwe, corruption actually increased from 2001 onward. This was the time when the Zimbabwean Catholic Church had intensified its popularization of the church's social teaching. In 2006, the Zimbabwean Catholic bishops collaborated with the Zimbabwe Council of Churches and the Evangelical Fellowship of Zimbabwe to produce a joint discussion document.[10] This effort represented a historical collaborative project combining the umbrella bodies of the main Christian episcopal bodies in Zimbabwe. The effort can be read as an attempt by the Zimbabwean church at large to respond to the political and economic crisis in Zimbabwe through Christian social teaching. It is a fact, however, that the Zimbabwean crisis intensified and deepened after this effort by the church. Part of the problem was the church's hesitancy to name names and push for corrupt leaders to take full responsibility for their actions. Nonetheless, some lay faithful, inspired by the general church principles, were forthright in naming names and challenging corrupt political authorities. However, the majority of the respective church authorities were irritated by their members who wanted to be vocal. These lay faithful, by their active engagement, were raising the important question, "Who is the church?"

Working at the level of general principles of Catholic social teaching, the Zimbabwe Catholic Bishops' Conference and the Catholic Commission for Justice and Peace in Zimbabwe issued powerful public statements and pastoral letters between 2005 and 2009. These statements decried increased political violence, bad governance, and the suffering of the poor and marginalized. This period, and especially 2007 and 2008, is now recognized as the period in which Zimbabweans experienced some of the worst political violence ever, the near total collapse of civil governance, and the worst forms of social marginalization and poverty in the country's history.

This trend has also been experienced in other African countries.[11] In South Africa, apartheid grew in the face of the church's social teaching. In countries such as Angola, Mozambique, the Democratic Republic of Congo, Uganda, Rwanda, Burundi, and recently in Kenya and Zimbabwe the general teaching of the church did not stop violence and social evils, many of which were perpetrated by the lay faithful, many of whom continued to attend holy Mass on Sundays.

There seems to be a disconnection between the general teaching of the church and the concrete lives of the lay faithful. The church, however, has also sometimes gone beyond the exposition of general principles into its second level by *involving itself in social policy debates*. In doing so, the church has tried to unpack its general values by illustrating their meaning in concrete policy development, policy monitoring, and evaluation processes. This role has meant direct engagement with the state and government in such areas as education, health, and social policy. Sometimes this engagement has been positive, but it has also resulted in negative confrontations with the state. Hence, many Catholic Church leaders have generally shied away from this approach for fear of reprisals from government.

Third, the church has sometimes gone even further than policy engagement by *witnessing to Christian values*. It has instituted development programs, organizations, and activities to restore justice and improve peoples' lives. In many countries in Africa where the state structures are weak if not non-existent, church schools, hospitals, and humanitarian organizations sustain peoples' lives.

All these levels of Catholic social teaching have been implemented by the church in different contexts. Yet the challenge is whether the church, in using these different approaches, has presented a consistent message at all these levels— and whether lessons from the experiences of witnessing Christian teaching and developing and implementing public policy inform the church's understanding of general values and principles. We have seen claims that the values and principles of Catholic social teaching never change. We are told that statements of Catholic social teaching build on but never contradict previous ones. Yet we know from the history of Catholic social teaching that the concept of human rights was once looked at with suspicion if not antipathy. The bishops of the Second Vatican Council talked about how "new avenues to truth are opened up"[12] by exchanges with the world. With greater participation of the lay faithful in the work of the church, and with greater visibility of Catholic social teaching, there is greater pressure for Catholic social teaching to develop in its insights and language and to become more relevant to peoples' concrete realities. This is certainly true in the African context where the colonial experience has not always benefited how the church and its practices are viewed, even by the lay faithful.

In my opinion, Catholic social teaching is at a crossroads. It must deal with the various ambivalences and ambiguities created by the development of social teaching at the three different levels just identified. If Catholic social teaching operates at the general level of values and principles, it will continue to be dominated by concerns for logical coherence and consistency, which may prevent it from becoming a transforming force. But if, on the other hand, it ventures into greater direct engagement with the world through policy development and witness of action, it may achieve a greater social impact but at the expense of logical unity and consistency.

If social teaching develops in the latter direction, as *Ecclesia in Africa* points out, "the church is aware that her social doctrine will gain credibility more immediately from the witness of action than as a result of its internal logic and consistency."[13] For social teaching to develop in this direction, the church's "witness of action" will need to recognize more formally and learn from the witness of action of the lay faithful. More thought will need to be given to clarifying not only the objectives of Catholic social teaching but also the roles of the various players and the instruments involved in "transforming humanity from within and making it new."[14] Clearly the development of Catholic social teaching demands a re-examination of Catholic institutions, organizations, and the respective roles and relationships of Catholics and those they work with. The church must therefore deal with several types of ambivalence in Catholic social teaching that involve the role of the lay faithful, including the following challenges.

1. The level of social responsibility that is given to the laity with one hand seems to be taken away by the other. For example, recognition is made of the priesthood of the laity[15] and the special role and relationship the laity have to the world. Yet the institutional and organizational arrangements in the church do not facilitate a concrete recognition of that role and responsibility. Effectively, Catholic social teaching is conveyed by the bishops to the lay faithful, who are then expected to implement or live the teaching. While the lay faithful are encouraged to be creative and take initiative in collaborating with others in society,[16] lay experiences do not seem to have added much to the general understanding and deepening of Catholic social teaching. There are signs that some Catholic professionals are beginning to confront this question.

2. Catholic social teaching encourages the lay faithful to bring "before the ecclesial community their own problems, world problems, and questions regarding man's salvation, to examine them together and solve them by general discussion."[17] While I can imagine cases where specific social problems could be solved "by general discussion," many situations need specific responses, which the "official" church sometimes selectively hesitates to give. We have seen this in the church's inability to use the social teaching to directly deal with racism, tribalism, class inequalities, poverty, the environment, education, health care, and community development. Part of the problem has been that the church itself has been implicated in these social vices. Therefore, the church is not institutionally organized in such a way that the lay faithful can fully live out in an unambiguous way some of the instructions of the Catholic social teaching.

3. Catholic social teaching encourages collaboration with "all people of good will," nationally, regionally, and internationally. In doing so we must be witnesses to our faith and the gospel values. Yet, by doing so, we are exposed to situations of learning and growth from others. More needs to be said about how we can positively learn from others and spiritually grow from our interaction with other faiths, scientists, and other Christians.

4. Catholic social teaching is presented in different ways. It is sometimes presented as *principles to be followed*. Examples include the principles of the dignity of persons, participation, subsidiarity, the common good, solidarity, and the option for the poor. These principles can be used to assess the justice of social situations and to suggest criteria for eliminating injustice. Yet, Catholic social teaching has also been presented in terms of *virtues to be cultivated* in individual persons, societies, and institutions. Further still, the principles of the common good, solidarity, participation and stewardship of creation have also been presented as ideal *goals to be pursued*.

As noted earlier, these three approaches are not always consistent with each other, and their social consequences are not always consistent. It is not clear what teaching we lay people can or should use in specific situations that require guidance. For example, Catholics have been divided on how to deal with specific social, political, and economic issues such as bad governance, traditional cultural practices, land reform, and economic reforms. Certainly more and more lay Catholics are beginning to reject the idea that they have to wait for ecclesial authorities to provide cookbook solutions to their problems. Some attempts to provide such solutions have been resisted—sometimes directly but most of the time quietly. It is not a great secret that many lay Catholics do not always follow the church's teaching. There was a time when it was easier for the church to ignore its lay faithful than for the faithful to ignore ecclesial authority. That time seems to be over as traditional ecclesial authority is challenged on the one hand when its authority is ignored by the laity, and on the other hand when lay people are ready to take up ecclesial responsibility.

Conclusion

Catholic social teaching has the potential to transform the temporal order. But this can happen only if there is the full participation of all people of faith and if church structures and processes unambiguously facilitate their participation. Since 2001, the African Forum for Catholic Social Teaching (AFCAST), which I coordinate, has been creating space and facilitating discussion on the meaning of the values and principles of Catholic social teaching in the African context. We have discovered many ambiguities and ambivalences in the understanding and practice of Catholic social teaching. What, for example, does solidarity mean in the context of land reform in Zimbabwe, election violence in Kenya, or xenophobia in South Africa? Catholics, and indeed Catholic leaders, have different views on these issues and episcopal conferences have taken differing positions.

These challenges cannot be solved by attempting to banish them from the top or by pretending they do not exist. The lay faithful do not have to walk away from the church, nor is it necessary to wage war against church authorities. Catholic social teaching is a rich locus for respectful engagement and deepening of the faith. Its principles could be debated while still guiding the clergy and lay faithful on how to build a more viable church and society. We must learn to cultivate new virtues that will facilitate greater participation of the laity in the authority of the church and promote the common good. Yet it is clear that the laity should not "expect the hierarchy to turn over power to the laity either on their own accord or in response to demands."[18]

For the church's social teaching to feel authentic and relevant to peoples' lives, there needs to be greater recognition of the role of the laity in assisting with the development of social teaching. Unless the lay faithful, in collaboration with all other members of the church, take full responsibility for the social teaching, church documents will continue to be written but only partially transform the social, political, economic, and cultural spheres. More needs to be done.

Notes

1. *Apostolicam actuositatem* (Decree on the Apostolate of the Laity), 24. See *Vatican Council II: The Conciliar and Post Conciliar Documents*, rev. ed., ed. Austin Flannery, O.P. (Grand Rapids, MI: Eerdmans, 1992).

2. Ibid., 20.

3. *Ecclesia in Africa* (Post-Synodal Exhortation of the Holy Father John Paul II) (Nairobi: Paulines Publications Africa, 1995), 75.

4. Ibid., citing *Relatio ante disceptationem* (The Gospel, Inculturation, and Dialogue), 8.

5. *Gaudium et spes* (Pastoral Constitution on the Church in the Modern World), 44.

6. Jonah Gokova, "Political Participation in Zimbabwe: An Ecumenical Perspective," in *Political Participation in Zimbabwe*, ed. David Kaulemu (Harare: African Forum for Catholic Social Teaching (AFCAST), 2010), 109-10.

7. *Gaudium et spes*, 1.

8. The Pontifical Council for Justice and Peace organized a Pan African Seminar on the theme: "Caritas in veritate: The Social Doctrine of the Church as a Leaven of Integral Development" at the Ghana Institute of Management and Public Administration (GIMPA), Achimota, Accra, Ghana, from September 24 to September 29, 2010.

9. See Catholic Commission for Justice and Peace, *Breaking the Silence: Building True Peace—A Report on the Disturbances in Matabeleland and the Midlands 1980-1988* (Harare: Catholic Commission for Justice and Peace, 1997).

10. See *The Zimbabwe We Want: Towards a National Vision for Zimbabwe* (Zimbabwe Catholic Bishops' Conference, Evangelical Fellowship of Zimbabwe, Zimbabwe Council of Churches, 2006). This document, also known as the *National Vision Discussion Document* (NVDD) of Zimbabwe, can be accessed at http:// www.kubatana.net/docs/ relig/zim_churches_national_zim_vision_060918.pdf.

11. Elisee Rutagambwa, S.J., "The Rwandan Church: The Challenge of Reconciliation," in *The Catholic Church and the Nation-State: Comparative Perspectives*, ed. Paul Christopher et al. (Washington, DC: Georgetown University Press, 2006), 181.

12. *Gaudium et spes*, 44.

13. *Ecclesia in Africa*, 21.

14. Ibid., 55.

15. *Apostolicam actuositatem*, 4.

16. Ibid.

17. Ibid., 10.

18. Mary Jo Bane, "Voice and Loyalty in the Church: The People of God, Politics, and Management," in *Common Calling: The Laity and Governance of the Catholic Church*, ed. Stephen J. Pope (Washington, DC: Georgetown University Press, 2004), 190.

Justice and Equity in the Health-Care World: An Ethical Cry from Latin America and the Caribbean

Leo Pessini

In the wish to be loved and to live longer (or forever!), good health is one of the most basic goals that human hearts seek. It is a question of building a future for humankind, and for the new and next generations that will follow us, that will provide a quality of life beyond simple survival. This domain has become an issue of salvation (with the possibility of living longer and with a greater quality of life) and of condemnation (premature death) for millions of people in the world.

Going beyond the definition of "health" by the World Health Organization as "complete wellbeing . . . and not just the absence of infirmities,"[1] health is the result of some very simple ingredients of our daily life, including (among other things) education, economic resources, employment, having land to cultivate, a sound environment, pure air, and water. Good health, a prerequisite for personal and community development, results from the integration of health-care services with programs for nutrition, education, employment, salaries, the promotion of women and children, ecology, and the environment, among others.

It is necessary to promote and protect human life and health not only because of the immediate needs of individuals, communities, and interpersonal relationships, but also because of the need to construct public policies and national, regional, and local development projects within a framework of equality, solidarity, and justice. The policies and projects should empower the poor to participate as fellow citizens. This dynamic of a socioecological conception of health helps us to understand not only the physical, mental, and spiritual causes of diseases but also the social and political factors that result in injustice as well as disease and illness. Often those in the greatest need of health care are simply excluded. This is an injustice that cries to the heavens!

Giant industrial and technological complexes with huge investments for research, equipment, and training for specialized professionals spend trillions of dollars. But we need to ask what values they prioritize. Are they Christian values or just free-market values?

185

Most health-care systems of the major nations in the world are in crisis: economic resources alone are not sufficient to provide all the health-care needs people have! There have been harsh political debates around this issue, most recently in the United States. The providing of health care is characterized by great injustices and inequalities, with poor people usually excluded and easily forgotten. Is there a role for ethics and its quest for justice and equity? Indeed, it has been said that the twenty-first century will put ethics on center stage of every kind of activity—otherwise we will simply disappear.

This essay begins with a discussion of the health of populations in the Latin American and Caribbean region, focusing on the primary problems and challenges. It then turns to an ethical-theological reflection about justice and equity in the field of health care.

The vision of the status of health care in the Latin American and Caribbean region is presented according to a privileged perspective, that of the task force for pastoral care of the *Department of Justice and Solidarity* of the *General Conference of the Bishops of Latin America and the Caribbean* (CELAM), in which I have taken part since 1994 as an expert in ethics and health. After many years of meetings in many countries of the region this task force has recently issued an important document approved by CELAM entitled *Discípulos Missionários no Mundo da Saúde: Guia para a Pastoral da Saúde na América Latina e no Caribe* (Missionary Disciples in the World of Health: Guidelines for Pastoral Care in Latin America and Caribbean).[2]

The Reality of Health in Latin America and the Caribbean[3]

Economic Aspects

In 2007, the population of Latin America and the Caribbean was around 565 million inhabitants, with almost 209 million living below the poverty line and millions suffering from extreme poverty.[4] The distance between rich and poor, which is steadily increasing, stems from structural causes. Inequity has increased due to the neoliberal adjustment policies applied in almost all our countries in order to further the insertion of Latin America and the Caribbean into the increasingly globalized and interdependent world, where great powers decide the fate of the planet.

Today, about 200 million people lack access to regular and appropriate health services because of geographic location, economic barriers, or a lack of accessible health facilities. Fifty-three million do not have fresh water systems, 127 million lack basic sanitation systems, and 100 million have no access to secure garbage collection.[5] Millions of people who suffer the ravages of crises and economic adjustments do not have state support; in addition, societal solidarity is insufficient in coping with the magnitude of socioeconomic problems.

Demographic Aspects

In Latin America and the Caribbean the demographic pyramid is inverted as a consequence of decreasing birth rates, infant mortality, and increasing life expectancy. There are also great migratory movements between countries and the forced internal displacement of populations due both to violence and the pursuit of better living conditions. Migration to the urban centers often results, creating trauma there with serious consequences for the health of the population.

It is important to reflect on and denounce the first-world concept of demographic explosion as the sole cause of poverty; such a perspective does not consider poverty as a result of injustice, corruption, and the misallocation of resources. It is a fact that although fertility and birth-rate indexes have declined in Latin America and the Caribbean, the quality-of-life indicators have not improved. Instead, there is an increase in poverty, which generates more and more diseases and death.

Social Aspects

In the *Document of Aparecida*,[6] the church mentions the *"suffering faces of Christ"* in Latina America and the Caribbean:

> Among them are the indigenous and Afro-American communities, which often are not treated with dignity and equality of conditions; many women who are excluded because of their sex, race, or socioeconomic situation; young people who receive a poor education and have no opportunities to advance in their studies or to enter into the labor market so as to move ahead and establish a family; many poor people, unemployed, migrants, displaced, landless peasants, who seek to survive on the informal market; boys and girls subjected to child prostitution, often linked to sex tourism; also children victims of abortion.[7]

Millions of individuals and families live in poverty and are severely malnourished. There are also people with dependencies on drugs, people with disabilities, and victims of serious preventable diseases such as malaria, Chagas disease, Leishmaniasis, tuberculosis, and HIV/AIDS who receive only inadequate treatments. Members of this latter group also suffer from loneliness and find themselves excluded from social and family life. There are also the abducted and those who are victims of violence, terrorism, armed conflict, and insecurity. Nor should we overlook the elderly, who, besides feeling excluded from the production system, are frequently rejected by their family as inconvenient and useless. We also regret, finally, the inhumane situation of the vast majority of prisoners. They also need our solidarity and fraternal aid.

Without the presence of solidarity, globalization negatively affects these poorest sectors.[8] The lack of comprehensive care and the situation of abandonment experienced by the elderly are of concern, as is the situation of the mentally ill, the terminally ill, and people with disabilities. The *Document of Aparecida* calls for special attention to five situations: people living on the street, immigrants, the disabled, drug addicts, and prison inmates.[9]

It is important to consider the factors that cause disease and death. In terms of longevity, major factors include lifestyle habits (53 percent), the environment and its influence on people (20 percent), genetics (17 percent), and the health-care system, the main concern here, only 10 percent. (These statistics and those in the following paragraphs are taken from *Health in the Americas,* vol. 1: *The Region,* a 2007 publication of the Pan-American Organization of Health [PAHO].)

PAHO data indicate that approximately 700,000 deaths in the regions of the Americas are due to causes that could be avoided, given adequate knowledge and available resources. Included are infections due to diarrhea, which are responsible for a high percentage of the deaths of children.

It is estimated that 40 million Latin Americans live in regions of moderate and high risk of malaria transmission, and more than a million people, mostly children under five years, die each year from malaria. In past years, there was also an increase in cases of dengue fever, with 430,000 in 2005; this reflects a serious oversight by authorities responsible for population and health statistics.

Likewise, tuberculosis affects more than 350,000 people and kills 50,000 every year. This situation has been aggravated by the co-infection of tuberculosis and HIV/AIDS as well as the resistance of tuberculosis to combined treatments. The so-called tropical diseases are directly linked to poverty, malnutrition, lack of education, and unemployment.

Almost all the countries of Latin America and the Caribbean have experienced a process of epidemiological transition in which chronic and degenerative diseases replace infectious and contagious transmitted diseases as the major causes of morbidity and mortality. Haiti remains an exception, as transmittable diseases remain the leading cause of mortality, with a total estimated rate of 351.2 deaths per 100,000 inhabitants; circulatory diseases are next, with a mortality rate of 227.9 per 100,000 inhabitants.

Malnutrition is a health problem that affects at least 10 percent of the population of the region: 52 million people in 2003 (there are no recent official reports), and about 7 million children under five years died because of inadequate nutrition. In some countries, the situation is more delicate, with malnutrition rates of 28 percent. Although the overall infant mortality has decreased, the rate of perinatal mortality is still a concern.

HIV/AIDS: A Big Challenge to Public Health Policies

An analysis of morbidity in the Americas in 2006 indicated that the main causes of death with the greatest effect in years of life lost among men are diabetes, HIV/AIDS, and homicides. According to estimates by the World Health Organization (WHO) and the Joint United Nations Programme on HIV/AIDS

(UNAIDS), by the end of 2005 there were approximately 3.23 million people with HIV/AIDS in the Americas, of which 1.94 million were in Latin America and the Caribbean. In 2005, 220,000 new cases were diagnosed, including 30,690 children less than fifteen years of age. It is estimated that these numbers are far below the reality, as not all cases are recorded, not to mention delays in notification of the disease. In 2005, 30 percent of adults having HIV/AIDS in the Americas were women, with 25 percent in North America, 31 percent in Latin America, and 51 percent in the Caribbean. Reported cases are increasing, especially for women. It is estimated, however, that 104,000 people die annually from HIV/AIDS infections in the Americas, which means that 285 people die every day.[10]

Ecological Aspects

Current threats to the environment in Latin America and the Caribbean are plentiful: deforestation, water and air pollution, soil erosion, desertification, acid rain, damage to the ozone layer, global warming, and so on. Natural disasters continue to impact several countries and, unfortunately, they lack a culture of impact prevention and of systematic action to care for the affected populations. The environment continues to be assaulted: land is vandalized and water is treated as a tradable commodity, as exploitation of these resources is transformed into a well-played game by the superpowers. A very important example is the Amazon.[11]

We must be aware of the devastating effects of uncontrolled industrialization and urbanization, which now take on alarming proportions as they deplete natural resources and contaminate the environment. Seventy-seven percent of the population (473 million) lives in cities, and the current trend continues to increase.[12]

After this overview of the harsh situation of health in Latin America and the Caribbean region, one that is similar to that in many African countries, let us turn now to an ethical theological reflection about equity and justice in the health-care field. The framework of ethical thought of the following session is based in the work that I have co-authored with James Drane, *Bioética, medicina e tecnologia: Desafios éticos na fronteira do conhecimento humano* (Bioethics, Medicine and Technology: Ethical Challenges in the Frontier of the Human Knowledge).[13]

Equality and Equity in the Field of Health Care

In the context of health care, equity refers to issues of distribution and access. At the most concrete level, it works out in the way patients are treated in health-care facilities.

High-tech scientific medicine today is better equipped than ever to cure and to prevent disease, but most individuals, industries, and even governments cannot afford the costs. Wealthy patients may experience the ecstasy of recovery from life-threatening illnesses, but increasingly greater numbers of economically less fortunate patients experience the anger and frustration of being left to die. The gap between the wealthy who have access and the poor who lack access to health care is a potentially explosive issue in countries with a predominantly free-market health-care system and those with a predominantly government-run system.

Any proposed solution to the issues of justice and inequity in health care will be full of ambiguities and uncertainties, and basic ethical components of the doctor-patient relationship cannot be violated without serious repercussions. Christianity, more than any other background belief system, provides the most solid foundation for a health-care system based upon solidarity and fraternity, equality and social justice: a health-care system for the rich and the poor, the intelligent and mentally disabled, the emotionally weak and emotionally strong, the lucky and the unlucky.

We intuitively recognize that basic bioethical values are being violated when richer people or persons from certain races or places have access to needed health care and survive, while poorer persons or people from other races or places do not have access and die. Equity and justice are violated; and whenever equity and justice are violated, human beings recognize the situation's immorality, experience anger, and suffer frustration. If political movements to remedy this immorality and frustration are unsuccessful, revolution can result. The ethical values of equality and justice may be abstract and theoretical, but there are potentially serious consequences if they are ignored or fail to be implemented.

Plainly stated, equity requires that essential goods and services that are provided to some persons in a society should be available to others similarly in need, as all human beings share the same human dignity. Essential health care should not be available only to some. Even if essential goods and services are so scarce or so expensive that they cannot be provided to all, then theoretically they should be made available through a form of lottery. The equal value of each person would thereby be protected.

The logic of such a conceptualization is admirable, but providing for essential human needs in an equal way is so complex that it is not easily put into practice. The logic is simple, but the realities are complex. Equality imposes obligations, but the principle of equality alone, even if applied without bias through a lottery, cannot solve basic health-care distribution problems. Overly simple schemes to implement equity provide no real help.

For equity to work, economics has to work, and many other ethical principles have to be put into practice. Autonomy, for example, cannot be ignored. Neither can the sanctity of life. And without compassion, equality could neither determine needed health care nor provide needed services. First, equity has to be clearly defined and then related to economics and to other ethical principles. These are challenging uncertainties to overcome.[14]

Understanding Equity

Equity and justice are closely related. Justice establishes the standards for the distribution of goods, and equity is one of these standards. Justice in the sense of distributive justice refers to the equal allocation of limited goods and services. Indeed, the distribution of goods and services to everyone on the same basis is one meaning of both justice and equity. Ideally, justice would strive to make all human beings as equal as possible. Justice, fairness, impartiality, equity—these are at the very least comparable categories. They are different ways of expressing the same ideals and objectives of natural law.

Measuring Equity

How efficient is a health-care system in providing basic goods and services to all? The answer to this question depends on how the basic goods and services are identified and measured.

Every society organizes, finances, and delivers health services somewhat differently. Health-care organizations attempt to provide this essential human good within the limits created by available resources, competing goods, and the reigning political perspectives. Comparing one health-care system with another is difficult because the very definition of health care may differ considerably from one culture to the next. In cultures like our own, health care may be synonymous with curing particular illnesses. In other cultures, health care may mean prevention. Similarly, judging the equality or inequality of health care cannot be separated from all kinds of background metaphors and sociocultural beliefs.

People generally agree that equity is important and should be pursued. But they also have other beliefs. Most North Americans prefer the free market over the government as the chief provider and distributor of medical goods and services. In other countries, people believe that health care is the responsibility of government. Given the different beliefs, the variety of delivery systems, the diversity of cultural values, different economic systems, and the different levels of care, equity becomes a value difficult to measure and difficult to implement.

A socialist theory of justice measures equity in health care one way, and a libertarian theory measures it differently. A socialist perspective leaves out of consideration individual freedom and hard work, while a libertarian vision does not consider influences such as genetics and environmental factors. While a socialist theory would maximize access, a libertarian theory would maximize personal responsibility. Libertarians would consider the intervention of the state in order to concretize equal treatment a violation of personal property and justice. A socialist view might discount ambition and hard work. Libertarianism tends to undermine the significance of the community and shared benefits, and socialism tends to create inadequate wealth to provide acceptable health care.

Equity and the Concept of Human Rights

Health insurance was introduced as a way to protect wage-earning workers who became vulnerable if they got sick. Workers with a basic health-care insur-

ance policy thereby attained a certain degree of equity in health care. Later, governments stepped in to extend basic coverage to other vulnerable groups, such as the
elderly and the poor. It was the concept of health care as a basic objective human
right that made insurance and its extensions possible. Broadly extended health-
care insurance gave flesh to the idea of equity in health care as a basic right, and it
provided the motivation for industrialists and politicians to implement health-care
programs for the needy.

The concept of human rights is linked with equity in health care both historically and philosophically. Equity is an old concept, but only in this century has it
been proposed as a universal human right. Equity in effect has been joined with
such basic requirements for decent human life as freedom from slavery and torture and arbitrary arrest. It is on the same level as freedom of speech, freedom of
assembly, and freedom of religion, and it is included under the general concept of
the right to equal treatment under law. The inclusion of equality among the most
basic human rights certainly puts the continuing campaign for equality in health
care on firm ground.[15]

The Right to Equality in Health Care

While equality as a right translates into the right to equality in health care,
it also means a right to be protected against serious health hazards and the right
of access to certain basic health-care benefits. Rights to health care begin as moral
rights, supported by ethical arguments and a natural-law vision of humane living.
Subsequently, human rights become legalized, that is, they become legal rights.
Legal rights to access to health care attempt to put the moral declaration into concrete practice, and health-care programs try to give concrete form to the ethical
vision of equality-based rights to health care for all.

Threats to Equality as a Basic Right

However, no matter how great the effort and how many of the already-limited
resources has been invested in extending health care to all, this ideal has rarely been
fully realized. Consequently, some have simply given up and substituted autonomy
for equity. Individual autonomy joined to free-market capitalism creates a vision
that makes health care something that each person pays for from his or her personal
wealth. No one is required to pay for anyone else in this vision. If equality—in the
sense that every person has a right to health protection and health care—cannot be
attained, then attempts to approximate the ideal may be abandoned. This would be
a classic example of the baby being thrown out with the bath water.

Paradoxically, the same concept of rights that once helped propel initiatives
toward equity in health care now challenges the hard-won advances. People are
concerned about rights, but the concept of rights is now employed more broadly.
Rights are not restricted but greatly extended. Besides individual patients who
claim a right to access health care, doctors too claim a right to decide whom they

will treat. Insurance companies and capitalist health-care institutions claim a right to satisfy the financial interests of their stockholders. Industrialists and corporations claim a right to compete worldwide and not be disadvantaged by having to pay for health-care benefits for workers. Drug companies claim a right to make a profit on the products of their research and therefore charge exorbitant prices for their medications. All these rights claims work against efforts to put into place a right to equal access to basic health care for all people.

Responding to the Threats

How are providers of health care to meet this challenge? One way to address inequality would be to downplay the concept of rights in order to focus on a concept of justice that balances equity and autonomy; in other words, to work out the concrete details of a health-care system that would balance micro-allocation with macro-allocation, primary care with curative medicine, acute therapeutic interventions with public health measures, and equality with autonomy.

Implementation of a rationing system for health-care services is another way to respond to the challenge. But rationing alone does not accomplish the goal of equity. Health-care costs always seem to exceed patient needs for health-care goods and services. No matter how much rationing is decreed, health benefits are not provided equally for all persons. The rich, the socially well-connected, celebrities, the imaginative, the persistent, and the less-than-honest always find a way around the rationing no matter how strongly the system tries to promote equity.

Every system of rationing is based on the concept of need: rationing attempts to meet essential health-care needs of all citizens. But how are such "needs" defined? Is any benefit a need? How about benefits that restore normal functioning? Could "need" be correlated with "significant" health benefits? Even if the concept of need is reduced to basic or essential or minimum need, it remains difficult both to define and to meet. What is meant by terms such as "basic" or "adequate" or "essential" or "minimum" needs in health care?

And there are other needs that make a claim on the same limited resources: food, education, shelter, transportation, police protection, drug prevention, water supply, and so on. While these are not considered health needs, they certainly impact health. Resource limits make equality in health care a challenge that may never be perfectly met. Yet it is a challenge that we confront, one that can generate creative initiatives, and one that can effect gradual improvements in the health care system.[16]

Specific Challenges to Equity in Health Care

We spoke earlier about equity as a more realizable ideal if health care is restricted to primary and preventive care. Is it possible to imagine a community that could reach a consensus about primary, preventive, and acute health care? If that consensus were reached, what would be essential or basic or adequate care for all? And what more should all persons have access to: dental care, rehabilitation services for alcohol and drug addiction, nursing home care, prenatal and postnatal care, family-planning services, and supplies?

Making basic or adequate or essential care equal and accessible to all is not impossible, but it requires a continuing effort. Equity must, however, remain a moral objective that drives efforts for change. Certain circumstances that create challenges to equity in health care have to be considered, including the following:

1. the need to maintain basic universal coverage in the face of steady increases in immigrant populations, some of whom migrate just for health reasons;
2. the problem of administrative costs that can quickly consume the resources assigned for care;
3. the problem that micro-management of physician decisions is seen as a necessity for managers and an intrusion by physicians;
4. astronomical malpractice payouts and, in reaction, wasteful defensive medical practices;
5. the restriction of rising health-care costs;
6. copayment requirements that can destroy equality and the handling of high-risk patients;
7. the need for effective monetary constraints on medical suppliers and pharmaceuticals;
8. the challenge of managing the expansion of mental-disease categories and payment for mental health care without downplaying the importance of care for the mentally ill; and
9. the difficulty of managing fraud and abuse, costs that are as high as $100 billion a year in the United States.

The responsibility to provide health care for all, especially the least advantaged, suggests that the more a society is founded on the values of justice and equality between human beings, the more it should reject unfair and avoidable social inequalities.[17] An egalitarian and just society must continuously stimulate collective solidarity that aims to promote the welfare of everybody, without distinction on the basis of origin, race, sex, color, age, or other forms of discrimination.

Toward the Future: Some Challenges

In order to move from our currents methods of providing health care, it is essential that government and civil authorities assess the needs of their population. Christian ethicists and theologians and all committed people of faith should place the following goals before their political and civil leaders:

- Nurture the "utopian" horizon of meaning (the evangelical concept of the *reign of God*) so that it becomes the guide for all our actions, choices, investments, searches and researches, thinking, and dreams in this field of the health care.

- Strive to implement social policies oriented by the ethical principles of justice, equity, and solidarity. The great goal is to *build a just and egalitarian society* that permanently stimulates a collective solidarity to protect the good for all without prejudices of any kind (origin, race, gender, color, religion, age, nationality, and so on).

- *Changing the concept of health* from "charity" to "right." Nowadays, this right is being transformed into a "business" in a free market without heart! There is a need to empower the poor in terms of speaking out and to make concrete and enforce the basic right to health care that is guaranteed by the constitutions of many countries (social control of the state by the civil society). Unfortunately, this is still a "theoretical and mere virtual right" in most countries of Latin America and the Caribbean region. In theory, everything is perfect, but all is perfect only in legal rhetoric; in reality, things are unjust.

The change that we all expect and are pursuing does not come from the *top* but from the *bottom*. Here the role of *pastoral care* is vital! In addition to taking care of the sick (the "Samaritan" dimension) we must also work to change unequal social structures and policies, as well as to preserve the Christian identity of the church institutions and Christian values in the formation of future health-care professionals.[18]

In summary, in the countries of Latin America and the Caribbean region the provision of health care requires a theological ethics of four "Ps": *promotion* of health, *prevention* of diseases, *protection* of the vulnerable ones, and the principle of *precaution*. The principle of precaution is essential, given the increasing interference of biotechnological developments in some vital issues for people, including such technologies as genetically modified organisms (GMOs), and so forth.

As Christian believers we see health as a gift from God, and we have a mission to be responsible with this gift. Taking care of the health of the poor is the main priority and the practical evangelical duty to which we are all called. In concluding, I recall a popular saying in Latin America: When I dream alone, my dreams remain just "dreams" (and frequently they turn into nightmares), but when at least two people start to dream together this is the beginning of a "new reality." We must not forget that any quest for health includes a nostalgic and sometimes unconscious quest for salvation!

Notes

1. World Health Organization (WHO), *Basic Documents* (Geneva: WHO, 1966), 1.

2. See CELAM, *Discípulos Missionários no Mundo da Saúde: Guia para a Pastoral da Saúde na América Latina e no Caribe* (São Paulo: Centro Universitário São Camilo, 2010).

3. The data mentioned in this section comes from the Pan-American Health Organization's *Health in the Americas: The Region*, vol. 1 (Washington, DC: PAHO, 2007). It

presents figures and statistics sent by the health authorities and government of each country. It is also available at http://www.paho.org.

4. Ibid.

5. Ibid.

6. *Document of Aparecida*, 393. See CELAM, *Documento de Aparecida: Texto conclusão da 5ª Conferência Geral do Episcopado Latino-Americano e do Caribe* (São Paulo: Paulinas, Paulus, 2007).

7. Ibid., 65.

8. Ibid.

9. Ibid.

10. PAHO, *Health in the Americas*.

11. *Document of Aparecida*, 84, 470-75.

12. Ibid., 126.

13. See James Drane and Leo Pessini, *Bioética, medicina e tecnologia: Desafios éticos na fronteira do conhecimento humano* (São Paulo: Centro Universitário São Camilo, 2005).

14. Daniel Callahan, "Equity, Quality and Patient Rights: Can They Be Reconciled?" in *Interfaces between Bioethics and the Empirical Social Sciences*, ed. Fernando Lolas Stepke and Lorenzo Agar (Santiago: World Health Organization, 1992).

15. See Paulo Antônio de Carvalho Fortes, "Bioética, equidade e políticas públicas," *O Mundo da Saúde* 1 (2002): 143-47; Paulo Antônio de Carvalho Fortes and Elma Lourdes Campos Pavone Zoboli, eds., *Bioética e Saúde Pública* (São Paulo: Centro Universitário São Camilo, 2003); and Paulo Antônio de Carvalho Fortes, "Orientações bioéticas de justiça distributiva aplicada às ações e aos sistemas de saúde," *Revista Bioética* 1 (2008): 25-39.

16. See Norman Daniels, "Why Justice Is Good for Our Health," in *Interfaces between Bioethics and the Empirical Social Sciences*, ed. Fernando Lolas Stepke and Lorenzo Agar.

17. See Margaret White, *The Concepts and Principles of Equity and Health* (Copenhagen: World Health Organization, 1991).

18. See Leo Pessini, Christian de Paul de Barchifontaine, and Fernando Lolas Stepke, eds., *Ibero-American Bioethics: History and Perspectives* (London: Springer, 2010); and Leo Pessini and Christian de Paul de Barchifontaine, "What Kind of Future Awaits Us? Some Challenging Questions for the Future of Bioethics in Ibero-America," in *Ibero-American Bioethics*, 369-75.

HEALTH ISSUES:
A GENDER PERSPECTIVE

Pushpa Joseph

Sex and gender are both important determinants of health. Biological sex and socially constructed gender interact to produce differential risks and vulnerability to ill health. Despite widespread recognition of these differences, health research has hitherto, more often than not, failed to address both sex and gender adequately. In India, as in many other parts of the world, a gender perspective brings into focus multiple public health issues facing urban and rural India today.

Health Scenario in India

There are about two to three million cases of cancer and approximately 700,000 to 900,000 cases are diagnosed each year. According to a study by the International Agency for Research on Cancer there will be approximately 250,000 new cases of breast cancer in India by 2015. At present, India reports around 100,000 new cases annually. Breast cancer will become an epidemic in India in another ten years if the country does not put in place vigorous mechanisms for early detection and awareness-building. Accordingly, the National Cancer Control Programme has proposed a centrally sponsored plan.

India accounts for 10 percent of the global HIV burden. An estimated 4.58 million men, women, and children were living with HIV/AIDS in the country at the end of 2008, with an adult (15 to 49 years) prevalence rate of 0.8 percent.

Other significant forms of diseases include dengue (haemorrhagic) fever. This fatal viral disease, caused by female *Aedes aegypti* mosquitoes, was first reported in Delhi in 1996 with 10,252 infected cases and 423 deaths. In 2009, 3,188 cases were reported with 53 deaths. It is now spreading to new areas. These and other diseases kill more people each year than conflict alone.

Challenges and Contradictions

A gender analysis of the health scenario in India presents us with a number of contradictions and challenges:

Inverse Care

People with the most means—whose needs for health care are often less frequent and less serious—consume the most care, whereas those with the least means and greatest health problems consume the least. Public spending on health services most often benefits the rich more than the poor in high- and low-income communities alike. As adults, women in India received less health care than men: they tend to be less likely to admit that they are sick, and they will wait until their sickness has progressed before they seek help or help is sought for them. Studies on attendance at rural primary health centers reveal that more males than females are treated in almost all parts of the country, with differences greater in northern hospitals than southern ones, pointing to regional differences in the value placed on women. Additional constraints on their receiving adequate health care include the cultural socialization of women to tolerate suffering and their reluctance to be examined by male personnel.

Impoverishing Care

People who lack social protection and who must pay for their own medical care can confront catastrophic expenses. At the global level, over 100 million people annually fall into poverty because they have to pay for health care. India, with a population of one billion, is the world's second most populous country. That number includes 120 million women who live in poverty. Over 70 percent of India's population currently derives its livelihood from land resources (primarily subsistence agriculture), and 84 percent of this population consists of economically active women.

Fragmented and Fragmenting Care

The excessive specialization of health-care providers and the narrow focus of many disease-control programs discourage a holistic approach to the individuals and the families they deal with and do not often result in any continuity in care. Health services for the poor and marginalized groups are often highly fragmented and severely under-resourced, and development aid often adds to the fragmentation. For example, mammogram technology and related equipment are available only in major metropolitan cities, while women who live in rural and semi-urban areas have no access to such facilities. The annual average income of Indian women is nearly Rs.11,500 (US$285), yet the cost incurred for a doctor's consultation, a mammogram, and a fine needle aspiration for a biopsy is nearly US$50, which is not affordable for the average Indian women.

In addition, an estimated 200 million women in India are illiterate, and even most educated women are unaware of the symptoms of breast cancer. Many women also shy away from doctors, fearing social embarrassment. In millions of villages and small towns across India, women with breast cancer are looked down upon by their spouses, families, and friends.

Unsafe Care

India's health-care systems suffer from inadequate design and regulation. Facilities that are unable to ensure safety and hygiene standards result in high rates of hospital-acquired infections, along with errors in medications and other avoidable adverse effects that are an underestimated cause of death and ill-health.

Misdirected Care

The expensive allocation of resources to curative services neglects primary preventive care and the promotion of health through education, which can potentially prevent up to 70 percent of the need for curative services. At the same time, the health sector lacks the expertise to mitigate the adverse effects on health from other sectors (for example, pesticides used in agriculture) and to make the most of what these other sectors can contribute to general well-being.

Health Care in India

Health inequality, which is quite common in India, often results from the inappropriate use of existing funds. Poverty is a major problem. Health facilities have improved considerably in India's cosmopolitan cities, creating a health divide where those who can afford it can receive good quality care. Health gaps typically mirror economic equality gaps. Corruption is also an ever-present problem. Corruption not only exacerbates the problem but some policies actually encourage corruption, as has the lack of health resources.

Another issue that plagues India is the "brain drain," whereby poor countries educate some of their population to key jobs such as in medical areas and other professions only to find that they are attracted to rich countries and move there to practice their professions. As a result, the number of health workers such as doctors and nurses in proportion to the population can be small; in many rural settings, it can be very difficult for people to access services.

Gender Bias in Health Concerns in India

In recent years the government of India has launched the National Rural Health Mission to correct rural inequities in the matter of health. It seeks to integrate health services with other services essential to health such as sanitation, hygiene, safe drinking water, and adequate nutrition. Most of the schemes and programs initiated by government look good, but they usually fail at the implementation level. Again, there is little to find fault with in the infrastructure devised for rural health-care delivery, yet the primary health-care centers and sub-centers are crumbling. Poor implementation haunts practically all of our well-intentioned plans and programs for the welfare of the people.

Women from infants to senior citizens get an unfair deal in matters of health. Throughout generations, women are conditioned to place themselves last within the family itself, even though they often put in the most labor without any financial gain. As such, their health concerns also get a very low priority. Women themselves bear pain and discomfort in silence for long periods of time without seeking relief.

India's sex-ratio speaks volumes about the importance given to women in this country. Women are discriminated against when it comes to the treatment of diseases and medical problems. If a man and a woman have the same problem that requires an expensive treatment, it is invariably the man who is treated first, and he is often the only person to receive care. All the possible treatments are usually explored for a man who is ill, but the situation is entirely different for a woman. And this allocation of resources and inherent preference for the male is not true just for the poor. Well-to-do families are equally prone to bias, and parents generally tend to spend more on health care for boys than for girls. It is these attitudes that are responsible for the inadequate levels of health care provided to India's women and girls.

Looking Back and Looking Forward at HIV/AIDS in Africa: Serodiscordant Couples, Re-infection, the Role of Women, and the Condom

Margaret A. Ogola

Twenty-five years ago, nearly a quarter century ago, the first case of HIV was diagnosed. A little later, in 1984, I did not know that I would begin my life's journey with the HIV pandemic. It would be the battle that I would engage with my most productive efforts. Then I did not know what I know now: it would be the journey that would most help to define my faith as a Catholic and a practicing physician. This has been quite a journey, and what I am going to share with you are the distilled thoughts of that battle and that journey, and where I think we are at the beginning of the twenty-first century. I am going to talk about the issue of discordancy and re-infection and the challenges of care and prevention of HIV today.

Let me just explain a few definitions so that we are all on the same page. *Discordancy* is the phenomenon whereby a couple is living together and engaging in regular sexual activity in an ordinary way, yet one partner is infected and the other is not. In Kenya about half the couples that come for HIV testing fall into this category. Many of them are couples who have lived for many years and even have children. The second phenomenon is *re-infection*, whereby a person is infected again due to exposure to the virus from the regular partner or some other partner.

The nature of this virus is such that it changes its face, so we are talking about different strains. An individual may start an HIV journey with one strain and end up with several strains. This particular state of affairs is called *co-infection* with different strains and may happen whether you are faithful or not to your partner. It depends whether another strain of the HIV virus has been introduced into that relationship; in other words, a person may be infected by different populations of viruses.

Over the last few years a major occurrence on the HIV/AIDS scene has been the introduction of massive outreach programs: the U.S. Presidential Emergency Program for AIDS Relief (PEPFAR) and the Global Fund to Fight AIDS, Tuberculosis, and Malaria.[1] Both are major epidemic-changing efforts to provide antiretroviral therapy (ART) to deserving populations, most of them living in Africa.

Because of these programs, we Africans stopped burying young people by the hundreds of thousands.

However, the main problem that follows closely at the heels of widespread efforts to provide ART is the advent of drug-resistant viruses and the danger of being re-infected with such viruses. For example, five years ago in Kenya we only had about five thousand patients on such therapy, and today we have scaled up to two hundred thousand patients on ART. This is in fact one of the success stories of PEPFAR and the Global Fund. The state, non-governmental organizations (NGOs), and the church have all been major contributors to this effort to scale up ART availability. For many years, I directed the effort of mission hospitals in this regard, with the Catholic Church being a major provider of health care in the developing world, and we were a vital part of that scaling up of care and support of people living with HIV.

However among other reasons, the drugs are toxic, making it difficult to adhere to schedules. Besides, many patients face various challenges, such as lack of food, shelter, and the arbitrary arrest of the poor, so that their drugs are not taken regularly or at all. What is happening now is that we are facing a major problem of resistance to first-line and sometimes even second-line regimes of ART. I personally have had a patient resistant to every drug known in Kenya.

The emergence of drug-resistant strains of HIV makes the problems of co-infection and re-infection a very real nightmare. It means that if a person is infected with the resistant virus, we have to start treatment at a higher level—with second-line or even third-line drugs. Remember that this was a country that could not afford treatment for many people during the many years that we have had HIV. We could do so only with the provision of massive funding from donors like PEPFAR and the Global Fund.

Having to start large numbers of patients on treatment with expensive drugs is an enormous public health problem. It is from this background that I am sharing these thoughts with you. In the decades of the 1980s and 1990s, the mortality rate from HIV and AIDS was extremely high. However, we did not have problems of re-infection because people died quite quickly after diagnosis, so that one did not even have to think too hard about the ethics of transmission and prevention. I realize that I am not an ethicist, nor am I a theologian. However, I am talking to you from the front lines of a battle in which I have been engaged from the very beginning.

As noted above, most patients were so ill or died so quickly that one did not have to agonize about whether they would infect anybody, whether they needed to abstain, or whether they needed to use condoms, because they would be very sick in the process of dying and then dead. HIV is a fast-developing disease among the poor because they do not have access to food, and they do not have very high levels of resistance.

When I was a young doctor, people suspected of having died from AIDS used to be buried under police escort. This was very hard because most African communities like to mourn their dead ceremoniously and at close quarters. In the above-mentioned situation, the mourners were made to stand far away, so it was a terrible way to die. Now all that has changed, and people are living longer.

With ART, people are living longer. Also the disease is better understood, and many programs giving ART are also in addition providing nutritious foods so that people can build up their immunity. The drugs alone cannot do it. With the reduction of stigma, it is possible for a woman to admit that her husband has died of HIV or that they have HIV. This used to be an absolute anathema; no one spoke about the disease.

However with these successes, new areas of concern have surfaced:

1. There are still an unacceptable number of new infections.

2. As old risk groups learn to take better care of themselves, new risk groups have emerged. For example previously the highest infection rate was among young women aged fifteen to twenty-four. Now the women most likely to be infected are women living in stable relationships such as marriage.

3. As more people use ARTs with different degrees of compliance, the problem of drug-resistant viruses emerges, necessitating treatment with even more costly drugs. Considering that the hardest-hit countries of Africa need massive international aid to buy drugs, this escalation of costs is a matter of urgent concern.

4. As more and more viruses become resistant, the risk of infection, re-infection, and co-infection with multi–drug-resistant viruses becomes a public health nightmare for planners.

Similarly, the problem of serodiscordance has become more apparent. In many African countries over half of couples living in a normal conjugal relationship are serodiscordant. The longer the serodiscordant couple lives together, the greater the likelihood and, in fact, the inevitability that all the uninfected will get infected. Again, even if both members of the couple are infected, re-infection and co-infection are sooner or later likely to occur. It is again inevitable that the more you expose a person, especially people who are challenged in various ways, as I have pointed out, the more likely they are to get infected.

When re-infection occurs in places where large numbers of people living with HIV are using, misusing, or under-using ART, the danger of being infected with drug-resistant HIV strains is extremely high. This creates a nightmare situation for a public health planner, and this poses an enormous problem for countries that depend on donor funding. If PEPFAR or the Global Fund, for example, were to stop their funding, a country such as Kenya would not be able to treat these two-hundred-thousand people, and most would be dead within a year or two.

In view of the above, particularly the question of transmission within marriage needs careful consideration. A few years back, statistics showed that for quite a while the highest rates of infection were among young people between the ages of fifteen and twenty-four. And women in that age group were three times more likely to be infected because our women are also poor. Women in Africa have few if any sexual rights, particularly married women who are socialized to give in to sexual demands. Sixty percent of all HIV cases are women.

Possibly due to massive education efforts, the latest statistics indicate that young people in the age group between fifteen and twenty-four are beginning to do better, and they are not getting infected as frequently as before. It is easier for young people to change: they "google" and they use Facebook to get information, and they smarten up. But women in marriage are in a different situation all together because they are owned; in much of Africa the dowry men pay when marrying represents a purchase price.

Women in Africa, particularly in Kenya (I cannot speak for all African countries), have little or no access to land or major production rights. Once they are married, they work on the land, but they do not actually get to own it, or have any real say on what is produced. If a woman leaves her husband, she has nowhere to go. Meanwhile the former husband may want to have back the cows and the sheep that were his dowry, so that he now can marry other women. Thus, a separated or divorced woman is not welcome at her parent's home and has little choice but to stay in a marriage, however difficult it is.

Therefore, I believe that the church needs the courage and honesty to look at whether affected couples—especially those vulnerable to infection and re-infection by their partners and taking into consideration the fact that in Africa women have few if any sexual rights—should be left to their fate.

This journey has taken me twenty-five years. I must confess that twenty-five years ago I was in the forefront of burning condoms, which indicates something about the journey I have had to make to be able to make this statement today: In view of the fact that people are living longer, the need to rethink the condom as a prophylactic is inescapable. As a church we have to look at this issue with greater clarity.

I worked for Kenyan bishops for over ten years and have helped write pastoral letters and strategic plans. Yet we are still arguing over the issue, leaving service providers who are actually dealing with patients on the front line in a fuzzy limbo over what to do with couples who come for advice, counseling, and support. As people live longer and couples live longer, they cannot be abandoned to their fate. Barrier methods such as the condom and virucidal jellies, which are being tested currently in South Africa, are now more than ever necessary for the control and prevention of infection and re-infection. Statistics show that jellies give a protection rate of 50 percent. Condoms, with all that has been said against them, provide a protection rate of 80 to 90 percent. In my view, both condoms and jellies may protect African women from their vulnerability to HIV and AIDS.

Conclusion

Prevention of new infections is critical for HIV control, but equally important is the need to prevent widespread dispersion of drug-resistant viruses. Furthermore, the issue remains of the continued vulnerability of married women who are lulled into a false sense of security by the fact that they are married or who are simply too disempowered to tackle partners who engage in risky behavior. African women are often poor and secondary citizens at the mercy of strong patriarchal systems. There is generally no place for them to turn because of the way society is structured. It is also found acceptable that a woman's life is expendable, particularly while engaging in conjugal duties or in childbirth. This thought appears to find approval even in church teaching where such "martyrdom" for women is considered very meritorious. However the death of a mother has severe psychosocial consequences for any children left behind whose prospects for survival, especially for younger ones, are greatly diminished by the passing on of a female parent. The mother may go to heaven, but the children remain in hell.

With this in mind all modalities for prevention should be weighed anew without the intrusion of prior mindsets that were previously argued out in the realm of agents of contraception. The argument must be elevated to the level of prophylaxis and be engaged in with a level of honesty and with less furtiveness. Holiness is not achieved by refusing to think through a problem, sweeping it under the table, or refusing to recognize that it exists even if it is like the proverbial elephant in the room.

The following steps may all help toward keeping infection rates low.

1. Abstinence is an almost foolproof method, though accidental infection can occur where a spouse is caring for an infected partner without proper protection. Latex rubber—whether worn as gloves or as condoms—does reduce infections. Though claims of viruses passing through condoms abound, no such claims exist for latex gloves. No one would wish to frighten health-care providers, of course. Patients might get abandoned en masse. Abstinence was attractive in the pre-antiretroviral era where infected persons lost ground quickly and died. But with couples living longer and healthier lives, and with so many of them serodiscordant, sexual activity is inevitable.

2. Strict compliance to treatment regimes is crucial and needs to be in the region of over 97 percent. A high level of compliance leads to low viral loads and less resistance. Infection of a partner is a function of the viral load. The lower the viral load, the less the likelihood of infection. However, among patients in settings with poor resources, this level of compliance is often impossible. My patients have missed treatment because they have no food, no bus fare to come to the clinic, because they were locked out by the landlord for not paying rent, because they were arrested by the city police after being found hawking in downtown Nairobi, and any number of other misfortunes.

3. The church has tried hard to wish away the condom. It is my contention—having been at the ringside of the war against HIV/AIDS for a quarter of a century, as a clinician, a lobbyist, and a defender of ecclesiastical teachings—that this is impossible. The condom is simply the most accessible and most effective way of keeping infection levels low. It has practically no side effects; and if one wishes to conceive, one simply stops wearing it—thus it can hardly be accused of being

anti-life. It is over 90 percent effective, and if combined with proper antiretroviral use it reduces infection very effectively.

4. In regard to virucidal gels, much effort has gone into gels with the hope that it may get those who reject condom use off the hook. Finally, there is a virucidal product that is 40 to 50 percent effective. But many virucidal gels also have spermicidal properties, making them even more anti-life than the condom, so it defies logic why the church would consider gels a better option unless it is for other reasons not related to faith and morals.

The HIV/AIDS epidemic is a battle that will eventually be won, but there will never be a single silver bullet for it. One of the things that HIV/AIDS has done for humanity has been to remove us from our comfort zones and un-thought-out dogmas. The human is a thinking being; one cannot stifle thought and still be fully human. Unless one wishes to continue in acceptable levels of casuistry, the inescapable conclusion is that latex rubber saves lives.

While it is true that we are all on an epic journey to eternity, eternity begins in this life. We cannot claim to value endless life while we hold the lives of others so cheaply as we sojourn here on earth. Every moment that we live longer is an eternity in microcosm.

Notes

1. For more information, see the U.S. President's Plan for AIDS Relief, http://www.pepfar.gov/; and the Global Fund to Fight AIDS, Tuberculosis, and Malaria, http://www.theglobalfund.org/en/.

Part IV
THE FUTURE

Identity, Reciprocity, and Familial Relations
A Vision of Marriage for Twenty-First-Century Christians:
Intimacy, Reciprocity, and Identity
   Julie Hanlon Rubio (United States)
Vulnerability, Reciprocity, and Familial-Care Relations:
A Socioethical Contribution
   Christa Schnabl (Austria)
The Abuse of Power in the Church: Its Impact on Identity,
Reciprocity, and Familial Relations
   Aloysius Cartagenas (Philippines)

Pressing Global Social Challenges
Economics as if People Mattered
   Peter J. Henriot (Zambia)
Sustainability: An Ethical-Theological Perspective
   Simone Morandini (Italy)
Citizenship
   Myroslav Marynovych (Ukraine)

Theological Ethics in the Future
An Archbishop's Perspective on the Future of Theological
Ethics
   Reinhard Cardinal Marx (Germany)
Gender and Moral Theology: A Shared Project
   Julie Clague (Scotland)
Context and the Future of Theological Ethics: The Task
of Building Bridges
   Shaji George Kochuthara (India)
Racialization and Racism in Theological Ethics
   María Teresa Dávila (Puerto Rico)

INTRODUCTION

The conference's final day began with two parallel plenaries, followed by the discourse of Reinhard Cardinal Marx, and then a plenary on the future of theological ethics as seen by the "newer" scholars.

The first parallel focused on our expectations for ways we will be related in the future. In place of the traditional traits of Catholic marriage as procreative, permanent, exclusive, and complementary, Julie Hanlon Rubio from the United States offers three other key concepts: intimacy, reciprocity, and identity, within the context of companionate marriage. She expands on an *intimacy* that grows through time within a promise of lifelong fidelity in the context of community, a *reciprocity* that does not allow for violations of justice, and an *identity* marked by discipleship that propels us out into the world, invigorated to embrace a mission even larger than love.

Austria's Christa Schnabl presents a remarkably sensitive reflection on the provision of care to children and to elders as at once integrating both reciprocity with autonomy and an ethics of care with an ethics of justice. Aloysius Cartagenas, from the Philippines, offers a very prophetic paper on the effects of the sexual abuse crisis on the church's ability to promote credibly honest and abiding relationships. His evident love for the church, in what it offers and in what it can offer, but also in the sins within it, reminds us of how we need to see the church as not only "the bride of Christ" but also as in need of reconciliation and reformation, both locally and universally.

The second parallel plenary addressed three issues on the horizon of the world church: economics, sustainability, and migration and citizenship. From Zambia, Peter Henriot considers three major papal encyclicals, Paul VI's *Progressio populorum*, John Paul II's *Sollicitudo rei socialis*, and Benedict XVI's *Caritas in veritate* in order to identify enduring insights from the Catholic social justice tradition that can animate an approach to ethics that guides economics to promote human dignity.

Italy's Simone Morandini develops the theological foundations for an environmental ethics and insists that sustainability designates a subject who is vulnerable and well aware of the relationality on which her or his life is based. He concludes by offering basic principles and virtues so as to realize this ethics in ordinary life.

Because of a year-long protest against the policies of the Schengen visa-treaty countries, Myroslav Marynovych presented his paper via a taped transmission from his native Ukraine. Marynovych raises two issues: the grounds for his protest against the way other nations receive migrating peoples and the responsibilities of nations that prompt their citizens to move beyond their borders in search of work. His Ukranian context serves as a microcosm for issues of migration and citizenship around the world.

Germany's Cardinal Marx prompted the participants in a fairly forthright presentation to ask questions of the universal notion of the claims of theological ethics. Attentive to the autonomy of particular cultures, he challenges us to find critical, engaging ways to offer anew a natural law that is normative and universal while able to appreciate the needs of the local in a globalized world. He closes by exhorting us to assist the church in the moral formation of its members.

The final plenary was designed to present new voices as we look to the future of theological ethics. From Scotland, Julie Clague enters into the encounter between theological ethics and gender. She helps us to appreciate how even though the category gender seems new, it has always been present in any anthropology. Clague invites us to see how in many ways gender captures the development of theological ethics in its past, present, and future. In facing the future, she suggests that to the extent that we are true to gender, we will develop an integral and viable theological ethics for the future. She closes her essay with a theatrical sketch of a delightful fiftieth-anniversary date between Theological Ethics and Gender in contemporary Trento.

India's Shaji George Kochuthara examines context and highlights the challenges of discourse when every person seems to have his or her own set of presuppositions about what constitutes the "moral"; when secular claims seek to reduce the claims of religious-minded people; and when more fundamentalist persons try to reduce the complexity of religious logic to a sound bite. By the same token, globalization offers a radically reductive autonomy as its worldview of ethics. Kochuthara advises us to return to our actual contexts but not as if we have not already learned the lessons of others in need. In many ways, his essay captures the challenge of Cardinal Marx.

Finally in a tour-de-force, María Teresa Dávila, from Puerto Rico, writes that "theological ethics must find a way to acknowledge the historical 'sin of the world,' the air we breathe and the sin embedded within, in order to highlight the human damage in which we continue to participate and of which we are complicit by virtue of our inadequate attempts at resistance." She concludes that with "respect to the sin of racism, theological ethics has missed the mark"; she urges "the coming together of theologians and ethicists from a variety of historically racialized groups to ask corporately the hard questions of privilege, institutional violence, racialization of the other, dehumanization of entire groups, and the essentialization of the white or the European as paradigmatically human." Fittingly, after four days of questions dealing with justice, migration, economics, and identity, the topic of racism, raised earlier by others such as Magesa and Massingale, became the final theme of our concern.

A Vision of Marriage
for Twenty-First-Century Christians:
Intimacy, Reciprocity, and Identity

Julie Hanlon Rubio

In 2009 after many drafts and much controversy, the United States Catholic bishops released a pastoral letter on marriage in which they identified four key threats to marriage: contraception, divorce, cohabitation, and same-sex marriage. Each of these practices is described as diminishing something fundamental to Christian marriage. According to the bishops, contraception separates the unitive and procreative meanings of sexuality and treats children as a lifestyle choice rather than a gift; cohabitation involves claiming the goods of marriage before making a commitment of exclusivity; divorce breaks the promise of lifelong fidelity; and same-sex marriage denies the centrality of gender complementarity to married love.[1] The bishops are "troubled by the fact that far too many people do not understand what it means to say that marriage—both as a natural institution and a Christian sacrament—is a blessing and gift from God."[2]

The bishops defend a traditional understanding of marriage as *procreative, permanent, exclusive,* and *complementary*.[3] Though the document includes some of the beautiful, personalist language that characterizes the work of Pope John Paul II (such as "total self-gift," "communion of persons," "become what you are"), it is dominated by more doctrinal language (such as frequent references to "God's plan for marriage," an insistence that marriage involves "the union of a man and a woman," and descriptions of marriage as "a sacramental sign of salvation").[4] Clearly, the bishops feel the need to define marriage in order to slow further cultural redefinition and to emphasize the structure and purpose of marriage as it has been traditionally understood, rather than focusing on its intrinsic or relational goods.

In the United States and across the industrialized world, however, many are beginning to question this traditional vision. Most historians and social scientists who study marriage characterize our time as one of great transition.[5] While the history of marriage is marked by diversity, certain features have been common in most cultures: heterosexual union, male authority, shared labor, the inclusion of wives and servants in the family, and common residence.[6] This is traditional, or institutional, marriage. The kind of marriage that became common in modern times (involving romantic relationships between spouses, limitation of family to parents and children, a division between work and home involving women's dominance in homemaking and child-rearing and men's labor outside the home) arose in the second half of the eighteenth century.[7]

Key contemporary changes to the companionate marriage model include declining birth and marriage rates, rising cohabitation and divorce rates, increasing gender equity, and support for the rights for same-sex couples.[8] In view of these changes, many identify a worldwide movement away from institutional marriage (supported and controlled by family, community, and the state) to companionate marriage in which the relationship between the spouses is more important than the concerns of extended family and extends beyond the raising of children.[9] Some see a further, problematic development toward individualistic marriage in which a focus on personal fulfillment excludes the possibility of sacrifice for the sake of one's spouse, children, or community.[10]

The church could respond to these changes by identifying threats and reasserting its traditional teaching. Certainly, it is important to criticize an excessive individualism that weakens families and communities and also truncates the mission of the Christian family to be a leaven for good in the world. In addition, decades of social science research have established that cohabitation is linked to higher divorce rates, and divorce is associated with lower levels of well-being for children and adults.[11] It is good for the bishops to call attention to these problems, which are especially acute in the United States.

In emphasizing the negative and reasserting the traditional, however, we may be missing a chance to celebrate positive changes and to put forward a compelling vision of marriage that ordinary men and women can recognize as valuable and worthy of their efforts. Falling back on traditional language upholding marriage as procreative, exclusive, permanent, and complementary and leading with condemnations is not an adequate response to the developing reality of marriage, nor does it capture the whole of the contemporary Catholic tradition. For the future, for the sake of marriage and families, we need a more inviting message.

At its core, marriage is about self-giving love, as married couples well know. In this essay, I suggest that a loving marriage embodies the values of *intimacy*, *reciprocity*, and *identity*. These are values married couples build over time through the practices that mark their everyday lives. *Intimacy* is sharing one's self with one's partner, *reciprocity* is maintaining a balance of giving and receiving, and *identity*, understood here as Christian identity, entails a shared, embodied commitment to the common good, rooted in discipleship with Christ. Today, though few connect marriage to the common good, growth in intimacy and reciprocity is worldwide. An inviting, contemporary Christian theology of marriage will rejoice in progress and inspire couples to embrace an even richer vision of married life.

Intimacy

Around the world, the desire for intimacy is increasing, and companionate marriage is on the rise.[12] In the industrialized West, passion draws people into marriage. Whereas previously families and communities played important roles in the selection of lifelong partners and delight in one's spouse was a pleasant but unexpected bonus, today many more see romantic love at the center of the choice to marry; they also understand its lack as a serious deficiency. Without denying significant, continuing cultural variations, most who study marriage would agree that "The notion of free choice and marriage for love [that] triumph[ed] as a cultural ideal" in Western Europe and the United States in the mid-eighteenth century is spreading to developing countries in the global South and East.[13]

Whereas institutional marriages required major input from the extended family and the community, neither have the same centrality in companionate marriage. The couple themselves is recognized as the center of marriage. Though most seek the blessing of family and plan to participate in an extended family, neither is required. Children are an important part of marriage and often the impetus for marriage, but they are no longer the only reason for getting married. Most couples still marry with the expectation that they will bring children into the world, adopt them, or co-parent those they already have, but their marriage often (though not always) precedes children and most will share long years together after their children are gone. Their partnership in life and love is the heart of their marriage, not their desire or duty to procreate.

In the United States, perhaps the epicenter of the movement toward companionate marriage, young adults overwhelmingly say that they would like to marry their "soul mate."[14] Only a small minority thinks that marriage is primarily about having and raising children.[15] To "settle" for someone who has the potential to be a good provider and partner would be, for most Americans, to deny something fundamental to marriage. Instead, they seek what sociologist Andrew Cherlin calls "a Superrelationship, an intensely private spiritualized union, combining sexual fidelity, romantic love, emotional intimacy, and togetherness."[16] Despite their knowledge of the fragility of marriage, the vast majority continues to marry and expects marriage to last a lifetime.

However, without the institutional structures, social norms, and family pressures that kept couples together in the past, marital breakdown has become pervasive. If one includes break-ups of marriages and cohabiting relationships, "[F]amily life in the United States has more transitions than anywhere else."[17] The troubling consequences for children of this instability are well documented.[18] Most Americans believe that marriage ought to be a permanent union and see divorce as a last resort.[19] Yet, the high rate of marital decline is an unsurprising result of the turn to a companionate model of marriage. When expectations for intimacy rise, disappointment is common, and more break-ups are inevitable.[20] The feelings that draw people into marriage and allow them to have happier marriages are the same ones that cause their marriages to be less stable.

In Western Europe, companionate marriage seems to be in decline, though a belief in companionate relationships continues to thrive. Today, cohabitation is much more prominent as an alternative to marriage.[21] Fewer couples eventually marry in state or church, and Europe may have transitioned to a society in which marriage is a choice but not one valued more than cohabitation, even for couples with children.[22] Yet, European unions are actually more stable than American ones. Europeans have a higher average age at first marriage, lower birth rates, and lower divorce rates.[23] While there are notable regional differences, the overall movement is toward acceptance of many different types of long-term, companionate relationships.[24] The growth in desire for intimacy is linked to a less enthusiastic embrace of marriage as an institution, but commitment and fidelity are far from dead.

Though the popularity of the companionate model of marriage is growing, it is less common in the developing world. In some Latin and South American countries, marriage is in serious decline. Many couples elect to remain *en junto* rather than marry in the state or the church.[25] In other countries, such as Mexico, marriage continues to be the norm.[26] Traditionally, many Latin American women hoped for little more from their partners than respect and money to support their children, while many men saw nothing wrong with infidelity. However, desire for companionate marriage is becoming more widespread. Jennifer Hirsch shows that younger Mexican couples on both sides of the U.S. border are rejecting the traditional norms of their elders and asking for more fulfillment from marriage.[27] While a marriage marked by mutual respect was acceptable to earlier generations, young adults seeking to differentiate themselves from their elders increasingly embrace modern ideas, including the idea that love is central to marriage.[28]

In Mexico, sexual intimacy and emotional closeness are particularly important, equality is still emerging, and parenting plays a more central role than it does in the European and the U.S. versions of companionate marriage.[29] However, the increasing importance of love is evident even in the language used by women to describe sex. Whereas in the past, the phase *cuando el me usa* was frequently employed, today it is more common to hear *hacer el amor*.[30] Though women are ahead of men in embracing the new ideas, men are not far behind them in a desire for more closeness than earlier generations would have imagined.[31] In Latin America, as in the United States and Europe, people are approaching marriage with expectations of love and intimacy. Even as couples around the world recognize the fragility of bonds chosen rather than imposed, few wish to return to earlier customs.

Christians ought to rejoice in this development, for contemporary Christian theology has increasingly come to appreciate the centrality of intimate companionship to marriage. Married theologians have been particularly good at describing how marriage can be "an intimate partnership of life and love," though few use either the language of bride and bridegroom sometimes favored in traditional theology or the hyperbolic language of popular culture.[32] Instead, they speak of spouses as best friends who belong to each other, of lovers who delight in each other's embrace, of partners who share a willingness to stretch and be changed for each other. Through the graced and the heartbreaking moments of marriage, theologians claim, we become who we are meant to be: people who can love through good times and bad.[33]

Christians, however, are rightly concerned that companionate marriage is more fragile than traditional marriage. Some social critics call upon parents to reject the ongoing search for intimacy and stay together for the sake of their children.[34] They celebrate those who are "willing to sacrifice the thrill of a love letter for the betterment of their children."[35] They assert that marriage is primarily about bringing up the next generation. Essentially, they seek a revival of traditional marriage. However, traditionalist critics undercut the force of their argument by assuming that divorce necessarily leads to greater happiness. Ironically, they sound very much like more radical thinkers who suggest that adults should abandon marriage altogether.[36] Both defenders and critics of marriage have low expectations for marriage.

The contemporary Catholic tradition can offer something richer by affirming the importance of intimacy *and* the centrality of commitment. It draws from the dominant companionate marriage model but insists that lifelong vows provide the framework that allows for vulnerability and maturity.[37] Vows to stay together through the darker times allow couples to grow both individually and together. From a Christian perspective, marriage is much more than a romance between soul mates who effortlessly remain passionate. It is a way of life structured by vows that offers a greater opportunity to experience and practice love than any short-term relationship ever could.

For Christians, the context of vowed intimacy is community. David Matzko McCarthy writes that marriage within the church "is a witness of faith. This great joy is ours because we are not alone; we are part of a people, a body, and a countersociety that sets itself to the task of living in light of God's self-giving love. . . . The promises of self-giving love are not our private possessions, but shared in the worship and works of the Church."[38] Human promises, though fragile, are taken up by God and supported by the faith of the community.[39] Community is not an externally imposed burden but a source of support and the context for Christian living.

Marriage is a sacrament not apart from but through intimate partnership. In an important sense, "Marriage is a statement against the isolationism of the world. This union is to empower people to live more fully, to connect and act together."[40] The marriage of two people who have found each other and decided to bind their futures together, knowing the difficulties they will inevitably face, can be a prophetic symbol for others.[41] A strong married couple symbolizes hope because they commit to care for each other and remain together even when it would be easier not to. "[T]o a world craving reconciliation and community," their continued striving for a better, deeper relationship can be an inspiration.[42] If they can overcome their differences and stay together, what more can be overcome? Their vowed, intimate partnership, lived not apart from but in the midst of community, is a tangible sign of God's enduring love for humanity.

Reciprocity

While affirming the centrality of love to marriage, Christians insist that love has to be reciprocal to be real. In *Caritas in veritate*, Benedict XVI uses reciprocity as a synonym for gratuity to describe a relational ethic in which we give and receive with respect for persons instead of always attempting to get the most we can without regard for someone else's well-being.[43] In feminist thought, reciprocity is understood as requiring respect and engagement, or being oneself while allowing another person to be her or his self.[44] Lisa Sowle Cahill names reciprocity as one of the central values of modern Christian family ethics. She notes that we cannot speak of "mutual self-gift" without acknowledging the social inequality that renders such mutuality practically impossible.[45] Reciprocity implies equality between men and women, which means that both partners give and receive.[46] As David Cloutier puts it, marriage is a promise "to give oneself to the other person [or] place one's life in the other's hands," and that kind of a promise has to be reciprocal to be just.[47]

As with intimacy, reciprocity in marriage is increasing. In the United States, as more women work outside the home, more women and men are sharing paid labor, housework, and decision making.[48] Traditional roles are being reformulated with more overlap and less distinction. Power is more evenly distributed. Most Americans now understand marriage as an equal partnership, and only a minority finds changes in gender roles problematic, though vestiges of separate-spheres ideology remain.[49]

Although the spread of gender equity is uneven, gender roles are changing everywhere. In developing economies, changes are often connected to migration patterns. In countries that send many women abroad to work, men are learning to do housework, and through their experience they are coming to see that work in less-gendered terms.[50] In Mexican and Mexican-American communities, women are gaining new power as workers or heads of household, and this is transforming their marriages.[51] Women are finding that work outside the home is often accompanied by power to make decisions within the home and increasing freedom to move around freely outside it.[52] Whereas traditional wives did not talk back to husbands, modern couples listen and talk together.[53] Hirsch claims that "sharing the *mando* [power] is a crack in the ideology of separate spheres" and the power imbalance that came with it.[54] Although change is still emerging, greater reciprocity can be seen in both developed and developing nations.

Christians should rejoice in the increase of reciprocity, because greater reciprocity means better marriages. With more balance between spouses, mutual understanding increases, and more intimacy is possible. Sociologists find that with shared roles come greater understanding and closeness.[55] Increases in reciprocity are associated with increased marital intimacy and stability in both developed and developing economies.[56] There is evidence that greater fluidity in roles allows for the creative adaptation and flexibility that can be crucial to surviving the more stressful times in a marriage.[57] Some argue that emphasizing the distinctiveness of each gender and the ways in which they complement each other is important to successful marriage.[58] However, reciprocity in marriage need not be feared. Marital happiness is associated with high levels of gender equity.[59] While conflicts can increase with greater role overlap, they have decreased in the last decade.[60] Moreover, entrenched roles are not the only way to guarantee a sense of purpose or marital stability. Christian women and men can be called to a balance of give-and-take that will strengthen their intimacy and cement their commitment to stay together.

Although significant progress has been made, the value of reciprocity is still violated everywhere. While the gaps are narrowing, disparities both in time spent on housework and in power in the exercise of decision making have yet to be eliminated.[61] Even more distressing, in the United States, one of every four women will be abused at some point.[62] In other parts of the world, these rates are tragically higher, and many women still believe it is their duty to stay with abusing husbands for the sake of their children.[63] Among Mexican-Americans, even though younger couples are sharing power, men often retain the privilege of using violence to keep women in their place.[64] Power imbalances exemplified in unequal work loads are at the root of domestic violence, yet discussion of both remains marginal to most theological treatments of marriage.[65]

Adultery is yet another violation of reciprocity that is curiously absent from most theological discussions of marriage. Infidelity is disapproved of by the vast majority of people in the United States but admitted by 15 percent of women and 25 percent of men. Opposition to infidelity is lower in Europe and Latin America and its prevalence is higher, especially for men.[66] Margaret Farley notes that in Africa there is asymmetry rather than reciprocity in the 30 to 40 percent of marriages that are polygynous, as "women's bodies belong to their husbands" while "husbands' bodies can be shared."[67] Infidelity and polygyny remain unchallenged because the assumptions behind them—men's need for sex and women's role in satisfying them—are still operative.[68]

Feminist theologians from all countries ask for more reciprocity in the family, for a balance of giving and taking so intimacy can flourish, for an end to abuse and infidelity. In the United States, Cahill writes that "the task of a Christian social ethic of sex is to imbue sexual and reproductive behavior with qualities of respect, empathy, reciprocity, and mutual fidelity, which would allow sexual and parental love to be transforming agents in society in general."[69] As Ada María Isasi-Díaz puts it, many Latina women are no longer willing "to remain married and/or living with men who oppress us and, yes, even mistreat us."[70] From Kenya, Anne Nasimiyu-Wasike argues, "Mutuality means entering into others' experience and trying to journey together to bring about transformation and change in equal human relationships. Justice is needed to put this into effect."[71] While rightfully worried about Western attempts to judge African Traditional Religion, Nasimiyu-Wasike, like most African women theologians, affirms "a global need for liberation of women."[72]

Christians need to affirm reciprocity wherever it is found.[73] Attempts to revive the traditionalist language of gender complementarity are simply inadequate to the contemporary situation in which flexibility in gender roles is associated with high marital quality, and inflexibility is associated with power imbalances, abuse, adultery, and infidelity. Violations of reciprocity—especially the most egregious—should be named as sins against justice. Rather than emphasizing the gender ideology of the past, Christians should affirm greater fluidity in gender roles that is associated with marital intimacy and satisfaction. As *Caritas in veritate* affirmed, both men and women are called to give of themselves in love.[74] Reciprocity is the ground of true intimacy in marriage.

Identity

If a theology of marriage is to be Christian, however, it must be about more than intimacy and reciprocity; it should call married people to reach beyond the microcosm of the family into the larger world. Traditional Catholic theology has often sought to give marriage a distinctive Christian identity by referencing Genesis 1:26-28 and 2:18-24, Matthew 19:6, Ephesians 5:21-25, and John 2:1-11.[75] The U.S. bishops' pastoral letter follows this trend with its cover depicting the wedding at Cana, "where Christ proclaimed the greatness of marriage."[76] Though these stories have held central places in the church's teaching, they do not fully capture the distinctiveness of Christian identity as it relates to marriage.

The Genesis creation narratives speak to the goodness of male-female lifelong companionship, characterizing their union as "one flesh." The goodness of this union is affirmed by Jesus in the Gospel of Matthew and by Paul in the Letter to the Ephesians, though little is said about how married life is to be lived. The story of the wedding at Cana has been the source of Catholic teaching on the sacramentality of marriage, though scripture scholars, both Catholic and Protestant, interpret the wedding setting as symbolic of the future messianic banquet, and rarely comment on the passage's relevance to marriage.[77] Though marriage is certainly viewed as natural and positive in scripture, these passages tell us little about how married Christians might approach daily life.

In contrast, in the writing of lay theologians, Christian identity is understood as discipleship, and discipleship entails a concern for the least linked to faith in Christ. This reality modifies and lifts up the relationship between two people, giving it a higher purpose. To understand what Jesus thought about marriage, we need to look beyond Cana and listen to his hard sayings.[78] In these often-shocking sayings, Jesus spoke to the potential of marriage to distract people from living out their faith, called his followers to leave their families (Luke 9:57-62), and even claimed they should hate their families (Luke 14:26-27) in comparison to their love for him and his mission.

As Lisa Cahill notes, while these sayings may seem baffling, they become clear when viewed in the context of Jesus' public ministry to the marginalized, for "loyalty to one's own group and dedication to the status of that group over all others and at the expense of whoever stands in the way are incompatible with a life of mercy, service, and compassion for the neighbor in need or for the social outcast and the poor."[79] If Jesus preaches that devotion to family can be dangerous to the person who wants to live a holy life marked by compassion, the implication is that his disciples who marry and become parents must resist the temptation to make care for kin their only mission in life. Jesus' witness and message should inspire contemporary Christians not to give up on marriage but to re-envision it.

Christian marriage begins with love in the home but extends that love into the world. Most couples will serve the world by bringing children into it. In the most prophetic of the church's teachings on marriage, *Familiaris consortio*, John Paul II calls "service to life" the most essential and irreplaceable social task of the family.[80] However, that service includes "spiritual fruitfulness" in serving others, and rearing children in Christian faith, which involves teaching them about the value of all life, including those of the poor and marginalized.[81] Not all Christian marriages involve children, though most do; and parenting as Christian spouses means attempting to form children as loving persons both inside the home and in the world.

Because families are "by nature and vocation open to other families and society," they must take up their appropriate role in the social and political realms.[82] Christian couples need to imagine how their lives can be of service to those Jesus held up in the last judgment of Matthew 25:31-46. In this parable, Jesus gives specific examples of how we respond to the needs of our "brethren," and in doing so draw close to God.[83] This parable offers a nice counterpoint to the hard sayings, for even as Jesus challenges his hearers to ask whether familial bonds stand in the way of serving God, he also offers an alternative practice that creates new kin relationships most would not have thought possible. Though families may begin feeding the hungry at our dinner tables, discipleship requires us to look outside our doors for others who may be in far greater need of nourishment and to rethink our ideas about who is our mother, our father, our brother, and our sister.

A Christian identity will shape marriage in profoundly counter-cultural ways. One does not have to be Christian to embrace a social mission for families, but this sort of focus is uncommon outside the church. It can be uncommon inside the church as well, as Christian families are as vulnerable as others to narrowing their focus to themselves. But if we rest there, even with greater intimacy and reciprocity, we fail to embrace the social implications of the sacrament of marriage as it was transformed by encounter with the life of Jesus of Nazareth, who healed, ate with, and lifted up the poor.

Conclusion: Beyond Threats to Invitations

Family life is in transition. Men and women increasingly desire a companionate marriage marked by intimacy and reciprocity. This growing focus on love and equality can be affirmed by Christians as more in keeping with human flourishing than is traditional marriage. But we also can invite people to more: to an *intimacy* that grows through time within a promise of lifelong fidelity in the context of community, a *reciprocity* that does not allow for violations of justice, and an *identity* marked by discipleship that propels us out into the world, invigorated to embrace a mission even larger than love.

Notes

1. United States Catholic Conference of Bishops, *Marriage: Love and Life in the Divine Plan* (Washington, DC: USCCB Publishing, 2009). Threats to marriage are outlined in the introduction, 3, and developed later in the document, 17-27.

2. USCCB, *Marriage*, 2-3.

3. Ibid., 7-8, 32-37.

4. The references to John Paul II can be found in USCCB, *Marriage*, 33, 12, and 45. More doctrinal language dominates the introduction (3-4) and the document as a whole.

5. Paul Amato et al., *Alone Together: How Marriage in America Is Changing* (Cambridge, MA: Harvard University Press, 2007). The authors place most scholars either in the "marital decline" (crisis) or the "marital resilience" (transition) camp before attempting to carve out some space in the middle (4-6).

6. Stephanie Coontz, "The Evolution of American Families," in *Families as They Really Are*, ed. Barbara J. Risman (New York: W. W. Norton, 2010), 30-47, here 33. Coontz emphasizes the diversity of families in history and across cultures.

7. Coontz, "Evolution of American Families," 39-40.

8. Stephanie Coontz, *Marriage: A History from Obedience to Intimacy or How Love Conquered Marriage* (New York: Viking, 2006). As more women work outside the home, women and men are sharing responsibilities for paid labor, housework, and decision making in the household. Traditional roles are being reformulated with more overlap and less distinction. See Scott Coltrane and Michelle Adams, *Gender and Families*, 2nd ed. (Lanham, MD: Rowman & Littlefield, 2008).

9. Amato et al., *Alone Together*, 246.

10. Ibid., 235-36. Evidence for this perspective includes declining marital interaction, and the participation of married couples in shared social networks, resulting in more separate lives.

11. On cohabitation, see Amato's analysis in *Alone Together*, 21-22. More recent studies differentiate between premarital cohabitation and less serious, more unstable arrangements, but the association between cohabitation and divorce has not diminished. For a comprehensive overview of the literature on the effects of divorce on children, see Paul Amato, "Children of Divorce in the 1990s: An Update of the Amato and Keith (1991) Meta-analysis," *Journal of Family Psychology* 15 (2001): 355-70. Forthcoming is Robert E. Emery, Christopher Beam, and Jenna Rowen, "Adolescents' Experiences of Parental

Divorce," in *Encyclopedia of Adolescence*, ed. B. Brown and M. Prinstein (New York: Academic Press, 2011).

12. Jennifer S. Hirsh, *A Courtship after Marriage: Sexuality and Love in Mexican Transnational Families* (Berkeley: University of California Press, 2007), 175-79, cites studies showing the spread of this trend from the industrialized West to countries as diverse as Nigeria, Papua New Guinea, Brazil, Spain, and China. This movement is also documented in Coontz, *Marriage*, and assumed by the vast majority of historians and social scientists who write about marriage.

13. Coontz, *Marriage*, 7.

14. Barbara Dafoe Whitehead and David Popenoe, *"Who Wants to Marry a Soulmate?" The State of Our Unions* (New Brunswick, NJ: National Marriage Project, 2001).

15. Andrew Cherlin, *The Marriage Go-Round: The State of Marriage and Family in America Today* (New York: Alfred Knopf, 2009), 139.

16. Ibid., 140.

17. Ibid., 9.

18. Ibid., 20.

19. Ibid., 26.

20. Ibid., 188.

21. Adrian Thatcher, "Living Together before Marriage: The Theological and Pastoral Opportunities," in *Celebrating Christian Marriage*, ed. Adrian Thatcher (Edinburgh: T & T Clark, 2001), 56. In the 1990s, 70 percent of couples in the United Kingdom cohabited before their first marriage.

22. Cherlin, *The Marriage Go-Round*, 17. Coontz, *Marriage*, 272.

23. Cherlin, *The Marriage Go-Round*, 272.

24. Marriage is more central to Italian and Spanish than to northern European cultures (Cherlin, *The Marriage Go-Round*, 33).

25. In 2008, 29 percent of Salvadorans identified themselves as single, 25 percent were married, and 29 percent, *en junto*. In rural communities, the marriage rates are lower, perhaps 10 percent. See National Reproductive Health Surveys, http://www.cdc.gov/reproductivehealth/surveys/SurveyCountries.htm#Latin%20America%20&%20Caribbean%20(y%20en%20Español.

26. Bron B. Ingoldsby, "Families in Latin America," in *Families in Global and Multicultural Perspective*, 2nd ed., ed. Bron B. Ingoldsby and Suzanna D. Smith (Thousand Oaks, CA: Sage Publications, 2006), 274-90, here 280. Ninety-five percent marry by age fifty.

27. Hirsch, *A Courtship after Marriage*, 16.

28. Ibid., 9.

29. Ibid., 178.

30. Ibid., 214.

31. Ibid., 154, 174.

32. *Gaudium et spes*, 48, http://www.vatican.va/archive/hist_councils/ii_vatican_council/documents/vat-ii_cons_19651207_gaudium-et-spes_en.html.

33. Some of the best theologians writing on marriage include Richard Gaillardetz, *A Daring Promise: A Spirituality of Christian Marriage* (New York: Crossroad, 2002); David Matkzo McCarthy, *Sex and Love in the Home*, new ed. (London: SCM, 2004); and John Grabowski, *Sex and Virtue: An Introduction to Sexual Ethics* (Washington, DC: Catholic University Press of America, 2003).

34. See, for instance, the publications of the Institute for American Values, including the annual report, *The State of Our Unions*, http://www.americanvalues.org.

35. Caitlin Flanagan, "Is There Hope for the American Marriage?" *Time* (July 2, 2009), http://www.time.com/time/nation/article/0,8599,1908243,00.html.

36. Cherlin, *The Marriage-Go-Round*, 192-99, counsels couples to "slow down" for the sake of their kids, which he sees as more realistic than seeking to revive marriage.

37. David Cloutier, *Love, Reason, and God's Story: An Introduction to Catholic Sexual Ethics* (Winona, MN: St. Mary's Press, 2008), 174-75.

38. Ibid.

39. On this theme, see also Jo McGowan, "Marriage versus Living Together," in *Perspectives on Marriage: A Reader*, 2nd ed., ed. Kieran Scott and Michael Warren (New York: Oxford University Press, 2001): 83-87. Of course, there are limits to the suffering human beings should be asked to bear; see David P. Gushee, *Getting Marriage Right: Realistic Counsel for Saving & Strengthening Relationships* (Grand Rapids, MI: Baker Books, 2004), 103, 167.

40. James L. Empereur, S.J., and Christopher G. Kiesling, O.P., *The Liturgy That Does Justice* (Collegeville, MD: Liturgical Press, 1990), 183.

41. Michael G. Lawler, "Marriage in the Bible," in *Perspectives on Marriage: A Reader*, 2nd ed., ed. Kieran Scott and Michael Warren (New York: Oxford University Press, 2001), 11-12.

42. Empereur and Kiesling, *The Liturgy That Does Justice*, 185.

43. Benedict XVI, *Caritas in veritate* (Washington, DC: United States Catholic Conference, 2009), 39.

44. Toinette Eugene et al., "Appropriation and Reciprocity in Womanist/Mujerista/Feminist Work," in *Feminist Theological Ethics: A Reader*, ed. Lois Daly (Louisville, KY: Westminster Press, 1994), 88-117, here 95.

45. Lisa Sowle Cahill, *Sex, Gender, and Christian Ethics* (Cambridge: Cambridge University Press, 1996), 119.

46. Cahill notes that magisterial teaching is sometimes compromised because mutual self-gift is counseled without attention to social equality (*Sex, Gender, and Christian Ethics*, 205).

47. Cloutier, *Love, Reason, and God's Story*, 174.

48. Amato et al., *Alone Together*, 28.

49. Eighty-five percent of Americans agree that most women have to work, and 81 percent approve of women working even if it is not necessary (Cherlin, *The Marriage Go-Round*, 125). Greater gender equity in decision making, jobs, care for children, and politics is approved of by most Americans as well (Scott Coltrane and Michele Adams, *Gender and Families*, 2nd ed. [Lanham, MD: Rowman & Littlefield, 2008], 331).

50. Hirsch, *A Courtship after Marriage*, 152.

51. Ibid., 149-50.

52. Ibid., 149.

53. Ibid., 132.

54. Ibid., 134.

55. Amato et al., *Alone Together*, 31, found that egalitarianism is associated with greater closeness and marital stability.

56. Hirsch, *A Courtship after Marriage*, 126-27, notes that traditional Mexican marriages were characterized by respect (but allowed for infidelity), while in modern marriages closeness is more valued and more common.

57. Amato et al., *Alone Together*, 27, 261-62.

58. Bradford W. Wilcox and Steven L. Nock, "What's Love Got to Do with It? Equality, Equity, Commitment and Women's Marital Quality," *Social Forces* 84, no. 3 (March 2006): 1321–45.

59. Amato et al., *Alone Together*, 212, found that what makes for a quality marriage is similar for men and women, despite the large literature on gender differences. The decline in traditional gender attitudes is positively associated with marital happiness (215). See also Kristen W. Springer, "Research or Rhetoric? A Response to Wilcox and Nock," *Sociological Forum* 22, no. 1 (March 2007): 111-16, who argues that the majority of current research shows that housework equity and emotional investment is linked to marital happiness, not gender complementarity.

60. Amato et al., *Alone Together*, 217.

61. Ibid., 27-28. Amato et al. note that more couples are sharing housework and decision making, but since women are progressing faster than men, disparities and conflicts remain common.

62. Patricia Tjaden and Nancy Thoennes, National Institute of Justice, and the Centers of Disease Control and Prevention, "Prevalence, Incidence, and Consequences of Violence against Women," http://www.ncjrs.gov/txtfiles1/nij/183781.txt.

63. Percentages of women who have ever experienced domestic violence range from a low of 13 percent in Japan to about 70 percent in Peru and Ethiopia. See the WHO study, http://www.who.int/gender/violence/who_multicountry_study/en/index.html. See also Hirsch, *A Courtship after Marriage*, 117.

64. Hirsch, *A Courtship after Marriage*, 135-39.

65. USCCB, *Marriage*, 24. The bishops do not name abuse as a threat to marriage and offer only one short paragraph on the subject.

66. Adrian J. Blow and Kelley Hartnett, "Adultery in Committed Relationships II: A Substantive Review," *Journal of Marital and Family Therapy* 31, no. 2 (2005): 221. In the United States, 80 percent of those surveyed say adultery is always wrong, but in other countries, the numbers of those disapproving are far lower: 67 percent in Britain and Italy, 36 percent in Russia, 58 percent in Japan, and even higher in Latin America and Africa; see Judith Treas, "Infidelity," in *International Encyclopedia of Marriage and Family Relationships*, vol. 4, 2nd ed., ed. James J. Ponzeti (New York: Macmillan Reference USA, 2000): 299-308. Hirsch, *A Courtship after Marriage*, 116-17, reports that many traditional Mexican men feel entitled to seek satisfaction elsewhere if their wives do not comply with their demands for sex. Infidelity is not necessarily seen as disrespectful by wives, as long as it is not flagrant.

67. Margaret A. Farley, *Just Love: A Framework for Christian Sexual Ethics* (New York: Continuum, 2006), 85.

68. Ibid., 81.

69. Cahill, *Sex, Gender, and Christian Ethics*, 119.

70. Ada María Isasi-Díaz, *Mujerista Theology: A Theology for the 21st Century* (Maryknoll, NY: Orbis Books, 2001), 137.

71. Anne Nasimiyu-Wasike, "Is Mutuality Possible? An African Response," *Missiology* 29, no. 1 (January 2001): 48. "Reciprocation" is used as a synonym for mutuality (45).

72. Ibid., 51.

73. Christianity is associated with the growth of companionate marriage in some developing countries (Hirsch, *A Courtship after Marriage*, 178-79).

74. Benedict XVI, *Caritas in veritate*, 53-54. Benedict claims that to be human is to live in relation with others, with "true openness" and "profound interpenetration."

75. USCCB, *Marriage*, 55, 8-12.

76. Ibid., 55.

77. See, for instance, Raymond Brown, *The Gospel According to John: I-XII: The Anchor Bible* (New York: Doubleday, 1966), who writes, "The dramatic action is set in the context of a wedding; in the Old Testament (Isa liv 4-8, lxii 4-5) this is used to symbolize the messianic days, and both the wedding and the banquet are symbols on which Jesus drew (Matt viii 11, xxii 1-14; Luke xxii 16-18)" (104-5); and Francis J. Maloney, S.D.B., *The Gospel of John: Sacra Pagina*, vol. 4 (Collegeville, MN: Liturgical Press, 1998), who states, "The setting of a marriage feast also summons up biblical images of the messianic era and the messianic fullness, marked by wine and abundance of fine foods (cf. Hos 2.19-20; Isa 25.6-8; Jer 2.2; Song of Songs)" (66).

78. See, for instance, David Matzko McCarthy, *The Good Life: Genuine Christianity for the Middle Class* (Grand Rapids, MI: Brazos, 2006); 49-57; Lisa Sowle Cahill, *Family: A Christian Social Perspective* (Minneapolis, MN: Fortress, 2000), 28-32, 44-47; Julie Hanlon Rubio, *A Christian Theology of Marriage and Family* (New York: Paulist Press, 2003), 26-43; Susan Calef, "The Radicalism of Jesus the Prophet," in Todd A. Salzman, Thomas M. Kelly, and John J. O'Keefe, *Marriage in the Catholic Tradition: Scripture, Tradition, and Experience* (New York: Crossroad, 2004): 53-65.

79. Cahill, *Family*, 29.

80. John Paul II, *Familiaris consortio* (Washington, DC: USCCB, 1981), 28.

81. Ibid., 37, 41.

82. Ibid., 42-44.

83. Cahill, *Family*, 130.

Vulnerability, Reciprocity, and Familial-Care Relations: A Socioethical Contribution

Christa Schnabl

This essay focuses on family relations from the perspective of care. What are the most pressing challenges with regard to families from an explicitly socioethical point of view? First, I mention a few of the most important developments that characterize the social situation of families from the perspective of a European, female, theological ethicist who looks at families, and particularly their care arrangements. Second, I elaborate on some of the characteristic elements that make care arrangements function in a just way. I summarize the ethical and theological consequences in the third section.

Social Challenges from the Perspective of Care Relations

Besides the marital partnership, fostering (and raising) children and organizing care for the elderly are two important responsibilities of families. Throughout history women have been primarily responsible for this kind of care work. However, at least since the postwar period, rising female participation rates in education and employment have increased the opportunities for women to choose an alternative.

In fact, a great number of women want to contribute in both fields: employment and care within the family. They try to avoid choosing only one of the two spheres of responsibilities. This desire to participate in both spheres leads to multiple responsibilities and often to multiple burdens, and some of the family troubles and conflicts between partners have their roots in this realignment. An increasing number of fathers and husbands bear familial duties in the field of care too. Today they spend more time looking after their children than previous generations have done. Nevertheless, since women started to participate in employed, paid work in increasing numbers, the contribution of fathers and husbands to familial care has not been sufficient to compensate for the amount of time women formerly devoted to such care.[1]

The changes in gender roles within families in the last decades raise a huge question: Who will take responsibility for people with care needs in the future, when women have increasingly chosen not to do this kind of unpaid work full time, work that often makes them dependent?

This topic is crucial for modern societies, particularly because intergenerational cooperation makes this future possible. Societies depend on care work, on the responsibility people are ready to take on in the fields of nurturing children and caring for the elderly. As Martha Nussbaum emphasizes, societies cannot disregard the fact that people can develop and cultivate feelings of care and sympathy.[2] Meanwhile, Western and Northern societies suffer from a lack of care giving, particularly in families and care institutions. Young women are aware of the risk of uncertainty and of financial and social dependency after becoming a mother, which is one of the main reasons why a lot of European countries have a relatively low birth rate.

The cause of many of today's political and social challenges in Europe is the gap in providing care for children and the elderly. This gap is caused by demographic changes, the precarious nature of different European retirement insurance systems, and the "emergency care" situation. These important topics are part of the political debate in many European countries. If you look below the surface, it becomes apparent that these topics have one concern in common: who cares for whom and what level of care is adequate, just, and available? A huge number of modern societies suffer from this so-called lack of care work as a consequence of the gender equality movement.

Given our context of globalization, one possible answer is global care chains that have become established throughout the world over the previous decades.[3] Women from the Philippines care for children in the United States, and women from Eastern Europe look after the older generation in Western Europe. Income and wage differences between the South and the North and the East and the West lead people to move from one region to another, hoping for an improvement in their financial and social situations.

These kinds of care chains, however, transmit the work of family care to people from lower social classes with the consequence that the value of care work itself is degraded continuously. Joan Tronto, an ethicist who writes about care politics, states that:

> Caring is often constituted socially in a way that makes caring work into the work of the least well off members of society. It is difficult to know whether the least well off are less well off because they care and caring is devalued, or because in order to devalue people, they are forced to do the caring work. . . . Care is devalued and the people who do caring work are devalued.[4]

Therefore, we have to rethink the relevance of caring in both our social and family lives. The increasing demand on care cannot be provided only by women in families or by the labor of migrants who often are undocumented. In the past, care was delegated primarily to women. The responsibilities for family care were incorporated into the family structure in accordance with the traditional "Haus-frauen-Ernährer" model (housewife-breadwinner model). This model enhanced dependency and gender injustice. This tendency to automatically delegate care to women should become a thing of the past. Today's circumstances offer a chance to redefine the position of caregiver and care needs within our societies as a demand that cannot be defined only as private or familial. As an important part of shared social responsibilities and politics, care should be offered in different ways and along different paths that support both care receivers and caregivers. We have to take a careful look at the field of care as a field of common responsibility, socially and politically.

This proposal was highlighted more than ten years ago in the 1999 United Nation Development Programme report:

> Studies of globalization and its impact on people focus on incomes, employment, education and other opportunities. Less visible, and often neglected, is the impact on care and caring labour—the task of providing for dependants, for children, the sick, the elderly and (do not forget) all the rest of us, exhausted from the demands of daily life. Human development is nourished not only by expanding incomes, schooling, health, empowerment and a clean environment but also by care. And the essence of care is in the human bonds that it creates and supplies. Care, sometimes referred to as social reproduction, is also essential for economic sustainability.[5]

How can we improve the recognition of the importance of care and how can we reorganize the redistribution of care in a just way? To answer these questions, we must analyze the characteristic form of care work and some of the particular elements of care situations. What characterizes care? What are the typical elements of care with regard to its anthropological dimension and ethical convictions?

Reflections on Care

Feminist ethics and care ethics regard *caring* as a prominent topic and over the last thirty years have emphasized the relevance of caring for ethical theory. The discussion started after Carol Gilligan published her book *In a Different Voice*, which describes the different kind of moral judgment observed primarily by women.[6] As a developmental psychologist, she criticized Lawrence Kohlberg's dominating male perspective. Gilligan called this type of female judgment the care orientation. The maintenance of human relations, the ability to judge the aims of another person, and the inclusion of emotions and specific situations are some of the elements of the Gilligan's so-called ethics of care. The reactions to Gilligan's book were very intensive and controversial. Despite the controversy, this critique essentially reshaped the debate, which will continue for the years ahead.

This debate was the starting point of a new discipline called "feminist ethics." From the perspective of care, different human conditions become crucial: the vulnerability of humans, asymmetry as an essential part of human relations, the facts of neediness and assistance and how these should be integrated, as well as the conditions of freedom, autonomy, and justice.

"Care" took on an important function as an umbrella category, summarizing various human and ethical aspects. The meaning and the use of care was broad: human bonding, responsibility, support for others, emotions such as compassion, sympathy, empathy, approachability, and so on. All who contributed to the debate used the category of "care" differently, and only a few defined their understanding precisely and in detail.

I want to focus particularly on the working dimension of care, which is part of the socioethical point of view. Despite the connections between both perspectives, care as a personal attitude or virtue is not my main interest in this essay. My focus is on care in practice, which is needed by many people because of their state of dependency and, second, on care as an ethical value that has to be integrated in a new way into our ethical theories.

When we focus on care as a need of dependent people, it becomes clear that families are institutions of care not only for children and elderly parents but also for those who are ill. Of course, families need not be the sole actors in this field, nor should they be the only ones; but in fact they remain one of the main institutions in the modern world to provide support, help, and care.

This brings us to the main elements of care relations, which can be called care activities rather than family activities to allow us to highlight the tasks that are *systematically* relevant and beyond simple personal concerns. Care relations consist of two elements: People who need help and others who provide help. This situation is characterized by a form of relation between the two "partners" that is structurally asymmetric because of the asymmetry of need on the one hand and help on the other. The actions (not the attitudes) that caregivers display when aiming to benefit people are important. I shall therefore define care as an interpersonal activity, acknowledging the irreducible vulnerability and dependency of human beings. Generally speaking, care is an asymmetrical act, oriented to the well-being and support of dependents.

We can distinguish care activities between adults on the same ability level (between partners or friends)[7] and care activities that deal with differing forms of ability and dependency. I call the latter typical care relations; both are important for our social life. Typical care relations are more relevant for our topic because of their radical asymmetry.

Typical care activities are one-way actions. Those who are providing help do not expect help back from the person in need. Forms of reciprocity could be developed (gratitude) but reciprocity is not essential. It may be present or practiced, but it is not obligatory.

Sometimes, reciprocity and symmetry are used as synonyms. To be precise, I have to illustrate a difference: to act reciprocally means to react or to answer to an activity in some way. A symmetrical activity requires an answer on the same level and given in the same way as the action itself. In typical care situations, giving and receiving care are not exchangeable because of the different levels of ability of caregivers and care receivers.

From a social point of view, it should be noted that caregivers can often become dependent themselves. Because they are obliged to care for the well-being of the dependent person and in comparison to people who are able to pursue their own goals, their opportunities are restricted. Particularly in private contexts where caregiving is unpaid work, caregivers sometimes need support to pursue their own goals. They can become dependent on a secondary level.[8]

In contrast to autonomous people who are often employed full-time and are economically autonomous, caregivers are often employed only part-time and have limited availability because of their responsibilities resulting from the dependency relationship. Thus, they often depend economically on others (for example, husbands) for their support and for the support of the people for whom they are responsible. This constellation makes caregivers vulnerable and puts them—in relation to the breadwinner—in a weaker position. As Eva Feder Kittay writes:

> As long as the dependency worker must rely on a provider to meet: 1) her own needs; 2) the needs of her charge (which in the self-understanding of the dependency worker gets taken up as—even as they stand in tension with—her own needs); 3) the resources required to sustain the dependency relation, the bargaining position of the dependency worker will be worse than that of the provider.[9]

The consequence of this situation is an asymmetric arrangement of power between the "dependency worker" position and the "breadwinner" position. This asymmetry of power that results from the prerequisites of the situation can easily turn into domination and subordination because of the structural background embedded in the care arrangements. To underline the difference in using the category of asymmetry, I want to stress that the dependency of the dependents results from differences related to their abilities, while asymmetry between caregivers and breadwinners results from the different status accorded to their responsibilities and activities.

When we look at political and social theories that dominate scientific debate and analyze the recognition of dependency workers using the theories of equality, autonomy, and justice, we can see that most of them ignore the asymmetrical relationship experienced by care workers. For example, equality is based on the idea of an individual who is free and autonomous and who is not obliged to care for dependents. For caregivers, this asymmetry contributes to and increases their degree of vulnerability, structural discrimination, and exploitation. To avoid and reduce the risk of structural exploitation, Kittay emphasizes the moral and political obligations of people not directly involved with care workers: "The moral features of dependency work, then, include both the moral responsibilities of the dependency worker to her charge, and the moral obligation of those who stand outside of the dependency relation to support such a relation."[10]

Having described key elements of the phenomenology of (asymmetric) care relations, let us examine the normative significance that results from asymmetric care relations. What are the most important challenges for social ethics today?

Consequences for Social Ethics[11]

First, I will consider consequences that deal with human nature: How we are to deal with vulnerability and dependency as a human condition is one of the most important ethical questions we can pose. According to the human condition, human beings are vulnerable on an existential level and dependant on a social level. In most of our ethical theories dependency is a term with primarily negative connotations. However, dependency was and obviously will be a part of all of our lives.

Dependency can be extensive or brief, with the extended dependency of early childhood or a temporarily incapacitating illness. Dependencies may be alleviated or aggravated by cultural practices and prejudices, but given the immutable facts of human development, disease, and decline, no culture that endures beyond one generation can be secure against the claims of human dependency.[12]

Therefore, we should overcome the primarily negative sense of dependency. Not all forms of dependency are avoidable. Full independency is an anthropological fiction. However, as the idea of autonomy shapes our ethical and practical self-understanding, we have to be aware of the reality of a dependency that cannot be avoided.

Most of our common-sense theories do not differentiate between avoidable and unavoidable dependencies. This leads to the position that almost every kind of dependency is negative or problematic. Only independence seems to be valued. On the other hand, an anthropology of recognized dependency would help to raise sufficient awareness of forms of unavoidable dependency, which in fact should obtain acceptance on an ethical level. An important consequence of this understanding is that actions based on this reality gain more acceptance and recognition and make more sense. Care work is not only exhausting and exploitative, but also a source of meaningful relations between people.

Selma Sevenhuijsen, an author from the Netherlands who deals with care theory, calls attention to the lack of awareness of care in theories with a socioliberal background. Care as represented in these theories reflects more a burden, and care seems to describe an aspect of heteronomy and alienation of women. Therefore, women who are determined to care for their children or care for elderly parents, giving up the opportunity of having a career, are often seen as old-fashioned and traditional in a negative sense. It could be that the negative drive in the judgment of care causes problems for the recognition of women in socioliberal theories. On the basis of socioliberal theories, a rational reason cannot be found to legitimize such care decisions as sensible. Selma Sevenhuijsen explains that such activities reflect a false "consciousness," and care misses a lack of positive appreciation.[13]

Philosopher Cornelia Klinger suggests that we should recognize both aspects of our care activities, the positive and the negative ones.

> The attraction, which is attributed to the conservative approach despite its more or less shameless establishment of traditional, unjust gender roles, should rather be understood as an indication of a shortcoming on the part of political theories, which promise women change and improvement without however taking into consideration the positive *and* negative aspects of the familial private sphere and thereby the situation in which very many women actually find themselves. They promise women liberation but only at a high price; giving up along with their "chains" that which for so long has represented their place, their identity and their purpose.[14]

Based on the insight that we can all become dependent, care work should be respected and highly esteemed. Therefore, this strong societal appreciation should be articulated in our practice to support caregivers. Caregivers should neither be degraded to dependents nor second-class people. Their care engagement should be recognized by the political and social frameworks that help care workers to fulfill care obligations.

> Questions of who takes on the responsibility of care, who does the hands-on care, who sees to it that the caring is done and done well, and who provides the support for the relationship of care and for both parties to the caring relationship—these are social and political questions. They are questions of social responsibility and political will. How these questions are answered will determine whether the facts of human dependency can be made compatible with the full equality of all citizens—that is, whether full citizenship can be extended to all.[15]

It is interesting to see that theological ethics is more sensitive than philosophical ethics in recognizing and responding to the reality of dependency. Here I am referring to the long and broad Christian tradition of *caritas* and *diakonia* in theory and in practice. Diaconal help, which fundamentally characterizes Christian ethics, describes an essential activity of the church.[16] In describing the church, care is one of the most important aspects that dominates present ecclesiastical discussions, as well as it did in previous centuries.[17] Organizations such as the Roman Catholic Caritas in Europe or the German Protestant Diakonie operate on multiple levels, providing support in individual situations on the one hand and criticizing structural injustices on the other.[18]

Since the beginning of modern times in the nineteenth century, the Catholic Church has fundamentally changed its thinking about providing and organizing help. During the Middle Ages, support for the poor and for those in need of help was considered to be the charitable work of the rich and affluent. Donating alms was the main form of assistance.[19]

The modern age brought a process of rethinking that has changed the way in which help is defined and practiced. This shift in mindset brought the structures of injustice that produced poverty to the fore. Thus, effective diaconal practice had to change these structures as well, structures that resulted in poverty. Diakonie and Caritas thus attempted to change understanding of the (social) causes of poverty. As such, criticism of society became an important aspect of providing assistance: "Were Caritas to only help people in time of need, it would become part of the system. In that case the church would betray the mission of Jesus Christ which states that Christians have to protest against all forms of social repression."[20]

The most important theological reasons to provide aid historically were the need to show mercy and the grace of charity. Since the onset of the modern age, a tradition of solidarity has developed, and since the late nineteenth century, solidarity has become one of the most important values, and it represents a new field of research in social ethics.[21] The preference for solidarity rather than the grace of charity can also be found in the exegesis of the New Testament. For example, Wolfgang Stegemann argues that the Christian love of one's neighbor should be understood as solidarity. The reason for Stegemann's reluctance to use the word charity is because of the paternalistic connotations of compassion and sympathy.[22] He writes:

It [i.e., the commandment to love thy neighbor] should not be confused with compassion as pitiful condescension of the economically and socially more powerful, towards the poor or the socially and economically weakest. The crucial point of the commandment... doesn't lie in the resolution or compensation of social inequality but rather the commandment to love thy neighbour enlarges the circle of "neighbors" that the ethics of solidarity encompasses to include those who would deserve to be hated or have revenge taken upon them because of their own negative social behaviour. ... Love thy neighbour is as such, through its origins, a command to show solidarity that overcomes social "hostility" within the same... sociological group.[23]

Understanding *diakonia* or *caritas* as an essential activity of an individual believer and as an institutional activity of the church is part of the Christian self-definition rooted in the mission of Jesus Christ. The theological tradition (for example, the enduring allegory of the Good Samaritan) offers a strong moral obligation to provide help and to provide care for people who need support, as noted in *Lumen gentium* (8 and 9) and *De justitia in mundo* (6).

The contractual model, which generally dominates discussions of ethical theories of bonding, is not adequate for relationships in the field of need and dependency. A contractual model focuses on independent and free actors who develop their commitments autonomously. If someone depends on help, however, the concept of a contract, which deals with the exchange of advantages, is not appropriate. What advantages can dependent people provide when it comes to the exchange of abilities?

The widespread theories of autonomy and justice that dominate ethical discussions underestimate circumstances of dependency and neediness. In fact, autonomy and one-way dependency should not be viewed antagonistically; human beings should practice autonomy on the basis of accepting structures and situations of dependency.

Eva Feder Kittay refers to John Rawls's theory of justice when she articulates the demand that care and the need for care should be part of theories of justice. She underlines the reasonable and sensible aspects of "dependency concerns" as part of the choice to follow the principles of justice. She terms this "reasonable" because dependency should be included in the conception of social cooperation even from the point of view of self-referential self-interest. Because people choose principles of justice as independent and active citizens, we cannot avoid times in which we are responsible for people in need. This need for care is "sensible" because we should conceptualize as connected the interests of the self and the interests of others.

For human beings who come into the world through birth and who leave the world through illness, accident, or old age, the idea of social cooperation and society has to integrate sensibly the neediness of dependent people. The most important goal of Eva Feder Kittay's approach is to embed dependency and care in the dominant liberal understanding of justice.

> [W]hen we reorient our political insights to see the centrality of human relationships to our happiness and well-being, we recognize dependency needs as basic motivations for creating a social order. This means that we cannot limit our understanding of social cooperation to interactions between independent and fully functioning persons because it obscures or minimizes the social contribution of dependents—who, even in their neediness, contribute to the ongoing nature of human relationships—and of those who care for dependents.[24]

Care relations and care demands should be reflected by social ethics. The need for justice, one of the most important normative approaches today, should also be applied to the recognition and the redistribution of care work. It is necessary to reflect on the division of labor within families. The gender shift of unpaid caregiving has to be resolved, and unpaid caregiving within the family should be divided between men and women in a just way. Just caregiving responsibilities should focus on the careers and relations within families. It is our care for others—and not only markets and companies—that drives the process of globalization. Establishing just social relationships between people from different regions throughout the world requires taking the force of needs for care into account. Caregivers should not be exploited by unfair conditions produced by international hierarchies.

Notes

1. See also Rüdiger Peuckert, *Familienformen im sozialen Wandel*, esp. chap. 8: "Der soziale Wandel der Rolle der Frau in Familie und Beruf" (Wiesbaden: Verlag für Sozialwissenschaften, 2008).

2. Martha C. Nussbaum, *Konstruktion der Liebe, des Begehrens und der Fürsorge: Drei philosophische Aufsätze* (The Construction of Love, Desire and Care: Three Philosophical Essays) (Stuttgart: Reclam, 2002), 12.

3. Arlie Russel Hochschild, "Global Care Chains and Emotional Surplus Value," in *On the Edge: Living with Global Capitalism*, ed. Will Hutton and Anthony Giddens (London: Vintage Books, 2001), 130-46.

4. Joan Tronto, *Moral Boundaries: A Political Argument for an Ethic of Care* (New York: Routledge Chapman & Hall, 1994), 112-13.

5. United Nations Development Programme, *Human Development Report 1999* (New York: Oxford University Press, 1999), 77. An entire chapter deals with this important topic: "The Invisible Heart—Care and the Global Economy."

6. See Carol Gilligan, *In a Different Voice: Psychological Theory and Women's Development* (Cambridge, MA: Harvard University Press, 1982).

7. See, for example, the feminist-ethical considerations of Helga Nagl-Docekal, "Ist Fürsorglichkeit mit Gleichbehandlung vereinbar?" in *Deutsche Zeitschrift für Philosophie* 42 (1994): 1045-50.

8. Eva Feder Kittay, *Love's Labor: Essays on Women, Equality, and Dependency* (London: Routledge, 1998), 45.

9. Ibid., 45.

10. Ibid., 50.

11. For a more detailed socioethical examination about "caring in a just way," see Christa Schnabl, *Gerecht sorgen: Grundlagen einer sozialethischen Theorie der Fürsorge* (Freiburg: Herder, 2005).

12. Kittay, *Love's Labor*, 1.

13. See Selma Sevenhuijsen, "Feministische Überlegungen zum Thema Care und Staatsbürgerschaft," in *Globale Gerechtigkeit? Feministische Debatte zur Krise des Sozialstaats*, ed. Helga Braun and Dörthe Jung (Hamburg: Konkret-Literatur Verlag, 1997), 74-95. See also the English translation of her Dutch book *Citizenship and the Ethics of Care: Feminist Considerations on Justice, Morality and Politics* (London: Routledge 1998).

14. Cornelia Klinger, "Zwischen allen Stühlen: Die politische Theoriediskussion der Gegenwart in einer feministischen Perspektive," in *Feministische Politikwissenschaft*, ed. Erna Appelt and Gerda Neyer (Vienna: Verlag für Gesellschaftskritik, 1994), 119-43, at 127. My emphasis.

15. Kittay, *Love's Labor*, 1.

16. Many theological publications and encyclopedias deal with the *caritas* tradition within the church. See, for example, Konrad Hilperts's book *Caritas und Sozialethik: Elemente einer theologischen Ethik des Helfens* (Paderborn: Verlag Ferdinand Schöningh, 1997), see esp. 17-32, 54-67.

17. *Diakonia* is one of the three main works of the Roman Catholic Church: *liturgia, martyria*, and *diakonia*.

18. See, for example, the self-understanding of the Roman Catholic European organization Caritas, http://www.caritas-europa.org/code/en/default.asp, or the German Protestant organization of Diakonie, http://www.diakonie.de/index.htm.

19. Thomas Aquinas, *Summa Theologiae* II-II, q. 23, a.8.

20. "Würde sich die Caritas damit abfinden, die Opfer des Gesellschaftssystems nur zu betreuen, bliebe sie letztlich ein Teil dieses Systems. Sie verriete ihren Auftrag, im Namen Jesu gegen jede Form von selbst oder gesellschaftlich verfügter Zerstörung von Menschen Einspruch zu erheben" (Norbert Mette, "Theologie der Caritas," in *Grundkurs Caritas*, ed. Erna Appelt and Gerda Neyer [Linz: Landesverlag, 1993], 115-18, at 136-37).

21. Markus Daniel Zürcher, *Solidarität, Anerkennung und Gemeinschaft: Zur Phänomenologie, Theorie und Kritik der Solidarität* (Tübingen: Francke, 1998).

22. See Wolfgang Stegemann, "Nächstenliebe oder Barmherzigkeit: Überlegungen zum ethischen und soziologischen Ort der Nächstenliebe," in *Spiritualität: Theologische Beiträge*, ed. Herwig Wagner (Stuttgart: Calwer, 1987), 59-82.

23. Ibid., 77-78.

24. Kittay, *Love's Labor*, 106.

The Abuse of Power in the Church: Its Impact on Identity, Reciprocity, and Familial Relations

Aloysius Cartagenas

The Roman Catholic Church is in deep crisis. Pope Benedict XVI publicly admits the church suffers from "problems of its own making... born from the sins within the Church," which we see today "in a truly terrifying way."[1] Among the attempts to give the crisis a name, none is as courageous and truthful as the one that calls it the "abuse of power."[2] The breadth and depth of the abuse is shaking the church to its foundations as it severely impacts the identity, reciprocity, and familial relations of the people of God.

A Corporate Identity in Crisis

There is something distinctive about the church as a community of disciples of Jesus the Christ. It is perhaps the only faith community that dares to call itself the "body" of its Lord and Savior. In recent times the phenomenon of clergy sexual abuse, the pattern of neglect if not outright cover-up by church leaders who have the responsibility to deal with it, and the appalling silence of those who knew about it, have seriously impaired the church's corporate identity. This is happening at the same time that the theological claims that underpin it are under close scrutiny.

These events not only call into question the structures of church governance and authority, but they also bleed the very heart of its identity as the "historical and mystical body" of its Lord and Savior. If "the question of power and authority in relation to Church governance is, in the last analysis, an ecclesiological question,"[3] the disturbing issue is what sort of embodiment is the church, as the "body of Christ," expressing in history, given the phenomenon of power abuse? If the body is comprised of both victims and perpetrators as part of all the faithful, what sort of body is it? If the present crisis is to point to a future hope, what sort of body could it be?[4]

Crisis of Identity, Crisis of Law

The foundational principle of the church's corporate identity is clear: all Christians, by reason of baptism, possess equal dignity and responsibility for the

church's life and mission.[5] The problem is, some would say, the lack of a legal application of this principle.[6] Despite the deep egalitarian spirit of the Christian sacraments of initiation, church laws continue to restrict, if not disregard, the rights of
the faithful. These include the ethical requirements of participatory governance,
collegial decision making, the selection process of officeholders, and mechanisms
of accountability, to name but a few.

The church's current system of laws makes it difficult for all—both ordained
and non-ordained—to recognize such equality or, at least, experience it in practice.
It is not the lack of correct doctrine that is in crisis, but the lack of truthfulness,
which is needed to give a structure commensurate with the interior reality of corporate identity. This huge gap needs to be confronted, considering that laws, from
the viewpoint of Catholic moral theology, "give expression to the inner reality of
the Church as a community of love empowered by the Spirit."[7] Laws may never
satisfy the full measure of moral responsibility, but nevertheless, as "repositories of
moral wisdom," they help shape and sustain a collective identity. In the same way
that bones support the body, laws provide the framework for the community of
believers to be able to identify and promote the basic values and ethical standards
without which it cannot live.

Crisis of Identity, Crisis of Authority

For others, the crisis of the church's corporate identity is due either to the
misunderstanding of what authority entails or to the actual misuse, perhaps even
abuse, of that authority. In the church, those vested with power and those who are
next in line are socialized by two accounts that seem contradictory.[8] One account,
perhaps the dominant one, says that church authority, like the proverbial key
received by Peter from Jesus, is solely received from Christ by the ordained. The
other holds that church authority is "granted by the community as an investiture
of certain rights held by the community, given in trust to the office-bearers to exercise."[9] The authority of the "believing church" as a whole is the prior condition of
the authority of officeholders.

To directly link the abuse of power with church identity and authority is to
call attention to the fact that every view of authority is "essentially bound up with
a system of ideas." The dominant system claims the primacy of the authority of the
ordained over the *sensus fidelium* of the believing community. The other asserts
that the authority of officeholders is an institutional tool to shape corporate identity by empowering those from whom their power comes instead of lording it over
them (1 Pet 5:3). The global phenomenon of church authority abuse ought to alert
us that neither "personal qualities" nor "assumed characteristics" of those invested
with power, or the "claim to be representing a tradition," are sufficient to establish legitimacy. The theological-ethical challenge, it seems, is for a world church
to engage critically the ideas that buttress a dominant system of authority that is
abuse prone.

Crisis of Identity, Crisis of Ethos

A third view speaks of a "body of Christ" made docile by the dominant ethos or "living processes" of clericalism.[10] Much of what impels all members of a social body to act comes from the surrounding influences and accepted practices. In the church, this is the power of clerical ascendancy. The clerical ethos accrues privilege, separateness, status, and entitlement for the members of "the Club." This includes the privilege of being able to fit into a ready-made and grandiose identity and to use the language of an all-male inner circle that excludes the competence or gender of those who allegedly lack the ability to be an icon of Christ the High Priest.[11] The result is advancement to a higher form of status, creating inferiors from whom unquestioning dependence is expected if not demanded. This entitlement to the "virtual identification of the holiness and grace of the Church with the clerical state and, thereby, with the cleric himself"[12] creates a pharisaical mindset. Even those excluded from the "the Club" are, in many ways, shaped by that power, inasmuch as it also constructs reality for them and defines their lives according to prescribed roles of a single drama.

To direct attention to the living processes by which corporate identity is constructed and sustained is to argue that the phenomenon of power abuse within the church is rooted in a highly dysfunctional church ethos. Locating power abuse in the clerical ethos appreciates power not as a possession, not as something the clergy alone "has," but as a mark that "rather permeates institutional life in complex and subtle ways."[13] Most significantly, it manifests itself in "the relationships of dominance and subordination within different roles and functions that are exercised within [the] organization." If power is "never in anybody's hands, never appropriated as a commodity or piece of wealth," then both the clergy and the laity "are not only [the] inert or consenting target" of power and its abuse but are "always also the element of its articulation."

In clericalism, the problem is not that power is in the wrong hands. Rather, all in the church are agents of the asymmetrical relations of power, not its points of application. Thus, the whole body of Christ is made docile and molded into "normality." The ones rewarded with more power are in fact the same ones who acquiesce docilely to the authority being administered. For this reason, much of the causation of the abuse of church power is unacknowledged and not easily accessible. This makes the clerical ethos highly resistant to change and so resilient that no one can fully anticipate its dysfunctional outcome.

The Appalling Deficit in Trinitarian Reciprocity

There is another thing peculiar about the church. It is the only faith community that claims to be a people made one in the unity of a God professed as Father, Son, and Spirit.[14] "In the trinity of persons" the church finds "the highest model and grounding mystery of (its) unity."[15] Divine revelation, therefore, presents us with an image of a God who is "a unity of reciprocal relations—different, unique, necessary relations."[16]

As with the Holy Trinity, so too the church's reality lies in the reciprocity of relationships. Being "united in the Spirit with the Son, in their missions, responding to the depth of God, who is for us Abba, we find individually and collectively our deepest reality."[17] That reality is "reciprocal relations" wherein, as in the Triune God, "identity does not destroy difference," and each member of the church is taken seriously "as the revelatory, holy, indwelt temple of the Spirit." But in recent times this "unity in reciprocity" has been very difficult to come by for God's people, and we are left to echo Jesus' prayer "that they may be one as you and I are one" (John 17:20-22).

A Church Living a Double Life

The root cause of the crisis in reciprocity, it seems, is that "theology is saying one thing while the organizational practice implies something else."[18] *Lumen gentium*, for instance, envisions that the "variety of local churches with one common aspiration is particularly splendid evidence of the catholicity of the undivided Church."[19] The restoration of Latin in the liturgy, the return to the Tridentine Mass, and the coming new translations of the Roman Missal are not just forms of cultural insensitivity, but modes of a systematic dismantling of the reciprocity of cultures and languages integral to the vision of the Second Vatican Council.[20]

Moreover, there "is not a lack of profound, well-reasoned, theologically sophisticated, and perfectly orthodox theologies of the laity and lay ministry."[21] However, if the 1997 Congregation for the Doctrine of the Faith "Instruction"[22] is at all an indication, lay involvement in church governance cannot in any way be institutionalized through deliberative structures. The surfeit of advisory and consultative bodies, convened in recent years to tame autocratic and paternalistic governance, is not working. The church's social teaching acknowledges the "aspirations to equality and participation" as "two expressions of human dignity and freedom"[23] and clearly prefers democracy over other forms of human organization.[24] While the church seems to want democratic structures everywhere else, it does not want them in the organizational aspects of its own life.

What seems clear, from an organizational standpoint, is "the unwillingness of the hierarchy, following the lead of the pope, to grant full consideration to such theologies, and to begin the process of restructuring the church."[25] As a result, there is no genuine reciprocity among local churches, on the one hand, and between clergy and laity in all aspects of Roman Catholic ministry, on the other. If no less than the Trinitarian reciprocity is the core reality that the church is called to witness in the world, democratic ethos and structures may well be the urgently needed organizational revisions in the church.

A Church of Two Competing Claims of Supreme Power

Other theologians see the crisis in two contending claims of supreme authority in the church.[26] Two agencies are endowed with "full, supreme and universal power": the supreme pontiff acting alone, and the college of bishops united with its papal head.[27] To complicate matters, the two seats of power are in disparity. While all bishops are called to a "pastoral solicitude" to the whole church, only the papal head of the episcopal college holds the "power of jurisdiction" over all.[28] Besides, there is no "firmly established institutionalized governmental mechanism capable of imposing constitutional restraints on the freewheeling exercise of (papal) authority."[29] Matters become worse as this lack is paralleled at every level of church leadership from bishops' synods powerless in governance all the way down to the merely consultative and/or advisory diocesan and parish councils.

To confront the crisis of reciprocity in the church is to revisit an unresolved tension between the "power of order" and the "power of jurisdiction." Classical canon law defines the former as "the capacity specifically conferred by ordination to administer the sacraments and to preach the Word of God with authority," while the latter refers to "the general authority to direct and govern the affairs of the Church, and also the right to obedience from the governed." However, church tradition does not indicate that the power to govern was always connected to the power of order, and neither is the former a derivative of the latter.[30]

Crisis of Reciprocity as the Exclusion of the Authority of the Poor

The fact that it has not been easy to pass from a model of church based on the power of order and jurisdiction to a body built on the power of reciprocal relations speaks volumes about the asymmetrical power relations in the church. But would a simple appeal to the moral will of those with competing claims be enough to free the church from the trajectory of self-destruction? Should the tension be soothed by a mere balancing of interests of those competing within the system? Or should a "decent consultation hierarchy"[31] be implemented to prevent power abuse or, at least, to mitigate its ill effects?

Perhaps the key to a church of reciprocity is not how but from whose vantage reciprocity is imagined. What of the voice of those excluded from the present authority structure and the ones left out by those who wish to reform or replace it? "What of those who do not have the economic, psychological, organizational or educational space or skills to participate in shaping any proposed model of authority and governance?"[32] What does it profit a church to have structures of reciprocity that express the imperatives of modern democratic society but that, at the same time, exclude the poor, the disadvantaged, and the marginalized? Divine revelation is clear and consistent: the Triune God welcomed the poor into its own reciprocal communion as first beneficiaries. Hence, the theological-ethical challenge is how authoritative their voice and experience will be in the conversation to determine structures of reciprocal relations.

The Crisis in the Church's Familial Relations with the World

One final thing is particular about us as church. Unlike other faith communities, we confess that the church and the world, like two human families of the same origin, are mutually related. Instead of fleeing from it or being indifferent to it, we take it upon ourselves as a "family of God's children" to serve "as a leaven and a kind of soul for human society" by fostering "mutual exchange and assistance" in our common concerns.[33] In return, we profess that a church not "enriched by the development of social life" may not be able to "understand itself more penetratingly, express itself better, and adjust itself more successfully to our times." The enrichment is mutual in that "whoever promotes the human family (in all its dimensions) . . . according to God's design, contributes greatly to the Church community as well."[34] But, as recent events are making lamentably clear, the envisioned familial relations of mutual exchange and assistance have been seriously compromised.

The Crisis of Its Privileged Sociopastoral Location

The location from which the church carries out its service to the world is of crucial importance. It can limit or expand its field of vision, reduce or increase the range of its choices, and determine the type of public interventions it ought to take. Not all social locations offer an angle of vision that is mutually beneficial for both church and society. Even in these postcolonial times, for instance, particularly in contexts where Roman Catholicism still enjoys social dominance and political influence, the nation-state continues to be the preferred locus of the church's public interventions in the world. In fact, much of how the church understands and carries out its relations with the modern world is framed with the state as a counterpart, the state being the conventional "container of society" and center of legitimate power.

The problem is that the territorial state itself is called into question by the process of globalization.[35] The problems and challenges of everyday life are now cutting across national frontiers. Networks of global interdependence and obligation are getting more expansive, and the contours of society are no longer coextensive with the geographical domains of states. Moreover, the legitimate power of states is increasingly embedded in a complex network of authority relations opening up new spaces of power and new levels of public intervention, birthing new transnational actors in the process. In short, the "architecture of thinking, acting, living within state-cum-social spaces and identities" is collapsing.

Given the fact that the nation-state, as the traditional location of the church's engagement with the world, is being put into question, from which new vantage point should the church take its place in the public sphere "as a form of practice oriented to the service of society and open to human need in all its variety"?[36] It does not appear enriching to the world if a world church in the twenty-first century continues to insist that its abuse of power is purely a domestic matter subject only to the power of its own laws. To claim the separation of church and state as a reason for not recognizing when abuse of power is a crime is, in itself, an abuse of power. To be a relevant moral community in a globalizing world, the church must recognize civil and other forms of authority as partners, and must not be afraid to be under the scrutiny of public legal and judicial institutions whether at national and international levels.

The Crisis in the Social Carriers of Catholicism in the Public Sphere

The crisis in the church's familial relations is also about the social carriers of its public role in the world. Modern history cannot turn its back on the long list of Catholic social movements that advocated for modern human values and democratic processes and championed economic justice and social betterment. If not for the critical interaction of such movements in the modernizing society, the world would not have been able to receive the help it urgently needed. The problem is that, in the face of vastly altered social and cultural settings that are now more pluralistic and global, these social carriers of the Catholic faith have either collapsed or have been secularized.[37]

The lay people of today are engaged far less in the service of the church's institutional interests than in the prophetic and compassionate service to society at large. Whereas before they allowed themselves to function as the hierarchy's "long arm," today their projects are no longer burdened by the need of hierarchical mandate or endorsement. Where before their organizations and movements passively waited for orders from a central authority and simply had to execute the papal or episcopal agenda, today they network to advocate for issues common to their regions and continents. Moreover, in other contexts where traditional expressions of faith convictions are breaking down, lay people are giving birth to new Catholic movements and are engaging their members in interfaith and/or ecumenical dialogue toward a global society based on common moral and spiritual values.

Behind the crisis in the traditional social carriers of Catholicism is actually a *kairos* moment. Their disintegration has spawned "spontaneous experiments in possibilities of new forms of life for Christianity and the church."[38] These experiments address what is faulty or obstructive, and sometimes even absurd, in the existing church organization, in light of radically altered circumstances. More importantly, their public engagement has thus far sparked renewed interest in religion. Some faith communities are increasingly being drawn into policy making, and their critiques of mainstream global institutions are appreciated.[39] The church's new social carriers and the initial contours of their public engagement are thus poised to arrest Catholicism's dismal participation in postmodern and postcolonial settings.

But even as new spaces for a mutual exchange with the world are opening up, the hierarchy does not see in them the proverbial "new wine" nor decipher from them the initial contours of the "new wineskins." Church officeholders have not until now recommended these new social carriers. Even interreligious movements of peace, justice, and ecology have been met with suspicion or lack of clarity by the

Vatican.[40] Benedict XVI's separation of justice as the task of the state and charity as the church's duty poses a serious problem to church–world relations anchored on mutual solidarity.[41] The moral system of dividing the expertise to formulate teachings as exclusive to the hierarchy, and the competence to apply them as belonging to the laity,[42] perpetuates hierarchical control and obscures the laity's ethical subjectivity in the exercise of their proper mission.

The Crisis of the "Roman Catholic" Culture

The church's familial relations with the world is in crisis lastly because, while the extent of the power of its "Roman Catholic" culture has shrunk, modernity, which was the church's declared enemy before it became its legitimate partner, appears to have won its rightful place in human society.[43] Modernity has evolved to become the "matrix in which all forms of social life exist," not excluding Roman Catholic life. Hence, by being "an evolving part of a likewise evolving modernity," Roman Catholicism is also in the process of "continuous religious modernization" and can therefore no longer claim immunity from change. One radical result is that, in many nation states and societies, not much is left of the "Roman Catholic" sub-culture that served as "container" of church identity and authority.

With this disintegration, what contours will a new form of Catholicism adopt? Will we end up with an "areligious society" without Catholic churches or with small churches that are but moribund reminders of the old glory? Or will there be a band of small "residue churches" fighting against an areligious society in which Catholicism has to operate? Will Catholic churches continue to decline in some contexts as many Catholics continue "believing without belonging" to a centralized institution? Or will these churches thrive vigorously in local and diverse contexts and play a key role on equal terms with other religious actors in a competitive religious field?

Even in nations where Christianity was imposed during the process of colonialization, "Roman Catholic" cultural identity also appears to be ending. Today "the continuity and historicity of identity are challenged by the immediacy and intensity of global confrontations."[44] Culture is increasingly evolving into a "third space" or "a place of fluidity, where former fixities and unities are dissolved and reformed, so that new negotiations of power can occur between people of difference."[45] What used to be the distinctly "Roman Catholic" identity of a Filipino, for instance, is now challenged by new and productive kinds of fusion or creation of new identities brought about by cultural encounters that cut across territorial, spiritual, and religious boundaries.

The present risk is to prolong the power game by reducing the church to "a site where conflicts and struggles which are colonial in origin continue to be played out in neo-colonial ways." The future hope, however, is for the church to take the forefront in becoming a "space of fluidity where former fixities and unities are dissolved and reformed so that new negotiations of power can occur between people of difference" and "the mixing or renewal of identity"[46] is possible. In this light, for ethics to deal adequately with the issue of power in the church, it will be hard put to show that being "Roman Catholic" is constitutive of being a truly "catholic church."

Conclusion

To admit that the terrifying "problems of our own making" are "born from the sins within the Church" places a most serious burden of ethical responsibility on the whole people of God to overcome the crisis over its own abuse of power. In order for the church's corporate identity to be the ethical embodiment of Christ's mystical body in history, the church must address the deficiencies of its legal system, the contradictions within its authority structure, and the hegemony of its clerical ethos. If the grounding mystery of the church's unity is the reciprocity of the Triune God, it has to embrace democratic ethos and structures into its own life, resolve the disparity between the power of order and the power of governance, and listen to the voice of the victims of power abuse as it builds a church of reciprocal relations. The church, as leaven for human society, must foster familial relations with a world that has radically changed. It has to be ready to subject itself to the same standards by which it judges all other forms of authority and public institutions. It should put an end to the proclivity of church leadership to control the laity and become a space where the diversity of a catholic identity is appreciated as constitutive of being truly church.

The trajectory of church renewal is irreversible, and a return to the past is not the way to take the church into the future.[47]

Notes

1. Nicole Winfield, "Pope Benedict Places Blame for Sex Scandals on Catholic Church," *The Washington Post*, May 12, 2010, http://www.washingtonpost.com/wp-dyn/content/article/2010/05/11/AR2010051104949.html.

2. James Keenan, "Sex Abuse, Power Abuse," *The Tablet* (May 2002): 9-10.

3. Agnes Cunningham, "Power and Authority in the Church," in *The Ministry of Governance*, ed. James Mallett (Washington, DC: Canon Law Society of America, 1986), 80-97, at 95.

4. In framing this theological-ethical question I am are helped by Frances Ward, "Theological Strand—Power," in *Studying Local Churches: A Handbook*, ed. Helen Cameron et al. (London: SCM, 2005), 221-33.

5. *Lumen gentium* (Dogmatic Constitution on the Church), 32.

6. See, for instance, Michael Fahey, "Diocesan Governance in Modern Catholic Theology and in the 1983 Code of Canon Law," in *The Ministry of Governance*, ed. James Mallett (Washington, DC: Canon Law Society of America, 1986), 121-39; and John Beal, "It Shall Not Be So among You! Crisis in the Church, Crisis in Church Law," in *Governance, Accountability and the Future of the Catholic Church*, ed. Francis Oakley and Bruce Russett (New York: Continuum, 2004), 88-102.

7. Richard Gula, *Reason Informed by Faith* (Mahwah, NJ: Paulist Press, 1989), 250.

8. See, for instance, Gerard Mannion, "What Do We Mean by Authority?" in *Authority in the Roman Catholic Church: Theory and Practice*, ed. Bernard Hoose (London: Ashgate, 2002), 19-36.

9. Ibid., 22, 32-33.

10. See Michael Papesh, *Clerical Culture: Contradiction and Transformation* (Collegeville, MN: Liturgical Press, 2004); and George Wilson, *Clericalism: The Death of Priesthood* (Collegeville, MN: Liturgical Press, 2008).

11. Mary Daly calls this "christolatry" while Dorothee Soelle warns us against "christofascism." See the discussion in Margaret Fraser, "Language of God, Gender and Authority," in *Authority in the Roman Catholic Church: Theory and Practice*, ed. Bernard Hoose (London: Ashgate, 2002), 193-215.

12. Donald Cozzens, *Sacred Silence: Denial and Crisis in the Church* (Collegeville, MN: Liturgical Press, 2004), 118.

13. We are borrowing here the insight of Michel Foucault as explained in Frances Ward, "Theological Strand—Power," 225. In a similar vein, see Karen Lebacqz, *Professional Ethics: Power and Paradox* (Nashville, TN: Abingdon, 1992), 137-51; also see Michel Foucault, "Pastoral Power and Political Reason," in *Power/Knowledge: Selected Interview and Writings 1972-77*, ed. C. Gordon (Hertfordshire: Harvester Press, 1980), 78-108, especially 98.

14. *Lumen gentium* (Dogmatic Constitution on the Church), 4.

15. *Unitatis redintegratio* (Decree on Ecumenism), 2.

16. David McLoughlin, "Communio Models of Church: Rhetoric or Reality?" in *Authority in the Roman Catholic Church: Theory and Practice*, ed. Bernard Hoose (London: Ashgate, 2002), 181-90, especially 185.

17. Ibid., 189.

18. Ibid., 187. In a similar vein, Francis Oakley contends that "if one views [the Second Vatican Council's] effort not in terms of abstract theological formulations but rather in concrete or operational terms as an attempt . . . to restore an effective constitutional balance in the governance of the church, then, . . . in that attempt it must be judged to have failed." See Francis Oakley, "Constitutionalism in the Church?" in *Governance, Accountability and the Future of the Catholic Church*, ed. Francis Oakley and Bruce Russett (New York: Continuum, 2004), 76-87, especially 79.

19. *Lumen gentium* (Dogmatic Constitution on the Church), 23.

20. *Lumen gentium* (Dogmatic Constitution on the Church), 13: "Within the Church particular Churches hold a rightful place. These Churches retain their own traditions without in any way lessening the primacy of the Chair of Peter. This Chair presided over the whole assembly of charity and protects legitimate differences, while at the same time it sees that such differences do not hinder unity but rather contribute toward it."

21. R. Scott Appleby, "From Autonomy to Alienation: Lay Involvement in the Governance of the Local Church," in *Common Calling: The Laity and Governance of the Catholic Church*, ed. Stephen Pope (Washington, DC: Georgetown University Press, 2004), 87-107, here at 105.

22. Congregation for the Doctrine of the Faith, "Instruction on Certain Questions Regarding the Collaboration of the Non-Ordained Faithful in the Sacred Ministry of the Priest," August 13, 1997, art. 5, para. 3.

23. *Octogesima adveniens* (On Catholic Social Teaching), 22, 24.

24. *Centesimus annus* (Hundredth Year), 44, 46-47.

25. Appleby, "From Autonomy to Alienation," 105.

26. Oakley, "Constitutionalism in the Church?" 79-80.

27. *Lumen gentium* (Dogmatic Constitution on the Church), 22.

28. Ibid., 23.

29. Oakley, "Constitutionalism in the Church?" 80.

30. Hugh Lawrence, "Ordination and Governance," in *Authority in the Roman Catholic Church: Theory and Practice*, ed. Bernard Hoose (London: Ashgate, 2002), 73-82, especially 78-80; John Beal describes the tension as between "juridic" and "communion" models of church in "It Shall Not Be So among You!" 95-96.

31. Following the eminent political theorist John Rawls, Russett suggests clear and predictable procedures of consultation to make a hierarchical society decent and well ordered. See Bruce Russett, "Conclusion: Monarchy, Democracy, or 'Decent Consultation Hierarchy'?" in *Governance, Accountability and the Future of the Catholic Church*, ed. Francis Oakley and Bruce Russett (New York: Continuum, 2004), 196-202, especially 199-200.

32. John O'Brien, "The Authority of the Poor," in *Authority in the Roman Catholic Church: Theory and Practice*, ed. Bernard Hoose (London: Ashgate, 2002), 217-30, especially 219-23.

33. *Gaudium et spes* (Pastoral Constitution on the Church in the Modern World), 40.

34. Ibid., 44.

35. Ulrich Beck, *What Is Globalization?* (Cambridge: Polity, 2000), especially 12, 21, 64; and David Held, "Cosmopolitanism: Taming Globalization," in *The Global Transformation Reader*, ed. David Held and Anthony McGrew (Cambridge: Polity, 2000), 514-29.

36. James Sweeney, "Catholic Social Thought as Political," in *Scrutinizing the Signs of the Times in the Light of the Gospel*, ed. Johan Verstraeten (Leuven: Peeters, 2007), 207-20, here at 213.

37. John Coleman, "The Future of Catholic Social Thought," in *Modern Catholic Social Teachings: Commentaries and Interpretations*, ed. Kenneth Himes (Washington, DC: Georgetown University Press, 2005), 522-44, esp. 532-37.

38. Robin Gill, *Theology and Society: A Reader* (London: Cassell, 1996), 399.

39. See, for instance, *Studying Local Churches: A Handbook*, ed. Helen Cameron et al. (London: SCM, 2005), 5-6, 10, 235; and Wendy Tyndale, "Some Reflections on a Dialogue between the World's Religions and the World Bank with Reference to Catholic Social Thought," in *Globalization and Catholic Social Thought: Present Crisis, Future Hope*, ed. John Coleman and William Ryan (Maryknoll, NY: Orbis Books, 2005), 157-71.

40. Gregory Baum, "Religion and Globalization," in *Globalization and Catholic Social Thought: Present Crisis, Future Hope*, ed. John Coleman and William Ryan (Maryknoll, NY: Orbis Books, 2005), 141-55, especially 150-54.

41. See Stephen Pope, "Benedict XVI's *Deus Caritas Est*: An Ethical Analysis" in *Applied Ethics in a World Church*, ed. Linda Hogan (Maryknoll, NY: Orbis Books, 2008), 271-77. "A just society," the pope contends, "must be the achievement of politics, not the church." The church rather contributes "to a better world only by personally doing good now, with full commitment and wherever we have the opportunity, independently of partisan parties and programs" (see *Deus caritas est* [God Is Love], 28 and 31).

42. See, for instance, Pontifical Council for Peace and Justice, *Compendium of the Social Doctrine of the Church* (Vatican City: Libreria Editrice Vaticana, 2004), nos. 539-40, and the earlier document by the Congregation for Catholic Education, "Guidelines for the Teaching of the Church's Social Doctrine in Forming Priests," nos. 58-63.

43. See the discussion in Staf Hellemans, "From 'Catholicism to Modernity' to the Problematic 'Modernity of Catholicism,'" *Ethical Perspectives* 8, no. 2 (2001):117-27; and Bill McSweeney, *Roman Catholicism: The Search for Relevance* (Oxford: Blackwell, 1980).

44. Kevin Robins, "Encountering Globalization," in *The Global Transformation Reader*, ed. David Held and Anthony McGrew (Cambridge: Polity, 2000), 239-45, here at 242.

45. Ward, "Theological Strand—Power," 229, citing a study by Homi Bhabha, "Cultural Diversity and Cultural Differences," in *The Post-Colonial Studies Reader*, ed. B. Ashcroft (New York: Routledge, 1995).

46. Ibid.

47. My most sincere gratitude goes to Denis Nolan, Deacon Michael Ghiorso, and Fr. Domingo Orimaco of Our Lady of Mercy Parish in Daly City (California, USA) for their insightful comments and helpful suggestions.

ECONOMICS AS IF PEOPLE MATTERED

Peter J. Henriot

What does one say about "economics" at a conference of Christian ethicists? Particularly if the one doing the saying is trained as a political scientist and not as an economist! Well, that is the challenging situation I find myself in here at Trento.

Let me begin by explaining why I have chosen "Economics as if People Mattered" as the title of my presentation. This is the subtitle of the extremely influential book of E. F. Schumacher, *Small Is Beautiful* (1973).[1] An economist, civil servant in post-war England, and one-time associate of John Maynard Keynes, in the 1950s Schumacher delved into what he called "Buddhist Economics," which emphasized the centrality in economic situations of good work for individuals: "Buddhism taught him that the purpose of work was more than fulfilling material needs, that it's function was also the development of human potential and man's relationship with his fellow beings and towards God."[2]

Schumacher became appreciative of early documents of the church's social teaching (CST), such as Pope Leo XIII's *Rerum novarum*; he drew inspiration from Catholic "distributist" thinkers such G. K. Chesterton and Hillaire Belloc; and he developed a close friendship with the prominent Catholic economist Barbara Ward. In the early 1970s, he converted to Catholicism.

My own academic training was in political science, with a specialty in constitutional law. I never did any formal studies in economics (thank God!), but Schumacher's arguments pushed my own minimal economic understanding, as I was drawn more into the area of the politics of socioeconomic development. And it was the central thesis of his work as summed up in the subtitle of his book that contributed strongly to both my thinking and my activism on development issues, even before I moved to live and work in a "developing" country.

I now live in Africa, having spent the past two decades involved with a faith-based civil society organization in Zambia that is dedicated to promoting in practical policies and human activities the triad of the church's social teaching: *justice, peace, and the integrity of creation*. I will return later to this particular Zambian challenge, which for me illustrates so well the importance of an emphasis on "economics as if people mattered." Now let me suggest why "economics as if people mattered" is a thesis so relevant, so very urgent, in our globalized world of today.

The Urgency of the Situation

Two huge problems currently undercut our human quest for progress in today's world. First, in the immediate past several months, we have faced a collapse of sustainable economic activity in the rich nations. I would argue that that collapse has come about basically because of a dominant dogma in market activities that "greed is great." Second, we continue to face a seemingly insurmountable problem of human deprivation in poor nations, primarily because of a grossly unfair process of globalization. This is a structured globalization favorable primarily to the rich nations of the so-called First World.

Readers of this essay who live in rich nations can tell better than I can the stories of the impact on ordinary life of the global economic crisis of the past few years. Independent of one's ideological inclination—right or left—one can surely agree that much of the crisis found a root cause in ignoring basic human values of rights and community, duties and solidarity. Immediate return on investment mattered more than secure economic structures for the future; individual profiting weighed more heavily in decision making than promotion of the common good.

My expression "greed is great" might appear to some to be overstated, but I would argue that the fundamental drive of unfettered markets bent on profit maximization has had dire consequences indeed. And central to such an economic approach is the systemic ignoring of the human dimension, of the lives of the people directly involved or indirectly affected by the economic activities around them.

Readers who share my geographical location of a poor nation will know what I refer to in critiquing both external and internal forces grossly unfair to the majority of people living in our midst. Global economic structures of trade and investment and global political structures of dominance in decision making have combined with national economic and political structures that have considered the human development indices of people as secondary to the gross national product indices of economies.

Efforts to restore some balance to a development picture dominated by fixation on economic measurements devoid of human considerations can be seen in the promotion of the Millennium Development Goals (MDG). Poverty and hunger reduction, promotion of education, empowerment of women, reduction in child mortality, and improvement in maternal health care—these are a few of the goals to be achieved by 2015 through national commitments and international cooperation. But progress toward achievement of the goals is a monumental task indeed! For many of the "developing" countries, this progress has been disappointing and illusory.[3]

The Need for an Ethical Voice

Is there an ethical voice, a moral stance, a principled argument that can contribute substantially to the promotion of a more human-centered development process in our world of today? Is there something contrary to these forces noted above and constructive of a vision attuned to making "economics as if people mattered" less of a slogan and more of a reality?

I believe there is and that it can be found in what we refer to as the CST. Therefore I want to explore the economic developmental ethics of three major papal social encyclicals. I choose to go to these documents not out of pious admiration, but rather intellectual appreciation. In other places and times I have emphasized the importance of rescuing our CST documents from their status of being "the church's best kept secret"![4]

Certainly the three documents I am looking at all have their deficiencies, both intellectually and politically. But for me they also highlight points I want to stress in arguing that "economics as if people mattered" is not only urgent and necessary but also possible in our globalized world.

Progress of Peoples

The first document is Pope Paul VI's *Populorum progressio* ("Progress of Peoples"; *PP*), published in 1967 with the freshness of Vatican II's winds blowing through its pages.[5] The strong emphasis of *PP* is that authentic development is "for each and for all, the transition from less human conditions to those which are more human" (20).

Paul VI expressed the aspirations of women and men, especially those living in misery, as "to seek to do more, know more and have more in order to be more" (6). For *PP*, development is much more than economic growth: "In order to be authentic, it must be complete: integral, that is, it has to promote the good of every person and of the whole person" (14). In other words, *people first*! The first and fundamental question to ask in any development planning and evaluation is, "What is happening to the *people*, and not what is happening to the *economy*?"

These words might sound to some like pious utterances without foundation or relevance. But they were written by a pope who relied heavily on very progressive thinkers (take a look at his footnotes!) who were exploring alternatives to the socio-economic situation of the day. These included prominent Vatican II theologians such as Marie-Dominique Chenu and Henri de Lubac, preliberation theology thinker Louis Joseph Lebret, world-renowned philosopher Jacques Maritain, and social theologian Otto Nell-Bruening. The highly influential woman economist Barbara Ward was also part of the group that influenced the document. (Would that more recent papal encyclicals followed such a good example of wider consultation!)

The dominant economic paradigm guiding so much of development thinking and planning in the 1960s was that of the growth model formulated by Walter Rostow, an economist from the United States. In his highly influential *The Stages of Economic Growth*,[6] Rostow described development primarily as a planned effort for a "developing" country to "take off" by increasing economic growth, which—

hopefully—would "trickle down" to the impoverished masses. These impoverished masses—the majority of people in the so-called Third World—were not the principal focus of development efforts. Rather, foreign investments, expanded trade, and major infrastructure were higher on the development agenda than social services (for example, education and health), employment generation, or food security.

The focus of Paul VI in *PP* on people as primary in any development thinking and action was, in my view, an emphasis that only a few decades later became prominent in more mainstream circles. Beginning in 1990, the annual reports of the United Nations Development Programmes (UNDP) turned attention away from gross national product (GNP) measurements of *economic* well-being to measurements of *people* well-being expressed in the Human Development Index (HDI).[7] In the construction of the HDI, life expectancy, literacy, and household security are seen as more realistic and accurate indications of societal development. Surely this emphasis echoes *PP*'s definition that authentic development is "for each and for all, the transition from less human conditions to those which are more human" (20).

This emphasis had been even more strongly influential because of the writings of Nobel Prize laureate Amartya Sen. Sen was a seminal figure in designing the HDI. In his major study *Development as Freedom*,[8] this widely respected economist proposes a "human capabilities" measurement of development. These capabilities are not simply the measures of income and wealth preferred by more orthodox development analysts, but rather they point to substantive human freedoms. These include a focus on the capabilities of people to do and to be what they personally value. Surely, Sen is a strong voice in pushing for an "economics as if people mattered"!

In citing these two prominent secular emphases on the human dimensions of development, I want to stress the great contribution made earlier by *PP* in situating the debate very centrally around "economics as if people mattered."

On Social Concern

In 1987, twenty years after *PP*, John Paul II's *Sollicitudo rei socialis* ("On Social Concern"; *SRS*) arrived. Coming just prior to the historical collapse of the bi-polar world of capitalism and communism, this document pleased many with its radical freshness. But it also upset many with what appeared to be a "moral equivalency" argument that implied that both the capitalist West and the communist East were causes of global development ills.

To demonstrate the relevance of *SRS* to the theme of "economics as if people mattered," let me pick two related points in the encyclical that lift up the priority of human focus in any development efforts.

The first point is the theme of the *option for the poor* (42), a mandate to give priority in concerns and commitments to that portion of the population living in conditions marked by the extreme deprivation of the basics for decent living.[9] In most countries of the so-called Third World, it is the poor that make up the majority of the population. Personally, I believe it is more accurate to refer to the "impoverished" than to the "poor." "Poverty" is a situation, a circumstance; "impoverishment" is a consequence, an effect.

The "option for the poor" had been most commonly associated with the writings of Latin American liberation theologians such as Gustavo Gutiérrez and Jon Sobrino.[10] Such theologians had been criticized by Vatican officials such as the head of the Congregation for the Doctrine of the Faith, Cardinal Josef Ratzinger.[11] I feel it is significant, therefore, that John Paul II lifted up the "option for the poor" as an important element in contemporary CST.

In Part VI of *SRS*, discussing some guidelines for dealing with international economic realities, John Paul II explicitly refers to the "option or love of preference for the poor" (42). What implications such an option has for the economics of development are then spelled out by the pope when he urges that it applies to "the logical decisions to be made concerning the ownership and use of goods." Furthermore, he expects that "our decisions in the political and economic fields must be marked" by the realities of increasing poverty in the world.

The pope does not hesitate to apply the implications of this option for the poor to very pressing international development issues. "The motivating concern for the poor—who are, in the very meaningful term, 'the Lord's poor'—must be translated at all levels into concrete actions, until it decisively attains a series of necessary reforms" (43). He goes on to mention specifically

> the *reform of the international trade system*, which is mortgaged to protectionism and increasing bilateralism; the *reform of the world monetary and financial system*, today recognized as inadequate; the *question of technological exchanges* and their proper use; the *need* for a *review of the structure of the existing international organizations*, in the framework of an international juridical order (43).

By quoting at length here John Paul II's focus on the option for the poor, I want to indicate a significant emphasis on putting people, especially the poor who are the majority of the people in the so-called developing world, in the priority spot of development economics.

If development is to succeed, I believe that this emphasis on paying primary attention to the poor is precisely the message of an important World Bank Report issued in 2005 entitled *Development and Equity*.[12] This report is notable in its departure from a priority on economic structures to direct attention to human factors, that is, to people. Its thesis is straightforward: without paying attention to equitable involvement of and benefit to the poor, no economic growth is sustainable, no enjoyment of common prosperity is possible. "Economics as if people mattered" therefore must put the poor first in analysis, mandate, process, and evaluation.

A second important point of *SRS* is *solidarity*. The Polish pope would of course be associated with this theme because of his key involvement in the revolutionary changes in his own country in the 1980s, spurred on by the Solidarity movement. As pope, he incorporated this theme of social teaching into his view of development by emphasizing that "the conviction is growing of a radical interdependence and consequently of the need for a solidarity which will take up interdependence and transfer it to the moral plane" (26). As noted above, John Paul II is not hesitant in *SRS* to discuss specifics in international development matters, But he stresses that "None of what has been said can be achieved without the collaboration of all—especially the international community—in the framework of a solidarity which includes everyone, beginning with the most neglected" (45).

The theological basis for such an emphasis is clear: "The exercise of solidarity within each society is valid when its members recognize one another as persons" (39). This means that solidarity is the recognition that the human person is made in the image of God, a Triune God who is existentially a community of relationships among persons. Hence, it is not possible for there to be a Christian "commitment to development and its application which excludes regard and respect for the unique dignity" of the human person (33). In such an expression, *SRS* is repeating the emphasis on promoting an "economics as if people mattered."

Charity in Truth

Finally, I take the most recent papal document, *Caritas in veritate* ("Charity in Truth"), 2009, as offering a unique contribution to this search for ethical support for "economics as if people mattered." I do not think it requires too much of a stretch of the imagination to comment that Pope Benedict XVI has surprised many of us with his strong social teaching manifested in his encyclicals, his World Day of Peace messages, and numerous addresses to various audiences.

While serving the church universal as Cardinal Josef Ratzinger, his best-known public contributions to the body of CST were his very sharp critiques of liberation theology. But as pope, he immediately began to emphasize strongly the requirements of social justice for fully living out the Christian vocation.

In his first encyclical letter, *Deus caritas est* ("God Is Love"), in 2005, Benedict made clear the essential link between charity and justice. And he emphasized the duty of the lay faithful to promote justice within the state (28-29).[13] *Spe salvi* ("Saved by Hope"), his second encyclical, appeared in 2007. It made clear that the love of God, which is the Christian vocation, necessarily "leads to participation in the justice and generosity of God towards others" (28).

Given this background, there was understandable eagerness when it was learned that Benedict was writing a major "social encyclical" to come out sometime in 2008. But with the sudden appearance of the global economic crisis, the document was delayed so that some thoughtful analysis and recommendations could be offered both to church people and to officials in the public sector. When

Caritas in veritate (*CV*) appeared in mid-2009, it immediately stirred interest and lively discussion, since it covered such a wide range of issues—admittedly in a rather dense style.

But of the many points that might be drawn from *CV* to elaborate more on the theme of "economics as if people mattered," I want to consider briefly what Benedict XVI refers to as the "economy of communion." I do so with some hesitancy, since I readily admit that I myself do not fully understand this interesting new economic model, and therefore I do not want to endorse it uncritically. In an excellent analytical overview of *CV*, Nigerian theologian A. E. Orobator expresses caution about acceptance of this model in light of some African cultural traditions.[14]

But it does seem to me that the challenge Benedict offers is to promote an intermediate area in the economy between private business firms pursuing profit and strictly non-profit organizations pursuing human improvements. Profits are to be made, the pope argues, but they are to be shared gratuitously, as gift, to fund development programs in places of need (47).

Listen to his challenge: "In order to defeat underdevelopment, action is required not only on improving exchange-based transactions and implanting public welfare structures, but above all on gradually increasing openness, in a world context, to forms of economic activity marked by quotas of gratuitousness and communion" (39). And, "Today's international economic scene, marked by grave deviations and failures, requires a profoundly new way of understanding business enterprise" (40).

Benedict wrote this encyclical in the midst of the global economic crisis. He is calling for something more than a continuation of the blind and brute market forces that brought about the crisis. He is calling for something more than an increase in mere charitable responses to the victims of the crisis. His intriguing invitation to explore further the "economy of communion," with its emphasis upon the contribution of "gift" to sustainable development, is something that needs further exploration, with both favorable and critical analyses expected.

I highlight this "economy of communion" discussion here because it seems to me to offer an approach that can be seen in the orientation of promoting "economics as if people mattered" and is deserving of further exploration.

African Wisdom

Before passing to some specific Zambian issues relating to the emphases I have drawn from the three social encyclicals, I turn my attention briefly to some links to African culture as I have experienced that culture during my stay on that beautiful and varied continent. Elements of that culture really are expressions of social wisdom, a wisdom that throws both complementary and critical light on the traditional CST elements I have been discussing here. I am particularly encouraged to discuss, even in very simple fashion, some cultural points after listening to Professor Bénézet Bujo's presentation here at Trento.[15]

For example, Paul VI's definition of *development* in *PP*, with its strong emphasis on a communal link that authentic development is "for each and for all" (20), resonates with a practical expression of African wisdom emphasizing community. This practical emphasis is found in many ways in the Zambian context I have experienced. One small way that has touched me is found in the clear social demand for "relationships before business." This is a priority shown by hand-shaking and greeting before getting into the agenda of the moment—whether meeting someone on the street or coming into an office. (Africans and visitors to Africa can confirm this custom!)

The *SRS* emphasis of John Paul II on *solidarity* rings true in expression and practice to a central thesis of African wisdom that is expressed in the first set of African proverbs I learned when I came to Zambia twenty-one years ago. These proverbs about *ubuntu,* or "humanness," express the truth of solidarity by stating, "A person is a person through other persons," and "I am because we are, and we are because I am." My potential and growth are achievable because I belong to a community, and a community's creativity and beauty are possible because it is made up of individuals like me.

Finally, Benedict XVI's highlighting of gratuity and gift as essential for economic growth reminds me of the centrality of *hospitality* within traditional African experiences. The welcoming to the village and home even of the stranger goes beyond mere profit motives or charitable instincts. It is simply central to the fullness of life within community.

Now I surely do not want to over-romanticize these bits of African wisdom and practice. Surely there are faults and failings in all of this, as could only be expected in any real-life situation. But I do believe that probing into these elements does point to some enrichments in what otherwise might be a rather dry treatise on economics! For each of these bits of African wisdom does highlight why "economics as if people mattered" is so important to the fullness of life.

Zambian Challenges

Let me conclude by suggesting the relevance of this theme of "economics as if people mattered" to my country of residence, my home of concern, Zambia. Zambia is a country rich in resources but with a majority of seriously impoverished people. Though we live in a peaceful country—indeed, the envy of our neighbors—the life experience of too many Zambians is far from kind and progressive.

Economics under pressure from the World Bank and the International Monetary Fund has meant the adoption of neo-liberal structural reforms that have omitted a focus on people, with disastrous declines in the standard of living. Reaction to the HIV and AIDS pandemic has focused more on medical-pharmaceutical and behavioral-change responses, neglecting the social justice dimensions of development.[16]

Agricultural policy sensitive to the primary role of small-scale farmers is threatened by imposition of industrialized and environmentally unfriendly policies through promotion of genetically modified organisms (GMO). Gender in development issues is only recently being discovered as central to equitable and sustainable development. Ecological survival is threatened not by Zambian practices but by Northern consumerism. And all too often, politics has operated as if people did not matter!

These and many more challenges face Zambia today.[17] And that is why the theme of "economics as if people mattered" is for me not simply attractive to explore in a scholarly paper for an international conference. I believe it is centrally related to that synthesis of the Good News of Jesus that we find expressed in John 10:10: "I have come that you may have life and have life to the full." For me, consideration of and response to the theme of "economics as if people mattered" is primarily a call to think and act and pray in a way that positively affects the people I have come to love.

I hope I am not too presumptuous in inviting you, the readers of this essay, to join me in that thought, that action, that prayer!

Notes

1. Ernst F. Schumacher, *Small Is Beautiful: Economics as if People Mattered* (New York: Harper & Row, 1973).

2. Barbara Wood, *E. F. Schumacher: His Life and Thought* (New York: Harper & Row, 1984), 12. Barbara Wood is Schumacher's daughter.

3. United Nations, *The Millennium Development Goals Report 2010* (New York: United Nations, 2010).

4. Edward P. DeBerri, James E. Hug, Peter J. Henriot, and Michael J. Schultheis, *Catholic Social Teaching: Our Best Kept Secret* (Maryknoll, NY: Orbis Books, 2003).

5. For all of the papal encyclicals cited in this essay, easy access can be found on the Vatican Web site, http://www.vatican.va.

6. Walt W. Rostow, *The Stages of Economic Growth: A Non-Communist Manifesto* (Cambridge : Cambridge University Press, 1960).

7. For the latest edition, see United Nations Development Programme, *Human Development Report 2010–20th Anniversary: The Real Wealth of Nations, Pathways to Human Development* (New York: Oxford University Press, 2010).

8. Amartya Sen, *Development as Freedom* (Oxford: Oxford University Press, 1999).

9. See Peter J. Henriot, *Opting for the Poor: The Challenge for the Twenty-First Century* (Washington, DC: Center of Concern, 2004).

10. See, for example, Gustavo Gutiérrez, *A Theology of Liberation: History, Politics, and Salvation*, 15th anniversary ed. (Maryknoll, NY: Orbis Books, 1988); and Jon Sobrino, *No Salvation outside the Poor: Prophetic-Utopian Essays* (Maryknoll, NY: Orbis Books, 2008).

11. See *Instruction on Certain Aspects of "Theology of Liberation,"* Sacred Congregation for the Doctrine of the Faith, August 6, 1984.

12. World Bank, *World Development Report 2006: Equity and Development* (Washington, DC: World Bank, 2005).

13. See Peter Henriot, "For the Love of Justice," *The Tablet*, February 11, 2006.

14. A. E. Orobator, "Caritas in Veritate and Africa's Burden of (Under)Development," *Theological Studies* 71, no. 2 (2010): 320-34.

15. See in this volume, Bénézet Bujo, "Reasoning and Method in African Ethics," 147-59.

16. For fuller discussion of this major issue, see Michael J. Kelly, *HIV and AIDS: A Social Justice Perspective* (Nairobi: Paulines Publications, 2010).

17. For fuller discussion of these challenges, see the Web site of the Jesuit Centre for Theological Reflection, http://www.jctr.org.zm.

SUSTAINABILITY:
AN ETHICAL-THEOLOGICAL PERSPECTIVE[1]

Simone Morandini

In Our Ecological Age

The word "sustainability" invites us to think ethically about the environmental question and to locate it within a temporal horizon that is attentive to the future. It recalls a topic that is no longer new, given that almost forty years have passed since the publication of the report of the Club of Rome entitled *The Limits to Growth*.[2] Sustainability has become a central topic in the time in which we now live, and it can be considered as both "risk" and a "shared threat."[3] The most recent decades have above all reinforced the urgency to respond to many environmental questions. In particular, climate change demonstrates the brevity of the time scale—only ten years or so—in which the dramatic effects are taking place and will continue to occur.

I wish to emphasize that humanity is going through an original ethical experience, albeit in contradictory and differentiated forms. This experience invites us to rediscover ourselves as a human family deeply involved in global solidarity and concerned with our origin and our destiny, a solidarity that looks beyond the present moment.[4] It is quite ironic that precisely in this critical phase when we ought to be identifying the energies and resources that will help us to tackle serious environmental challenges, the global economic crisis appears to be suffocating any long-term objectives and tempting us instead with short-term policies. For faith communities, and especially for the ethical reflection that finds expression in them, the challenge is therefore to meditate attentively on the crisis in its complexity in order to discover the contributions that they can make to the growth of a human race genuinely capable of inhabiting the earth.

The Complexity of the Challenge

In order to proceed competently, we must remember that the devastating phenomenon of global warming is only one dimension of the environmental question. A number of other dimensions are also involved. There are threats to biodiversity and to the availability and accessibility of resources (water, food, energy, and so on), and the challenge posed by environmental refugees. These themes have dramatic implications, and each deserves treatment.[5]

257

I can merely mention them here. My intention in doing so is primarily to direct our attention to the complexity of a profound theme, one that cannot be approached in a one-dimensional manner. Doing justice to the theme of sustainability requires looking at a number of separate dimensions: theological and philosophical, scientific, sociopolitical and economic, and educational (the list is not exhaustive).[6] It is important to note that the same complexity is reflected in individual ecological questions. Even when dramatic questions have a more strongly local character, such as desertification in Africa or the impact on the marine ecosystem of the oil spill from the BP platform in the Gulf of Mexico, the only context in which one can adequately reflect on them is globally; the planetary effect of these occurrences must always be considered.

All of these varied factors, however, must not prevent us from perceiving precisely in and through their existence the "groaning" of the *ktisis,* of God's creation (Rom 8:19-23), which is interconnected with the cry of human beings, and especially of the poor.[7] It is this perspective that can concretize an ethical-theological approach, even before such an approach produces any normative guidelines.

An Anthropogenic Phenomenon

A truly adequate treatment of sustainability demands above all that we explicitly consider its anthropogenic nature. The environmental question and the groan associated with it do not spring from an inevitable fate, but rather are linked to human conduct and actions, both personal and social. We can point to roots in the dynamics of a consumer society or in the structural characteristics of nineteenth-century capitalism, or even in some tendencies of the philosophical anthropocentrism of the modern age. An eco-feminist approach might also see links between an exploitative anthropocentrism of this kind and patriarchal androcentrism.

There are undeniable elements of truth in each of these approaches. In the present context, however, it seems most relevant to view the crisis that we are living in as a manifestation of the cultural nature of human beings who alone are capable of escaping the bonds that confine other living beings to their delimited ecological niche. Human beings can shape their own environment.[8] This dynamic reaches its high point in the emergence of technical ability, which has reached a wholly unprecedented level of development in our time.

It is precisely this reality that led Paul Crutzen, winner of the Nobel Prize for chemistry in 1995, to speak of the "Anthropocene," the epoch in which human activity is one of the principal factors in the biological and geological evolution of the planet.[9] In *Something New under the Sun*, John McNeill, a historian of the environment, underlines the novelty of the condition of the planet in the twentieth century. By now, the planet is almost completely hominized.[10]

Those who grasp the anthropological novelty of the Anthropocene will also understand the dramatic discrepancy between the immense power that is available to the human race and our ability to assess the goals toward which this power ought to be directed. Recent popes have rightly pointed out that the ecological crisis has not only technological and political dimensions, but also poses a great moral question. The lives of millions of men and women of the present and future generations are at stake, beginning with the poor who are the first to pay the price of an unsustainable way of life.

The Environmental Question and the Church's Social Teaching

The social teaching of the Catholic Church has taken up the environmental question in an increasingly assertive manner, particularly in drawing attention to the future generations of the human race. As there are too many texts produced by the magisterium to be analyzed here, I mention only a few that are particularly relevant, including chapter 10 of *The Compendium of the Social Doctrine of the Church*,[11] the Messages for the World Days of Peace in 1990 and 2010, and paragraphs 48 through 51 of the encyclical *Caritas in veritate*.

It is interesting to note that none of these documents explicitly employs the concept of sustainability, although the Pontifical Council for Justice and Peace examined it carefully during the preparation of *The Compendium*. In the end, it preferred the less-demanding concept of "environmental compatibility." In *Caritas in veritate*, however, Benedict XVI employs a concept very similar to that of sustainability. Benedict speaks of the "grave duty to hand the earth on to future generations in such a condition that they too can worthily inhabit it and continue to cultivate it."[12]

These words use strong moral language to define a goal that is, in effect, the equivalent of sustainability. We may recall here the customary definition of sustainability goes back to the report presented to the United Nations by the Brundtland Commission.[13] This report spoke of sustainability in terms of the ability to satisfy the needs of the present generation without prejudice to an analogous possibility for the future. Accordingly, it is first and foremost the attention to the human family understood in its future dimension and in its inescapable relation to the Earth that underlies the concept of sustainability. The concrete proposals of the Brundtland Report on the capacities of the ecosystem of the Earth must be evaluated on the basis of this fundamental anthropological dimension.

If Catholic theology is to evaluate correctly this concept and its implications, it must not forget that the World Council of Churches employed it to make a similar point as long ago as 1975, when it called on the Christian world to collaborate in the construction of a "just, participatory, and sustainable society."[14] This perspective was elaborated in the course of a lively process deeply rooted in both the Protestant and the Orthodox approaches. Remembering this initiative could help the Catholic magisterium better appreciate the great moral and theological importance of sustainability. This concept has already been employed in many texts drawn up by various episcopal conferences, with the German and American conferences leading the way.

An Ethical and Theological Perspective

There is an immediate need for a perspective on the need for sustainability that can confront the current ecological challenges with a resolutely anthropocentric approach. This perspective is undeniably different from the holistic perspective of Earth ethics or the biocentrism of life ethics,[15] but it is no less demanding. Making the future generations of the human race the key reference point for environmental ethics means interpreting the centrality of the *anthrōpos* in responsible and relational forms that are very remote from the absolute forms of the modern age. What is involved here is thus neither the anthropocentrism of the *homo oeconomicus* with its insatiable thirst for good things, nor the Promethean anthropocentrism that ignores every limit on one's own transformative technological action. Nor is it the "anthropocentrism" of the "consumer of sensations" in this fluid modern age.

Sustainability requires a subject who is vulnerable and well aware of the relationality on which his or her life is based. This subject is conscious of being a member of a human family that is located on a finite planet and that understands well the ecosystemic impact of one's behavior and consumption on this generation and the generations to come. This subject must be aware of the power that believers see as part of the vocation conferred on them by God, but also of the burdensome task of giving this power a responsible orientation to life—that is to say, human life, but not only human life.

It is clear that a subject of this kind does not see biological and ecosystemic nature as a mere quarry to be mined as one pleases. On the other hand, neither does nature constitute an immediate source of norms that one could simply apply in one's own conduct. Rather, nature is the sphere of life, both glorious and vulnerable, that demands prudent action. Such action can transform nature to make it inhabitable but without undermining the very structures of support that make inhabitability possible. Such action will know how to cultivate and take care of the garden that is entrusted to it (to use the language of Gen 2:15) in a wise equilibrium between innovation and conservation.

These few remarks suffice to show that reflection on sustainability has a radical anthropological significance that goes beyond sociopolitical dimensions. But it also has a corresponding theological dimension, and this too is important. The Nicene-Constantinopolitan creed expresses this dimension when it calls the creator *Pantokratōr*. This term is usually translated as "omnipotent," but the root noun *kratos* not only indicates the dimension of absolute power but also introduces the dimension of sustaining and conserving. In other words, the Creator is the *Pantokratōr* because he sustains everything. It is the Creator who in the covenant after the flood guaranteed the stability of the climate and of the seasons of the year, without which a genuinely human existence is impossible (Gen 8:2). For the

believer, therefore, the responsible praxis of sustainability is an essential component of the way in which human beings correspond to the image of the God who
lives in them and whose providence takes active care of the Earth and its inhabitants.

This fundamental affirmation does not allow us to forget that believers themselves also behave in ways that show a grave lack of attention to God's Earth. Nor
can we deny that the theological interpretation of the position of the human being
in creation has sometimes been marked by ambivalence.[16] But the American historian Lynn White was completely wrong to claim that such elements show that an
anti-ecological stance is constitutive of Christian anthropocentrism.[17] The opposite
is true. The trained theological eye will see that such elements are an utter betrayal
of the true and genuine "ecological promise"[18] that runs through the whole of scripture. One important element in the task of theological ethics today is to explore the
meaning of this promise and to rediscover its spiritual and normative power.

Principles Needed in Order to Promote Sustainability

Sustainability should be of urgent concern to all believers. At the same time,
it provides an orientation for praxis that by its very nature involves the various
components of the entire human family. This is why it is important to offer some
concrete ethical guidelines.

We must begin by emphasizing that the principle of sustainability is not an
invitation to abstain from action, as if there were a contradiction between sustainability and human creativity and the integral human development that is so power-
fully evoked by *Caritas in veritate*. On the contrary, our conduct must seek justice
as it explicitly considers the environmental dimension in *all* the relevant choices it
makes, whether societal or personal. In other words, sustainability must become an
indispensable element of the continuous praxis of discernment that is at the heart
of moral behavior (Rom 12:1-2).

It is not a question of deriving rigid normative directives from a predefined
concept of sustainability. Instead, the emphasis should be on learning how to
approach sustainability in an adaptable and well-structured manner. Then such
a perspective can function as an interpretative criterion in the complex concrete
situations that involve human and environmental values.

Five principles can help concretize this requirement. These guidelines,
although not exhaustive, are generated by the concept of sustainability, but they are
also wholly consonant with the social teaching of the Catholic Church. The first
two are very general, but experience indicates that they are also fundamental. The
third and the fourth principles draw on *The Compendium of the Social Doctrine of
the Church*, and the final point takes up a theme emphasized by John Paul II on a
number of occasions.

First, sustainability is an *intergenerational extension of justice*. Justice demands
that we consider the needs of succeeding generations. Justice must guarantee that

all the components of the human family, and especially the poor, have adequate access to the goods of the earth, beginning with the vital goods of water, energy, and nutritional resources. Today's oligarchic distribution must be overcome, since the unequal sharing of responsibilities, goods, and risks that characterizes the condition of the human family is a dramatic negation of sustainability. Similarly, ethical reflections on how to mitigate climate change and on the contributions that the various nations can and ought to make must be based on justice.[19] The scanty attention paid to this dimension was one of the factors that led to the failure of the conference on the environment held in Copenhagen in December 2009.

Second, sustainability entails an *appeal to subsidiarity* so that personal, social, and institutional responsibilities are structured in forms that are "common but differentiated." Subsidiarity concerns not only institutions—supranational, national, and local—but also the various expressions of civil society, including churches, as well as the world of scientific and technological research and the sphere of economics. It follows that an environmental ethics must be articulated on different levels, giving careful expression to the responsibility that is shared in the various areas in which it is exercised.

Third, for attention to be truly paid to justice, the human race must view sustainability in terms of the *global solidarity* of the human family. Precious national and local characteristics should certainly be appreciated, but we must learn that a global challenge such as sustainability demands commitments from all. Sustainability involves individual feelings and actions, but it also demands an adequate expression on the level of political institutions. Individual national subjects must unilaterally undertake actions that are necessary, but these must be integrated into a multilateral framework, into what we might call a pact for the Earth and for future generations.

Fourth, the encyclical *Sollicitudo rei socialis* invites us to take an *ecosystemic perspective*, that is, to "take into account the nature of each being and its mutual connection in an ordered system."[20] This point is taken up by *The Compendium of the Social Doctrine of the Church*, which invites us to consider everything that exists, whether living or inanimate, not only in terms of its individual value but also in its role with regard to the stability and vitality of the local and global ecosystem. We must bear in mind that even a limited alteration in individual factors can have immense consequences. And this means that ethics must learn to "think like a mountain"—to borrow the well-known expression of Aldo Leopold, one of the founding fathers of environmental ethics in the United States. In other words, we must learn from the ecological sciences how to perceive the complex interweaving of factors that interact, even in a local ecosystem.[21]

Fifth, *prevention and precaution* teach us that it is a much more difficult to repair damage to the environment (particularly when this damage is substantial) than to take prudent measures to prevent such damage. This makes preventive action a duty, especially when the consequences may be vast. This remains true even if scientific knowledge of the factors involved is not yet complete. Today, the principle of precaution[22] is proving relevant in many spheres of environmental ethics, particularly in areas such as climate change and the use of genetically modified organisms.

Virtues Needed in Order to Promote Sustainability

The principles mentioned above are most relevant when making important socioeconomic choices. However, an environmental ethics must also appeal to a number of ecological virtues that help to shape the hearts of those who are summoned to practice sustainability in their daily praxis, in other words, their lifestyle.[23] One global factor in the current environmental crisis is the increasing spread of the unsustainable behavior typical of the *homo oeconomicus* of the consumerist model of Western societies.

A subject working toward sustainability must pass through what John Paul II called an "ecological conversion," which requires an evaluation of one's praxis in terms of radically different parameters.[24] This possibility too is rooted in the cultural nature of human beings and in their ability to modify behavior that is no longer appropriate. Our societies must prepare themselves for a profound transformation in order to make the transition to sustainability. This perhaps critical passage in the dynamic of evolution must be based on a renewal of the behavior of individual persons, families, and communities. Such renewal can be expressed by a number of virtues.

The first ecological virtue is certainly *gratitude*. Gratitude expresses our recognition of the finitude of the human subject who comes from a human community and from a biological evolution that makes possible the sheer fact of existence. It is the consciousness of being a guest, of having received a gift that surpasses any possibility of giving an equivalent gift in return, and a gift that must be handed on intact to future generations.

The second virtue is embedded in gratitude. *Sobriety* is required for a sustainable personal and communal lifestyle. This is the ability to lead a life free of all that is inessential. In the Western world, such a life is necessarily in conscious opposition to contemporary culture, which focuses on maximizing consumption. Sobriety involves two dimensions. The first is eco-sufficiency, which is the ability to examine one's own consumption attentively in order to see whether it genuinely corresponds to the requirements of a good life, or whether it is a type of behavior generated by imitating others or by the seduction of advertising. The ethical-theological tradition must continue to insist that one can have a good life even with a quantity of goods (and an impact on the environment) much smaller than is customary for the citizens of Western societies.

A second condition of sobriety is eco-efficiency. We may indeed recognize that some needs are both genuine and essential, but we must be able to satisfy these needs in such a way that the impact on the environment is minimal and that it makes use of the best developments in science and technology. An ethical-theological perspective must also affirm the vital role of technological innovation with regard to sustainability, since technology can help to reduce the consumption of energy and materials for the production of goods and services. If we are to lead to the full a sustainable lifestyle, a third virtue demands that we *go beyond the anthropocentrism* that has guided our reflections on sustainability up to this point. In other words, the construction of sustainable existence must also look to figures such as Francis of Assisi or Seraphim of Sarov and rediscover these saints' experience of *eschatological siblinghood* with other creatures. This points us toward an ethics that pays attention to the animals who are our companions in creation, but also to a spirituality on a cosmic scale that is capable of situating human action and emotion within the vast horizon of the creation of God.

Fourth, one who experiences such universal siblinghood must fully live the virtue of *caring*. Ethical and theological reflection by women has paid great attention to this topic. Care for human beings and for human relationships is accompanied by care for the Earth, since one cannot bear to see it laid waste.

The principles or virtues evoked above are relevant to ethical-social reflection, but they are directly relevant to the concrete existence of individuals and communities. This is why it is vital that they be integrated into moral reflection and into the pastoral praxis of the communities of believers, in order to recover the concrete, lived relationship with the Earth that is an important dimension of the Christian life. The Day for Creation on September 1 each year, initially proposed by the Ecumenical Patriarchate of Constantinople and since adopted by many Protestant churches and by numerous Catholic episcopal conferences, offers a great opportunity to put these principles into practice.

Conclusions

Although environmental ethics certainly belongs to the sphere of applied ethics,[25] it has anthropological and pastoral implications that greatly exceed this sphere, since it is relevant to systematic theology on the doctrine of creation. Sustainability, often thought of as a "cold" term, has led us through an ethical reflection that has evoked the technological, political, and economical dimensions, but it also contains an intense and significant theological and spiritual component. This is because the house of life that is bestowed on us is also the precious space in which the word has erected its tent (John 1:14) and in which the Spirit gives life to all living things, renewing the face of the earth (Psalm 104:30). This perspective does not in any way contradict the description of reality that is offered by contemporary science. It seeks only to demonstrate that faith can discern the expression of a cosmic creative love in the dynamics that science reveals to us.[26]

The Christian faith presents a Trinitarian horizon that can sustain an ecological ethics and spirituality. As Jürgen Moltmann likes to point out, Christian faith also locates a hope that embraces the whole of creation.[27] A believer's ethics of sustainability will not be motivated only by the concern the believer necessarily shares with others about the threat that looms over the human family. Above all, our ethics will be inspired by a radical love that is addressed to the Earth and to all those who live on it and are our companions on the path toward an *eschaton* in which God will be "all in all" (1 Cor 15:28).

I conclude with the words of Father Zossima in *The Brothers Karamazov*:

Love all God's creation, the whole and every grain of sand in it. Love every leaf, every ray of God's light. Love the animals, love the plants, love everything. If you love everything, you will perceive the divine mystery in things. Once you perceive it, you will begin to comprehend it better every day. And you will come at last to love the whole world with an all-embracing love.[28]

Notes

1. English translation by Brian McNeil.

2. Donella H. Meadows et al., *The Limits of Growth* (New York: Universe Books, 1972).

3. In addition to a classic such as Hans Jonas, *Das Prinzip Verantwortung* (Frankfurt: Insel, 1979), I refer to the fine study by Elena Pulcini, *La cura del mondo: Paura e responsabilità nell'età globale* (Turin: Bollati Boringhieri, 2009).

4. I have discussed this perspective in Simone Morandini, *Da credenti nella globalizzazione: Etica e teologia in prospettiva ecumenica* (Bologna: EDB, 2007).

5. For an overview, see the report *Global Environment Outlook: Environment for Development (GEO-4)*. This document can be accessed on the home page of the United Nations Environment Programme (UNEP), http://www.unep.org/geo/geo4/media/.

6. For some indications here, see Simone Morandini, ed., *Per la sostenibilità: Etica ambientale ed antropologia* (Padua: Gregoriana, 2007); and Simone Morandini, *Nel tempo dell'ecologia: Etica teologica e questione ambientale* (Bologna: EDB, 1999).

7. See Leonardo Boff, *Cry of the Earth, Cry of the Poor* (Maryknoll, NY: Orbis Books, 1997), but this does not mean that I agree with every element of the theology Boff proposes.

8. For a more ample consideration of this perspective, see Simone Morandini, *Etica ed evoluzione* (Assisi: Citadella, 2010).

9. Paul Crutzen and Eugene F. Stoermer, *International Geosphere-Biosphere Programme Newsletter* 41 (May 2000): 17-18.

10. John R. McNeill, *Something New under the Sun: An Environmental History of the Twentieth-Century World* (New York: Norton, 2000).

11. Pontifical Council for Justice and Peace, *Compendium of the Social Doctrine of the Church* (Vatican City: Libreria Editrice Vaticana, 2004).

12. *Caritas in veritate* (Charity in Truth), 50.

13. Gro Harlem Brundtland, ed., *Our Common Future: The World Commission on Environment and Development* (Oxford: Oxford University Press, 1987).

14. See the relevant articles in Nicholas Lossky et al., eds., *Dictionary of the Ecumenical Movement* (Geneva: World Council of Churches, 1991).

At the time of my protest, however, there was a gap between the ideas declared and the reality experienced. There were a number of provisions of the Schengen visa legislation that might satisfy bureaucratic logic but violated the vastly more important principle of human dignity.

Especially denigrating to the citizens of Ukraine was the requirement, practiced by the majority of Schengen Agreement embassies (at least by the time of my protest), that persons who apply for visas must subject themselves each time to personal interviews and provide evidence of their declared professions. As a result, there were countless instances when Ukrainians were forced to do this on the premises of embassy buildings: children had to dance to prove that they were really members of a dance ensemble; writers were required to bring copies of their books; and singers had to show that they had professional voices. Sometimes the applicants were forced to bring documents confirming that they were not infected with HIV or tuberculosis and so on. This was humiliating for the persons in question, but it was also a violation of the basic democratic principle of the inadmissibility of collective responsibility for those who violated visa requirements. Blame for violations of visa regimes should be ascribed exclusively to those individuals who committed these violations.

It was not only my personal observation. According to the EUobserver Web page, "a survey by a consortium of Ukrainian think tanks found that people face queues, days-long delays, mysterious extra fees and unexplained refusals when trying to visit the EU."[2] Jan de Ceuster, head of the European Commission's visa issuance department, said changes were sorely needed: "I think we should admit that in the past sometimes the visa process was not always customer-friendly."

Since that time, Schengen authorities made some significant steps toward normalizing the situation. The European Commission has introduced draft legislation to move Albania and Bosnia and Herzegovina to the list of visa-exempt countries. Most important, a new EU visa code came into force on April 5, 2010, which is aimed at coordinating the practices in all the Schengen countries and, as was promised, "is meant to be more fair, transparent and precise."

It would be justified, therefore, to say that now the ball is in the Ukrainian court. The Ukrainian Parliament and the Ukrainian government have a list of Ukrainian obligations waiting for their approval.

However, another problem can be identified. On some occasions, the entire issue of the EU visa system seems to be politically flavored. As euobserver.com reports,

> [T]he EU is likely to take a big step toward visa-free travel with Russia. But Poland wants to make sure that other post-Soviet countries, especially Ukraine, are also included. Polish foreign minister Radek Sikorski said the EU should not leave out in the cold the six post-Soviet countries in its Eastern Partnership scheme, however. The scheme covers Armenia, Azerbaijan, Belarus, Georgia, Moldova and Ukraine.... Georgia had for years

complained that the EU is undermining its territorial integrity by letting people with Russian passports, including those in its breakaway Abkhazia and South Ossetia regions, travel on easier terms than people with Georgian passports. Ukrainian diplomats are bitter that the EU is happy to open borders with Russia but not with Ukraine, despite Ukraine's democratic transformation.

So the problem still remains.

In my opinion and in the opinion of my colleagues, the time has come to change the very philosophy that governs the practical protection of the rights of citizens to free and unobstructed travel in Europe and to remove degrading bureaucratic obstacles relating to the issuance of visas. At one time the European security system, represented by the OSCE (Organization for Security and Cooperation in Europe) and Helsinki Agreement, opened the borders of Europe and facilitated interpersonal contact. As a then-imprisoned human right activist, I was proud of such a Europe and grateful to it for calling to me to fight for human rights. Today, I appeal to the theological ethicists of the world to ensure that official Europe and other regions of our planet will not create a security system in which new "iron curtains" are created and to which basic democratic values are subordinated.

Emigration

Now let me turn to my second concern, the issue of emigration. I am primarily addressing the Ukrainian experience, but I am sure representatives of many countries taking part in this conference will recognize similar social contexts.

Having experienced over the last century four major waves of emigration, Ukraine has, in its own eyes, become a huge reserve of people; from time to time, geopolitical tsunamis have forced surges in emigration, with the last wave caused by the collapse of the Soviet Union.

The communist system collapsed in part because it could not withstand competition with the capitalist system. The glittering advertisements and glossy shop windows were all too alluring to citizens of the USSR, who gazed with envy from behind the Iron Curtain at the trappings of the Western world. In this sense the envious gaze of Ukrainians did not differ in any way from the equally envious looks of those who leaped over the Berlin Wall or filled boats of illegal migrants in the Mediterranean. Socioeconomic elements cannot be disputed as motivation for those who at the first opportunity headed West in search of prosperity and a happy life. Western Europe presented a far-too-tempting civilization and, like Ancient Rome, it could not fail to be besieged by the surrounding so-called barbarians.

Socioeconomic motivations for leaving Ukraine were even strengthened when the economic problems of the Soviet system were replaced with the economic crises of the first years of independence. Ukrainians of all generations suffered psychological trauma. Older people whose youth had been scarred by war had lived through all the years that followed with the hope of a "light at the end of the tunnel."

for the West and especially for Europe. One of the main reasons was the uncontrolled migration of the population. Therefore, it is not surprising that in place of the Iron Curtain, which had been established by totalitarian states and that fell between 1989 and 1991, now an "emigration curtain" appeared, raised this time by democratic Europe. More and more, Ukraine seemed to be encapsulated to prevent eventual troubles.

In the end, however, awareness grew that in the global world it was impossible to isolate a population of forty-eight million. Globalization not only brings benefits to Western economies; it also encourages their governments to share responsibility for situations in less-successful countries. It is precisely for this reason that Pope John Paul II spoke so much about how the globalization of the world economy needs to be balanced by the globalization of world solidarity.

Today, therefore, the fate of Ukrainian emigration cannot be resolved solely within the framework of Ukraine alone. Earlier we analyzed the direct dependence of this emigration on the success or lack of success of the global project of "independent Ukraine." And the fate of this project, although first and foremost lying in the hands of Ukrainians, is implemented on a global field and depends significantly on international factors. The project "independent democratic Ukraine" is in direct opposition to the project "the restored greatness and strength of Russia." More than anything, Russia wishes to renew its monopoly on the post-Soviet realm. Its allies are those forces in the West that recall with nostalgia the situation of "one predictable player against fifteen that are unpredictable." In principle, it is possible to push the East European genie into a Russian authoritarian "bottle." However, doing so will resolve Europe's lesser difficulties while creating much greater problems.

On the other hand, I am well aware that it would be equally dangerous for Europe to take the side of the Ukrainian project blindly and recklessly, ignoring the Russians. Trying to avoid exclusion of ourselves, we cannot propose to exclude others. However, what we face today is a global change of the geopolitical status quo. We Ukrainians stand at the crossroads. The previous status quo, despite its backwardness, retains nonetheless a certain attraction. The future status quo, despite its allure, still lacks clear features and is therefore fraught with certain dangers. At the moment, the political leadership of the West, searching for stability and energy security, seems to prefer sinking back into the illusory comfort of the old status quo. I have strong doubts that this will succeed because the restoration of the previous comfort will inevitably bring back to life the demons of the past against which Europe measured its strength so long and with such difficulty. I am afraid that the priority given to stability and security will threaten the very basis of Western civilization, that is, the strength of its moral values.

However, a new world order will inevitably evolve, and one of the roads to this maturing process is international support for Ukraine's democratic project. This is worth the resources invested since its success will help to civilize and humanize the entire post-Soviet space.

Allow me to conclude my paper with the following observation. On the one hand, I would ask forgiveness from our European colleagues for the fact that the difficult and thorny ascent of my country to the heights of democracy is causing difficult problems in European countries. It is the duty of our government and our society to cooperate with you to soften this geopolitical blow. On the other hand, I would like to assure you that, at the present time, Ukraine, while enduring its postcommunist transformation, is undertaking a difficult civilization-linked mission of significance for all of Europe. It is extremely important that we achieve this mission not *despite* the fleeting illusions of Europe, but with its clearly understood and strategically determined *support*.

An Update

On November 22, 2010, the European Union commission issued an Action Plan for Ukraine leading to visa-free travel. It listed specific reforms that Ukraine must fulfill before the European Union opens its doors. According to European Commission President Jose Manuel Barroso, the plan will aim at "establishing a visa-free regime for short-stay travel as a long-term perspective."[3] It also envisaged a breakthrough in time for the Euro 2012 football championship in Poland and Ukraine. But there is little progress on the Ukrainian side in fulfilling the requirements necessary.

Moreover, new difficulties appeared recently. The Europol study (EU Organized Crime Threat Assessment 2011) says that southeast Europe is a hub for smuggling arms, drugs, and people into the union.[4] According to the document, the projected introduction of a visa-free regime for Ukraine may facilitate these negative trends. Ukraine's ambassador to the European Union, Kostiantyn Yelisieiev, labeled the statement as "non-acceptable" and "urged the Europol to revise its statements."[5]

The political situation in Ukraine does not seem to be favorable for the success of the EU–Ukraine negotiations. In spite of the claims by Ukrainian President Viktor Yanukovych to make stability and the rule of law his top domestic priority, the reality of Ukraine is drifting away from democracy and, consequently, from the West. It will be difficult for the present Ukrainian administration to reconcile the EU Action Plan requirements with ever-growing pressure from Russia.

It puts the European Union in a rather ambiguous situation. As Andreas Umland, a teacher at the Kyiv Mohyla Academy in Ukraine said, "Brussels will now have to find a new tone in its negotiations with Kyiv. It needs to make sure that it neither pushes away the Ukrainian leadership as a negotiation partner for the near future, nor loses the Ukrainian state as a member of the European community of democratic countries."[6]

What is important for us in this situation is to safeguard the freedom of writers and academic researchers, sportsmen and people of art—in general, all those who are natural promoters of democratic values and interpersonal relations—so they do not become hostages of these undoubtedly difficult negotiations.

Notes

1. See http://www.schengenvisa.cc/.
2. http://euobserver.com/?aid=31316.
3. Ibid.
4. http://www.europol.europa.eu/publications/European_Organised_Crime_Threat_Assessment_%28OCTA%29/OCTA_2011.pdf.
5. http://news.kievukraine.info/2011/05/ukraine-attacks-europol-over-organised.html.
6. http://euobserver.com/9/31316.

An Archbishop's Perspective on the Future of Theological Ethics

Reinhard Cardinal Marx

It is a great honor for me to address such a distinguished audience.[1] When I read the impressive conference program and the list of participants, I wondered what contribution I could make to this international congress. The title of my lecture indicates that I do not intend to discuss one special topic in moral theology or social ethics. I should like to speak more generally, from the perspective of a bishop, about the future of theological ethics in the context of the Catholic Church. My remarks are no more than an outline; they are meant as an invitation to a discussion.

We moral theologians and social ethicists have become in many ways specialists for individual topics, with the risk that we lose sight of the search for a holistic concept or (let me venture to say) a vision for a better world, for a good life. This makes conferences like our present meeting in Trento all the more important. The fruits of your work and reflection here will be brought back to the societies from which you come.

Biographical Approaches to Ethics

Let me begin by indicating some biographical approaches to my topic. The question of justice has played an important role in the course of my life. I come from a family in which societal involvement was central. My father was an employee representative, and this meant that the debates about work and capital and the question of workers' participation in management had a profound impact on me.

Another formative influence was my work in the *Kommende*, the Social Institute of the Archdiocese of Paderborn, where I became conscious of how the church's social teaching, and indeed basically the whole of moral theology, rests on three columns. The first column is the teaching of the magisterium. The second column is the academic debate and the formulation of normative propositions by social ethicists and moral theologians. The third column consists of those who also translate the social teaching into reality in specific movements and political actions—significant but sometimes forgotten by moral theologians and social ethicists. It is not enough to write beautiful books. All three columns are exceptionally important for the future of Catholic ethics. If we concentrate our attention on only one of these columns, we will not succeed in shaping the future in the manner required by the situation of the world today.

Let me mention a third biographical approach to this topic. As the director of the Social Institute, I faced the question as to how I as a priest could work in an organization that was concerned with themes such as the social market economy, pension insurance, and health care. I was helped at that time by the concept of discipleship proposed by Johann Baptist Metz, that is to say, the conviction that there is no antithesis between mysticism and politics, or between active responsibility for the world and spirituality. Rather, these are two sides of one and the same coin. This approach taken by political theology left its mark on me and has been a continual source of encouragement; it is still extraordinarily important for the future of moral theology and for an ethical vision of what the church is. It does not entail any reduction of the rational claim made by ethics. On the contrary, the link between mysticism and politics constitutes the heart of ethical thinking, and this approach will remain important in the future too, as the encyclical *Caritas in veritate* confirms.

I was surprised to see that the encyclical's text begins with the theme of love; but after I had read it several times, I realized that this approach is perfectly logical. It follows the tradition of the church's social teaching by taking its starting point in that which is constitutive of the human person. We exist in this world because God said, "You shall love!" This is the starting point of ethics, and this is basically the starting point of this encyclical, in which we can see something of the piety of ethics. This too is important for the future of ethics. I found this insight very liberating and encouraging. It is only natural that the theme of justice should find its place here too.

Future Fields of Investigation and Challenges

After presenting these biographical approaches to our topic, I should now like to mention some future fields of investigation and challenges that I believe now face Catholic theological ethics.

The first challenge is the question of justification. We must seek plausible justifications for theological ethics in a global context. It must be possible for all persons of good will to grasp the positions that are maintained by moral theology and social ethics. This may seem obvious, but you all know from your academic work that it cannot simply be taken for granted. We must continue to work on the theological foundations of our ethical thinking. We know that Catholic ethics is theology, since it has its source in belief in the Triune God. Its criterion is the word of Jesus and the example of his life, and it does not shrink from facing the claim made by universal reason. In recent decades, however, it has not become clear what this reason means. On the contrary, it has become even less clear. We cannot assert that our European conception of reason appears plausible to everyone and finds acceptance everywhere.

This is why I consider reflection on the concept of reason to be another great challenge. If we do not arrive at a shared way of thinking about reason, we shall be unable to find a common language—even within Catholic theological ethics. Despite all the diversification of theological approaches, we need a rediscovery and a reformulation of our normative claims, which have their source in the Gospel, but at the same time do justice to the claim made by universal reason. However, as Pope Benedict XVI says in his encyclical, this demands a fresh examination of natural law. The goal here is to formulate the personal dignity of the human being anew, in keeping with the approach elaborated by Thomas Aquinas in terms of *natura ut ratio*. The discussion between Jürgen Habermas and Joseph Cardinal Ratzinger in 2004 clarified both the problems and the challenge that are inherent in this undertaking.[2] We must accept this challenge.

I believe that a new discussion of natural law is important for the future of Catholic theological ethics, both in social ethics and in moral theology, for otherwise we shall not find common formulations in the bioethical debates. I cannot predict whether or not this endeavor will be successful, but our aspirations ought at least to tend in this direction.

The same applies to the concepts of autonomy and freedom. I cannot imagine any Catholic ethics that would disregard freedom and see it primarily as a danger. And we can carry conviction in a global context only if we make it clear that we as Catholic ethicists regard freedom as the absolute hallmark of human dignity. Freedom is also the precondition for love. Human dignity depends on freedom, as does the idea that the human person is made in the image of God—an idea that, as far as I know, is found only in the biblical tradition. This means that freedom is first and foremost something positive and important. It follows that our preaching must promote and facilitate freedom, while of course indicating the boundaries of freedom and bringing freedom and responsibility together. We should not elaborate a hermeneutic of suspicion with regard to freedom; rather, we must encourage people to live freedom in responsibility. Such encouragement is one of the tasks of theological ethics. The central message—that the human person can lead a good life because God has called him or her into life out of love—must become clear.

Another challenge concerns particularity and universality. Let me put it somewhat critically: Some parts of the program of your congress look like a "feast of particularism." The immersion in specific ethical fields may have been, and may still be, a necessary process of clarification, since it is only in this way that we can appropriately reflect on the ethical claim and formulate it. Nevertheless, the goal of theological ethics must surely be to find a global formulation that lies beyond all particularisms, for who else could put forward a universalistic claim of this kind?

But how does Catholic ethics arrive at universal justifications that are held in common? Let me begin by stating that if all we do is to thematize the plurality of cultural and other particularisms, we are not rendering the world a good service.

Nor are we doing justice to our task of finding a common language for the one family of humankind. In the future, it will be decisively important to demonstrate that Catholic ethics genuinely has something special to contribute, something that everyone can understand, something that is lived and attested to in the church. At the same time, we must hold fast to the necessary differentiations and encourage these. The autonomy of the various cultural spheres must be genuinely preserved in Catholic social ethics. All I want to do is to indicate this briefly, since my impression is that this congress takes this task seriously and intensively.

In Germany, we have a traditional differentiation between moral theology, social teaching, and social ethics. This distinction may seem alien to some people in the worldwide church, but I believe that it is not unimportant. These differentiations make it possible to come to social ethics or institutional ethics from a different access road than we use for individual ethics. This certainly does not amount to driving a wedge between them, but we ought to maintain the differentiation.

In the future, there must also be more intensive reflection on theological language. Normative propositions are rational propositions, not *paraenesis*. They must match the claims of reason; and naturally, they must also be presented with the justification that is authorized by the magisterium. *Paraenesis*, asceticism, and prophecy are complementary but completely different forms of speech, even if it is not always possible to separate them entirely from rational discourse. Perhaps we must become more accustomed to keeping these differentiations in view in our theological language.

Let me mention one further challenge. If Catholic ethics is to have a future, the church must be perceived more strongly as a movement and as the sacrament of comprehensive salvation, in every sense. The Catholic social movement changed society. It is true that this movement is no longer as strong as it once was, since everything has its own historical context. At any rate, however, we can say that the three columns I have mentioned complemented one another well. That was not always easy, but it led to a greater measure of justice in society and made wider participation possible.

This is why I believe that the question of the future of theological ethics also entails the question of ethical formation. The question of how people arrive at convictions is decisive, but it receives far too little attention and study today. What is the genesis of values and convictions? The sociologist Hans Jonas replies by pointing to the necessity of an interpretative framework and powerful experiences. In other words, one must possess ideas and images and then experience the rightness of these images.

I would like to encourage us not to neglect completely the question of how people come to act morally and to get involved in politics and society. In this perspective, the moral theology of the future must be open to the ecclesial dimension and to the entire realm of theology, and it must be open to interdisciplinary work, for only in this way can we find the answer to the question of ethical formation and communicate the complete picture of our understanding of a right and good life.

The preaching of the Gospel is in fact the most important "enlightenment" that ever occurred; but we must make it clear that even today, the Gospel brings light and a perspective on life, and that the Gospel represents a quantum leap in quality.

In his important address at the University of the Sorbonne in Paris, Pope Benedict said that Christianity is "enlightenment" guided by reason, and I want to emphasize this point. Theology must make its voice heard in the debate with the great intellectual projects of our age, and a great deal remains to be done here. This is also linked to the crisis that afflicts us at present. I do not in any way wish to deny this crisis, which requires a proper response, but I sense again and again that nothing can replace religious language and that it cannot be transformed into philosophical language. In recent years, Jürgen Habermas has frequently under-lined this point: there exist genuinely theological propositions that are necessary. This is something new, and we ought to seize the opportunity to take our part in this discourse.

I have spoken of the church as the sacrament of comprehensive salvation. In my reflections on moral theology, I have always been impressed by the fact that Jesus' first step was not to deliver moral sermons. The great difficulty that is so often found in the church's preaching is the reduction of faith to morality. How-ever, Jesus surprises us by reversing the sequence of indicative and imperative. He does not say, "You must lead good lives, and then God will be good to you." Rather, he says: "You are to live, and God is good to you. And now you can live differently, precisely because God is good to you." The order of things is reversed: God's good-ness has the priority, and this goodness can be experienced in worship and sacra-ment.

What does this mean for the future of moral theology? We must not put the sacramental and cultic dimension of our faith in second place, for that would be to accept the erroneous opinion that Christianity is first of all morality and only sec-ondarily the celebration of the love of God. In his book on the function of religion,[3] the German sociologist Niklas Luhmann takes up the question of how a religion can be constructed in the modern world. His answer: a combination of Marxism and addictive intoxication. This is, of course, somewhat ironic, but Luhmann wants to make it clear that what intoxicates, what dissolves boundaries—the experience that I live in another, indestructible world—belongs to the essential foundations of religion, and of Christianity in any case. This is also connected to our moral capacity. I can only mention this briefly here, but it is very important for the future.

Examples of Challenges

Let me conclude by presenting three examples that show the challenges that face us in the future. First of all, of course, we have globalization. The financial crisis has shown that the world is growing together in a way that we did not want. I must however occasionally remind the opponents of globalization in our church that it was Catholic social ethics that spoke of the one family of humankind and the common good of the world as a whole. The challenge that confronts us is to identify the core of this common good. We can formulate the question in provocative terms: Does the common good find its center in capital or in the human person? This reformulates the question that emerged from Catholic social teaching in the nineteenth century.

As a bishop, I travel a great deal, and I have observed that there are not many movements that thematize this problem with the same intensity as Catholic social ethics. This is why it is essential to build up networks within the church. Let me once again emphasize here how important it is to think globally. The Catholic Church is truly a global institution, and no other institution in the world can be compared to it. Doubtless this is why the rejection of the church and the fight against it are sometimes very vehement.

I believe that we, as a worldwide organization, have not yet arrived at the level that is necessary today, and this is an important point. In order to achieve this, we need not only a center in Rome but also congresses like this, meetings between Catholic universities, and networks of social movements throughout the world. All this already exists in an incipient fashion, but it must be consolidated. As the example of the financial crisis shows, this would make it possible for us truly to *shape* globalization.

In his encyclical *Caritas in veritate*, Pope Benedict rightly affirms that a new cooperation on the world level between the state, the market, and society is necessary. However, political frameworks and ideas about a world order do not come only from above. They need to be corrected and accompanied by civil society, and this is where we as the church have a role to play. This work must be intensified, and that is why I welcome congresses like this that bring inspiration to work in local contexts.

A second example is the personal dignity of the human being. The encyclical has very fine words for this topic too. It involves the holistic development of the human being, following an anthropology that not only selects particular parts but sees the human being as a whole. This is why development policy, justice, and the protection of life belong together. Some people in the past wondered why John Paul II maintained progressive theses in social ethics while at the same time taking a strict position with regard to the dignity of the human person from the very beginning of life and also calling for the abolition of the death penalty. In his encyclical *Evangelium vitae*, he stated with great clarity that this is the result of a holistic picture of the dignity of the human person, both in the struggle against poverty and for justice and in the struggle on behalf of life. We will continue to work on central issues in this context, such as the following: What is "personal dignity"? What does it mean to speak of human rights from the very beginning of life? This will also generate vigorous debates in the future with regard to the natural law.

My third example is democracy and its presuppositions. Our unconditional affirmation of democracy and freedom must be unequivocal throughout the whole world. However, it is not basically clear how a free and plural society can be formed without ending up in what Pope Benedict XVI has called a "dictatorship of relativism." For political ethics, the discussion of the presuppositions of democracy is exceedingly important. For us as Christians, the goal must be to collaborate in the establishment of a free society while holding fast to common principles for the sake of the dignity of the human person. I believe that this is a uniquely important historical challenge that we as the church must tackle.

We may not say that things were better in the past, since that is not correct. Democracy is better, plurality is better, freedom is better. Responsibility is needed, but to set limitations on freedom is not the message that we should be proclaiming in the present-day situation of the world. Here, I can only mention this challenge, which will of course be seen differently according to the various cultures that you yourselves represent. What is democracy? What does plurality mean? What does it mean to unite responsibility and freedom? What attitude do we take to our cultural traditions? What do they mean to us? What normative powers do they unfold? We shall have to go on thinking about these questions.

I have only been able to indicate briefly many points that I find important as I reflect on the future of Catholic theological ethics, and I have the impression that many of these ideas have already occurred to you and have been included in the conference program. As a bishop, I am repeatedly asked to state my position; and, as a bishop, I want to emphasize how important such congresses are and how vital it is for us to share our thoughts with one another. Only in this way can we show that the church is truly one worldwide voice and movement, and that we ourselves can make a contribution to this. Let me once again cite Pope Benedict, at that time Cardinal Ratzinger: Christianity as an "enlightenment" guided by the reason is a qualitative leap that expands and deepens the possibilities of the human person. We can unite across the continents in our participation in this task.[4]

Notes

1. Cardinal Marx spoke without a manuscript. The oral style has been preserved in this translation of his address.

2. There are many references to this exchange on the Internet. See also Jürgen Habermas and Joseph Ratzinger, *The Dialectics of Secularization* (San Francisco: Ignatius Press, 2005).

3. Niklas Luhmann, *Funktion der Religion* (Frankfurt: Suhrkamp, 1977); see the Eng. trans. of pp. 72–181 in Niklas Luhmann, *Religious Dogmatics and the Evolution of Societies*, trans. Peter Beyr (New York/Toronto: Edwin Mellen, 1984).

4. English translation by Brian McNeil.

GENDER AND MORAL THEOLOGY: A SHARED PROJECT

Julie Clague

Prologue

Once, there was no gender. There were boys and girls, women and men, but there was no gender. We were male and female. For many that was enough. That was our end—*and therefore* the *end. For others, it was just a beginning.*

At a time when it seemed as though there was no gender, gender had to be invented. It came about as a response to an emerging consciousness at a particular moment of human history. We had been in a deep sleep. When we awoke we saw the world differently; we saw one another differently. Our eyes were opened, and we knew we were not naked (and never could be). We were clothed—with all manner of layers of meaning. We were embodied and ensexed and engendered, with thoughts and feelings, fantasies and dreams, desires and behaviors. We were a mystery to ourselves. We were not in a state of nature (and never had been). We were connected to others in highly patterned and formally regulated social webs of gendered cultures. And we knew we were complex.

Now we were awake, but we did not understand. We were in a garden of earthly delights, unsure of our bearings. There stood the tree of the knowledge of male and female. So we went up to the tree and began to climb. And as we climbed we began to see that gender had been there from the very beginning.

In the beginning was gender. It was in the beginning with God. All human things came into being through it, and without it not one human thing came into being. What has come into being is life: a life that is gendered. Gender was in the world, and the world came into being through it; yet the world did not know it. Gender became flesh and lives among us. But we are blind and fail to recognize it. Gender offers us the means of becoming. But we distort and misappropriate it, in order to rule and maim. Yet, when gender reveals itself to us in its fullness, we catch glimpses of its glory, and its potential as a channel for grace and truth.

Moral Theology's Embrace of the *Humanum*

When we look at moral theology today, what do we see? Variety and vitality. If moral theology was monochrome in the pre-Vatican II days, then you do not need to be a friend of Dorothy to know that "we are not in Kansas anymore, Toto."[1] Moral theology is a colorful and transformed discipline undergoing an important phase of creativity and productivity. In part, this is because—as a necessarily interdisciplinary subject—moral theology has opened its doors to expertise drawn from the gamut of academic discourses and disciplines—including the academic study of gender. This new phase of development has also come about because unprecedented numbers are teaching and studying moral theology, and those scholars are more heterogeneous than in any previous era. They come from the four corners of the Earth and from all walks of life. Priests have been joined by religious sisters and brothers and by large numbers of lay people. Women work alongside men and may one day outnumber their male counterparts. As a college of theologians it is not yet fully representative of a world church, but that goal is now seen as a necessary and achievable objective.

When new people join the club, the club changes. Moral theology has benefited in immeasurable ways from being a more gender-inclusive subject area. The entry of female ethicists has led to major contributions across the "specialisms." The rich tapestry of moral theology has been extended, renovated, redesigned where appropriate, and dethreaded and re-embroidered where necessary. Social and political and sexual and biomedical ethics all bear the imprint of this development, with significant work on body theology, human sexuality, marriage, family, childhood, divorce, fertility control, reproductive technologies, abortion, the ethics of care, theories of moral development, the theology of work, HIV and AIDS, conscience, virtue, love, sin, and so on. Feminist ethics has developed as a subject in its own right. Feminist liberation theologies and eco-feminism have also emerged. Feminist biblical scholarship and historical research have both offered critiques but also alternative readings and ways of recovering tradition. Along the way, women have been at the forefront of exploring concepts such as nature, experience, subjectivity, and sexual difference. In half a century, the women who have engaged with moral theology have enriched all areas of the discipline.

A characteristic of these theologians and ethicists has been their general reluctance to be content with study for study's sake and retreat to the dreaming spires and ivory towers of academia. More often than not, these scholars demonstrate a strong impetus to apply their learning to concrete historical contexts in order to transform situations of diminished human agency and structural injustice. Taking a cue from the women's liberation movement, activism and social engagement have been central concerns for moral theology. It is axiomatic that moral theologians must "walk the walk" as well as "talk the talk," for it would be a strange form of moral engagement if witness did not accompany words. This vocational commit-

and as gender studies confirm, the personal growth and development of the human subject into the fullness of his or her divine calling can never be a self-creating act of will but is always contingent upon the person's inherent capacities and limitations, as well as forces outside of and beyond that person's direct and sole control. Here, new opportunities arise for more experientially resonant reflection on theological concepts such as sin, finitude, grace, and salvation.

At the same time, gender study requires moral theologians to become more critically conscious of unthinking notions of abstract truth, and to look more deeply into the effects of history and culture on humanity's moral norms. Gender studies uncover variation and diversity in patterns of behavior and belief, and this de facto variety can, for some, become a norm with which to destabilize all other social norms, thereby potentially undermining all our categories and certainties. In this respect, cultural relativism can quickly dissolve into moral relativism. This can make gender study appear an inappropriate bedfellow for moral theology. It is incumbent on moral theologians to engage with these challenges rather than to allow the center ground of reflection on humankind's values to be undermined by an "anything goes" subjectivity.

This task is made complex by the loss of confidence in traditional accounts of human nature, which a fuller understanding of gender has further undermined. Gender analysis is intolerant of scientifically untenable, essentialist theories of natural law that tie eternal truths to the supposedly fixed bedrock of human nature. Timeless truths and unchanging givens are the ideological currency of religions, and for an historical and transcultural religion such as Christianity, they have a unifying appeal. Yet, studies of history and culture can demonstrate the time-bound and culture-bound nature of a religion's abstract ideals. And gender studies show that, concerning human sexuality, there are multiple variables and few fixed constants. Religions are among the social groups that have found it hardest to adapt to this more complex and dynamic model of reality, and what it entails; for herein lies the most serious threat to traditional understandings of morality (based on natural order and natural laws) and theology (based on a Creator of law and order).

Natural law theories assume that human nature follows nature's laws, and that these laws can be easily apprehended (co-naturally) and agreed upon always, everywhere, and by all. Historically, culturally, and scientifically attentive gender study has complicated this picture of an orderly, Newtonian-type model universe of natural and observable sex laws, designed and inscribed in nature by the Divine. This mechanistic understanding of divine agency, with its knowable natural laws, has allowed religious groups to claim—as Newton did of his laws of motion—that one can think God's thoughts after Him [*sic*]. It is hardly surprising that religions that claim the authority of truth find it difficult to relinquish such nomological notions. Yet, as the deists of the eighteenth century recognized, such a diminished understanding of the Divine is scarcely worth human attention. Something of greater theological import must be affirmed.

In order to do more justice to what is at stake theologically, it is necessary to think less abstractly and nomologically, and more experientially and sacramentally. It is part of the religious impulse of humans to sanctify and sacralize human realities, allowing them to be viewed *sub specie aeternitatis*. The sexual difference of male and female is a potent "natural symbol" that religions have divinized since the earliest of times, sublimating its worldly associations and giving them religious meaning. Since for Christianity there can be no part of life that falls outside the loving embrace and concern of the Divine, it cannot but make sense of this fundamental element of human life in terms of its overarching Christian narrative, symbol system, and (for Catholic Christianity) sacramental framework. With such a rich and fertile subject, however, it is inevitable that there are various ways to read and interpret, in the light of the gospel, the theological meanings written into the human body. Can this be done in relation to the sexes in a way that avoids reductionist and essentializing traps? Or must anthropology always be made to solidify into ontology as a means of hardening sexual norms and forcing the gender symbolism to perform as required?

Since the papacy of John Paul II, in particular, there have been a number of attempts to articulate a richer theological anthropology in Catholic teaching, one that is more closely attuned to the Christian narrative while incorporating some degree of gender analysis. Detailed exposition and analysis of these texts is beyond the scope of this study. The statements treat topics such as marriage and family life, the status of women in the church and the world, sexual ethics, and the sacrament of orders. Whatever the respective merits of these individual statements, many are found wanting in terms of the images of God that are portrayed in these accounts, and the unsatisfactory understanding of gender upon which they rely. A document of the Pontifical Council for the Family, *The Family and Human Rights* (1999), for example, attempts to explain humankind's createdness in the image and likeness of God (Gen 1:27-28), not in terms of characteristics or attributes of persons, but in terms of an assertion about how masculine and feminine complementarity is said to reflect the immanent communion of the Triune God. It states:

> They [men and women] are complementary: "God created man in his image; in the divine image he created him; male and female he created them" (Gen 1:27). In order to manifest that human beings are the image of the trinitary God, they [men and women] must unfold their existence according to two complementary modes: the masculine and the feminine. Human existence is thus sharing in the existence of a God who is a communion of love.[5]

Male-female complementarity—a modern idea absent from biblical and traditional Christian sources—does not enter into Catholic teaching until the papacy of John Paul II, who introduces the language of complementarity in the context of his general audiences on the theology of the body.[6] Since that time there have been arguments put forward in favor of the elimination of sex discrimination command widespread support. Recognition of the equality of the sexes, human dignity, and the rights and responsibilities that flow from it, respect for personal agency and rejection of the objectification and instrumentalization of human subjects are touchstone issues for modernity and no longer assumed to be contentious. Yet, sex discrimination lives on—in part because it is bound up with the stubborn tendency to gender stereotype. Gender stereotyping is a complicated phenomenon. Its roots lie in three utterly central and interrelated ways with which humans interact and make sense of their world and one another: through meaning making and valuing, through ordering and classifying, and through symbolizing and decoding. These were not matters that overly concerned modernity. They are, however, subject to intensive and disputatious hermeneutical scrutiny in the classrooms and playgrounds of postmodernity. They are also of immense significance to religions and their theologies.

In moral theology the human search for meaning and value and the human tendency to order and classify are abundantly evident. Humanity's capacity to experience and communicate about the significance of the world through metaphor and symbol pervades religiosity and is reflected in the Catholic tradition's sacramental view of divine mediation. Gender has prompted us to consider anew these three epistemological imperatives. In so doing, it has brought to the surface the promise and the perils of our moralizing and theologizing. Consider, for example, the creation narrative: a story of the emergence of order out of chaos, of separation into different kinds, of classifying on the basis of naming, of God's valuation of creation as "very good," and much more besides. When humans both interpret and re-stage this drama, gender plays its part as both accessory and victim. Sometimes, for example, we are confronted with a gender fundamentalism based on a notion of hardwired biological sex. This prioritizes certain notions of masculinity and femininity while ignoring, pitying, or condemning the not insignificant part of humanity that is embodied and ensexed differently.

We can also see gender taken advantage of in the service of a hermeneutics of order. This can occur because Christians tend to believe that God's creation of the earthling as female and male is not a chance accident of evolution, but a reflection of the divine will for humankind: a design classic, fit for purpose, ordered both to the pleasure of the present and the fecundity of the future. It is a compelling narrative. Yet, it is one in which "is" can quickly dress itself up as "ought," spawning sexual moralities based on a religious myth of natural "law and order." This reading of the myth risks reducing the divinity to a grotesquely sexist and homophobic judge. And it encourages dutiful religious leaders to assume the authority to police the transgressors and their accomplices.

How will theologians of the future rewrite the divine *Logos* of "law and order" and create experientially resonant theological anthropologies? Will more supple understandings of sacramentality and mediation emerge to accommodate what we are learning about the expressive symbolism of embodied and engraced (gendered) subjects? Gender can perform many roles for moral theology. It can lead us astray. But it can also lead us on to a fuller understanding of how the divine is re-embodied in and through our gendered bodies, and wounded once more, with every act of gender injustice. Gender is bringing us face to face with questions about fundamental theological understandings and deepest religious hopes. "Tread softly," wrote Irish poet W. B. Yeats, "because you tread on my dreams."[13] The door that opens onto the future of moral theology is one that we—women and men—with faith in one another are helping to push open—even if we can neither fully appreciate nor dare to dream what lies beyond.

Epilogue: Gender and Moral Theology: A Love Story

Location: A bar, somewhere in Trento.[14]

Gender and Moral Theology are coming up to their fiftieth anniversary. For their friends it was an unlikely relationship. And like many that began back in the heady days of the 1960s, it was a tempestuous affair when they first met—but they do say, opposites attract!

I ran into them soaking up the sun in Trento and, over a drink, decided to find out how they were getting along these days. They looked happier than I had ever seen them. Moral Theology was certainly larger than he was back then! He had lost the awkward arrogance of youth and was looking older and wiser. Gender had retained her good looks, and waspish sense of humor, but something about her had changed too. She'd had it tough back then. Now she seemed more centered and content than I had seen her in a long time.

"Look at you two! You look great! It is so good to see you both thriving after all these years. Who could have predicted that you two oddballs would stick together!"

Gender: To be honest, a relationship with Moral Theology was the last thing I was expecting. He didn't have any experience of women—and he was so naive about sex!

Moral Theology: I can't deny you certainly put me right about a thing or two. Back then, I was a little square. I thought I had life all figured out; but I couldn't relate to people. Gender changed all that. She opened my eyes, and I began to think differently. She was totally wild! She was like this massive force of nature that I couldn't resist—that no one could resist. (But that's another story.) Gender wanted to fight the system, and she wasn't going to stop until she'd won. She's still fighting now. Where do you get all that energy from, darling?

Gender: A woman's work is never done, dear.

Moral Theology: Compared to her I felt boring and old fashioned.

Gender: That's because you were, honey. You were totally out of touch. But I couldn't resist your charming innocence!

Moral Theology: I have to admit, before Gender came along I was a little lost. I just didn't know who I was anymore. I had lost sight of my goals. I needed a new direction; a new challenge—and when Gender came along, boy, did I get one!

Gender: You still ignore most things I say.

Moral Theology: I know; but I wouldn't be without you now, darling.

Gender: That's because you wouldn't survive without me!

Moral Theology: Ha! That's probably true, but at least I gave you something to work on.

Gender: And some! I certainly got more than I bargained for. But your heart is in the right place, and you mean well. Moral Theology is a work in progress. Then again, aren't we all? After all this time, I still don't feel like I've got him all worked out. Like they say, there is always something new to discover about one another. Ultimately, what counts is that we share the same values and want to leave this world a better place.

Moral Theology: We are certainly better together than we would be apart.

Gender: Yes, we get on pretty well now, don't we, darling? But our kids are forever fighting!

Moral Theology: We've got to go now. Gender wants me to see the "bearded woman" fresco in the Castle.[15]

With that they headed off together, arms entwined, looking inseparable.

Notes

1. Words spoken by Dorothy to her pet dog, Toto, when they find themselves transported from the black-and-white representation of Kansas to the colorful world of Oz in the film *The Wizard of Oz* (1939) based on the children's novel *The Wonderful Wizard of Oz,* by L. Frank Baum (1900).

2. "Profile," The Circle of Concerned African Women Theologians, Pan African Meeting, 2002, http://www.thecirclecawt.org/profile.html.

3. *Gaudium et spes* (Pastoral Constitution of the Church in the Modern World), 3.

4. See, for example, the documents *Letter to the Bishops of the Catholic Church on the Collaboration of Men and Women in the Church and in the World,* 3; and Pope Benedict XVI, *Address to the Members of the Roman Curia for the Traditional Exchange of Christmas Greetings,* 1. The papal documents referred to in this essay are accessible at http://www. vatican.va.

5. Pontifical Council for the Family, *The Family and Human Rights,* 59.

6. John Paul II, *General Audience, Wednesday 7 November 1979,* note 5.

7. Pope John Paul II, *Letter to Women,* 11.

8. Ibid.

9. Ibid.

10. Ibid.

11. Pontifical Council for the Family, *The Family and Human Rights,* 74. Other discussions of gender can be found in Pontifical Council for the Family, *Family, Marriage and*

"*De Facto*" *Unions* (2000); Congregation for the Doctrine of the Faith, *Letter to the Bishops of the Catholic Church on the Collaboration of Men and Women in the Church and in the World* (2004); Pope Benedict XVI, *Address to the Members of the Roman Curia for the Traditional Exchange of Christmas Greetings* (2008); and in the discussions of the Fifth General Congregation of the Second Special Assembly for Africa of the Synod of Bishops in October 2009, an account of which can be found at: "Gender Theory's Dangers Exposed," Zenit news agency, October 15, 2009, http://www.zenit.org/article-27213?l=english.

   12. *Family, Marriage and "De Facto" Unions*, 8.

   13. The phrase appears in the poem *Aedh Wishes for the Cloths of Heaven*, published in W. B. Yeats, *The Wind among the Reeds* (London: E. Mathews, 1899).

   14. This paper was first presented at the "Catholic Theological Ethics in the World Church" conference in Trento, Italy in July 2010, which was attended by some six hundred male and female moral theologians from around the globe. Understandably, many took full advantage of Trento's excellent bars and gelaterias in the short respites between sessions. It is important to stress, therefore, that the characters who appear in the following tale, while they may appear to resemble actual moral theologians, are wholly fictional, and any similarities to persons living or dead are entirely coincidental.

   15. The Castello del Buonconsiglio, Trento, now a museum, was formerly residence of the prince bishops of the region. During the years of the Council of Trent, the castle housed a number of the Council's participants. They would have undoubtedly admired the late-fourteenth-century artistic masterpiece housed in the Castle's Torre Aquila (Eagle's Tower). The "Cycle of the Months," a series of frescos in the international gothic style, depicts life in the region over the course of a year. The June fresco shows a procession of noble couples arm in arm. One comprises a male religious in his habit accompanied by an ostensibly female character whose facial features are those of a bearded male. While various theories have been proposed to explain this gender puzzle, its precise origins remain unexplained.

Context and the Future of Theological Ethics: The Task of Building Bridges

Shaji George Kochuthara

In Catholic theology, we have entered the "Age of Christian Ethics." Clearly, ethics was always an important and integral part of Christian theology. In the first millennium doctrinal and dogmatic questions occupied the central stage. In the second millennium theological discussions over the authority of the church (especially political), the primacy of the pope, the relationship of the church with the state and the conflict with different political ideologies, and the debate over the importance of scripture and tradition were the main theological concerns. Toward the end of the second millennium, especially in the twentieth century, developments in biblical interpretation brought about drastic changes.

With the instruction given by the Second Vatican Council[1] and the publication of *Humanae vitae* begins the "Age of Catholic Theological Ethics." Though in the beginning the controversy was over contraception, discussions gradually entered into new realms. The conflict between "autonomous ethics" and "faith ethics" and the debate over proportionalism are only a few of them. Theological ethicists have reflected on the sources and methods in fundamental moral theology, biomedical issues, sexuality and marital issues, social justice, and so on. From a confession-oriented theology focusing on sin, a theology practically meant only for the preparation of future priests, Christian ethics today addresses every area of Christian life, and it has come out of the enclosure of a seminary curriculum.

Similarly, a number of magisterial and official documents, completely or partially dedicated to theological ethics in general[2] or to specific areas such as sexual ethics, bioethics, and social justice,[3] have been promulgated. Ethical issues occupy one of the major areas of theological debate within the church, between the churches, and between the church and the state. Christians look to theological ethicists for answers to the different problems and issues that they confront. They feel that theological ethics, understood as the practical dimension of theology, responds to their actual life situations.

There is a steady growth in the number of moral theologians on all the continents. Not only priests and religious, but also lay people—both men and women—pursue study and research in the field of moral theology. Similarly, new departments or faculties of moral theology are being established around the world.

When we look into the wider society as well, we can say that we are in an "Age of Ethics." Today there is a broader interest in ethics. Different branches of ethics develop independently of religions—for example, human rights movements, bioethics, economic and business ethics, professional ethics, sexual ethics, feminist ethics, gender ethics, and political ethics. Ethics has become a central concern in all human activity; it need not be limited to the religious dimension of a person.

Today civil society and political authorities often lead the debate on ethical issues such as same-sex unions, de facto unions, cloning, stem-cell research, and genetic engineering, whereas in the past such issues would be left to the authority of religions. This is true not only with regard to the Western secularized states but also with regard to Asian and African countries, where religion continues to be normatively important. Moreover, as in many other areas, decision making on ethical issues is not left only to those in authority, but (autonomous) people actively participate in the decision-making process. While the future of theological ethics is bright, this also implies tremendous responsibilities, considering these developments within the church and in the society as a whole. The future is the continuation of the present, which is the continuation of the past. Through this light, we look toward the future.

Theological Ethics within the Christian Community

The Challenge of Dialogue among Different Approaches and Methods

After the manuals, theological ethics began to develop closer ties with systematic, biblical, and spiritual theology. The Second Vatican Council gave further momentum to this movement. Christian ethicists began to feel the need for a deeper dialogue with the different branches of philosophical ethics, physical and social sciences, scientific and technological advancements, and the ever-changing life situation. All these have resulted in a number of approaches and methodologies. Whereas the manuals followed a single methodology, Christian ethics today follow a variety of methodologies.

In a recent article, Raphael Gallagher identifies four "systems of moral theology"[4] and defines the field as a moral science but with different purposes.

1. Developed primarily from revelatory sources, it provides the necessary Christian means to reach happiness through our moral choices and actions.
2. Developed primarily from the ethical insights of human intelligence and practical reasoning, it aims to explain human fulfillment in our Christian vocation.
3. Developed primarily through a dialectical and hermeneutical use of its various sources, it seeks to communicate the essence of the tradition to a new cultural situation.

is a strong sense of the equality and freedom of all human beings, the dignity of
the human person, and the fundamental rights of everyone. The church has also
creatively responded to this thirst for justice, as can be seen in the developments in
the social doctrine of the church in the twentieth century. The church's attempts
to ensure justice in society are held in high esteem. However, there is a growing
skepticism about the church's sincerity in ensuring justice.

One of the criticisms raised against the church in the wake of the recent cases
of the abuse of minors by the clergy centers on administering justice within the
church. Often we see that the church employs different norms distinguishing those
who are in authority from others. Such disparity in meting out justice creates a
negative image of the church's commitment to justice. Catholics who share this
view prefer civil procedures in cases of abuse, and they believe that the ecclesiastical system will not ensure justice.[11] While we cannot ignore the concerted efforts
from different corners to tarnish the image and to weaken the moral power of the
church, the loss of trust in the church's administration of justice is a matter of serious concern for ethicists.

This skepticism about the administration of justice within the church is not a
new situation. In recent decades, theological ethicists such as Charles E. Curran,
Richard A. McCormick, and many others have pointed out the need for transparency and justice in dealing with theologians who differ from the magisterial
stances. Recently, James Keenan and others have underscored the need to "practice
what you preach."[12] One of the tasks of theological ethics will be to raise a voice
relentlessly and fearlessly for justice within the church and to stand for the collegial
nature of the church.[13]

Another aspect of this issue also needs attention: Theological ethicists are
uncomfortable discussing many issues—including such concerns as biomedical
issues, HIV/AIDS prevention, and contraception. As a member of the institutional ethical review board of a Catholic medical college, I often face this difficulty. There are also those who insist that the only role of theological ethicists is
to defend the official teaching of the church. This difficulty is more acutely felt by
those at seminaries and pontifical institutes. The lack of freedom to discern the
will of God in the "signs of the times" and "too much control of theological imagination and thought"[14] frequently discourage the continuing development of the
Catholic moral tradition. This atmosphere will not help theological ethics to carry
out its duty in the present or in the future. There is no doubt that the theological
ethicist should remember that he/she belongs to a community, which is the basic
context for theological reflection and discernment. Authority is a sign of unity, and
attempts to ensure unity have to be respected, but this should not be at the cost of
the collegial nature of the church and its communitarian dimension. Otherwise,
unity will become a superficial uniformity.

The Christian faith is entrusted to a community in which the authority, the
theologian, and each member has his/her unique role. The lack of proper dialogue

will only weaken attempts to respond to the complex ethical dilemmas in our ever-changing life situations. Bridging the gaps between the authority and theological ethics and between people and theological ethics are challenges to be faced in the years to come.

Developing Theological Ethics in Asia, Africa and Latin America

There is an urgent need to develop more departments of theological ethics in Asia, Africa, and Latin America to facilitate research and writing in indigenous contexts and to bring a new dimension to moral theology in future. Within a couple of decades, more than 75 percent of the world's Catholics will be living on these continents.[15] At present the possibilities of specialization in theological ethics on these continents are limited. Partnership programs with Western universities can be of great help, and this is one of the urgent needs for the development of theological ethics. The West has a long tradition of moral theological education. Sharing this experience and expertise can help support moral theological education in Africa, Asia, and Latin America. It will also help to maintain a balance between the particular context and the universal nature of Catholic moral theology. Besides, the challenge of specialization will facilitate moral theologians to come out of the confines of a seminary curriculum,[16] because at present in most of the countries on these continents, the only or the major role of the moral theologians is to prepare future priests.

Theological Ethics in a Globalized World

The Political System

A good number of nations follow a democratic system. Compared to other systems, democracy can be said to be rather new, but so far we do not have a better alternative. However, we are witnessing a politicization of democracy that is resulting in its degeneration, a denial of justice, and a promotion of favoritism, nepotism, uncontrolled corruption, and the corrosion of values.[17] Democratically elected governments themselves often become the greatest violator of human rights.[18] The legal system is not an exception: "There are thousands of poor people fighting the legal system. The legal system is very colonial and access to justice for the poor is impossible. In fact, the legal system is a great engine of oppression of the poor."[19] In many countries, democracy is no more the rule by the people, but the rule by a few politicians, often elected by power and economic gain.[20]

According to the United Nations, the global price tag for corruption every year comes to $1.6 trillion, which is much more than the combined annual amount of foreign aid that flows from the industrialized to the developing world. For example,

In the coming years, theological ethicists will have to engage in resolving the conflict between globalization and the indigenous cultures, because these conflicts have their roots in the new ethics inherent in globalization. These ethical issues range from poverty, inequality, and the breakdown of traditional occupations to drastic changes in lifestyle, sexual life, family life, and religious practices.

Conclusion

In short, theological ethics in the future needs to be more and more objective, scientific, open to human experience, committed to justice, and ready to dialogue with different branches of ethics and different cultures, while keeping the uniqueness of the Christian vision. This is possible.

Since human experience was accepted as a valid source of moral theological reflection, moral theologians have become increasingly aware of the fragility of so-called certainties. This does not mean that they have given away to relativism. Rather, they have become aware of the complexity of what constitutes objectivity and the real situations of life, the uniqueness of each person, and the need of an ongoing dialogue—mutually challenging and enriching—between the norms and human experience. Arbitrary application of the so-called inalterable norms formed on the basis of a physicalist approach to natural law are no longer convincing. Theological ethics will be accepted as relevant and life related only if the dialogue between human experience and norms continues.

After the Second Vatican Council, especially in the debate following *Humanae vitae*, we find that moral theologians understand their vocation in terms of compassion for their fragile and weak fellow human beings who, in spite of their sincere intentions, do not always succeed fully in living up to the prescribed norms. The "situation of tension" proposed by Peter Chirico, the "conflict situation" solutions proposed by Charles Robert, and the "compromise" situation proposed by Conrad van Ouwerkerk and later defended and elaborated by Charles Curran, and "the law of graduality" are all attempts to understand with compassion the fragility of humans, without denouncing them.[26] This mission of compassion undertaken by theological ethicists will be more significant in the future for people who will continue to confront more and more complex and conflicting situations and opinions, and for people who are broken-hearted and confused. Yet, there must be an awareness that we also share the same fragility.

Finally, I would like to emphasize that we are a people of hope. We are not discouraged by the complexity of the situation or the engulfing presence of evil. Instead, we explore new possibilities with the hope in the Risen Lord, and we believe that the Lord is with us to guide us in our pilgrimage forward. It must be with hope that theological ethicists look toward the future.

Notes

1. Second Vatican Council, *Optatam totius*, 16; *Gaudium et spes*, 46.

2. For example, *Veritatis splendor*.

3. For example, *Humanae vitae, persona humana, Letter on the Pastoral Care of Homosexual Persons, Donum vitae, Familiaris consortio, Gratissimam sane, The Truth and Meaning of Human Sexuality, Evangelium vitae, Reflections on Cloning, Populorum progressio, Laborem exercens, Sollicitudo rei socialis*, and *Centesimus annus*.

4. Raphael Gallagher, "Moral Theology from a European Perspective: Emerging Methodologies Attentive to Tradition and Learning from Asia," *Asian Horizons* 4 (2010): 149-50.

5. Marciano Vidal, "Theological Ethics in Europe," in *Catholic Theological Ethics in the World Church: The Plenary Papers from the First Cross-cultural Conference on Catholic Theological Ethics* (Bangalore: Asian Trading Corporation, 2009), 94 (hereafter *CTEWC*).

6. See James F. Keenan, *Towards a Global Vision of Catholic Moral Theology: Reflections on the Twentieth Century* (Bangalore: Dharmaram Publications, 2007), 101-45.

7. For example, "Secular bioethicists and policymakers seem anxious to keep explicitly religious views off the table and assume that religion leads in a socially conservative direction, obstructing scientific advancement and going against the tide of enlightened social policy" (Lisa Sowle Cahill, *Theological Bioethics: Participation, Justice, and Change* [Washington: Georgetown University Press, 2005], 1).

8. See Vidal, "Theological Ethics in Europe," in *CTEWC*, 97.

9. For a description and analysis of this trend, see John L. Allen Jr., *The Future Church: How Ten Trends Are Revolutionizing the Catholic Church* (New York: Doubleday, 2009), 54-94.

10. For example, see Ronaldo Zacharias, "Dreaming of a New Moral Theology for Brazil," in *CTEWC*, 118.

11. Aaron Milavec, "Reflections on the Sexual Abuse of Minors by Priests," *Asian Horizons* 4 (2010): 179-91.

12. For example, James F. Keenan, *Practice What You Preach: The Need for Ethics in Church Leadership* (Milwaukee, WI: Marquette University Press, 2000); M. Shawn Copeland, "Collegiality as a Moral and Ethical Practice," in *Practice What You Preach: Virtues, Ethics, and Power in the Lives of Pastoral Ministers and Their Congregations*, ed. James F. Keenan and Joseph Kotva (Lanham, MD: Sheed & Ward, 1999), 315-32.

13. Please note: "The 21st century could well create a 'boom market' for movements seeking to foster greater accountability, collaboration and transparency in the church, if activists and entrepreneurs understand how to make the pitch in a global key." (John L. Allen Jr., "A Global Case for Good Government in the Church," in *National Catholic Reporter*, June 25, 2010, http://www.ncronline.org, accessed 11-07-2010.

14. Laurenti Magesa, "Locating the Church among the Wretched of the Earth," in *CTEWC*, 56.

15. See Allen, *The Future Church*, 141-77.

16. Clement Campos, "Doing Christian Ethics in India's World of Cultural Complexity and Social Inequality," in *CTEWC*, 90; Zacharias, "Dreaming of a New Moral Theology for Brazil," 121.

17. "Politics have been identified as a propitious place for thieves and robbers" (Zacharias, "Dreaming of a New Moral Theology for Brazil," 116).

18. See Antonio Papisca, "The Needs of the World and the Signs of the Times," in *CTEWC*, 15-16.

19. Payal Saxena, "David vs Goliath," in *The Week* 28, 33 (July 11, 2010): 21. This cover story is about ordinary people who took on the high and mighty in their fight for justice and emerged victorious.

20. Thomas Hong-Soon Han, "Moral Challenges and the Church in Asia Today, with a Specific Consideration of Korea," in *CTEWC*, 67-68; Sebastian Mier, "Hope in the Midst of Enormous Challenges in Mexico," in *CTEWC*, 128.

21. John L. Allen Jr., "A Global Case for Good Government in the Church."

22. Benedict XVI, *Deus caritas est*, 42.

23. John Mary Waliggo, "A Call for Prophetic Action," in *CTEWC*, 254, referring to Cecil McGarry, "The Impact of Globalization on African Culture and Society: Dangers and Opportunities," in *The New Strategies for a New Evangelization in Africa*, ed. Patrick Ryan (Nairobi: Paulines Publications Africa, 2002), 13-22.

24. Benedict XVI, *Deus caritas est*, 26.

25. Ibid., 42.

26. James F. Keenan, *A History of Catholic Moral Theology in the Twentieth Century: From Confessing Sins to Liberating Consciences* (New York: Continuum, 2010): 146-51.

RACIALIZATION AND RACISM
IN THEOLOGICAL ETHICS

María Teresa Dávila

How does theological ethics responsibly engage history as a necessary part of ethical reflection? Spanish Jesuit José Ignacio González-Faus raises the basic question of the role of history in our understanding of our humanity, the power of grace, and the role of forgiveness when he speaks about the irreparable damage of sin in history. He maintains that the infinite gravity of sin does not lie in a direct (or even religious) offense against God but in the injury done to the image of God in the person. There is something irreparable about sin, and only grace embodied in the forgiveness of one person (or group) to another can offer redemption. This irreparability is described as the effects of sin that cannot be undone: even if justice and solidarity were to create a world without concentration camps, wars, killing fields, and acts of terrorism, the fact remains that we are left with a world in which these things did exist.[1]

For González-Faus, our basic theological and ethical principles—and particularly our understanding of our humanity, our filial relationship with God and our relationship as sisters and brothers in the human family, and of our becoming like Christ—must be grounded in the incarnational principle that takes the salvation of human history as central.[2] The "sin of the world," then, is not some abstract theological principle restricted to the recitation of the *Agnus Dei* during our liturgies. "The sin of the world" is the individual and corporate consequence of the evil we do to one another in the course of human history.

If, as González-Faus claims, a perfectly just world would still exhibit the scars of historical evil and sin, what then should be the place in theological ethics for reflection on the process of racialization and the evil of racism? How should we integrate the histories of institutionalized and systemic oppression and ideologies of the superiority of one group and the inferiority of another? How do we address the direct violence and dehumanization imposed on groups classified strictly on the basis of an irrational fear of difference and a violently developed sense of the existential import of group boundaries, national borders, religious uniqueness, ethnic markers, and skin color?

The goal of this reflection is to give some consideration to these important questions. First, I consider the social tendency of the "racialization" of groups and its effects on the construction of what it means to be human in society. Second, given that the process of racialization grounds societies in a web of groups in conflict for resources, political autonomy and agency, and cultural validation, I revisit the long-standing tension between Catholic social teaching and liberation theologies regarding the role of conflict in human history and in approaches to justice with respect to the question of racism. This leads to a third point: discussing "facing history" with the scars and still open wounds of racism as a basic principle for theological ethics.

Finally, I consider two concrete cases, the United States (and the anti-immigrant law in the state of Arizona) and France. I conclude with the principle of incarnation as intimately linked to hope *in this world*, which must be the goal of most of our work. Throughout this reflection, I hope to remain grounded in the option for the poor, the Christian principle that demands that incarnation and history be central elements of following the gospel by attending to the voices of those considered invisible or unimportant in most societies but who share with us a common destiny as human family.

The Process of Racialization and Human Being and Becoming[3]

How do we interpret race as a formative social category determinative of social location and privilege? Anthropologist Marisol de la Cadena considers race as a "constitutive tool of modernity."[4] She states, "[Race] operates, among other things, as a way of abstracting humanity from the conceptual regime of a dominating God. ... It places the human being within nature, making knowledge of the human accessible from within biology and science, outside of God."[5]

According to de la Cadena, "race" as a social and political concept is developed in the political, cultural, and economic relationships between those subjects who are doing the classifying and those being classified. These relationships are organized around principles of *power* and *domination*; racism, then, systematizes the classifications that enshrine these relationships of power and the domination in ideologies of the nation and citizenship, borders and laws, cultural belonging and exclusion.

The process of the racialization of the other in society leads to the institutionalization of the superiority of one group over the perceived inferiority of another, within a spectrum of social, political, and economic relations that include the dehumanization of the inferior other. In some cases it even results in their philosophical and, unfortunately, often concrete and very real elimination from history. The racialized other is thus excluded from history or perceived as outside of history, as *pre*historic.

Race, the process of racialization, and racism operate in the false binomial of "culture/nature," which holds "culture" (quite narrowly defined) as the highest expression of human achievement, and "nature" as that which is outside of history, not proper for the political or social realm of human activity. The racialized other is characteristically placed in the rubric of "nature" and therefore excluded from history.[6]

The development of the concept of whiteness and the racialized other in the Americas serves as an example of this process. While people of color, indigenous people, African slaves, and their descendants are reduced to their corporeal or "natural" state in much of sixteenth- and seventeenth-century artwork—their appearances are hypersexualized and their cultural expressions, religious traditions, and political organizations are dismissed as subhuman expressions of primitive instincts. At the same time Europeans and those of European descent making their way in the New World are depicted as possessing the power of reason and culture in their very essence.[7]

According to cultural theorist and artist Coco Fusco, "whiteness was understood as a spirit that manifests itself in a dynamic relation to the physical world."[8] She continues, "whiteness, then, does not need to be made visible to be present in an image; it can be expressed as the spirit of enterprise, as the power to organize the material world, and as an expansive relation to the environment."[9] In short, the post-Enlightenment period came to perceive "whiteness" as all that signified progress in human history and as the rational domination of the natural world for the purpose of furthering the civilizing trend of history; the racialized other was subjugated to the natural world that was to be conquered and domesticated. This very violent worldview seeped into society's most basic relationships: among neighbors, within the churches, in the workplace, the market, education, and across nations.

The conquest of the Americas, as well as every other project of racialization of the other, is marked by the explicit establishment of relationships of domination between those in power and those at the bottom of a society (or excluded from it altogether). But what is more important for theological ethics, the process of racialization has historically meant the essentializing of certain traits, such as whiteness and Europeanization, as the truly "human," while other traits, such as brown skin and an Earth-based religion, are considered as less than human and outside of history. The institutional and corporate consequences of this process have been systemic oppressive and violent relationships between groups that believe themselves to be representations of the essential nature of the human being and those considered to be less than human and therefore disposable.[10]

The formation of nations in the Americas proceeded to essentialize the characteristics and traits that originally differentiated the European from the indigenous.[11] The "citizen"—identified by a set of characteristics such as speaking the official language, dressing a certain way, learning a certain way, even worshiping and raising their families a certain way defined by the colonial heritage of the nation—was considered the paradigmatic human being. Those falling outside the rubric of citizen had their very humanity questioned; and, in the case of the United States, many laws were put in place during the nineteenth and the early part of the twentieth century in order to ensure that anyone who threatened the homogeneous definition of "citizen"—because of differences in language, physiognomy,

well as accessing the social benefits that come with home ownership such as better neighborhood schools).[19]

Stated succinctly, "Racism is not merely or primarily a sin of ignorance, but one of advantage and privilege. Privileged groups seldom relinquish their advantages voluntarily because of dialogue and education."[20] Catholic social teaching's insistence on conversion of heart glosses over the reality lived by so many people in diverse societies today, societies where the long-standing historical process of the racialization of the other embeds each new generation in relationships of conflict, domination, and power. Such relationships are hard to dismantle without engaging in concrete confrontation with unjust privilege. While new generations may not be consciously engaging in the process of racialization or in overt practices of exclusion and dehumanization, theological ethics must find a way to acknowledge the historical "sin of the world," the air we breathe, and the sin embedded within, in order to highlight the human damage in which we continue to participate and of which we are complicit by virtue of our inadequate resistance.[21]

The conflict of history must continue to inform us. It represents a counter-epistemology or counter-identity[22] in theological ethics that is grounded in the incarnational principle. I believe that theologies developed from the underside of contemporary empires, from the multitudes of the racialized other in developed nations, will offer great insight into the role of Jesus' own experiences of racialization within history.

In his book *Galilean Journey* Latino theologian Virgilio Elizondo pays close attention to Jesus' context as a Galilean who lived on the periphery of the centers of political and cultural power and on the receiving end of the structures of domination and victimization that were institutionalized and formalized in the legal and political relationships of that historical moment.[23] Jesus' passion and death on the cross is an expression of the tools used at the time to relate to the racialized other, those dehumanized and disposable elements considered threatening to the system of power.

Christ's victory over death is a victory over a particular type of death, an unjust death, the death of someone considered a threat to the status quo. Therefore, in his resurrection we are no longer Gentile or Jew, servant or free. Christ's victory is the victory over the conditions of existence that are the source of the violence we do to one another. These particular details of the history of salvation need to be key elements in the development of a Catholic ethic that can begin to transform the historical violence of racialization in authentic and effective ways.

"Facing History": Theological Ethics and the Scars of History

A deeply ingrained allergy to attending to conflict in history by the official church and its documents on racial justice notwithstanding, "facing history" has proven to be a basic element of many efforts at restorative justice between groups that have suffered the violent effects of the racialization of the other as well as institutionalized racist laws and social norms. This points to the fact that authenticity, honesty, charity, and concern for both victim and oppressor and proper care not to repeat history are highly important to challenging oppressive systems and transforming relationships ruled by domination and power.

I mention not only the Truth and Reconciliation Commission in South Africa, but similar commissions in other parts of the world (such as in El Salvador, Rwanda, and Chile). In addition, a number of countries have enacted similar projects to deal with the genocide of their native populations at the hands of conquering powers. However, this is something that the United States sorely lacks. Violent as our own apartheid was for centuries during and after slavery, and evident as was our wholesale mistreatment of Native Americans during American expansionism and still today, the United States continually rejects the idea that we could engage in the process known as facing history or establishing a truth and reconciliation commission. Only very recently, and under the direction of the first president of African descent, has the United States decided to review its original position against the United Nations Declaration on the Rights of Indigenous Peoples (2007).[24]

The human family is in desperate need for a theological ethic that takes into account the scars of history, an ethic of humanization that is grounded in honesty. Virtue ethics, for example, and in particular Jim Keenan's treatise on mercy—the particular Christian virtue of entering the chaos of another—is well poised to the type of truth telling, common lamentation, and compassionate accompaniment that facing history requires.[25]

Bryan Massingale describes "authentic solidarity" as one that "cannot evade social conflict, resistance, and recalcitrance if it is to be of genuine service in the quest for social transformation"; he later terms this "conflictual solidarity."[26] Indeed, decades ago at Medellín the Latin American bishops articulated that solidarity with the poor, the third understanding of poverty in the "preferential option for the poor," required that we take on some part of the suffering of the poor—so often the racialized other—as we walk with them in the struggle for justice.

Solidarity as taking on the suffering of the poor and mercy as entering the chaos of another are but two examples of the way theological ethics intersects and interrupts the conflicts of history. But this process necessitates sharing difficult stories, common lamentation, and confession of our complicity in systemic oppression—efforts that are not often appreciated by our peers or by the institutions in which we work. I mention just two examples, Alex Mikulich's work on white privilege and the seminal paper "Confessions of a White Racist Catholic Theologian," by former Catholic Theological Society of America president Jon Nilson,[27] but there are many others.

Scholarship on the topics of antiracism or white privilege among white and non-white Catholic scholars in the United States is a very dangerous task. To openly acknowledge the conflicts in our history and the violence through which we have often forged our progress—or to comment on the complicity of the church in the silence that perpetuates relationships of oppression—can have severe negative professional consequences for scholars in the United States and elsewhere. Much more work needs to be done, and a primary requirement is for theologians and ethicists from a variety of historically racialized groups to come together and corporately take on the hard questions of privilege, institutional violence, racialization of the other, dehumanization of entire groups, and the essentialization of the white or the European as paradigmatically human. How we ask and answer these questions as ethicists will have great consequences in the theological academy and in the church for future generations.

If, as I have stated, the process of racialization and racism as an ideology informs the dominant epistemology that not only gathers and privileges certain information but that also shapes how we organize and reconstruct what we consider to be history or important for our reflection, then our task as ethicists is to construct an epistemology of resistance. We must expand history to include what the dominant groups would have us ignore as ahistorical or too primitive to belong to history or the political process. Indeed, as liberation theology pointed out in the 1960s, the "irruption of the poor in history" is that process of correcting history by turning to its missing protagonists, the racialized other, demanding that we make whole a very twisted and incomplete vision of the human person as the European conqueror.

The historical wholeness of the human family needs to be wrought out of and within a conflicted history, a wounded humanity, a scarred society. Wholeness assumes an original paradise-like existence from which we have strayed but that continues to shape the most basic part of ourselves. If this were easy, it would also be inauthentic. Human being and becoming whole follow the path of a resurrection that does not deny the marks of the cross. The open wounds of Jesus in the resurrection appearances remind the apostles that the conflict of history is present, however joyfully reversed, in salvation. An ethic of authentic human being and becoming, whether in its social/corporate or in its individual/personal dimensions, gives all the more glory to God's transforming justice and love when it bears fruit within a history marked by the scars of its racialized past. As Christian ethicists we are beholden to a gospel narrative that does not conceal or deny conflict, but in fact transforms conflict into wholeness.

"On the Ground": Anti-Immigration Sentiment in the United States and France

Unfortunately, in our globalized world one does not have to search too long to find contemporary examples of the ongoing effects of the racialization of the other. An important task for ethicists is to defeat the false claim that the violent effects of the racialization of the other in history have been overcome or at least corrected for future generations. This will be difficult because many constitutions and laws have been changed to attempt to legislate some measure of cosmopolitanism, equal opportunity, or even a postracial sensibility into a reality. Statements such as "this

fight has been won" (also often used to refer to feminist concerns about the treatment of women) or "slavery happened many generations ago and does not involve
me directly" fail to recognize the deep and formative roots that racism has in many
societies. The church must confront these false illusions about our ability to overcome the evil of racism at a corporate or institutional level; this cannot happen
without the work of facing history and understanding the conflict that we have
long avoided.

Two examples witness to the fact that the struggle against racism is far from
over and that the church has a clear role to play. It must be informed by ethicists
who have dedicated their craft and intellectual care to explore the deeper roots of
these issues and to address them through a diversity of Christian ethical perspectives. Both examples give evidence to the effects of the process of racialization of
the other and the establishment of the "citizen" as normative.[28]

A Racialized United States

In the United States, the passing of strict anti-immigration measures (SB 1070)
in the state of Arizona has surfaced much anti-immigrant sentiment nationwide,
with many media pundits repeating false claims about the deleterious effects of
wave upon wave of illegal immigrants. This new controversial law will have, among
other things, law enforcement officials stopping individuals to request evidence of
their legal presence in the country. While law enforcement in general is encouraged
to include consideration of a person's citizenship status in any encounter of a crimi-
nal nature, this new law takes it a step further by demanding that law enforcement
agents routinely stop and demand documentation from drivers, workers, and even
students.

Additional provisions in the law ask that landlords refuse to rent to persons
unable to produce documentation of their status as citizens, demand that immigrants carry proof of their citizenship status at all times, and allow for legal action
against agencies believed not to be in compliance with federal immigration law.[29]
In comparison with other industrialized countries, the demand that people carry
citizenship documentation at all times is not too outrageous. However, what is evident in the passing of this law is the deep fissure in the country that considers the
racialized other undesirable on its soil. While the history of the development and
progress of the United States is marked by the ongoing presence of a laboring class
composed mainly of migrant labor, the presence of these groups has more often
than not been accompanied by legislation to limit that particular group's achievement of that essential paradigm of human being, the citizen.[30]

Conversations in the media that preceded these decisions and those that followed have been marked by vast misunderstandings of the role of migrant groups
and often resulted in their vilification. Immigrants are described as unable to
assimilate, lacking in a desire to adapt, hungry for the plethora of social services
available to them through government agencies, responsible for importing disease

and crime into the continental United States, and unable to contribute to "American society," a society that is characterized by the dominant ethos of national belonging and exclusion.[31]

The pages of this part of our history are still being written. Although there are those who claim that the effects of racialization and racism are part of our past, such laws continue to be enacted throughout the United States. My children and I would be vulnerable to being stopped by law enforcement, having to provide proof of citizenship, and being subject to the potential of a search and detention. That is some of what awaits many of us in the United States simply because we belong to groups of racialized others.

A Racialized France

The case of France struggling with its immigrant African population holds some similarities with the United States while being unique in other ways. At the heart of both cases is the irruption of the racialized other on a national stage in which national identity has played out as the essential paradigm of being human. All that is worthy and good about human being and becoming has been annexed to the identity of citizen and nationality and vice versa.

Indeed, in the recent decision to not allow the wearing of a face covering or veil in France, Justice Minister Michèle Alliot-Marie stated that this decision protected "French values," which include the "values of freedom against all oppressions that try to humiliate individuals; values of equality between men and women, against those who push for inequality and injustice."[32] President Sarkozy is quoted as stating that "the Burqa is not welcome in France because it is contrary to our values and contrary to the ideals we have of a woman's dignity."[33]

In both the United States and France, language about the racialized other that emphasizes an inability to adapt or *adopt* national values of freedom, enterprise, and equality expresses a deeply ingrained belief that national identity—including language, a certain type of appearance, and family values—is a reflection of essential human nature. Such language appears to maintain that such values should be upheld by all universally, without the need to consider or value the racialized other's circumstances, preferences, or ways of knowing. These beliefs and the rhetoric that they incite provide evidence that we often create idols of national identity, idols that inevitably will demand sacrifices that include the disposal of those elements considered not human and outside of history.

This experience is not limited to a one-time event in a nation's history. Unfortunately, it is repeated at various times throughout the ages as long as the racialization of the other, with its concomitant violent state, continues to inform national and cultural identity. In the words of performance artist and critical thinker Guillermo Gomez-Peña, a U.S. citizen of Mexican heritage, "what begins as inflammatory rhetoric eventually becomes accepted dictum, justifying racial violence against suspected illegal immigrants."[34]

Conclusion: Incarnational Hope and
the Task of Theological Ethics

The following quote by Marisol de la Cadena summarizes the ongoing influence of the process of racialization and the sin of racism in our societies:

> The discrimination that was sanctioned in the 19th century continues acting with security, recklessness, and arrogance, even through the age of multiculturalism, within the space where race collaborates with history in order to define who has a right to political self-determination, to citizenship, who does not, and the degrees to which these rights can be enacted.[35]

Indeed, we are continually confronted with situations where human being and becoming have been essentialized to represent a specific group of people, often bearing the privileges afforded to people of a lighter complexion. The damage this has effected throughout history has resulted in millions of victims of domination and oppression. At issue here is the very essence of "being human," whether or not the racialized other is included in our paradigmatic vision of the essential human person and is therefore a legitimate participant in history.

Christian ethics is charged with identifying those elements that interrupt our relationship with God and our relationships with one another. This task is inadequately addressed if we do not evidence in our work a deep awareness of the conflictive nature of history, the violent effects of racialization and racism in society, and the ongoing and current episodes of institutional violence directed against those who do not fit the dominant conception of national values or citizenship.

Theological ethics will always need to carefully and adequately define what it is to live in Christian hope and love in a broken world. Traditionally, though, this has been done from a standpoint that lacks a proper appreciation of the stories and lived realities of those victimized and dehumanized because of the color of our skin. As such, it cannot be seen as an incarnational hope.

With respect to the sin of racism, although theological ethics has missed the mark, present hope is vibrant. I am greatly encouraged by the work of thinkers such as Bryan Massingale, Alex Mikulich, and Virgilio Elizondo. These and many others begin to offer a glimpse of what it is to ground our theological and ethical reflection in concrete history, suggesting ways of living the Christian call of love of neighbor, compassion, solidarity, and mercy. Their work is often undertaken at great cost to them professionally and personally. And so, there is great hope that indeed there will surface a corporately derived, historically grounded, conflict-aware incarnational theological ethics to aid in the process of humanization, making whole what racialization and racism have violated throughout history, the image of God.

Notes

1. José Ignacio González-Faus, *Proyecto de Hermano: Visión Creyente del Hombre* (Bilbao, Spain: Editorial Sal Terrae, 1987), 397-98.

2. For a detailed discussion in English of González-Faus's anthropology and Christology, especially his treatment of original sin and the sin of the world with respect to the doctrine of the option for the poor, see María Teresa Dávila, "A Liberation Ethic for the One-Third World: The Preferential Option for the Poor and Challenges to Middle-Class Christianity in the United States" (Ph.D. diss., Boston College, 2006).

3. A clarification of the concept of "racialization" is in order. In Michael Omi and Howard Winant's essay "Racial Formations," racialization is described as "the extension of racial meaning to a previously racially unclassified relationship, social practice or group. Racialization is an ideological process, a historically specific one. Racial ideology is constructed from pre-existing conceptual (or, if one prefers, 'discursive') elements and emerges from the struggles of competing political projects and ideas seeking to articulate similar elements differently." See Michael Omi and Howard Winant, "Racial Formations," in *The Social Construction of Difference and Inequality: Race, Class, Gender, and Sexuality*, ed. Traci E. Ore (Mountain View, CA: Mayfield, 2000), 18. According to the Kirwan Institute for the Study of Race and Ethnicity at Ohio State University, "Structural racism/racialization refers to a system of social structures that produces cumulative, durable, race-based inequalities." See Kirwan Institute for the Study of Race and Ethnicity, "Structural Racism/Racialization," Ohio State University, http://kirwaninstitute.org/research/structural-racism.php. Use of the term "racialization" refers to a systemic process of social and cultural "othering" (the process of securing one's positive identity through the stigmatization and negative characterization of those considered other to one's group), the effects of which are embodied in political and economic structures. It inherently represents differentiation, exclusion, and victimization of the racially other. While Omi and Winant consider racialization as a modern process, their essay and the use of the term in other literature and in this essay include the process of othering that has marked the encounter of different social groups throughout history.

4. Marisol de la Cadena, "Anterioridades y Externalidades: Más Allá de la Raza en America Latina," in "Race and Its Others," special issue, *e-misférica* 5, no. 2 (December 2008), http://www.emisferica.org. Translations are my own.

5. Ibid.

6. Ibid. A very telling example provided by de la Cadena is the historical impact of the Haitian revolution for independence. This event in the early nineteenth century went "under the radar" of most European historians and thinkers. De la Cadena attributes this to the dominant view that anything indigenous or black was considered outside of history, especially that which pertained to European-dominated America.

7. See Ronald Takaki, *A Different Mirror: A History of Multicultural America* (Boston: Back Bay Books, 2008).

8. Coco Fusco, "Framing Whiteness," in "Race and Its Others," special issue, *e-misférica* 5, no. 2 (December 2008), http://www.emisferica.org.

9. Ibid.

10. De la Cadena, "Anterioridades y Externalidades." The concept of disposable people is presented by various liberation theologians. Notable is the work of José Comblin,

Called for Freedom: The Changing Context of Liberation Theology (Maryknoll, NY: Orbis Books, 1998), and Jon Sobrino, *Christ the Liberator: A View from the Victims* (Maryknoll, NY: Orbis Books, 2001), among others.

11. De la Cadena, "Anterioridades y Externalidades." While Latina/o theologians in the United States have for the most part considered the concept of *mestizaje* as a term emphasizing the hybridity of Latina/o people and as such a positive force against the hegemony of the colonizer, de la Cadena proposes that *mestizaje* is not so much a hybridizing process that breaks down the false essentialism of the European; rather, she see that in some instances *mestizaje* has served as a force to water down black and indigenous cultural and ethnic forces in society.

12. Bryan Massingale, *Racial Justice and the Catholic Church* (Maryknoll, NY: Orbis Books: 2010), chap. 1.

13. De la Cadena, "Anterioridades y Externalidades."

14. The concept of sin as human damage is taken from José Ignacio González-Faus, "Sin," in *Mysterium Liberationis*, ed. Jon Sobrino and Ignacio Ellacuría (Maryknoll, NY: Orbis Books, 1993).

15. Congregation for the Doctrine of the Faith, *Instruction on Certain Aspects of the "Theology of Liberation"* (1984), and *Instruction on Human Freedom and Liberation* (1986), http://www.vatican.va. Two basic elements of both instructions are important for the current discussion. First, the instructions object to what they see as a tendency in liberation theology to utilize tools of analysis from the social sciences, such as Marxist theory but not limited to it, that explain human development and history as an inherently conflictive process. A second major concern is that Christian liberation is first and foremost liberation from sin, a truth to which all hearts must be converted in order to achieve integral liberation and social transformation.

16. Massingale, *Racial Justice and the Catholic Church*, 74-75.

17. Bryan Massingale, *"Vox Victimarum Vox Dei*: Malcom X as Neglected 'Classic' for North American Liberationist Reflection (What Catholic Theology Should Learn from Malcolm X)," CTSA Presidential address, June 13, 2010. Unpublished draft provided by the author.

18. See, for example, Adam Gordon, "The Creation of Homeownership: How New Deal Banking Regulation Simultaneously Made Homeownership Accessible to Whites and Out of Reach of Blacks," *Yale Law Journal* 115, no. 1 (October 2005): 186-226; and Melvin L. Oliver and Thomas M. Shapiro, "A Sociology of Wealth and Racial Inequality," in *Redress for Historical Injustices in the United States: On Reparations for Slavery, Jim Crow, and Segregation*, ed. Michael T. Martin and Marilyn Yaquinto (Durham, NC: Duke University Press, 2007), 91-117. For a more specific treatment of inclusion and exclusion in asset development from the perspective of Catholic social teaching, see James P. Bailey, "Asset Development for the Poor," *Journal for the Society of Christian Ethics* 24, no. 1 (2004): 51-72.

19. Lizabeth Cohen, *A Consumers' Republic: The Politics of Mass Consumption in Post-War America* (New York: Vintage, 2003). Cohen's treatment of exclusionary homeownership programs in the United States, particularly those connected with the GI Bill after World War II, point to how African Americans and women were systematically excluded from the basic tools of wealth creation and financial independence in the second half of the twentieth century.

20. Massingale, *Racism and the Catholic Church*, 75.

21. Ibid., 75, and 97-100. For a treatment of structural sin as part of "the sin of the world" and as it negatively affects an anthropology grounded on being for others, see González-Faus' *Proyecto de Hermano*, 230-300. For a discussion in English on this material in González-Faus, see Dávila, *A Liberation Ethic for the One-Third World*.

22. Massingale, *Racism and the Catholic Church*, 84-89.

23. Virgilio Elizondo, *Galilean Journey: The Mexican-American Promise* (Maryknoll, NY: Orbis Books, 2000).

24. Other countries that voted against the original declaration in 2007 include Canada, Australia, and New Zealand.

25. James F. Keenan, *The Works of Mercy: The Heart of Catholicism*, 2nd ed. (Lanham, MD: Rowman & Littlefield, 2007).

26. Massingale, *"Vox Victimarum Vox Dei."*

27. See Jon Nilson, "Confessions of a White Racist Catholic Theologian," *Proceedings of the Catholic Theological Society of America* 58 (2003): 64-82.

28. A caution on these two cases is in order. The processes of racialization with respect to immigration in the United States and in France and other European countries are very different. In addition, these two examples are contemporary highlights of long and complex histories of cultural, racial, and religious xenophobia. For example, in the case of France it is important to consider current sentiment against public displays of religious zeal, such as the Muslim *hijab* or *burqa,* against the backdrop of a long history of secularization and the establishment of French national cultural and political identity since the French Revolution. The context of anti-immigration sentiment in the United States is equally complex, covering centuries of interactions with peoples across many borders, the conquest of the "American Southwest" in the mid-nineteenth century, and the role of immigrant peoples in economic development. However, the long-standing complexity of these two cases is, in fact, evidence of the hard and cumbersome work that must be done by ethicists working on racism and taking history seriously. It signals a call to careful scholarship, not a call to abandon hope.

29. Randal C. Archibold, "Arizona Enacts Stringent Law on Immigration," *New York Times*, April 23, 2010, http://www.nytimes.com/2010/04/24/us/politics/24immig. html. There are numerous court challenges to these laws so that even after the law went into effect its full intent has not been carried out.

30. Takaki, *A Different Mirror*, pts. 3 and 4. Takaki specifically treats the different laws that were put in place to limit the extent to which different groups already present in the United States—primarily to perform the arduous labor of building railroads or displaced Native Americans—could gain citizenship or be excluded based on certain physiognomic traits, such as skin color and parentage.

31. For an extreme example of the essentialization of an "American" ideal citizen, see Samuel Huntington, *Who Are We? The Challenges to America's National Identity* (New York: Simon & Schuster, 2005).

32. Steven Erlanger, "Parliament Moves France Closer to a Ban on Facial Veils," *New York Times*, July 13, 2010, http://www.nytimes.com/2010/07/14/world/europe/14burqa. html.

33. Ibid. The presentation of this material at this conference has brought me into dialogue with a number of international ethicists, including French nationals, about the complexities of this topic. The French raised the complexities of France's secular society as

well as French efforts to counter religious extremism of any kind within its borders. Counterparts from the United States noted that current laws follow a pattern of anti-immigrant sentiment that is due primarily to the growing influx of African Muslim immigrants. A feminist ethicist from yet another country defended the French laws as ways of furthering a liberation agenda among Muslim women. The exchange of these perspectives must continue and deepen if such topics are to influence authentically theological ethics in the world church.

34. See Guillermo Gómez-Peña, "The '90s Culture of Xenophobia: Beyond the Tortilla Curtain," in *The New World Border: Prophecies, Poems and* Loqueras *for the End of the Century*, quoted in José Palafox, "Opening Up Border Studies: A Review of U.S.-Mexico Border Militarization Discourse," History Is a Weapon, http://www.historyisaweapon.com.

35. De la Cadena, "Anterioridades y Externalidades."

CONTRIBUTORS

DIEGO ALONSO-LASHERAS, S.J., teaches theological ethics at the Pontificia Università Gregoriana. He studied law and empirical sciences at ICADE, Madrid. He did his theological studies at the Universidad Pontificia Comillas (Madrid), the Pontificia Università Gregoriana (Roma), and the Weston Jesuit School of Theology (Cambridge, Massachusetts) where he defended his dissertation "Justice as Virtue in an Economic Context: *De Iustitiae et Iure* from Luis de Molina," forthcoming from Brill.

REGINA AMMICHT-QUINN did her dissertation on ethics and theodicy and her habilitation on the body, sexuality, and religion. She is professor of ethics at the International Centre for Ethics in the Sciences and Humanities, University of Tübingen, Germany.

ALBERTO BONDOLFI is professor of ethics in the Theology Faculty of the University of Geneva. He is a member of the Swiss National Commission on Bioethical Problems. He was president of *Societas ethica* and was founding president of the *Società svizzera di etica biomedica*.

LUIGI BRESSAN is Archbishop of Trento, Italy. He was Apostolic Nuncio to Singapore, Thailand, and Cambodia, and Apostolic Delegate to Malaysia, Myanmar, and Laos.

BÉNÉZET BUJO is a Catholic priest of the Diocese of Bunia (Democratic Republic of Congo). He has been Ordinary Professor of Moral Theology and Social Ethics at the University of Fribourg/Switzerland (1989-2010). His research field is African theology and ethics, and he has published several books and articles, including *Foundations of an African Ethic* (2001) and *Plea for Change of Models for Marriage* (2009).

ROGER BURGGRAEVE is Professor Emeritus of Theological Ethics at the Faculty of Theology, Catholic University Leuven (Belgium). A Levinas scholar, he is cofounder and honorary chair of the Centre for Peace Ethics at the KU Leuven and has been visiting professor at Lumen Vitae (Brussels), Dharmaram College (Bangalore, India), and elsewhere.

ALOYSIUS CARTAGENAS earned a doctoral degree from the Katholieke Universiteit in Leuven (Belgium). He teaches at the SMSC Graduate School of Theology (Cebu City, Philippines).

JULIE CLAGUE lectures in Christian theology and ethics at the University of Glasgow, UK. She co-edits the journal *Political Theology*.

MARÍA TERESA DÁVILA is a native of Puerto Rico and teaches Christian ethics at Andover Newton Theological School. Her publications include works on social justice in the lectionary, Latino/a Catholic theology in the United States, Latino/a public theology, and the use of force in the ethics of Reinhold Niebuhr. Her current interests are Christian ethics and U.S. civil society, immigration and race, the use of force, public theology, and liberation ethics.

MARGARET A. FARLEY is the Gilbert L. Stark Professor Emerita of Christian Ethics at Yale University Divinity School. She is the author, co-author, and co-editor of seven books, including *Just Love: A Framework for Christian Sexual Ethics* (2006), as well as numerous articles and chapters of books. She is past president of both the Catholic Theological Society of America and the Society of Christian Ethics.

BRUNO FORTE is Archbishop of Chieti-Vasto, Italy, and is known for his work on aesthetics and the ethics of transcendence. He is a member of the newly formed Pontifical Council for Promoting the New Evangelization. His many books include *The Portal of Beauty: Towards a Theology of Aesthetics* (2008) and *L'Uno per L'altro: Per un'etica della transcendenza* (2003).

ÉRIC GAZIAUX is a professor of fundamental moral theology at the Université Catholique de Louvain (Louvain-la-Neuve) and president of the Association de Théologiens pour l'Étude de la Morale (ATEM) since 2005. His works include *Morale de la foi et morale autonome: Confrontation entre P. Delhaye et J. Fuchs* (1995); *L'autonomie en morale: Au croisement de la philosophie et de la théologie* (1998); and as editor, *Philosophie et théologie: Festschrift Emilio Brito* (2007).

PETER J. HENRIOT is a member of the Zambia-Malawi Province of the Society of Jesus. Before moving to Zambia in 1989, he served as director of the Center of Concern in Washington, DC. From 1990 until 2010, he was the director of the Jesuit Centre for Theological Reflection in Lusaka, Zambia, where he specialized in the politics of development and church social teaching. He currently is director of development for the newly founded Loyola Jesuit Secondary School in Kasungu, Malawi.

BRIAN V. JOHNSTONE is a professor of moral theology/Christian ethics at the Catholic University of America.

PUSHPA JOSEPH is a professor in the Department of Christian Studies at the University of Madras.

DAVID KAULEMU is the regional coordinator for eastern and southern Africa of the African Forum for Catholic Social Teaching (AFCAST). He was a lecturer in philosophy and chair of the Department of Religious Studies, Classics and Philosophy at the University of Zimbabwe. He has taught, researched, facilitated workshops, and published on social ethics, development, human rights, good governance, and Christian social teaching.

JAMES F. KEENAN is Founders Professor in Theology at Boston College and co-chair of Catholic Theological Ethics in the World Church. His most recent book is *A History of Catholic Moral Theology in the Twentieth Century: From Confessing Sins to Liberating Consciences* (2010).

SHAJI GEORGE KOCHUTHARA, C.M.I., teaches moral theology at Dharmaram Vidya Kshetram, Bangalore. He is the editor-in-chief of *Asian Horizons* and the chairperson of the Institutional Ethical Review Board of St John's Medical College, Bangalore. His publications include *The Concept of Sexual Pleasure in the Catholic Moral Tradition* (2007).

AHMAD SYAFII MA'ARIF completed his Ph.D. at the University of Chicago. He is the founder of the Jakarta Maarif Institute, former president of the Muhammadi-yah Islamic Movement, and emeritus professor of Yogyakarta State University.

LAURENTI MAGESA teaches African theology at Hekima College Jesuit School of Theology, Nairobi, Kenya. He belongs to the Catholic Diocese of Musoma in Tanzania. His most recent book is *African Religion in the Dialogue Debate: From Intolerance to Coexistence* (2010).

REINHARD MARX is Cardinal Archbishop of Munich-Freising, Germany. He is a member of the Pontifical Council for Justice and Peace and the Congregation for Catholic Education. He authored *Das Kapital* (2008).

MYROSLAV MARYNOVYCH is vice rector for University Mission of the Ukrainian Catholic University in Lviv, Ukraine, and president of the Institute of Religion and Society of the same university. A founding member of the Ukrainian Helsinki Group and a prisoner of conscience (1977-1987), he headed the Amnesty International structures in Ukraine (1991-1996) and is president of the Ukrainian Center of the PEN International.

BRYAN MASSINGALE is a priest of the diocese of Milwaukee, Wisconsin, and associate professor of moral theology at Marquette University in Milwaukee. He also teaches in the Institute of Black Catholic Studies at Xavier University, New Orleans, and is a convener of the Black Catholic Theological Symposium and a past president of the Catholic Theological Society of America. He is the author of many articles and of *Racial Justice in the Catholic Church* (Orbis Books, 2010).

SIMONE MORANDINI is the coordinator of the project "Ethics, Philosophy and Theology" of the Fondazione Lanza, teaches the theology of creation at the Theological Faculty of Triveneto, and has written and edited books on environmental ethics and the dialogue between science and theology.

ANTÔNIO MOSER has his doctorate in moral theology and has published twenty-six books. He is director of Editora Vozes de Petrópolis-Brasil; president of Centro Educacional Terra Santa, Petrópolis; assessor for bioethics of the National Conference of Bishops and of the Catholic University in Petrópolis.

ANNE NASIMIYU-WASIKE was born in Kenya and is a member of the Religious Institute of the Little Sisters of St. Francis. She has served her community as General Superior from 1992 to 1998 and was elected again in 2010 for another six years. She holds a Ph.D. in systematic theology from Duquesne University, Pittsburgh. She has taught at Kenyatta University and is a visiting lecturer at Tangaza College, Hekima College, and the Maryknoll School of Theology.

MERCY AMBA ODUYOYE, long identified with the Circle of Concerned African Women Theologians, is at the Institute of Women in Religion and Culture at Trinity Theological Seminary, Legon, in Ghana. Among the books she has written are *Daughters of Anowa: African Women and Patriarchy* (1995); *Introducing African Women's Theology* (2001); *Beads and Strands: Reflections of an African Woman on Christianity in Africa* (2004); *Hearing and Knowing: Theological Reflections on Christianity in Africa* (2009).

MARGARET A. OGOLA is a pediatrician and the director of the Cottolengo Center for Children with HIV/AIDS, Kenya. She is also the mother of four and the celebrated author of several novels, including the award-winning *The River and the Source* and *I Swear by Apollo*.

LEO PESSINI has a Ph.D. in moral theology and is a professor in the Graduate Program in Bioethics at Centro Universitário São Camilo. He is author of several books in the area of pastoral care and bioethics, including *Distanásia: Até quando prolongar a vida?* (2001) and *Eutanásia: Por que abreviar a vida?* (2004). With Luciana Bertachini he edited *Humanização e Cuidados Paliativos* (2001).

PAOLO PRODI is Professor Emeritus in Modern History at the University of Bologna. Among his works are *Il sovrano pontefice* (1982, 2006); *Il sacramento del potere* (1992); *Una storia della giustizia* (2000); *Furto e mercato nella storia dell'Occidente* (2009); and *Il paradigma tridentino: Un'epoca della storia della Chiesa* (2010)

JULIE HANLON RUBIO is an associate professor of Christian ethics at St. Louis University, St. Louis, Missouri. Her most recent book is *Family Ethics: Practices for Christians* (2010).

MIGUEL ÁNGEL SÁNCHEZ CARLOS holds a doctorate in theology from the Theology Faculty of Grenada, Spain. He teaches Christian ethics at the Universidad Iberoamericana and edits the journal *Revista Iberoamericana de Teología*.

CHRISTA SCHNABL is vice rector of the University of Vienna and associate professor at the Institute of Social Ethics at the Faculty of Catholic Theology in Vienna. Her fields of research are ethical fundamentals, care ethics, gender ethics, political ethics, and ethics of the welfare state. She is the author of *Gerecht sorgen: Grundlagen einer sozialethischen Theorie der Fürsorge* (2005).

INDEX

abortion, 43, 77, 172, 178, 179, 187, 299,
    302
academics, and moral theology, 275
Africa
    Catholic Church as Tridentine church
        in, 57
    and Catholic social teaching, 178, 179
    and Christian evangelization, 48-57
    clerical structure of church in, 56
    division among Christian groups in, 53,
        54, 55
    faith communities in, 20-22
    HIV/AIDS in, 201-6
    wisdom of, and Catholic social teaching,
        253, 254
African Forum for Catholic Social
    Teaching (AFCAST), 183
African history, missing voice of women in,
    110-12
African Traditional Religion (ATR), 20, 21,
    22, 23, 25, 26, 152
Alliot-Marie, Michèle, 316
Alonso-Lasheras, Diego, 38
altruism, 48, 49, 53
anathemas, and Council of Trent, 104
ancestors, role of, in palaver, 155
Angesicht, as metaphor in ethics, 65, 66
Annales school, 74
Anthropocene epoch, 258
anthropocentrism, 29, 30
anti-immigration, in France, 316
anti-immigration, in the United States, 314,
    315, 316
anti-retroviral therapy (ART), 201-3
Apel, Karl-Otto, 155
Aquinas, Thomas, 73, 90, 91, 126, 138,
    161, 277
Aristotle, 90, 161
Auer, Alfons, 128
Augustine of Hippo, 81
authority
    crisis of, in church, 236, 237

competing claims for, in church, 239
    and just war theory, 163
Autiero, Antonio, 2, 4
autonomy
    and Catholic theological ethics, 277
    and dependency workers, 228, 229, 232
    and equity and equality of health care,
        190, 192, 193
    and gender studies, 287
    and human spirit, 135
    and rationality, 129, 130
    and urban phenomenon, 126
Azumah, John, 21

Babel, tower of, as metaphor, and ethics,
    14-15
Barroso, Jose Manuel, 273
Baumann, Zygmunt, 12
believers, and non-believers, 34
Belloc, Hillaire, 247
Benedict XVI, 215, 235, 242, 252, 253,
    254, 259, 277, 279, 280, 281
Benedict, Ruth, 67
Berger, Peter, 170
Bible, missing voice of women in, 108-9
bioethics, 24, 25
birth control, 89, 91, 210, 211
Black Power Movement, 117
blacks
    absence of, in Catholic ethical
        reflection, 116-22
    as objects of white sympathy, 118
Blumenberg, Hans, 11
Bondolfi, Alberto, 38
Bonhoeffer, Dietrich, 12, 135
Boniface VIII, 71
borders, open, 267, 268, 269
Bouillard, Henri, 131
Branch, Taylor, 119
Bressan, Luigi, 2, 3
Brundtland Commission, 259

328